Luminos is the open access monograph publishing program from UC Press. Luminos provides a framework for preserving and reinvigorating monograph publishing for the future and increases the reach and visibility of important scholarly work. Titles published in the UC Press Luminos model are published with the same high standards for selection, peer review, production, and marketing as those in our traditional program. *www.luminosoa.org*

Imperial Matter

The publisher gratefully acknowledges the support for this book provided by Cornell University's Hull Memorial Publication Fund, Open Access Publishing Fund, and Department of Near Eastern Studies.

Imperial Matter

Ancient Persia and the Archaeology of Empires

Lori Khatchadourian

UNIVERSITY OF CALIFORNIA PRESS

University of California Press, one of the most distinguished university presses in the United States, enriches lives around the world by advancing scholarship in the humanities, social sciences, and natural sciences. Its activities are supported by the UC Press Foundation and by philanthropic contributions from individuals and institutions. For more information, visit www.ucpress.edu.

University of California Press
Oakland, California

Suggested citation: Khatchadourian, Lori. *Imperial Matter: Ancient Persia and the Archaeology of Empires*. Oakland: University of California Press, 2016. doi: http://dx.doi.org/10.1525/luminos.13

Library of Congress Cataloging-in-Publication Data

Names: Khatchadourian, Lori, 1975- author.
Title: Imperial matter : ancient Persia and the archaeology of empires / Lori Khatchadourian.
Other titles: Ancient Persia and the archaeology of empires
Description: Oakland, California : University of California Press, [2016] | "2016 | Includes bibliographical references and index.
Identifiers: LCCN 2015044540| ISBN 9780520290525 (pbk. : alk. paper) | ISBN 9780520964952 (ebook)
Subjects: LCSH: Imperialism—Social aspects. | Sovereignty. | Archaeology and history—Iran. | Archaeology and history—Caucasus, South. | Architecture and state. | Architecture and society. | Commercial products—Social aspects.
Classification: LCC JC359 .K475 2016 | DDC 935/.7—dc23
LC record available at http://lccn.loc.gov/2015044540

25 24 23 22 21 20 19 18 17 16
10 9 8 7 6 5 4 3 2 1

For Adam

CONTENTS

LIST OF ILLUSTRATIONS

FIGURES

MAPS

Maps

[illegible] Achaemenid Empire [illegible]
[illegible] Map showing sites mentioned in the text [illegible]
[illegible] The [illegible] regions [illegible]
[illegible] showing the [illegible]

PREFACE

This book is an extended investigation into the power of things to make a difference in shaping the conditions of imperial power. It is also an effort to bring together an eclectic range of scholarly conversations on imperialism and matter, and draw forth from this convergence what might be called a uniquely archaeological approach to explaining both the perdurance and the fragility of imperial sovereignty. It may come as little surprise to learn that a book under the title *Imperial Matter* presses anthropological engagements with problems of empire and colonialism up against the growing body of social and political thought that has come to be known as the "material turn." But perhaps less anticipated, and maybe even a bit jarring to our disciplinary sensibilities, is the intrusion of ancient Persia into this encounter of otherwise steadfastly contemporary bodies of thought. One of my main intentions in writing *Imperial Matter* is to demonstrate that the cultural production of ancient Persia can be taken seriously as an untapped wellspring for theoretical reflection on the material constitution of imperial sovereignty. Ancient Persia figures here neither as a misrepresented "Other" calling out for post-Orientalist rediscovery, nor merely as a compelling archaeological case study for extending ideas that derive from the canons of Western philosophy and social theory. Rather, my goal is to explore how the earliest politico-religious thought of ancient Persia, long marginal in the Western academy, can profitably contribute to political and material theory as we know it today. At the center of this effort is what I am calling the "satrapal condition," an analytic framework built out of the Old Persian word for sovereignty. The term plays on the dual meanings of the word *condition,* calling up the variable work of material things both in reproducing "conditions" of subjection and subordination, and in placing limits or "conditions" on imperial sovereignty, thus rendering it perpetually aspirational and incomplete. An investigation of satrapal conditions entails a close examination of the practical entanglements among humans and a range of political things that I call *delegates, proxies, captives,* and *affiliates,* whose capacities for action depend on their material properties as well as the cultural and political logics in which they are enlisted.

Empirically, these ideas are put to work through an archaeological examination of the Achaemenid Persian Empire (ca. 550–330 B.C.) and especially its northern territory of Armenia and neighboring regions. The data in this book include both my own findings from excavations of a settlement in the modern Republic of Armenia known as Tsaghkahovit, as well as the discoveries from new and old investigations conducted by others in Iran, Turkey, and the South Caucasus. Given various evidentiary limitations that will become clear in due course, Achaemenid Armenia offers difficult terrain for an examination of satrapal conditions. In a sense, the time and place under view represent an archaeological no man's land, geographically distant from the contemporary cities of ancient Greece, Mesopotamia, and Iran, sociologically removed from the transformative developments in human history that have long captivated archaeological attention (e.g. the emergence of social complexity), and largely unseen in the eventful pages of Eurasia's documentary history in the mid-first millennium B.C. Moreover, during the centuries in question, the people of the mountains appear to have been resolutely uninterested in the kinds of social technologies that make ancient societies most visible to us today: writing, ostentatious burials, large visible settlements, and so on. There is, in short, little glamor in this kind of archaeology at the extreme margins. But there is the opportunity to shift our vantage on the ancient world and denormalize the empirical and conceptual sources of contemporary archaeological thought. It can only be hoped that, in time, future fieldwork and methodological advances will bring to light new data to support or force a reconsideration of the arguments advanced in these pages.

The deep origins of this book reside in my doctoral dissertation, completed at the University of Michigan in 2008. While *Imperial Matter* bears resemblance to that project in its empirical commitments rather more than its conceptual ambitions, the kernels of an argument on the capacity of material things to exert their own force in the lived experience of empire can be found in that earlier work. The dissertation came about under the guidance of a number of advisors who played a critical role in shaping my thinking on complex societies of the ancient world. I am deeply grateful to Norman Yoffee, both for his friendship and for his unstinting support for a career that has taken shape at the intersection of anthropological and Near Eastern archaeology. I also owe a tremendous debt to Margaret Cool Root for leading me to discover the sublime pleasure of studying ancient Persia, and for a pioneering body of scholarship on the visual production of the Achaemenids whose influence can be felt across this book. The work and guidance of Carla

Sinopoli and Susan Alcock urged me to think concertedly about what might constitute a distinctly archaeological contribution to the study of empires. I also owe a great thanks to John Cherry for his years of mentorship. Unbeknownst to them all, these individuals "visited" me regularly in the writing of this book as shoulder angels, pressing me to refine my ideas and cautioning me to pursue new lines of reasoning with care and clarity.

In its current form, this book came together in earnest once I joined the vibrant intellectual community at Cornell University, first as a Hirsch Post-Doctoral Fellow in Archaeology (and visiting professor in anthropology), and then as a member of the faculty in the Department of Near Eastern Studies. A number of colleagues at Cornell offered guidance and encouragement throughout the writing process. As a mentor, Kim Haines-Eitzen provided invaluable advice at various stages of this project, and I am truly appreciative of her and the current chair of Near Eastern Studies, Lauren Monroe, for their unflinching support and friendship. I also thank Sturt Manning for his constant encouragement, and Catherine Kearns, who helped me as a research assistant in 2011–12. The Bret de Bary Interdisciplinary Mellon Writing Group on Material Culture in 2011–12 provided an extended opportunity to gather with fellow scholars who share an interest in matters of ontology and materiality, and I am grateful to Elizabeth Anker, Elisha Cohn, Renate Ferro, Noor Hashem, Stacey Langwick, Adam T. Smith, and Saiba Varma for many engaging conversations around stimulating texts, some of which found their way into this work. The introduction and chapter 1 of *Imperial Matter* were discussed at a workshop of the Cornell Institute of Archaeology and Material Studies, and I am particularly thankful to John Henderson for sharing thoughts that helped me sharpen my concepts. I also want to thank colleagues in an anthropology writing group for their comments on those same two chapters, namely Chris Garces, Saida Hodžić, Hiroku Miyazaki, Paul Nadasdy, Lucinda Rainberg, and Marina Welker.

It would be difficult to overstate how influential the fieldwork conducted at Tsaghkahovit was in formulating the ideas that lie at the heart of this book, quite apart from the intriguing data generated at the site. The excavations were carried out under the auspices of the Project for the Archaeology and Geography of Ancient Transcaucasian Societies (Project ArAGATS), and I am deeply grateful to my friends and fellow co-directors, Ruben Badalyan, Adam T. Smith, and Ian Lindsay, for ensuring that Project ArAGATS continues to thrive as the longest-standing international archaeological research initiative in the South Caucasus. It could have become isolating to be one of the lone historical archaeologists on a team of prehistorians if not for their unfailing support for the work at the Iron Age settlement of Tsaghkahovit. I am especially grateful to Ruben Badalyan for securing the permits for fieldwork, and for facilitating artifact restoration, illustration, and photography. I also thank team members Roman Hovsepyan, Belinda

Monahan, and Maureen Marshall for their archaeobotanical, zooarchaeological, and bioarchaeological analyses, and Lilit Ter-Minasyan and Hasmik Sargsyan for their architectural and artifact drawings. I was lucky to welcome a wonderful group of trench supervisors over the years, including Catherine Kearns, Kathryn Weber, Jacob Nabel, Elizabeth Hardy, and most especially Elizabeth Fagan, a trusted colleague who periodically directed the excavations when family obligations pulled me away. As director of the Institute of Archaeology and Ethnography and former co-director of Project ArAGATS, Pavel Avetisyan has been a steadfast supporter of our investigations on the Tsaghkahovit Plain, and I thank him genuinely for that. I have benefited greatly from conversations with fellow historical archaeologists in Armenia, Mkrditch Zardaryan and Inessa Karapetyan. I am also especially thankful to the people of the village of Tsaghkahovit for their tireless work in the trenches, their friendship, and their hospitality. The Tsaghkahovit community's needs are great, and it is unfortunately the case that the employment opportunities Project ArAGATS has afforded over the years have not enhanced the community's prosperity to the same degree that the community has enhanced our understanding of their region's rich past.

The fieldwork and research for this book were made possible by the financial support of a number of institutions, to which I am most appreciative, including the National Endowment for the Humanities, the National Science Foundation, the President's Council of Cornell Women, the Fulbright Scholar's Program, the University of Michigan Rackham Graduate School and Center for Russian and East European Studies, and the Social Science Research Council. Much of this book was written during the 2013–14 academic year, while I was a fellow with the American Council of Learned Societies. The ACLS afforded me the time to develop part 1 of this book in a way that would not have been possible without a year's leave from teaching.

I had the benefit of several opportunities to experiment publicly with the ideas in this book, when they were still germinating, through lectures at the University of Binghamton's Department of Anthropology, Columbia University's Seminar on the Ancient Near East, and a comparative conference on imperial states at the University of Chicago. I thank the organizers for providing these forums to present the concepts in this book when they were still in development.

In no small measure, the book is stronger thanks to the suggestions and assistance of a great many colleagues too numerous to list. I would especially like to single out Margaret Cool Root, whose close readings of various draft chapters saved me from many embarrassing missteps. I also extend my thanks to Bruce Lincoln, who was generous enough to indulge an archaeologist wanting to explore various crevices of Persian studies in which, without the requisite languages, she arguably has no business. Rémy Boucharlat helped me tremendously in securing illustrations of sites in the Achaemenid imperial heartland. The two anonymous reviewers and the reader for the University of California editorial committee offered much insightful feedback, for which I am greatly appreciative. Any remaining errors are of course my own alone. I am also thankful to Eric Schmidt and Maeve Cornell-Taylor at University of California Press for their efforts in seeing this book to production, to Roy Sablosky for his skillful copyediting, and to project editor Francisco Reinking for shepherding the book through the final stages.

It is my remarkable good fortune to have a family that has been endlessly supportive throughout the process of researching and writing this book. I often recall a quiet twilight car ride in Armenia in the summer of 2014, when my four-year-old son, Avedis, broke the silence to ask how my book was coming along. It was one of many such occasions when I felt overwhelming gratitude for Avedis's uncanny maturity, genuine curiosity, and basic trust that it was all just a matter of time. My daughter, Ani, was quite literally by my side throughout the writing process. When it comes to meeting a deadline, there is no better incentive than a pregnancy. Ani's newborn presence in my life provided much needed perspective during the final months of this project. All the while, from the very beginning, my dear parents and in-laws have been a constant source of love and support.

Finally, this book simply would not have been possible if not for my colleague, collaborator, and husband, Adam T. Smith. I thank him for his unwavering encouragement and enthusiasm, for the care with which he commented on draft chapters, for his penetrating insights on matters of politics, materiality, and much else besides, and for his impactful scholarly oeuvre, which has so profoundly shaped my own thinking. Adam repeatedly gave me the one precious thing that is in shortest supply for parents of small children: time. On countless days and nights, and with unrelenting patience and good humor, he kept the ship afloat while I disappeared to write. For all these reasons and more, I dedicate this book to him.

Introduction

An old and obscure word has recently acquired new currency in the lexicon of contemporary world politics, summoning the attention of anyone who follows the matter of empire. By all accounts, we live in an age of peculiar political entities that go by the names "satrap" and "satrapy." If the words sound archaic and only vaguely English, it is because they are. To locate their origins is to traverse over two and a half millennia of human history, and arrive at the earliest imperial formations of ancient Persia. Yet these arcane political entities are apparently still among us, in an era in which the newest technologies of postindustrial capitalism exist alongside the oldest technologies of macropolitical power. If mainstream print media is any gauge, since 9/11 satraps and satrapies have proliferated around the globe, putting a great many of the world's political communities under conditions of partial sovereignty (figure 1a). However ethereally, ancient Persia's singularly novel experiment with imperial dominion on a continental scale has come to haunt much of the world today.

It was not always so. In the simpler days of the Cold War, "satrapy" was a pejorative largely reserved for Soviet republics, protectorates, and allies, from Cuba to Czechoslovakia, Albania to Afghanistan. Yet these days, nearly every country has been said to either have one, or be one. It perhaps comes as no surprise that on the ledger of putative satrapal sovereigns, the United States tops the charts (figure 1b). In the decade that followed the 2003 Iraq War, commentators in leading world newspapers and across the blogosphere repeatedly opined that the U.S. had made satrapies out of Iraq, Afghanistan, and Pakistan, along with Britain, Australia, Canada, and other states conventionally considered allies. The *Guardian* anticipated the trend: "A collection of American satrapies" was how one

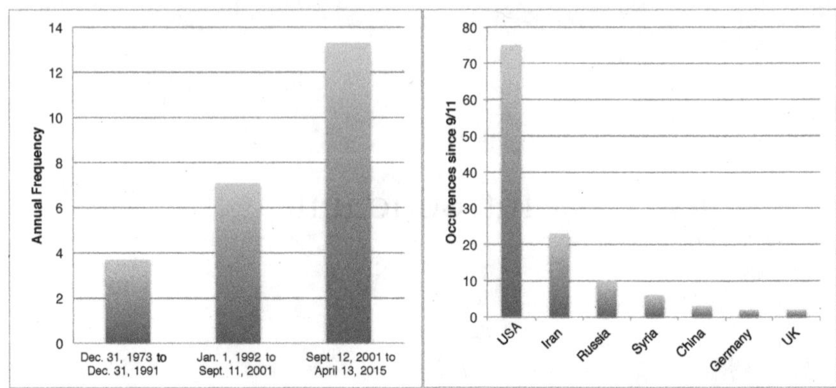

FIGURE 1. Left: Tracking occurrences of the words "satrap" and "satrapy" in major world newspapers and magazines from December 1973 to April 2015. Right: states said to have satrapies today. (Data source: LexisNexis Academic).

correspondent writing in those pages described George H. W. Bush's hoped-for outcome in the Middle East after the first Gulf War (Woollacott 1991), in which Iraq lost its own "satrapy" in Kuwait (Haig 1991). Beyond the Middle East, journalists have remarked that Britain has long maintained its "satrapy" of Scotland (e.g. Liddle 2011; Young 1997), that China has made "satrapies" of Myanmar and parts of Sub-Saharan Africa (Applebaum 2008; Thompson 2011), and that financial crisis has allowed Germany to make a "satrapy" out of Greece (Johnson 2011). Meanwhile, post-Soviet Russia has tried to reestablish "satrapies" in the Caucasus, Central Asia, Ukraine, and beyond (e.g. Black 2011; Champion 1994; Reeves 1995; Traynor 2008), even as one analyst once asked whether this former superpower could itself become an "American satrapy" (Trenin and Dolgin 2010). Some architects of contemporary geopolitics have themselves used this unconventional term, preferring to project it onto an adversary with perceived imperial designs. According to Steven Lee Myers (2009) of the *New York Times*, in 2009 defense secretary Robert Gates assured Congress that Iraq's leaders "do not intend for the new, post-Saddam Iraq to become a satrapy of its neighbor to the east" (that is, Iran). Others in the media soon joined him in returning satrapy to its place of origin, signaling the politically compromised condition in which Iraq would find itself if Tehran's ambitions were to be realized (e.g. Diehl 2011; Fisk 2011; Hughes 2011). The modern precedent is, of course, the Iranian "satrapy" of Syria (e.g. Ajami 2011; Harris 2013), itself at times overlord to satrapal Lebanon.[1] "Iran must know . . . that the Sunni Arab world cannot be transformed into a series of satrapies subservient to Tehran," the editors of the *Guardian* recently admonished.[2] The list could go on.[3]

How are we to reckon with this lively if at times sardonic appropriation of the ancient Persian past to the global present? It is, to be sure, easily dismissed as nothing more than a quaint and taunting archaism that is gaining fashion in the argot of punditry. But *Imperial Matter* opens with this word because the rhetorical trafficking of satrapies in the public sphere unwittingly conjures a term of rich but unrealized analytical potential derived from a sophisticated if obscure body of ancient Persian political philosophy. It is a term that will be pressed into service in this book to refigure the theoretical terrain of imperial sovereignty, and particularly its relation to the infinite world of physical matter. While materiality may not seem germane to the colloquial connotations that "satrapy" vaguely calls to mind—the subjugated provinces of bygone eastern despots, perhaps—this is only because satrapy's material associations were long ago abandoned, lost in translation, and left behind in the obscurity of early Persian theology. The word's potential for setting the terms of an archaeology of imperialism is therefore by no means self-evident. As we shall see in chapter 1, to discover it requires delving deep into satrapy's etymological and historical anatomy, and making new alignments with contemporary social and material theory, only then to emerge with the outlines of a heuristic framework that pushes to the fore the relations of humans and things in the reproduction and attenuation of imperial sovereignty. Such relations are the central concern of this book.

WE ARE SOMETIMES LIKE THEM

One need not plumb such etymological depths to sense the poignancy of this curious lexical resurgence for students of empire. For one, talk of satrapies implicitly unsettles the modernist conceit that imperialism's latest incarnations represent entirely novel forms of macropolitical ambition. It pushes us to ask how the trajectories of empires past can "help us to appreciate the importance of thinking clearly about what is and what is not possible in the present conjuncture" (Calhoun et al. 2006: 15). The resurrection of satrapies in contemporary political discourse therefore also adds new urgency to the oft-heard critique of colonial studies for its "exclusionary model of temporality" that has tended to "seal off" premodern periods (Loomba et al. 2005: 25), and treat the "'distant' past . . . as a field of undifferentiated alterity" (Cohen 2000: 3). In the words of other critics, the anthropology of colonialism has evinced a "temporal myopia" (Dietler 2010: 22) that has left it "rather uncurious about exploring the implications of looking backwards in time" (Cooper 2005: 409). Western social thought has worked assiduously to establish the intellectual ramparts that today separate notions of modern and ancient. But talk of contemporary satrapies represents a breach in that convention, denying the possibility of an autonomous account of the imperial present entirely unfettered by the political repertoires of the past.[4]

This is not the first time that a challenge to the ancient/modern divide has pivoted on the Achaemenid Persian Empire, a dynastic polity centered in today's southwestern Iran that spanned much of southwest Asia during the sixth through fourth centuries B.C. It was perhaps Hegel who first defied the division through recourse to ancient Persia, provocatively claiming in his *Lectures on the Philosophy of History* (1956: 187) that "the Persian empire is an empire in the *modern* sense." To Hegel, Persia's satrapies were the earthly expression of a Zoroastrian religious philosophy that allowed for humanity's discovery of the self-conscious Spirit as free and independent from matter and nature. Hegel held that the Persian political system entailed not only an interdependent unity, but also the possibility for a kind of freedom, manifested in the ability of each satrapal community to retain its distinctive customs and laws. This dialectic of unity and freedom Hegel associated with "Zoroaster's Light."[5] It is the unifying essence of light that Hegel tied to the beginnings of an awareness of the self-conscious Spirit. Light "enables the individual human being, together with other beings, to achieve freedom to act in as many ways as their natural propensities allow" (Azadpour 2003: 140), in contrast to the state of darkness, in which Spirit and matter are still immersed in nature. "As light illuminates everything—imparting to each object its peculiar vitality—so the Persian Empire extends over a multitude of nations, and leaves to each one its particular character" (Hegel 1956: 187). Since the objectification of the Spirit was to Hegel the precondition of history, the Achaemenid Persian Empire "constitutes strictly speaking the beginning of world history" (174), and therefore the start of the modern era.

In Hegel's orientalist teleology, the torch of civilization would thence pass to the Greco-Roman world and onward to Europe, leaving Persia's primordial modernity behind in what Zainab Bahrani (2003) has called the "extraterrestrial Orient." But viewed through the lens of contemporary political thought, Hegel seems downright heterodox to have located an early moment of political enlightenment in the mountains and lowlands of ancient Persia. Yet today's invocations of American or Russian or Chinese satrapies go even further than Hegel in upsetting our historical sensibilities; they intimate that some *modern* empires are sometimes imperial *in the ancient sense.* Put another way, not only were they something like us, but we are sometimes like them (Latour 1993).

POLITICAL AND MATERIAL THEORY FROM A STILL-ENCHANTED WORLD

What makes the contemporary journalistic usage so exceptionally provocative is not only the transhistorical bridge that it builds but also the unseemly baggage that it brings. As we shall see in chapter 1, the word "satrapy" has a thick semantic geology. Sedimented strata of meaning have accrued ever since Herodotus first adapted an Old Persian word and introduced his neologism into the Greek vocabulary to describe Persia's territorial possessions. These meanings have come to link the term inextricably with corruption, venality, brutality, greed, sycophancy, duplicity, authoritarianism, corruption, arrogance, feudalism, gluttony, and sloth—the full trait list of "oriental despotism" and then some. "A pile of satrap," wrote the editors of the *Independent,* in a rare scatological invocation.[6] In modern political discourse, satraps and satrapies have traditionally been consigned to the Middle East. At times farcically modified with terms like "desert" or "robed," they are code words for that region's perceived pathological politics. As it turns out, however, satrapies are also things of the West, the Far East, and other places besides. Globalizing the term "satrapy" to describe all arenas of partial sovereignty that inhere in today's macropolities grates at our political sensibilities because the squalid orientalist meanings linger just beneath the surface. They threaten to suggest that a mode of politics the West has worked discursively to curtail and contain since the Greco-Persian Wars of the fifth century B.C. has spilled out across time and space.

By all popular accounts, Persia's political habit entailed mainly the savage instruments of violence. Consider a cover story that appeared in the authoritative weekly news magazine the *Economist* in the summer of 2013, as America and its allies flirted with intervention in the Syrian civil war in the face of mounting Iranian influence over the regime of Bashar al-Assad and his neighbors (figure 2). "Can Iran be Stopped?" ran the headline, in a rhetorical turn of phrase that recalls a much earlier contemplation of the rampant advance of Persian power across the world stage.[7] This was no accident. The cover image of the *Economist* featured a stone sculptural relief from a palatial structure at the Achaemenid capital, Persepolis, in today's southwestern Iran. It showed a brawny lion digging its fangs and claws into the rump of a rearing bull. In the learned opinion of the magazine, the West should enter the Syrian fray to check the ambitions of a "Persian lion" that "has not lost its claws."

What is most fascinating about this tableau is neither the facile analogy of violence that it draws between the Islamic Republic of Iran and the Achaemenid Persian Empire, nor the way in which the *Economist* strives to awaken long-dormant anxieties of unleashed Persian despotism that reside deep in the Western historical consciousness—as if to say, "Old specters haunt modern politics in new guises" (Euben 1999: 7). Rather, the magazine's cover is of particular interest for how succinctly, if inadvertently, it encapsulates why it is difficult to fathom a serious contribution to political thought that derives from the cultural production of ancient Persia. The selected image of the grisly lion and the helpless bull is meant to invoke a primordial and untamable violence. The *Economist*'s glib metaphor seems to elide predatory ferocity with state aggression (awkwardly casting the dangerous bull as the Syrian prey in need of the West's protection), and thus calls up a visceral exercise of archaic political power that precedes and is closed off to rational

FIGURE 2. Economist cover. (© The Economist Newspaper Limited, London, June 22, 2013).

thought—one that is animalistic, motivated by innate compulsion rather than mindful reflection on the nature of sovereignty and its means of reproduction. As it turns out, the metaphor could not be further from the scholarly understanding of the lion-and-bull symplegma, as art historians call such unusual pairings with both combative and erotic connotations.[8] But this is the ancient Persia that most of us have come to know. It is a Persia that is quintessentially despotic in the sense that Montesquieu meant it, a regime driven only by passions, one that paradoxically "renounces the order of the political" and thus subscribes to "*the abdication of politics itself*" (Althusser 2007 [1972]: 81–82). It is the Persia we encounter in comic books and major motion pictures like the award-winning *300* and its prequel, *300: Rise of an Empire* (figure 3). It is the Persia of popular political histories like Tom

FIGURE 3. Movie poster for *300: Rise of an Empire.*

Holland's *Persian Fire: The First World Empire and the Battle for the West* or any one of a number of popular books and films that belong to the virtual cottage industry surrounding Alexander the Great. Hegel aside, theorists have generally hesitated to look conceptually at ancient Persian thought as a means to stimulate productive abstractions for the humanistic social sciences because of a prevailing suspicion of Persian political reflection as primeval, pre-rational, and grounded in nothing more than an insatiable thirst for power.

This is, of course, your garden-variety orientalism, as Edward Said (1978) famously called the West's style of thought, system of knowledge, and modes of discourse concerning the Orient. But my critique of the *Economist* serves here not as a prelude to a corrective, "indigenous" history that works to rewrite the Persian past on its own terms. Scholars of Mesopotamia and ancient Persia have made great strides in recent decades in advancing accounts of the region's history that demolish a metanarrative of Western civilization hinged on Near Eastern foils.[9] *Imperial Matter* takes a different approach, one that nevertheless emerges in no small measure out of the opening cleared by that important turn to forge new paths into the southwest Asian past. This alternative asks whether there are fertile fields on the other side of the Saidian critique in which to sow the seeds for a political and archaeological theory that builds on ancient Persia's studied "metaphysics of power" (Lincoln 2007: xv). To the extent that it seems unthinkable to turn to such thought as a means to amplify our concepts of imperialism and materiality, it is in part because Western political theory long ago left the business of what Roxanne Euben (1999: 3, 7) has called "metaphysical truths" and "transcendent foundations" in favor of a "profoundly this-worldly scholarly discourse that sees no place for such foundationalist certainties in modern political life."

The project to lift the perspicacious intuitions of pious (and powerful) intellectuals who believed in "divine truths unknowable by purely human means" (Euben 1999: 4) from the particularist domain of history to the general plane of theory is thus perhaps audacious. But as I hope will become clear in chapter 1, taking seriously political thought forged in a still "enchanted" world (Euben 1999: 15) is a legitimate endeavor if one accepts a broad understanding of political theory as an inquiry into such matters as the nature of legitimate sovereignty, the relationship between moral and political life, and the relationship of individual to society and polity (9–10, 51). To adapt Euben's judicious formulation, it might be best to speak not of an Achaemenid political theory, but of an engagement with Achaemenid premises of political life "*in terms of political theory*" (52). Such an endeavor is also an extension of the recognition, to which Bruce Lincoln (2007, 2012) has attended with particular delicacy, that the cultural production of the Achaemenids is not reducible to a crudely instrumentalist logic of propaganda, but instead acutely forged out of a complex set of religious and political values—values that provided powerful justification for empire, to be sure. Insofar as theirs was, in its own historical and cultural context, an investigation of certainties and principles of being and power, it was as much a theoretical project as any in the equally situated but more familiar and largely secular canon of post-Enlightenment Western thought.

It is with this in mind that in chapter 1 I dwell further on the word "satrapy," embarking on a project to wrest it from both the opinion pages of the broadsheets and the obscure remove of ancient studies. Through winding dissection of language, text, and image, that chapter probes the complex bearings of a word that reverberated across various spheres of ancient Persian thought. I offer neither a complete analysis of Achaemenid political philosophy, nor a thorough account of Zoroastrian (or more accurately Avestan) religion, but instead undertake a series of opportunistic forays into very particular dimensions of these corpora for the specific purpose of grasping some of the earliest recorded reflections on both sovereignty and its relation to matter. This kind of selective engagement is undertaken in the conviction that early Persian thinkers captured something in their exploration of these themes that can be abstracted to construct new concepts without succumbing to complete immersion in the historical or theological context of their genesis.

What results from this are key tenets that lie at the heart of what I call the "satrapal condition." The first is an understanding of imperial sovereignty as co-constituted in both sublime principles and material practices, which is to say both prior to and conditional on lived, earthly experience. Cast another way, the satrapal condition concerns the fragility of sovereignty, its persistently aspirational quality, as a paradoxical condition of its very existence, and the reciprocal constitution of imperial orders in ruling sovereigns and ruled subjects. The second critical insight to which a social scientific biography of satrapy gives rise is one that recognizes an absolute ontological indivisibility of sovereignty and physical matters as hard as rock crystal and as vital as molten metal.

Such an inquiry emerges, of course, out of its own historical conjuncture. In recent years, a distributed array of approaches across the humanities and social sciences have pushed to the fore careful reflection on the ontology of things, long banished by human-centered Cartesian thought to the margins of philosophy and social theory (e.g. Bennett 2010; Harman 2010; Latour 2005b; Olsen 2010). This "material turn" has not only claimed a place for things at the center of our conscious efforts to make sense of social worlds brimming with matter, but has also sharpened our appreciation of how things were once recognized as vibrant and autonomous participants in human affairs (e.g. Bynum 2011; Smith 2015). Against this backdrop, it is on the one hand not surprising that we should discern in certain dimensions of ancient Persian cultural production the kind of serious contemplation of the material world that is brought forward in the next chapter. On the other hand, what is perhaps most distinctive about Persian metaphysics as it pertains to these concerns—what distinguishes it from other traditions that gave purposeful thought to things, whether in transcendent or practical experience—is the tantalizing way in which thinkers of ancient Persia appear to have recognized a relation between things and the reproduction of imperial dominion. It is of no small consequence that this realization, which was both political and theological in nature, emerged alongside the earliest experiment in what Hannah Arendt (1951) called "continental imperialism." And it is because of this recognition that, with due respect to those who might prefer to reserve the arcane materials of ancient Persia's past for a strictly philological, historical, or theological enterprise, I take liberties in this book to redeploy satrapy as a heuristic concept—one that can refine our questions on imperial formations and their things.[10] Out of this gentle but unapologetic bending of satrapy's meanings emerges the satrapal condition, an analytical platform from which to grapple with the relations among sovereigns, subjects, and things that I pull through subsequent theoretical and empirical chapters of this book.

COLONIAL BODIES, SATRAPAL THINGS

It is in still one last respect that talk of satrapies today strikes a discordant chord, and this final dissonance provides an additional point of entry into the concerns that lie at the heart of this book. Satrapy denotes an alien category of subjection that is entirely unrectified to the familiar coordinate systems of Western imperial rule. Why resort to this peculiar and esoteric word—one recovered from the depths of a pre-Enlightenment political tradition guided more by metaphysics than by rationalist epistemology—when there is another term in the glossary of empire that is both less abstruse and ostensibly more fitting in the aftermath of an imperial age guided by Western liberalism (Mehta 1999; Pitts 2005)? Surely "colonies," long regarded by anthropologists, historians, and publics alike as the constitutive instruments of modern imperial dominion, would suffice.

Or perhaps not. Indeed, this particular citational reverberation of the ancient in the modern poses a challenge to the archaeology and anthropology of colonialism, just as it does to political theories of empire. It calls on us to confront the heretical notion that Europe may not be the only source of the fundamental concepts we use to organize knowledge concerning the conditions of imperialism across time and space. In recent years, from some quarters in sociocultural anthropology and history, calls have been sounded to rethink the study of empires in ways that peer deeper into the past and more expansively around the globe than familiar conventions of colonial and imperial studies previously encouraged. The time has come, some have said, to "expand our notion of imperial force fields to early modern forms of empire, to imperialism without colonialism, to empires by other names, and to imperial formations outside of Europe" (Stoler and McGranahan 2007: 11). Yet, by all accounts, we are to do this without fundamentally rethinking the workability of existing analytical terms that are so deeply entangled in the problems of

European colonialism that there is scarcely sufficient consensus to speak for their analytical integrity and global applicability (but see Stoler 2006b).

Michael Dietler (2010: 17) recently confessed to suppressing an inclination to abandon the existing vocabulary of colonialism altogether in favor of "a less compromised and entangled set of analytical terms." He concluded that we are "condemned to continue grappling pragmatically with the terms current in the disciplines of colonial analysis" because inventing "a new lexicon . . . that avoids any Greco-Roman terms that have been incorporated into modern discourse seems a cumbersome and quixotic endeavor at best—the intellectual equivalent of spitting into the wind" (17, 18). To the extent that "the satrapal" can be said to be "new" to the lexicon of empire, his point is, even if a bit defeatist, well taken. But even with every effort at definitional precision, it remains difficult if not impossible to evade the ideological and historical smog that surrounds the conceptual space of the colonial. The only alternative to (re)inventing our terms is to recast colonialism exceptionally broadly, as "a pragmatically general and inherently plural analytical rubric employed to focus critical attention and facilitate the comparative analysis of a wide range of practices and strategies by which peoples try to make subjects of other peoples" (19).

The difference that is at stake with my (re)invention of the satrapal rests on the question of *how* peoples try to make subjects of other peoples, or more precisely *what* makes subjects of peoples, under conditions of formal asymmetries of power. I mean to mark the distinction between what many studies of colonialism have broadly understood as the body politics of cultural interaction, which occurs through law, discourse, and practical intercultural encounters, and the transformation of persons and communities through the mediation of nonhuman things. Historical ethnography's theoretical and empirical contributions to the study of empire have centered largely on human–human relations—on the intimate proximities and regular encounters of European, "native," and mixed-race populations with different subjective and affective dispositions to a dominant polity. The anthropological archaeology of colonialism has likewise fixed its gaze on the entangled relations that emerge from direct, sustained encounters between colonists and "native" peoples (e.g. Dietler 2010; Voss 2008a; Voss and Vasella 2010; see also chapter 2). Hansen and Stepputat (2006: 297) have captured this disciplinary priority and the intimate concerns of colonial sovereignty: "The anthropology of colonialism has demonstrated that the anxieties of colonial rule were centered on its body politics, the imprinting of rule in the bodies of natives, and the protection of white bodies: the fears of miscegenation, the performance of European dignity, of the presentation of the European family and domesticity, the taming and disciplining of immoral practices, etc."

But what happens when the politics at issue is not particularly invested in such forms of bodily or social (e.g., racial, gendered) reengineering? There are, I suggest, at least two reasons to broaden anthropology and archaeology's priorities in the study of imperial formations beyond intimate human encounters and toward the politics of nonhuman things, and the first is that a focus on the body politics of colonial control dramatically constricts the anthropological gaze to a narrow range of historical phenomena. It leaves us ill-equipped to make sense of the instruments of sovereignty in numerous imperial contexts where everyday encounters between pluralities of imperial subjects and agents—the bureaucrats, missionaries, soldiers, and other settlers and their descendants that anthropologists of the colonial have long studied—are limited, and where law, discourse, and bodily affect are not the most effective tools for the definition and maintenance of inequalities. What happens when the "distinctive experience . . . of coming to feel, and to *re-cognize* one's self as, a 'native'" (Sartre 1955: 215, quoted in Comaroff and Comaroff 1997: 19) is not inflected with the rhetoric of an aggressive, post-Enlightenment civilizing mission intended to correct and change that affect and identity, to create particular moralities? In other words, the satrapal condition is put into service in part to help answer the question, "What sort of subjects does an empire without colonialism produce?" (Stoler and McGranahan 2007: 26), or more precisely, what sort of subject is produced in imperial spaces where interpersonal colonial encounters are far and few between?

And yet the analytical utility of the satrapal condition does not rest on an unproductive typological fetish. The point is less to reinstate the ontologically solid and monolithic imperial state through a crude typology than it is to provide a new optic that is trained on the vast world of durable matter long sidelined in contemporary theories of imperial sovereignty. I do not mean to emphasize the differences between, on the one hand, imperial formations involving settler communities, or civilizing missions, or large bureaucracies and, on the other, the protectorates, dependencies, and other semi-autonomous, indeterminate, or ambiguous spaces of formally compromised sovereignty that make up imperialism's uneven political geographies (Benton 2010; Stoler 2006a: 55). It is certainly the case that the contemporary sense of satrapy with which this chapter began captures non-settler forms of "decentralized despotism" (Mamdani 1996). And it is also the case that the Achaemenid Empire did not itself have colonies to any significant extent, much like other Eurasian empires that would follow, from the Sasanian to the Soviets.[11] But the second and indeed dominant reason for recalibrating the conceptual orientation beyond the body politics of intercultural encounter is to clear epistemological space for the autonomous capacities of nonhuman things in the reproduction and attenuation of imperial rule. An inquiry into satrapal conditions takes seriously the ways in which matter makes its own difference in imperial worlds—whether colonial or non-colonial—irrespective of the designs and assignments of its makers and users. As we shall see in chapter 3, in this respect the satrapal condition extends, sharpens, and revises a conversation on materiality already well underway in the anthropology and archaeology of colonialism (e.g. Cohn 1996; Comaroff and Comaroff 1997; Dietler 2010; Gosden 2004; McClintock 1995; Mintz 1985; Thomas 1991; Wright 1991). To the extent that a non-European, pre-modern, continental empire animates the conceptual apparatus of this book and provides the empirical terrain for its elaboration, it is less to set historical or typological limits on this project's defining concepts, than to detail those concepts through one of humanity's earliest experiments in macropolitical power.

Imperial Matter offers an archaeological account of the conditions of partial sovereignty entailed in imperial formations that hinges on the work of objects and built landscapes in the reproduction of sovereigns and subjects. It is for this emphasis on the material entanglements of imperialism that colonialism is here rhetorically and analytically unseated. As we shall discover in the chapters that follow, such a targeted inquiry into the "matter" of imperialism has few precedents. It is thus appropriate that, in terms of its empirical engagements, this book should begin at the beginning, with what Sheldon Pollock (2006: 180) in an apt material metaphor has called "the imperial toolbox first assembled by the Achaemenids."

THE FIRST "WORLD" EMPIRE

At the time of its ascendancy, the Achaemenid Persian Empire (ca. 550–330 B.C.) was, by all accounts, the largest polity the world had ever known. From its imperial heartland in modern southwestern Iran, the Achaemenid dynasty maintained ever-shifting degrees of control over an enormous realm that stretched from the Aegean Sea to the Indus River, and from Egypt and Arabia to the Caucasus Mountains and Central Asia (map 1). As charismatic conquerors, ideologues, conspirators, and builders of cities and monuments, the Achaemenid sovereigns—Cyrus and Darius, Xerxes and Artaxerxes (the names are so iconic of popular antiquity as to seem almost fictional)—in many ways provide the archetype of "great men" Rankean history, and narratives of their exploits, defeats, and habits of rule have been recounted for centuries.[12] At incalculable cost to human life, but also through collusion, threat, and the dispensation of pledges (both material and divine) within a system of reciprocity that was variously rhetorical and real, the dynasty attained and maintained a geographic scale of political integration never before achieved in world history. Like many empires since, the Persians dispatched and co-opted individuals to form a far-reaching imperial bureaucracy that worked through, and modified, pre-existing economic structures and built landscapes for the collection of taxes, the maintenance of a military force, and the implementation of royal decrees. Persians manifestly enjoyed a privileged status above other groups, although in certain respects special standing may likewise have extended to other populations enveloped within a possibly emergent "pan-Iranian" identity, particularly the Medes and Elamites (Root, forthcoming). Yet, as we shall see in

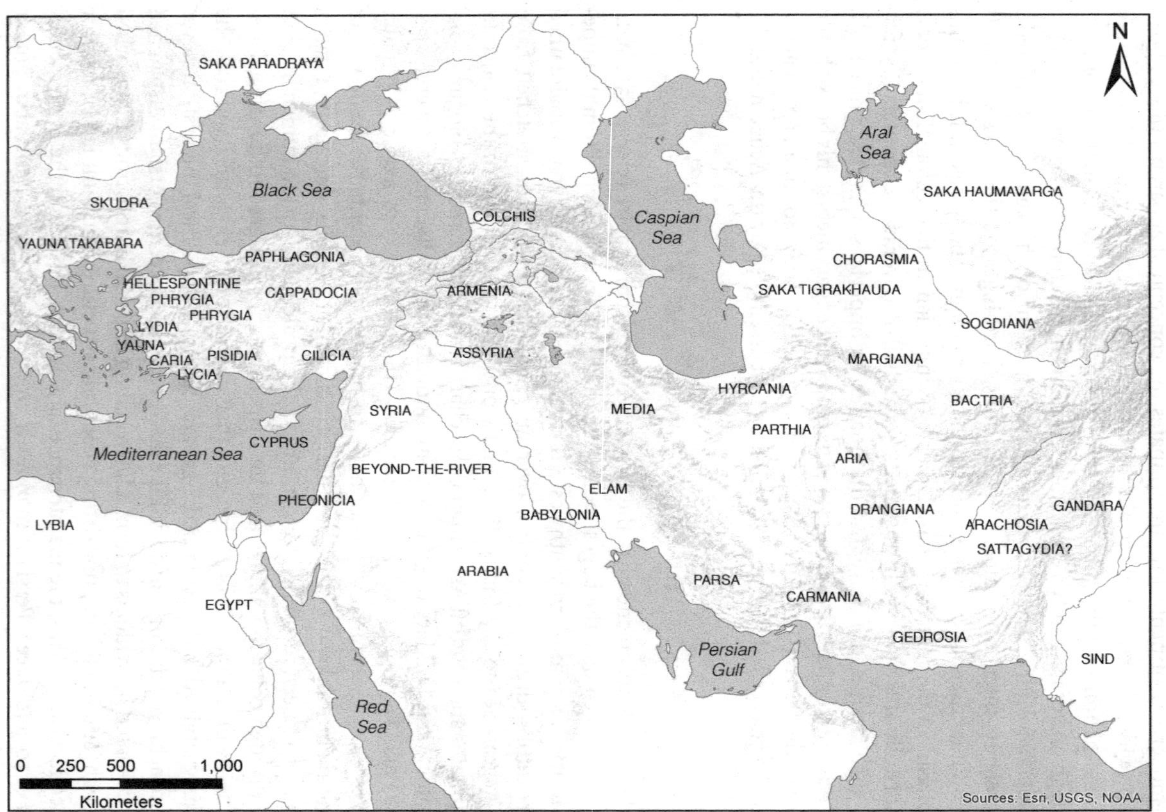

MAP 1. The Achaemenid Empire (created by Lori Khatchadourian and Adam T. Smith).

chapter 1, theirs was not a stridently eradicative civilizing mission. It was one that offered salvation yet permitted religious self-expression. It was one that, like many imperial projects, tolerated diversity yet dealt mercilessly with dissent. And it was one that, backed by a proven, effective apparatus of force, bound subjects to the polity for over two centuries, until Macedonian forces invaded Persia's territories, marched on Persepolis, and replaced the Achaemenid model of imperial rule with another.

A GUIDE TO IMPERIAL MATTER

Imperial Matter is written with multiple audiences in mind and, as such, it is a book that invites different kinds of encounter, accepting that the depth of engagement across the various chapters of the book will modulate depending on the commitments of different readerships. This roadmap is meant not only to provide a synopsis of the book, but also to alert its readers to the different intellectual bearings of each chapter, so that they may decide how they wish to read it. I hope this guide will help readers know where to expect the stakes to be high or low in relation to their own scholarly investments, where they will find themselves "at home" with the style of argumentation, and where they should be prepared for entry into a foreign scholarly jungle dense with either the esoteric idioms of theory or the arcane particulars of Near Eastern archaeology. While I have made every effort to make the path through these various jungles a clear one, there is of course still overgrowth on both sides of the route, which readers will choose either to venture into or to skirt past depending on their own interests.

Because this book is intended as much for audiences beyond Near Eastern archaeology as for those within it, I have made a terminological choice that requires a brief explanation. "Ancient Persia" is a term that specialists may regard as inapt, simultaneously too expansive and too narrow for the context in which I use it. In its most expansive connotation, "ancient Persia" could encapsulate a tremendous sweep of time, from late prehistory until the rise of Islam. At the same time, the term can be understood as geographically restricted, referring narrowly to the heartland of the Achaemenid Empire. My usage (in the title of this book and elsewhere) conforms to neither of these temporal or geographic extremes. In the main, I use "ancient Persia" broadly, in reference to a religio-political culture that stiches together the related (but very far from identical) political thought of the Achaemenid Empire and that of the later Avestan tradition of the Sasanian era. In this sense, ancient Persia is not exhausted by the centuries of Achaemenid ascendancy, although the latter is obviously an extremely important part of the former. Hence, what grounds the term "ancient Persia" is neither a dynasty nor a region, but a tradition of political reflection whose wellspring, to the best of our knowledge, lies in the imperial project of the Achaemenids. Insofar as, on a more temporally restricted scale, the empirical commitments of this book center on the Achaemenid Persian Empire, "ancient Persia" also denotes this particular historical phenomenon. In this usage I am referring to a political association conceived, maintained, and shaped through an imperial ideology emanating from what is today southwestern Iran. Specialists may find this archaic usage particularly discomfiting, for it may seem to imply that this far-reaching realm was a homogeneous, ethnically construed "Persian" unity. No such subtext is intended. My purpose, especially in the title of this book, is instead to simultaneously train the reader's attention on a cultural tradition of political thought and at the same time welcome a community of nonspecialist readers for whom "ancient Persia" may offer a somewhat better purchase on the empirical concerns of this book than would the more esoteric "Achaemenid Empire."

Imperial Matter is organized into two parts. The first (chapters 1–3) develops a theoretical project centered on the relationship between imperialism and things. The second (chapters 4–6) works to demonstrate the merits of that project through an in-depth examination of the working of things in the Achaemenid Empire and its northern lands of Armenia. In its overall design, chapter 1 alone may have the quality of being at once foreign and "homey" to all readers. Here I provide a detailed account of the "satrapal condition," working through a diverse corpus of textual and sculptural materials pertinent to the term "satrapy." To those unfamiliar with ancient Persian cultural production, these materials, while hopefully engaging, may also at times feel heavy with the weight that humanity's venerable but defunct antiquity can inflict on the present. At the same time, the approach taken is a social scientific analysis intent on deriving broad political concepts from the rich particulars of ancient Persian thought, and in this way is quite at odds with existing genres of practice in the humanistic endeavor of Iranian studies.

Part 1 positions the analytic of the satrapal condition in relation to related concepts and conversations in archaeology, anthropology, and the material turn. I begin with archaeology. Chapter 2 presents a critical historiography of the archaeology of empires and its engagements with the world of matter. Archaeologists will discern in this study an effort to theorize a subfield of our discipline not principally according to established categories (e.g., "processual" versus "post-processual," economy versus society, structure versus agency) but according to our shifting figurations of things. Should they choose to venture deeply into this chapter, non-archaeologist readers concerned with problems of empire and colonialism will gain a sense of how this peer discipline has carved out a space in the study of phenomena that refuse to be contained within any single disciplinary home.

In this chapter I make the case that the lingering evolutionary approaches of the 1990s, as well as those of the new millennium that have focused on problems of colonialism, while both decisive in bringing anthropological attention to early imperial and colonial formations, have not gone quite far enough in defining a distinctly archaeological epistemic of imperialism dedicated to understanding the work of things in reproducing the layered sovereignties of empire. Whether on account of an overemphasis on the strategies of the putatively tidy and omnipotent state, or the centering of the colonial subject to such degree as to hold the "matter" of empire at the margins of analysis, I suggest that both approaches stop short of realizing archaeology's own armature for elucidating the force and frailty of imperial sovereignty. This chapter thus develops a critical appraisal of "where things stand" in archaeology's account of imperial reproduction and the colonial encounter over the course of three and a half decades of sustained inquiry into the provinces and colonies of these expansive macropolities. As the chapter moves broadly from problems of empire to colonialism, from the actions of imperial agents to the agency of imperial subjects, a range of perspectives on things will emerge that cast them variously as goods of the good laborer, signifiers of the pliant subject, and artifacts and media of the agentive subject.

Chapter 2's effort to detail archaeology's prevailing perspectives on imperial things establishes a baseline from which an explicit theorization of the relations among humans, things, and the layered sovereignties of empire can take shape in the next chapter. In conversation with the ontological concerns of the material turn, chapter 3 conceptualizes the work of things in the production of satrapal conditions. Readers can approach the first half of this chapter expecting to discover what I regard as lacunae in both material and colonial thought, gaps that have left us without an adequate theory of imperial things. While several recent political theories of matter have heterodoxically asserted the determinative role of things in making political association possible, they have at the same time set the limits of the political quite narrowly, in such a way as to exclude imperial polities from the reach of their concepts. Conversely, while anthropologies of colonialism have placed at the center of their analyses precisely the unique relations of power that obtain in imperial formations, those that cast objects prominently in the theater of colonialism tend to shortchange things in their abilities to shape imperial projects, quite apart from the intentions of the humans who make them, use them, and conscript them to the work of signification. To fill these lacunae requires an analytic framework that is expressly centered on the politics of matter in imperial formations.

Such is the extended focus of the latter half of the chapter, which develops a schema for imperial things that pivots around political materials that I call *delegates, proxies, captives,* and *affiliates.* Readers who chose to move briskly along the main path in the first half of the chapter may here entertain a slower pace, in order to consider a suite of concepts that will frame all subsequent chapters of the book. *Delegates* are nonhuman political entities whose material substances and forms matter greatly to imperial agents. Sovereigns rely on delegates for the preservation of the terms of imperial sovereignty and, in turn, in a certain sense, come to be "governed" by them. Can we imagine Roman supremacy in the absence of the empire's marble architectural and sculptural delegates, or Incan sovereignty without delegates of textile? *Proxies* are things that come about through the mimetic arts. They echo delegates in aspects of their form, but distinguish themselves in their materials and production. Proxies can, under certain conditions, erode or undermine the efficacy of the delegates from which they derive. We often call such things imitations, copies, or replicas, but as we shall see, these terms do not adequately capture their material affordances. *Captives* are things in states of displacement and dislocation. They are the consequence of imperial theft—both the theft of material things, like the antiquities that European empires purloined from colonial lands, and the theft of ideas about matter and form. *Affiliates* are the great masses of everyday things that reproduce social life under empire, even as they preserve an inviolable space of experience within it.

Delegates, proxies, captives, and affiliates are modes of material being that override more conventional schemas for classifying the material world, be it objects versus landscapes, imports versus local productions, luxuries versus utilitarian goods. They are formulated instead to forward the distinctive interventions of different kinds of matter in sociopolitical life under empire, and to accentuate the differing relations both among these various modes and with their human makers and users, from the most privileged imperial agents to the subjugated whom they rule. Yet despite the varying ways in which delegates, proxies, captives, and affiliates make and modify imperial projects, they emerge analytically out of the well-founded postulate that virtually all matter is bound up in human–thing assemblages that palpably make some sort of difference in the world. Chapter 3 in part works to come to grips with these capacities, as a prerequisite for recognizing delegates, proxies, captives, and affiliates as the serious matter that lies at the heart of the satrapal condition.

Part 2 of *Imperial Matter* draws the theoretical concerns of the first three chapters into an investigation of satrapal conditions in the Achaemenid Empire and its northern "land/peoples" (Old Persian *dahyu*, pl. *dahyāva*) of Armenia. The jungle gets denser here for those outside of Near Eastern archaeology, and I acknowledge the formidable challenge of keeping the path clear for the nonspecialist while engaging closely with forms of evidence that matter greatly for those of us committed to thinking through the deep past. Readers less invested in the Achaemenid Empire should hopefully find sufficient signposting to help keep them on the main road. In chapters 4–6, the discussion tacks back and forth between the imperial heartland—in the foothills of southwestern Iran's southern Zagros Mountains (Fars) and the neighboring low-lying plains of Khuzistan—and the rugged uplands that stretch from the headwaters of the Euphrates River eastward to the mountains of the South Caucasus, and southward to the central Zagros (modern eastern Turkey, Armenia, Georgia, Azerbaijan, and northern Iran). The decision to concentrate on the provincial territory known to the Persians as Armenia at the expense of other regions of the empire was both a pragmatic and a principled one. Unlike, say, the Roman or Incan Empires, in the Persian case there has been a true and unfortunate dearth of targeted, sustained, systematic archaeological survey and excavation outside the imperial center, despite the longevity and tremendous territorial extent of the empire (Khatchadourian 2012). But thanks to the convergence of a number of factors—among them relative political stability, interest in the period on the part of scholars in the region, and a welcoming atmosphere for foreign archaeologists who are committed to genuine collaboration—the South Caucasus (Armenia, Azerbaijan, and Georgia) has emerged in the last decade as an area of heightened activity, where original, research-driven fieldwork into the period of Persian rule (or what I shall be calling the Iron 3 period) is being undertaken by a handful of international research teams. Counted among these initiatives are the long-term excavations that colleagues and I carried out at the central Armenian site of Tsaghkahovit under the auspices of the Project for the Archaeology and Geography of Ancient Transcaucasian Societies (Project ArAGATS). Begun in 1998, Project ArAGATS is the longest-standing collaborative archaeological research project in the South Caucasus. The findings from Tsaghkahovit, which are the subject of chapter 6, are particularly notable for the rare light they shed on village life in a remote corner of the empire.

Even more importantly, the research carried out at Tsaghkahovit was crucial in giving shape to the conceptual apparatus at the heart of *Imperial Matter.* The settlement and the larger sociopolitical sphere of Achaemenid Armenia to which it belongs therefore serve as a kind of laboratory for experimenting with the concepts developed in part 1 of this book. In the case study, in other words, I opt for depth over breadth. This is less a book dedicated to the archaeology of the Achaemenid Empire per se, than one that regards this early experiment in continental rule as especially well suited to a foundational account of the workings of imperial matter. I leave it to others to assess how well the central concepts of this book hold up elsewhere, not only in other regions of this particular empire, but in other imperial formations across time.

Part 2 opens with an examination of acts of material capture undertaken by the Achaemenid kings in relation to the highland zone of the northern Zagros and Caucasia, and the transformation of captives into delegates. Key to this analysis is a distinctive architectural form known as the columned hall, which became fundamental to the reproduction of Achaemenid sovereignty. The columned hall was first devised in the highlands during the eighth century B.C. as a material repudiation of the complex polity and the attendant hierarchical ordering of political association. From its relatively modest beginnings, the hall later appeared in more opulent form in the imperial centers of Iran as the result of Persian acts of capture and appropriation. Reincarnated as a delegate, the columned hall both enabled the reproduction of certain core principles and practices of Achaemenid authority and, in exchange, imposed unrelenting demands on the sovereign establishment.

In chapter 5, attention turns from delegates in the imperial heartland to the making of satrapal conditions in the Armenian *dahyu* by means of a host of delegates and proxies. The analysis in this chapter hovers at a broad, regional scale, offering a general picture of the contours of Achaemenid rule in this mountain region, to the extent that it can be pieced together from important but imperfect datasets derived from systematic and unsystematic surveys and excavations. The tensions of subjection and its limits that define the satrapal condition are here discernable through such things as Achaemenid silver drinking vessels from Turkey and Armenia (delegates), an elaborate columned hall in Azerbaijan (a delegate), and columned halls built in the highland style in both Turkey and Armenia (proxies). I make the case that these delegates and proxies worked variously to both reinforce and undermine imperial control over an upland zone of the empire that was evidently only lightly governed.

Following this regional scale of analysis, the resolution of inquiry increases in chapter 6 with a close examination of delegates, proxies, and affiliates at the settlement of Tsaghkahovit. In a field of inquiry that has long privileged imperial centers, urban hubs, and palatial residences, the work at Tsaghkahovit provides the most in-depth picture to date of life in an ordinary village of the empire. The settlement was peaceably abandoned in the fourth century B.C., and therefore largely denuded of its things. But nine seasons of excavation have yielded tantalizing hints of the community's involvement in the wider Achaemenid project. The primary affiliate at Tsaghkahovit was its distinctive semi-subterranean architecture, which provided the community's concealment and partial autonomy from the designs of imperial governance. Yet, in these underground havens, inhabitants made use of ceramic and stone delegates and proxies that, in their materials, forms, and practical affordances, extended the reach of Achaemenid sovereignty while at the same time limiting its efficacy. Places such as these bring to the fore the conjoint work of humans and things in the everyday making of satrapal conditions and the paradoxes of imperial rule.

Empires are critically shaped by a vast world of things. But they are not themselves things. In using the term "empire" throughout this book I do not mean to call up the old sense of the term as an ontologically solid entity that is fixed and bounded in space and time. Rather, empires are contingent and unfolding processes, ultimately grounded in structured violence, whose directions are critically shaped by the practical entailments of human–thing relations. I use the terms "empires" and "imperial formations" in this book to capture both the powerful institutions and ideologies of dominance *and* what Stoler and McGranahan (2007) have called the "blurred genres of rule" that account for imperialism's partial sovereignties. How deeply and persistently the destructive forces of imperial formations penetrate societies is historically and spatially contingent, yet such violence is a foundational and enduring quality of their very existence. Neither "empire" nor "imperial formations" denotes "steady states, but states of becoming, macropolities in states of solution and constant formation" (8–9). This is a book about the role of nonhuman things in partnering with imperial agents and subjects alike in confederacies that influence the course of such perpetually shifting and intricate configurations of macropolitical power.

PART ONE

1

The Satrapal Condition

Hushang ascended the throne after his grandfather and declared himself the king of the seven realms. During the forty years of his reign, Hushang spread justice and enriched the world as he was commanded to do so by God. He melted iron and inaugurated the use of instruments such as hatchets, axes, saws, and maces. But all of these new inventions were made possible only after he accidentally discovered the secret of making fire.

—FERDOWSI, *SHAHNAMEH: THE EPIC OF THE PERSIAN KINGS*[1]

In his celebrated epic poem the *Shahnameh,* the Persian poet Ferdowsi put to verse a history of the kings of Persia whose mythical beginnings establish in no uncertain terms the infrangible link between the material devices of work and war and the just and good imperial sovereign. Hushang, the second mythical king of yore, who took to the throne after defeating a horde of black demons, inadvertently discovers fire while attempting to strike a snake with a piece of flint. Missing the target, the flint instead hits a nearby stone, producing a spark, which leads first to Hushang's discovery of flames, and onward ineluctably to humankind's reliance on metal instruments. Once Hushang masters fire and introduces to humanity the metallurgical arts, he goes on to teach irrigation, agriculture, hunting, and the domestication of animals. He dies a peaceful death, forever remembered as a great king who transformed human experience for the better.

It is difficult to read Ferdowsi's verses on Hushang, the second king of the seven realms, without recalling the better-known Greek myth of the fire-stealing titan, Prometheus, which Adam T. Smith (2015: 27) recently described as an "urtext for today's material turn." In the ancient Promethian cycle, just as in the tenth-century *Shahnameh,* the introduction of fire is tied to the invention and use of material implements that dramatically improved the human condition, while at the same time leaving us hopelessly obliged to labor with this sophisticated new world of material things (Smith 2015: 28). And in both stories, such advances are attributed to figures credited with humanity's salvation—in the Greek case from the wrath of Zeus, and in the Persian case from the evil spirit Ahiraman, creator of demons and source of all darkness in the universe.

But the Greek and Persian tales differ in at least two critically important respects. First, unlike Prometheus, the heroic figure of the *Shahnameh* is a blameless savior. Hushang commits no transgression, angers no tyrant god, and faces no tragic fate. On the contrary, in putting his accidental discovery of fire to profitable use, he acts in accordance with God's will. The Hushang story asserts the connection between imperial sovereignty and metal as the natural and divinely ordained order of things. Second, the Prometheus legend is nearly cosmogonic in its temporality, unfolding in a fully mythic age when a titan still walked the earth and humankind had not yet assembled into political association. The *Shahnameh,* in contrast, sets the invention of fire, metallurgy, and the attendant enrichment of the world in the quasi-profane realm of primordial political history, in which the first kings not only walked the earth, but ruled it. The Hushang verses of the *Shahnameh,* in other words, represent an early rumination not principally on the general relationship between humans and things, but more specifically on the links that bind monarchal sovereigns, subjects, and things.

This is no isolated or coincidental convergence. As we return now to the word "satrapy" and a close dissection of its meanings and associations, what comes to the fore is a prevailing concern across various strands of Persian cultural production—sometimes explicit, often not—to grapple with this nexus of phenomena. The exploration that follows dwells on selected texts and sculptural reliefs of the Persian sovereigns, before moving forward in time to examine innovations in Mazdean religious scripture that postdate the Achaemenid fall by several hundred years. In the final section of this chapter, the insights from these esoteric bodies of ancient Persian thought are brought into conversation with contemporary anthropological reflection on imperial sovereignty, giving rise to a full elaboration of the satrapal condition as a productive heuristic for an archaeology of empires.

SOVEREIGNTY CO-CONSTITUTED AND CONDITIONAL

The primary lexical unit on which the word *satrapy* is built belongs to a language now called Old Persian, one of two textually preserved Old Iranian languages (the other being Avestan, the language of Zoroastrian scripture), which occurs in written form in the royal inscriptions of the Achaemenid Persian kings. It is in one of the oldest, if not the first, such Old Persian inscription, carved into the cliff face of Mount Bisitun, where this root word, *xšaça,* makes its first appearance (figure 4).[2] This foundational text of Achaemenid history recounts the story of how the charismatic king Darius rose to power and restored order in the aftermath of a series of rebellions and purported court intrigues that threatened the dynasty and the imperial realm. In the first column of the rock-carved text, we learn that an imposter claimant to the throne brazenly "seized *xšaça*" (DB I.11).[3] Then, by the grace

FIGURE 4. Photograph of the rock relief on Mt. Bisitun (courtesy of Rémy Boucharlat).

of the god Ahuramazda, Darius and a small band of nobles killed this so-called imposter and the god "bestowed *xšaça*" on Darius (DB I.13). The denouement of these tumultuous events is visually depicted in a stirring relief composition—the only part of the monument that would have been intelligible to most observers—in which Darius, with his foot pressed firmly on the chest of the imposter, stands facing the various troublemakers whom he successfully suppressed. Awaiting the king's judgment, all stand on the brink of exclusion from the body politic (Agamben 1998), their bodies stooped, their hands tied, their political identities stripped of dignity by "bio-political fiat" (Hansen and Stepputat 2006: 297) that sanctions the acts of torture recounted in the accompanying text.[4]

Scholars of Old Iranian languages have labored to arrive at a satisfactory definition of this weighty little word, and have been divided as to the ontological status of its referent as either an abstract principle (sovereignty/kingship) or a material entity (dominion/kingdom) (e.g. Gnoli 1972, 2005, 2007; Kellens 2002; Kent 1953; Schmitt 1998). The most lasting resolution to this semantic struggle has been to recognize *xšaça* as both (e.g. Bartholomae 1904: 542; Kellens 1992: 439). Linguist and semiotician Émile Benveniste (1969: 19) captured this duality in his formulation of *xšaça,* saying, "C'est à la fois le pouvoir et le domain où s'exerce ce pouvoir, la royauté et le royaume."[5] Echoing Benveniste, Lincoln (2007: 45) defines *xšaça* as "a term that fuses the senses of 'kingship' and 'kingdom,' denoting both royal power and the multiple provinces over which that power is exercised." This semantic unity suggests that Achaemenid political thinkers posited an ontological indivisibility of sovereignty as a prerogative of rule and a sphere of earthly exertion. Power is constituted through a physical, terrestrial world that is governed by its force; yet this animated physical world can be governed (qua dominion) only through the force of sublime power. In a slightly different manner, the duality finds expression in the contrasting uses of *xšaça* in the Bisitun text, where it is both given by God, and thus prior to the polity itself ("Ahuramazda bestowed *xšaça* on me"), and at the same time violable (as by rebels and imposters)—open to alteration, theft, or displacement by practical, human action—an a posteriori power that is dependent on experience. This acute intuition of the fragility of sovereignty as a paradoxical condition of its very existence was expressed in religious terms through the notion of the Lie, an evil force that embodies nothing less than "the negation of proper sovereignty" (Benveniste 1938, discussed in Lincoln 2012: 12). The very appearance of the Lie, a might that limits the possibility of absolute sovereignty on earth, marked the end of cosmic perfection and the beginning of history. The Lie is what necessitated the God-given imperial prerogative of the Achaemenid kings, who were tasked by Ahuramazda with the eschatological struggle to see to its eradication. Here is a case, if ever there was one, of an empire exercising "the privilege . . . to make [its history] appear as History" (Coronil 2007: 245). Achaemenid thinkers might not have been prepared "to abandon sovereignty as an ontological ground of power and order," but they might nevertheless have begrudgingly recognized "a view of sovereignty as a tentative and always emergent form of authority" (Hansen and Stepputat 2006: 297). Their task was less to deny the challenge of absolute sovereignty than to confidently work to overcome the circumstances (or, from their perspective, evil perversions) that made it all but unattainable.

There is one further layer to *xšaça*'s signification that contributes to its exquisite conceptual force. We have seen that Lincoln defined the term as one that denotes "both royal power and the multiple provinces over which that power is exercised." But strictly speaking, as Lincoln himself elsewhere notes (2007: 70), the earthly referent of *xšaça* in the Persian royal sources is not the "multiple provinces" of the empire, but one realm in particular, the imperial heartland of Persia, its people and society. It is only insofar as Persian cosmology under Darius viewed the entire empire as, in Clarisse Herrenschmidt's (1976: 45) words, "the generalized reproduction of Persian society" that the full extent of the imperial dominion can be semantically contained in *xšaça,* through a kind of synecdoche where the whole stands in for the part. Dominion in its entirety is in some sense replicative and regenerative of the heartland. In this *totum pro parte* relation between the empire and its "metropole," satrapy and center emerge co-constitutively rather than dichotomously. In a sense, this dimension of *xšaça* prefigures a key realization in postcolonial studies: that long-dichotomized centers and peripheries in fact emerge simultaneously, rather than in a teleological, imperialized sequence (e.g. Cohn 1996: 4; Comaroff and Comaroff 1997; Stoler and Cooper 1997).

How did early political thought lose hold of the richly nuanced understanding of imperial sovereignty contained in the semantic field of *xšaça?* How did a word that captured the notion of imperial sovereignty as conditional and co-constituted in principle and practice devolve into the banal and sordid sense of "satrapy" that has come down to us today—a technical term to denote a province of empire conscripted into the dirty work of imperial dominion? To answer this question we turn once again to the Bisitun inscription, where in addition to the word *xšaça* there appears its etymological relation, *xšaçapāvan*—literally meaning "a protector of *xšaça.*" The protectors of sovereignty/dominion were individuals whom Darius dispatched to distant lands (like Bactria and Arachosia, in modern Afghanistan) to quell the revolts that threatened the empire (DBIII.38, 45). These guardians of the royal and the realm were the advance guard in the cosmic and tellurian struggle against the Lie, their very appellation yet another indication of the recognition that sovereignty is provisional, in constant need of vigilant defense. The fragmentary evidence seems to suggest that the duty of the *xšaçapāvan* to protect the sovereign and his realm existed prior to any particular territorial jurisdiction that might also be assigned, at least in certain periods of Achaemenid history (Briant 2002: 65). Nowhere in the extant Old Persian corpus is there a term that fixes and partitions the work of the *xšaçapāvan* into distinct territorial units. The entailments of the *xšaçapāvan* were, it seems, more spatially elastic, much like conceptions of sovereignty that obtained in early modern Europe (Benton 2010: 288). The administrative notion of a "province" simply does not exist within the semantic scope of *xšaça* or *xšaçapāvan.*[6]

Such, it would appear, was the Greek historian Herodotus' contribution to the vernacular of empire. It is in his *Histories* that the word "satrapy" (*σατράπης*) makes its first appearance, where it is glossed as an alien political term meaning province or magistracy (*ἀρχή*): "[Darius] established twenty satrapies, *which is what they call provinces in Persia,* and after he designated the provinces and the governors in charge of them, he assigned to each nation the tribute it would pay to him" (Herodotus 2007: *Hist.* 3.89, 1.192, emphasis added). The satrapies of the Achaemenid Empire, a reading of Herodotus teaches us, are neatly divisible spatial units—the administrative apparatus that facilitated the extraction of resources from lands and peoples in the form of such things as silver and gold, horses and humans.[7] Entailed in this creative lexical innovation is a flattening of *xšaça*'s ontological status into a unidimensional concept, a partitioning and fixing in space of a notion of sovereignty not meant, it would appear, to be construed strictly territorially or partitively. It is of course possible that the Achaemenids indeed maintained such an administrative and geographic notion of satrapy, as Herodotus would have us believe, and we simply have no record of it. But I am inclined to think otherwise.[8] A great deal of the semantic sophistication contained in the Old Persian conception of *xšaça* and *xšaçapāvan* was thus single-handedly stripped away with this Herodotean neologism, as an embodied role in the preservation of sovereignty came to be linked to the mundane trappings of government.[9] It is this sense of the word "satrapy," later to be adopted by numerous Greek and Roman authors from Thucydides to Plutarch, that has come down to us today, now tinged in popular parlance with a derision (not to be found in Herodotus) that has accumulated around satrapy over centuries of civilizational discourse pitting democratic classical "West" against despotic Persian "East."

As might be expected with any novel political experiment, there was nothing accidental about the language of the first "world empire" (Kuhrt 2001: 93). Achaemenid thinkers took great care to devise a vocabulary of empire that met the needs of the imperial project and was consistent with their worldview, and in time *xšaça* no longer met those requirements (Lincoln 2007: 45, 70).[10] Yet the fundamental postulate of the co-constitution of kingship and kingdom, ultimate authority and the limiting conditions of practical action, endured in material form in an iconographic device that provides something of a visual allegory for *xšaça*. The scene occurs repeatedly, with some variation, on a number of the best-known Achaemenid monuments in and around Persepolis, from the doorjambs of two royal buildings in the grandiose metropolis (figure 5) to the façade that adorns the tomb of Darius and those of his successors (figure 6).[11] The tableau consists of four recurrent components: in the uppermost field there hovers the god Ahuramazda in a winged disk; in the central panel, the Persian king is depicted either enthroned or standing on a three-stepped platform before a fire altar; below the standing or seated king, there is a platform-like object with elaborate vertical struts; and in the lower part stand two or three registers of figures, each a personification of an incorporated people of the empire, with their arms upraised and interlocked in a pose that recalls the primordial titan Atlas, who was eternally condemned to hold up the celestial sphere.[12] In this case, however, the human bodies of the subjugated bear the platform or "throne-platform" above them (Root 1979). To the Achaemenids, the metaphorical task of holding up the figurative weight of imperial order was, to be sure, no sentence to punishment. It was rather an opportunity for those persons belonging to the political community to partake in what Bruce Grant (2009), writing in a very different context, has called the "gift of empire"—in this case no mere gift of civilization, but nothing less than the promise of cosmic happiness for all mankind. In contradistinction to Bisitun, these are the bodies included in the polity (Agamben 1998).

Much has been written about this composition. In perhaps the most authoritative account, Root has carefully dissected the scene's debts to, and creative modifications of, earlier iconographic traditions of kingship in Egypt and ancient Iraq, as well as its potential real-world referents and metaphorical claims. Based on

FIGURE 5. Illustration of the stone relief from the east jamb of the eastern doorway in the southern wall of the Hall of 100 Columns at Persepolis (source: Curtis and Tallis 2005, fig. 38, courtesy of John Curtis, drawing by Ann Searight).

her analysis of the motif's antecedents and the meaning of the various genuflections, from the "atlas posture" to the hand gestures of king and god, Root (1979: 131–181) concluded that the personifications of the subject peoples are portrayed as voluntary participants in a cooperative effort, at once religious and political, to support and pay homage to the king. The thrust of her interpretation stressed less the literal ceremonial event that it may portray—a royal procession involving the transport of the king on a monumental platform—than its symbolic work in representing a carefully conceived, hierarchical relationship between king and

FIGURE 6. Tomb of Darius at Naqsh-i Rustam (courtesy of Lloyd Llewellyn-Jones).

subjects (131). The "throne-bearing" scene, as it is called (though it is not literally a throne that is borne), fits neatly within the larger visual and rhetorical repertoire of the Achaemenids, which consistently projects a vision of a harmonious, participatory, and reciprocally constituted imperial order (Root 2000). Yet it is worth always remembering that such visual language of reciprocity "requires little or no actual reception among the conquered. It is the logic of sovereign rule where the act of taking—of lands, persons, and goods—is enabled by the language of giving" (Grant 2009: 44).

As an enlargement of the interpretive space surrounding the throne-bearing scene, two additional aspects of the tableau can be drawn forth by expanding on key insights in the work of both Root and Lincoln. First, it is possible to see in its arrangement the same postulate contained in the semantic field of *xšaça*—one that regards sovereignty as co-constituted, through the mediation of the sovereign, by that which is a priori (the rights and obligations conferred by the Wise Lord) and a posteriori (the profane realm of imperial subjection), by that which is independent of and dependent on experience, by both predestination and practical action. If this particular approach to the composition de-emphasizes somewhat the distinction of the king, it brings to the fore the embodied work of the upward hoist as an exertion of the body politic. In her analysis of the atlas motif in the Achaemenid reliefs, Root noted a significant shift from preceding Near Eastern traditions. Whereas in the earlier art of ancient Iraq and Egypt the posture was reserved almost exclusively for mythical beings, cosmic creatures, and gods, the

Achaemenids passed the pose on from daemons to mortals, and not merely to humans as such, but more specifically to political subjects—the embodied collectivities incorporated into the imperial community (Root 1979: 147–153). Root is no doubt correct in suggesting that the Achaemenids meant to draw on the motif's earlier associations with rituals of cosmological support, and thus engage the subjugated in a collective "song of praise" for king and kingdom (160). She has also stressed that in recasting the bearers as mortal political subjects, the Achaemenids developed a notion of earthly imperial power premised explicitly on reciprocity between the sovereign and the body politic.

I would like to press further this harmonious notion of reciprocity toward a more sharp-edged idea of *dependency* (with all the attendant connotations of susceptibility to disruption), to which I suggest the thinkers behind the motif were also keenly attuned. Lincoln (2012: 144) has picked up on this idea of dependence, writing that "The platforms Darius and his successors occupy . . . represent the entire imperial apparatus, which encompasses, contains, organizes, disciplines, and also quite literally *de-pends* on the lands/peoples of the empire" (emphasis added). Unlike mythical beings scripted into cosmic roles, the figures engaged in upholding the metaphorical imperial realm retained the capacity to exercise political choices. "The man who cooperates," one of Darius's more famous tomb inscriptions reads, "him according to his cooperative *action*, him thus do I reward" (DNb.2c, emphasis added).[13] This emphasis on purposeful action introduces unspoken into these scenes the looming metaphorical possibility that the figures could drop their arms, that human agency (when unconstrained by fear and the force of law, or blind to righteousness, which is all to say contaminated by the Lie) could entail letting go of the imperial apparatus and undermining proper sovereignty. The inscription and image betray a quiet concession that the entire structure could become unstable or, worse yet, come tumbling down. Herein, perhaps, lies the fundamental distinction between the daemon and the demos when cast in the guise of atlas.[14] That such a concession should be worked into this corpus of Achaemenid political art is hardly surprising; by the time the throne-bearing scenes were crafted, the lessons from the events recounted on the Bisitun monument were already learned. The possibility of an unruly body politic was well understood. In visually representing the inescapable dependency of the polity on the embodied, practical actions of the political community, Achaemenid political thinkers once again intuited a notion of sovereignty as a question not yet settled.

The second unexplored aspect of this visual trope that merits consideration (before we move closer once again into *xšaça*'s semantic orbit) is the considerable prominence accorded to the material object that makes possible the entailments of imperial sovereignty and the association of deity, dynast, and demos. There was a time when much of the scholarly attention surrounding these scenes focused on the actuality of the representation and the details of the ritual that would have required the ceremonial transport of the Persian king (summarized in Root 1979: 153–161). If Root was the first to emphasize the political metaphor behind the image, Lincoln (2012: 142) has most explicitly emblemized the central object itself: "Not a throne like any other, this is a metaphorical throne, a point the relief and inscription both make, each in its fashion." The inscription to which Lincoln refers is one that accompanies the tomb of Darius and includes the following injunction: "If now you should think, 'How many are the countries which King Darius held?,' look at the sculptures of those who bear the throne" (DNa.4).[15] Complicating matters, however, is the fact that the Old Persian word here translated as "throne" is somewhat ambiguous, its etymology and other appearances suggesting that it instead means "place" (Lincoln 2012: 143).

Thanks to Lincoln (2012: 127–144), we can appreciate the significance of this elision. He has observed that Achaemenid political thinkers took care to develop and express the acutely spatial notion of "putting things 'in place.'" Putting things "in place" captured the totality of the Achaemenid project of "reunifying humanity, conquering evil, restoring happiness, and ushering the final eternity" (128). It is what Darius claims to have done in various inscriptions after the sociopolitical unrest narrated on Bisitun. Yet putting things "in place" also entailed a manifestly material effort, as Darius makes clear from an inscription at the imperial capital of Susa: "By the Wise Lord's will, much handiwork that previously was not *in place*, that I made *in place*. In Susa, a wall had fallen down as a result of its old age. Formerly it was unrepaired. I made another wall (that will endure) from that time into the future" (DSe.5, emphasis added).[16] The rebuilding of the wall at Susa was no mundane act, but a reversal of the entropic momentum initiated by the arrival of the Lie: "By repairing the wall, Darius understood himself to have helped reverse processes of natural and moral decay, and to have restored things-as-they-once-were-and-forever-ought-be" (Lincoln 2012: 128).

Just as the wall at Susa was a participant in the work of putting things "in place," so too were the platforms of the throne-bearing scenes, which held "firmly 'in place'" the subjugated communities (144). The platforms in these tableaux are no mere props or incidental paraphernalia used to express a notion of kingship, but are instead the very scaffolding that makes the imperial project possible. Each stands quite literally as the material deputy of sovereignty itself, representing the unrepresentable, a frame—materially present but itself unframed—that delimits the inside from the outside (Bartelson 1995: 51). Viewed in conjunction, the throne-bearing scenes and the language of "placedness" reveal an unmistakable supposition in Achaemenid political thought on the interrelation of imperial sovereignty and materiality. The material world brings order to the political community, just as its decay threatens a promise of a utopian future that only the sovereign can secure.

While it may seem that we have strayed rather far from *xšaça* to arrive at this finding, other strands of thought from within the broader corpus of Persian metaphysics leave little doubt that early scholars of this religio-political tradition gave careful scrutiny to the link between *xšaça* and things. It is to these tantalizing and undisputedly difficult materials that I now turn.

CHOICE SOVEREIGNTY: HARD AS METAL AND CRYSTAL SKY

Every field of study has its own divisive yet defining debates whose vicissitudes would seem to outside observers like the scholarly equivalent of a merry-go-round turning continuously in place, but to their participants hold the very highest intellectual stakes. For ancient Iranian studies, one such debate has long centered on the relation of the religion of the Avesta, commonly known as Zoroastrianism, to that of the Achaemenids. Why precisely the stakes are perceived to be so high defies a simple brief, since the controversy has been waged through the observation of general resemblances as much as detailed doctrinal differences.[17] There is a sense that to regard the Achaemenids as the first to adopt Zoroastrian tenets into something like a state religion would be both to reach beyond what Achaemenid sources have to tell us about the dynasty's system of beliefs and, more troublingly, to presume a more codified Zoroastrian creed than we know to have existed in the sixth century B.C. on the basis of extant scripture. If the debate still seems thoroughly arcane, consider the broader context: Zoroastrianism is quite possibly the earliest recorded religion in the Indo-European tradition with clear, though by no means aggressive, monotheistic features, and it is one that, in ways much debated, influenced Judaism and Christianity (Gafni 2002: 234–247; Russell 1964: 19, 266, 384; Mark Smith 2001: 166). Its own history of emergence thus has a number of cascading implications (see also Lincoln 2012: 42). For present purposes, this debate matters relatively little; it suffices to accept the view that the Achaemenian and Zoroastrian were two traditions (among others) in a broader, pan-Iranian system of "Mazdean" belief that centered on the worship of the Wise Lord, Ahuramazda (Knäpper 2011; Lincoln 2007, 2012).

It is in this body of Mazdean religious scripture and associated interpretation that *xšaça* appears yet again, this time in a rather different guise, in connection with a group of six divine entities known as the Aməša Spənta (in Avestan), or Amahrspandān (in Middle Persian), meaning Bounteous Immortals. In Zoroastrian sacred texts, the Bounteous Immortals are abstract emanations that Ahuramazda created to assist him in the work of accomplishing creation and overcoming evil. While there are hints that the Bounteous Immortals were to some degree conceived on the composition of the earliest segments of the Avesta (the primary collection of Zoroastrianism's sacred scripture), the evidence is highly fragmentary, and it is only in the later hymns and subsequent commentaries that the Bounteous Immortals are explicitly listed and given their fullest elaboration (Boyce 1983; Geiger 1916; Kellens 2014; Kotwal 1969: 62–63; Narten 1982).[18] Thus, in the later additions to the liturgical texts of the Avesta, the Bounteous Immortals as a distinct group of abstractions are named for the first time (*Y.* 47.1), and it is here that we encounter the one divine entity that is of singular importance to the present discussion: Xšaθra Vairya, or Choice Sovereignty, *xšaθra* being the Avestan equivalent of the Old Persian *xšaça,* and likewise generally thought to have abstract and concrete connotations, though its meaning has been much discussed (see e.g. Gnoli 2005, 2007; Kellens 2002).[19] Sovereignty (or dominion or rulership or power) is in this context in part a divine, "otherworldly" (Lommel 1970 [1959]: 264), "almost magical power" (Gnoli 2007: 109), yet personification also accords a certain concreteness. In an effort to capture this duality, Herman Lommel (1970 [1959]: 257) wrote: "In a dynamic sense, dominion [*Herrschaft*] is the practice of rule and sovereign power. The more existential [*zuständliche*] view of the term is empire. One word combines both in itself: rule and empire. . . . Thus God's all-encompassing sovereignty obtains with respect to both world domination and the kingdom of God" (author's translation). It also obtains with respect to the right, legitimate rule that each person can exercise individually according to his or her place in the world. In a sense, therefore, Choice Sovereignty relates to the spheres of the sacred and the profane, to the heavenly, political, and personal.

At some point in the development of Zoroastrian thought, each of the Bounteous Immortals acquired a material quality that mirrored the various components of the original creations regarded by ancient Persian scholars as the foundation of the universe: sky and water, earth and plants, animals (specifically cattle), and sometimes fire (Lommel 1970 [1964]; Narten 1982: 103–106). Much consideration appears to have been directed toward this effort to relate the spiritual and material dimensions and domains of the Bounteous Immortals. Scholar-priests scrupulously analyzed the verses of the Older Avesta to detect correlations between the divine abstractions and some piece of the material world. They devised a system of correspondences that was present to an uncertain degree in the early history of Zoroastrian thought (Narten 1982). The end result, most clearly laid out in a corpus of language paraphrases and commentaries of the Avesta written in Pahlavi, or Middle Persian, was a schema that understood the material instantiations of each spiritual entity as that which made the qualities of the entity "perceptible to the senses and effective in the world" (Lincoln, personal communication).

The dualisms of spirit and matter that constituted the Bounteous Immortals are absolutely essential to the understanding of Zoroastrianism (Lommel 1970 [1959]: 256), although they differ fundamentally from the distinctions of the Cartesian schema. The divine entities linked to each abstract concept are not themselves abstractions, which is to say not virtues that reside in the interior mind of the person. They are instead active forces in the world that guide and act on the individual from the outside.[20] And each of these active forces is a "spiritual archetype or patron" of a part of the material world, so that, for example, Best Truth is the patron of fire and Good Purpose is the patron of cattle (260). Yet the material correlates of the Bounteous Immortals are not quite ontologically distinct from their personified abstraction. As Lommel labors to explain, it is inadequate to reduce the relation of the material elements to the active, personified value to one of symbolism. We might more properly construe the element as an emissary, representative, or proxy (Stellvertreter), as Goethe poetically described fire in his essay on ancient Persia in West-East Divan (2010: 184, quoted in Lommel 1970[1959]: 1266).

Of all the Bounteous Immortals, Choice Sovereignty presented the greatest challenge to the ancient scholar-priests. Its material embodiment is the most enigmatic and unstable in the entire schema. In the Middle Persian texts to which I just alluded, Choice Sovereignty is very clearly associated with metals (Narten 1982: 127–133). The association appears somehow to derive from earlier Zoroastrian theorizations of metals, since even in the earliest texts, before the schema of the Bounteous Immortals was codified, molten metal figures in judiciary and eschatological trials as a thing "through which sovereign powers test the truth and burn away the falsehood of those subject to their judgments" (Lincoln, personal communication). Yet the linkage of Choice Sovereignty to metals is nevertheless rather confounding, since metal plays no part in ancient Persian cosmogony. At the same time, the earliest old Avestan text (the Gathas) from which later interpreters discerned the material correlates of the Bounteous Immortals does mention sky as the first of the primordial creations; however, sky is left without a divine guardian in the Middle Persian commentaries. Modern scholars have worked to explain this apparent disjuncture. The prevailing resolution has been to recognize that, in a number of Zoroastrian texts of different periods, the sky is variously defined as made up of a positively hard substance, whether metal itself (e.g., *Yt.*13.2; *Bundahišn* 1a.16), "hardest stone" (*Y.* 30.5), or "the hardest and most beautiful stone," which is to say crystal (Boyce 1983: 935). With regard to the latter, Mary Boyce (1983: 935) has suggested that, in an act of "apparent sophistry," the scholar-priests responsible for interpreting the primary liturgical texts defined crystal as itself both metal and stone (crystal being mined like metal ores) to try to reconcile the ancient teachings of the Gathas, in which the association of sky as stone predominates, with contemporary interest in conjoining Choice Sovereignty to metals.

Matters become particularly speculative when trying to explain this interest, yet modern scholarly opinion often converges in one way or another on the practical entailments of earthly, political sovereignty. The scholar-priests who likely codified the material instantiations of the Bounteous Immortals were writing in the time of the Sasanian Empire (224–654 A.D.), a polity guided by Zoroastrian cosmology, and thus motivated in the imperial endeavor in similar ways by the eschatological notion we have already seen with respect to the Achaemenids—one that regards the reach of political power on earth and in historical time as an essential step toward the restoration of Ahuramazda's perfect original creation (Payne 2013). Against this backdrop, Choice Sovereignty as a spiritual entity responsible for assisting Ahuramazda in subduing evil implicitly aligns with the project of preserving and expanding the eminently just reach of kingly power—a project in which metals, whether bronze or iron, silver or gold, were by the time of these writings without question the most effective partners. In attempting to reconstruct the specific aspects of metal that were intended in the association with Choice Sovereignty, some scholars have examined the evidence for metal in the form of bronze or iron implements or weapons (Lommel 1970 [1959]: 264; Narten 1982), used for the defense of that which is good in a legitimate political system of martial kingship (Boyce 1983; Lincoln, personal communication; Lommel 1970 [1964]: 388–389), while others have considered the importance of precious metal luxuries—particularly vessels—for the display of the fortunes that accrue in a legitimate economic system of extraction (Boyce 1983; Kotwal 1969: 15.14–19; Lincoln, personal communication).

Yet Lommel (1970[1964]: 395) has pointed out that the particular instantiations of metal, their external forms and shapes, are less consequential than the compositional quality of the element itself—metal substance as a universal category "since time immemorial" that gathers together into one "concrete universality" all the forms it has taken and all the forms it can take. Such a stress on substance over form may relate to an acute metallurgical awareness that metal is dynamic, that it is irreducible to a single solid state, but is both rigid and fluid, possessed of its own, continuously modulating vitalism (Barry 2010: 93). It is an idea to which philosophy would later return. Gilles Deleuze and Félix Guattari (1987: 411), for example, wrote of this vitalism, this inherent alterability, that contravenes our intuitive sense of metal as hard and unrelentingly solid:

> Matter and form have never seemed more rigid than in metallurgy; yet the succession of forms tends to be replaced by the form of a continuous development, and the variability of matters tends to be replaced by the matter of a continuous variation. . . . In short, what metal and metallurgy bring to light is a life proper to matter, a vital state of matter as such, a material vitalism. . . . As expressed in panmetallism, metal is coextensive to the whole of matter, and the whole of matter to metallurgy. Even the waters, the grasses and varieties of wood, the animals are populated by salts or mineral elements. Not everything is metal, but metal is everywhere. Metal is the conductor of all matter.

Zoroastrian scholar-priests may not have recognized such vitalism, such omnipresent primacy, in these particular terms. They may not have conceived of a "metallic life" (Bennett 2010: 53), or of Deleuze and Guattari's elementally justified conceptual commingling of metal and *all* matter, as I will in subsequent chapters of this book, in which inquiry engages material objects that we would conventionally describe as both metallic (e.g. silver, bronze, iron) and non-metallic (e.g. stones, clays, bones). But following Lommel, it can be said that a concern for the ontology of "metal as matter" over "metal as form" is palpable. In the end, through whatever twists of metaphysical, political, and scientific reasoning, metal as matter came to be the physical embodiment of the spiritual and earthly force known scripturally as Choice Sovereignty. The association is so strongly conceived that Choice Sovereignty could almost be an expression for metal (Lommel 1970 [1964]: 377). Metal was rendered naturally, inherently, and inseparably religious and political.

It is interesting to note that while the relevant sources are highly lacunal, what might be called "Zoroastrian materiality" appears to have differed considerably from its Christian counterpart. Caroline Bynum has shown that, in the late Middle Ages, a profound sense of ambivalence surrounded Christian materiality. Matter was, for Christian theology, a "problematic locus of the sacred" (Bynum 2011: 19). It appears that early Zoroastrian theologians regarded the matter of the Bounteous Immortals as quite the opposite: the salvific locus of the sacred. In late medieval Christian theology, on the one hand, "the entire material world was created by and could therefore manifest God" (17). Moreover, the acceptance of a Christ "whose substance (in the Eucharist) and even whose particles (in blood relics) might be present on earth" (17) made it difficult to deny the possibility that an omnipotent God could signal such presence in multiple ways (158). And indeed, church leaders and theologians had no choice but to grapple with a world of holy matter that appealed greatly to the faithful—animated devotional images, relics, contact relics, sacramentals, the material of the Eucharist, and so on. Yet, on the other hand, to accept the presence of the holy in "dead" matter (which the faithful, in any case, did not accept as inert) and therefore to adore it, was "undignified and counter to the glory and transcendence of God" (46). Such an acceptance was even threatening, because matter was capable of change. "Miraculous matter was simultaneously—hence paradoxically—the changeable stuff of not-God and the locus of a God revealed" (35). Theologians and ecclesiastical authorities often forwarded contradictory views as they worked to establish whether holy images and objects merely conjured up and "gestured toward the unseen" or actually contained the sacred, manifested its power, and *shared being* with the eternal, transcendent One, even if at a tremendous remove (28, 50). Some Christian theologians were deeply uncomfortable with the later propositions (154–162).

Zoroastrian theologians, in contrast, codified the material instantiations of sacred beings without such anxiety. Confusion on the relation of sky to metal notwithstanding, there is no sense in the Zoroastrian corpus that the material correlate of Choice Sovereignty was seen merely as a channel for representing or gesturing toward the divine. The material elements of the Bounteous Immortals are quite clearly bound in relations of co-constitution with their respective entities, each segment of matter not so much something apart that comes to be possessed of the divine spirit through contact or blessing, but instead part of a divine unity, *itself an aspect of* the personified abstraction in all its material *thingness*. Metals are not the conduit for the realization of Choice Sovereignty, they are *themselves* Choice Sovereignty, and thus by their very existence (without regard to their animacy) further its purpose. In sum, what we find in these reflections is an ontologic disposition that, unlike the dominant strands of Western thought (see discussion in A. T. Smith 2015), categorically refuses the separation of spirit, matter, and power, of the abstract and the concrete (Lommel 1970 [1964]). In reformulation of these penetrating ideas for an archaeological epistemic of empire, we can consider this relation of inseparability as the material constitution of aspirational sovereignty.

As a final installment in this account of ancient Persian reflection on the partnership between sovereignty and matter, we turn our attention once again to the cultural production of the Achaemenids. With one possible exception (see Razmjou 2001), the Bounteous Immortals are nowhere mentioned in the Old Persian inscriptions, even though there are concepts that correspond to the abstractions themselves (much like *xšaça/xšaθra*), just as there are cosmogonic correspondences between the two schemes with respect to the original creations, of which sky is one (Knäpper 2011: 137; Lincoln 2012: 17). However, in one of the most exceptional visual representations of Achaemenid political thought, it is quite possible to discern an unmistakable acknowledgment of an intimacy between matter and imperial power. The largest building at Persepolis, known as the Apadana, presents an exquisitely conceived amplification of this affinity. The square building consists predominately of a spacious columned hall, about which much more will be said in chapter 4, perched atop a podium that rises over two meters above the surrounding terrace (figure 7). Of immediate concern here is the elaborate arrangement of reliefs that adorns the monumental staircases on the north and east sides of this imposing building. The two reliefs are virtually mirror images of one another and consist of three main elements. The central panel of the composition portrays an enthroned king, crown prince, and other courtly figures under a baldachin, receiving a bowing official. On one wing of the staircase a larger court entourage of Persian nobles disposed in three registers comes toward the king from the rear. Approaching him on the opposite wing are twenty-three groups of people, once again arranged in three registers, each group led by a Persian usher and each representing an incorporated people of the empire (figure 8). The groups are distinguished through differences of physiognomy and distinctive features of dress and headwear—the standard Achaemenid visual grammar of difference (figure 9). At the end of each wing and on either side of the central panel is the bull and lion symplegma that we have already seen (figure 2, p. xxiv), a possibly sexualized image redolent of "fecund dynasty" (Root, forthcoming).

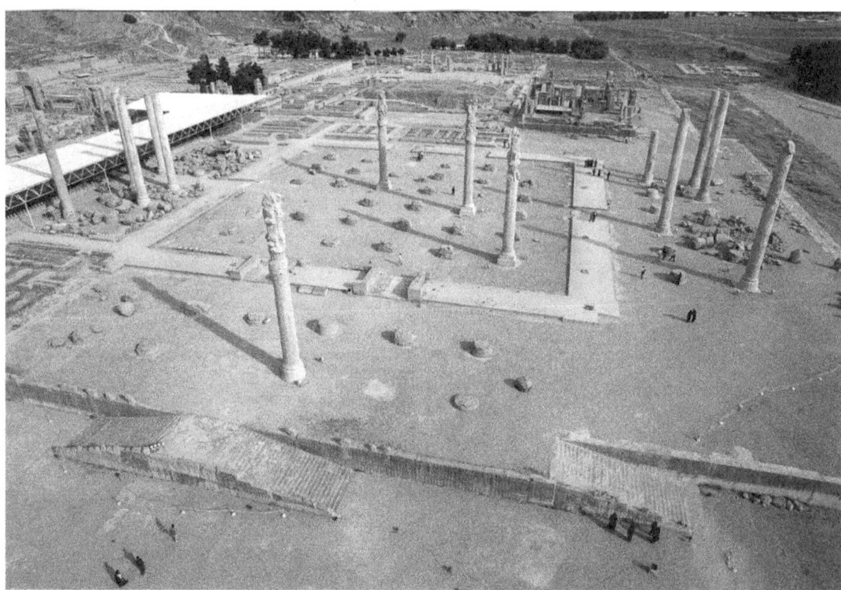

FIGURE 7. Aerial photograph of the Apadana at Persepolis, with a view of the north staircase façade in the foreground (courtesy of B. N. Chagny, French-Iranian Mission at Persepolis).

FIGURE 8. Tribute procession on the northern stairway of the Apadana at Persepolis (courtesy of the Oriental Institute of the University of Chicago).

FIGURE 9. Armenian delegation on the eastern stairway of the Apadana at Persepolis (courtesy of the Oriental Institute of the University of Chicago).

The delegations of subject peoples that approach the king bring various sorts of highly valued things—vessels and weapons, riding costumes and other textiles, skins and furs, and an array of animals, from horses and camels to bulls and lion cubs—in what is thought to be a metaphorical representation of a highly scripted tribute procession in which gifts serve as "a type of political encomium—an expression of gratitude and continued allegiance" (Root 1979: 228).[21] Taken as a whole, Root (1979: 279) has argued, the intent of the Apadana is not merely to portray a ceremonial event, but to use the tribute procession as a medium through which to convey "an abstract vision of empire and of imperial harmony" grounded in the putatively voluntary praise of the king. Root (forthcoming) has also probed the Apadana reliefs as a liminal moment of judgment, in which the king weighs the formidable weight of "Persianness", marked by the court entourage behind him, against the weight of the bounty brought by the peoples of the empire, assessing whether equilibrium has been achieved. The reliefs also speak in complex ways to the indistinguishably ritual and political performances that occurred in the hall itself (Root 2015). Without contradicting these penetrating interpretations, and himself drawing on Root's work, Lincoln has brought the Apadana closer into the frame of the Achaemenid metaphysics of power, viewing it less as a symbol of kingship per se than as a theorization of tribute in the context of the struggle against the Lie and the restoration of perfect sovereignty. The Apadana is no mere celebration of diversity, but an early visual representation of the tension between incorporation and differentiation that lies at the heart of a great many imperial projects (Cooper 2005: 415; Mehta 1999; Stoler 1997).[22] The relief presents a "theology of empire" that

> captures all these people, animals, and objects as they mount the stairs, which is to say, in the very last moment of existence in the state of fragmentation and diaspora that has marked history since the assault of the Lie. Directly they stand assembled upon the platform of the Apadana itself, all of them—animate and inanimate—will have left their provincial identities behind and been absorbed (or dissolved) into the imperial whole. At that moment, the state of unity and "happiness for mankind" that the Wise Lord made the crown of his original creation will have been restored. . . . At that point . . . history ends and a state of eschatological perfection opens onto eternity, thanks to the work of the Achaemenid king, the Persian army, and the tribute bearers of every land/people. (Lincoln 2012: 186)

In this more cosmological interpretation of the reliefs, the objects themselves—metal and otherwise—take on a different significance from when they are seen strictly as tribute for the furtherance of kingship (much less political economy). To quote from Lincoln (2012: 184) once more, "the tribute bearers depicted on the Apadana stairs bore *con*-tributions of things that had been *dis*-tributed as the result of the Lie's assault, and the *con*-centration of these goods—also of those peoples—at the imperial center was the means of reversing the fragmentation and strife that had characterized existence ever since." The objects thus participate in the *completion* of an as yet incomplete project toward the realization of imperial sovereignty.

There is reason to suggest that Persian thinkers accorded a privileged role to metal in this project. It is notable that, of the twenty-three delegations included on the Apadana relief, no less than sixteen, and possibly as many as twenty, come before the king bearing gifts of metal—jugs and bowls (figure 10), daggers, spears, axes, shields, and rings (Schmidt 1953, 1970; Walser 1966).[23] Metals make up approximately 54 percent of all objects depicted on the Apadana, as compared to 24 percent animals, 20 percent textiles, and 13 percent other things like bows, firs, tusks, and chariots. Beyond the Apadana, metallic elements make an appearance in Achaemenid architecture in other, rather more enigmatic ways. For instance, in the palace of King Artaxerxes II at Susa, in multiple courses of a wall belonging to a large columned hall, excavators discovered droplets of liquid mercury deposited in the mud bricks, as well as in the underlying shingle foundation. Given their localized presence, it is quite clear that these mercury deposits played no utilitarian function, but instead were part of a foundation ritual associated with the construction of the building (Boucharlat 2013a). As we shall see in chapter 4, columned

FIGURE 10. Detail of the zoomorphic amphorae carried by the Armenian and Lydian delegates on the Apadana at Persepolis (courtesy of the Oriental Institute of the University of Chicago).

halls such as these were of paramount importance in the practical reproduction of Achaemenid sovereignty. The deliberate, ritual deposition of quicksilver in the bricks of such a building speaks tantalizingly to a gesture of recognition that metal plays a vital part in the realization of this work.[24]

The attention that the Achaemenids appear to have directed toward metal in its various forms and states calls up a perspective on imperial power and authority that would later be contained in the Zoroastrian concept of Choice Sovereignty. There is absolutely no need to draw a direct line from the Mazdean politico-religious thinkers of the Achaemenid court to the Zoroastrian scholar-priests of later centuries. Yet it would be no less absurd to chalk up apparent parallels in the conception of the material (and metallic) constitution of sovereignty to mere coincidence. We may have to be content to realize a shared, ancient Persian interest in variously contending and representing this relation between substance and supreme power. The Apadana offers an early reflection on political association that is quite at odds with what Western political theory would later devise—one that, far from vesting the emergence of political order in the purification of humans from the material world (see A. T. Smith 2015), instead establishes things as the binding agents and very *raison d'etre* of political association. This in itself marks a significant contribution to political theory and a springboard from which to conceive a distinctly material approach to empire.

THE SATRAPAL CONDITION

The satrapal condition gathers the intuitions that orbit around *xšaça* into an analytic of empire for the "discipline of things" (Olsen et al. 2012). It registers at one and the same time the *experience* and the *limits* of imperial sovereignty, as these are produced in the relations of humans and "vibrant" matter (Bennett 2010), from the prosaic to the sublime. In this sense, the satrapal condition as a theoretical orientation toward empire is dialectical; it conjures two countervailing and mutually reinforcing senses of the word "condition." As will become clear, this is different from, but not contrary to, what anthropologists have conceived as the dialectic of colonialism, which pivots on the mutual "making" of metropole and colony (Comaroff and Comaroff 1997; Stoler and Cooper 1997).

On the one hand, the satrapal condition registers a political community's experience of subjection, as it is generated through human encounters with the material world. Such states of compromised sovereignty, which all imperial formations create as a fundamental imperative of rule, can of course differ dramatically in degree and kind. For the time being, let it be said that I am unconcerned to hitch the satrapal condition to any one of the prevailing categories often conjured to capture that variability—"formal" versus "informal" imperialism, "direct" versus "indirect" rule—terms that are themselves the discursive products of empires and thus, as Ann Stoler (2006a: 54) puts it, "unhelpful euphemisms, not working concepts." My purpose is rather to task the satrapal condition to bring to the fore the variable work of things in the production of imperial subjects. In the first of two senses, an inquiry into the satrapal "condition" fixes its gaze on the interventions of objects as efficacious participants in the distributed work of aspirational sovereignty, a task undertaken primarily by extraordinary and ordinary things that I call *delegates, captives, proxies,* and *affiliates* (see chapter 3). In this sense, the satrapal condition concerns itself with the ongoing, everyday making of acquiescent subjects who, like Atlas, "uphold" the imperial project through imposed, encouraged, or even chosen "entanglements" (Hodder 2012) with things that, to varying degrees, transform habits, persons, and political and social lives.

On the other hand, the satrapal condition is not exhausted by experiences of subjection, but refers as well to the inherent limitations on imperial sovereignty that arise from the inevitable *dependencies* on the practical action and material entanglements of its subjects. That is, contained in the second sense of the satrapal "condition" is a restricting or modifying force, a stipulation that registers the quiet bargains on which hegemony hangs. In this second sense, the satrapal "condition" recognizes the contradiction at the heart of imperial sovereignty: it is continuously in a state of potential attenuation or unraveling. Rephrased in an Achaemenid frame of reference, the satrapal condition indexes the constant need for sovereignty's protection, lest the subjects who uphold it drop their weary arms and let the "throne" tumble to the ground. Inquiry into this dimension of the satrapal condition entails scrutinizing the roles of things, the "missing masses" (Latour 1992), in producing the limits of sovereign prerogative and enabling everyday forms of semi-autonomous action. Such "missing masses," theorized in chapter 3 as *proxies* and *affiliates,* conspire with *delegates* and humans as players in the work of regulated autonomy.

Of course, as the ultimate imperial agents, Achaemenid thinkers did not go particularly far in elaborating the limitations of imperial sovereignty. Nor, for that matter, should students of empire become too caught up in romantic narratives of power's frailty or the equal distribution of agentive capacity when there is all too much evidence for the real, coercive, at times all-pervasive effects of domination on the human condition. But the conditionals of sovereignty speak less to its fragility per se than to a "will to mastery" (Dirks 1992: 23) that accords *xšaça* a quality of continuous emergence. It would be left to modern scholars to flesh out the intuition that the conditionality of sovereignty arises in practical life out of the very efforts intended to sustain it, that imperial projects are "made possible and vulnerable at the same time" (Cooper and Stoler 1997a: viii). These modern accounts, to their detriment, usually write things out of their theorizations of empire and sovereignty. But they are nevertheless helpful to elaborating the second sense of the satrapal condition, for they bring us down from the lofty heights of political metaphysics to the sordid world of the social, and they establish that such conditionals are written into the cards of imperialism, being only historically contingent in their details and degrees. As Stoler (2006b: 128) has written, all imperial formations are "scaled genres of rule that produce and count on different degrees of sovereignty and gradations of rights." Cross-cultural histories of imperialism have established the recurrence of layered, nested, or "partial" sovereignty (Stoler and McGranahan 2007), the existence of spaces of autonomous action that are less "a temporary concession to particular challenges of administering empire and more as a general premise of rule" (Benton 2010: 297). The countless impediments to anything as coherent as absolute imperial sovereignty create the conditions of possibility for such autonomous actions. These impediments of course include the oft-cited administrative reliance on, and compromises with, local institutions and authorities that allow for imperial stability. But such dependency is not only, as James Tully (2008: 160) portrays it with respect to modern empires, a matter of *efficiency,* economic or otherwise. Hegemons do not cede, only at their own discretion, spaces for "tactical" action in a field that they "strategically" structure (Tully 2008: 160–161, invoking de Certeau 1984); rather, they accede to such spaces as an inevitable imperative of imperial reproduction. It is as much a function of practical, inescapable necessity as of efficiency that the subject is to a certain degree governed "*through* his or her own freedom—his or her own participation in relations of governance, production, consumption, militarisation, securitisation, leisure and so on—by incorporating degrees of subaltern legality (customary law), democracy, and self-determination into informal and indirect modes of governance of political and economic life" (Tully 2008: 160).

Autonomous actions also emerge out of what Steven Wernke (2013: 7) has called the struggle between "analogy and erasure," in which the appropriation of indigenous analogs for foreign practices can result in the reproduction of the very institutions that imperial projects aimed to replace. And finally, conditionals of sovereignty derive from the complex temporalities of social life; that is, the terms of limitation that conquered communities place on imperial projects are not only reactive in the momentary sense of responding to the present, but also continuous in the enduring sense of arising from the past. As Tully (2008: 164) notes, the kinds of indirect and informal rule on which all imperialisms rely for their very existence entail "leaving local alterative worlds in operation to some constrained extent, and building its relationships of control and exploitation parasitically on them." Or, to adopt Caroline Humphrey's (2004: 420, 435) formulation, it could be said that such projects are in part conditioned by countless "localized forms of sovereignty" that are themselves shaped by "prior experiences and alternative lives" whose continuing life forms become something not outside the imperial "real" but part and parcel of it.

The semi-autonomous actions and unintended appropriations that the investigations of satrapal conditions may reveal do not necessarily amount to forms of resistance, even in its everyday hidden forms (Scott 1985, 1990). They arise not necessarily as critiques of dominant imperial structures but in the spaces of social and political life that such structures do not or cannot "see" (Scott 1998). Acting differently within bounds, bending rules without breaking them, keeping alive older ways of being and doing, such that they become a part of the new ways, too—all these count as the conditionals of satrapalism that occur in the spaces between life's regulated arenas under empire. In her work on law and geography in European empires, Lauren Benton (2010: 294) touches on the noncorrosive (or not necessarily corrosive) aspect of divided sovereignty: "What happens . . . if we view usurpation of elements of sovereign power as a recurring tendency, structurally even more prominent than the rejection of authority or the movement toward a substitute totalizing power? . . . Sites of bare sovereignty, a partial and often-minimalist construction of sovereign authority, pervaded empires."

The second sense of the satrapal condition, then, directs archaeology's attention to how this recurring, structurally determined "usurpation of elements of sovereign power" takes effect not through institutions of law, as is Benton's concern, but in the practical interactions between imperial subjects and imperial things that forge affective attachments alternative to those encouraged by imperial norms. Such alternative attachments have the *potential* to be mobilized toward counter-hegemonic ends. In this sense, the satrapal condition calls on us to detail how such human–thing interactions contribute to the "irregularities" that "political space everywhere generates," and the "peculiar forms of attenuated and partial sovereignty" that are common to political life under empire (279).

How does such an emphasis on the material and practical forces that produce, but also undermine, imperial power articulate with contemporary accounts of sovereignty that are firmly grounded in the corporeal human? I wish here only to note a point of divergence from Agamben's (1998: 6) well-known effort to locate the nucleus of sovereign power in the "production of the biopolitical body." His is, on the one hand, a vigorously human-centered view of sovereignty that insists on the inseparability of biological or "bare" life and the politicized life. But Agamben's biopolitical body is also a curiously lifeless one, insofar as its production appears to be essentially a metaphysical task. Humphrey's (2004: 420) anthropological reading of Agamben has gone part of the way toward highlighting this deficiency, noting his anemic understanding of "ways of life" and calling for a focus on practices, "actualities of relations," and lifeways that "do not simply acquiesce to the menace of sovereignty but interpose a solid existence of their own that operates collaterally or against it." To push the critique one step further, it could be said that, in his work *Homo Sacer,* Agamben's biopolitical body seems not only asocial but entirely unmoored, not unlike a "suspended" human surrounded by *no-thing* whatsoever, not even the strings to suspend it (Hodder 2012: 10)—a "bare life" indeed, if even that could be managed. As others have noted, Agamben's examination of the relation of power and life is "unable to account for the retinue of objects and technical knowledges that condition the vitality of bodies and avail them to political calculability" (Braun and Whatmore 2010b: xi). The satrapal condition aims to account for just such retinues of objects that subsume human lives in a politics of empire. But before moving any further in this effort, it is first necessary to ask in what ways such an analytic framework can be said to be new to archaeology.

2

Where Things Stand

At issue is the political life of imperial debris.
—ANN LAURA STOLER, "IMPERIAL DEBRIS: REFLECTIONS ON RUINS AND RUINATION"

The question of how to reckon with the detritus of empire is by no means a uniquely modern one. No sooner did the dust settle on old Rome than the *things* of empire came into focus as a matter of concern in the West. In town and country alike, during the sixth and seventh centuries A.D., for those who lived amid the debris of Roman dominion decisions had to be made on how to deal with the clutter of old power. In the ruins of imperium some saw only the promise of treasure, others a useful stock of processed raw materials, and others still the undesirable vestiges of pagan idolatry that the Christian relics of the new order would soon replace (Schnapp 1997: 85–88). This too was not the first time humans had to come to terms with the things of empires past.[1] But the early medieval era was a moment for which we have testimony to how people, from commoners to clerics, came to engage with imperial ruins in ways that would eventually call for institutional (e.g. ecclesiastical) intervention and sustained scholarly pursuit. In the millennium that followed, these same material remnants of the Roman past would come to play a leading role in the gradual birth of archaeology and its humanist and antiquarian beginnings (Schnapp 1997). What most animated generations of Europe's antiquaries was, to be sure, not imperialism as an economic, political, or social process, but Roman "civilization" as a cultural and aesthetic inheritance. Yet it is nevertheless ironic that a field of inquiry built in no small measure on the material things of empire would discover *empire* as a targeted object of inquiry rather late in its disciplinary formation. In a by now familiar story, the rupture with antiquarian tradition that attended the emergence of a scientific archaeology eventually relegated classical archaeology (and other textually bound forms) to its parochial historicist pursuits, and established global prehistory as the laboratory for a unified science of archaeological method and theory (Dyson 2006; Schnapp 1997; Trigger 1989). Throughout the nineteenth century and much of the twentieth, while archaeology's attention was directed elsewhere, empire and imperialism were left to historians, revolutionaries, and, not least of all, imperialists themselves.

ORIGINS AND ORIENTATIONS

Empire as a matter of conceptual theorization made a belated appearance in archaeological thought only in the early 1990s, as the neglected stepchild in the metahistory of social evolution. This was still an age in which mainstream anthropological archaeology was devotedly in thrall to the evolutionary *firsts* of the so-called chiefdom and the pristine state—those illusory taxonomic forms that had acquired currency as real and *sui generis* historical experiments in sociopolitical complexity (Pauketat 2007; A. T. Smith 2003a; Yoffee 2005). Neither the prevailing commitment to political life in its primordial condition, nor the historicist particularism of the Classical and Near Eastern archaeological traditions, with their abiding fealty to the idiosyncrasies of time and place, were adequate to the task of theorizing "secondary" sociopolitical phenomena that, however varied, were plainly regenerative and transhistorical. Yet the story of social evolution still provided the obvious plot line in which empire was to appear (Service 1975: 192–193; Steward 1955: 189; Steward and Faron 1959: 100–110). In the epilogue to that story, empire arose as the culmination of a long trajectory of development—the sublime apogee of the state, its most sophisticated instantiation before the Industrial Revolution. Empires shared with other states such defining attributes as intricate hierarchies and specialized administration and information processing (Schreiber 1992; Wright and Johnson 1975). But added to these standard indices of complexity, the evolutionary narrative went, were the capacities to absorb the full range of sociopolitical forms, from "band" to "simple chiefdom" to "state-level society," and to manage the cultural and ecological diversity that results from far-flung expansion (Schreiber 1992: 4, 18–26). Herein lay the unique "evolutionary significance" of empire (D'Altroy 1992: 1), its rightful claim to a rung (above the pristine state) on the ladder of social evolution, and thus its status as a proper object of archaeological inquiry. However obsolete these ideas may now seem in the twilight of neo-evolutionary archaeology, at the time they provoked a significant expansion of the scope of the discipline, and created a foundation on which much subsequent work could build.[2]

But the move to stake the significance of empire in social evolutionary terms came at a cost. It committed the emerging enterprise to priorities handed down from that theoretical tradition. For instance, like the less complex sociopolitical formations of tribes, chiefdoms, and pristine states, empires were to be subject to rigorous classificatory procedures. Concerns with definition and typology also led archaeology to ultimately defer developing a conceptual framework for empire that was appropriate to the discipline's epistemology, and instead import its theoretical terms and tools from political science and historical sociology. The result was that, throughout the 1990s and into the new millennium, a rather idiosyncratic set of key texts provided the theoretical foundations for a developing archaeology of empire broadly dedicated to sorting out matters of classification, enumerating the "material correlates" of empire, and modeling the strategies of imperial expansion and organization (D'Altroy 1992; Mantha 2013; Matthews 2003: 127–132; Ohnersorgen 2006; Schreiber 1992, 2001; Sinopoli 1994a; M. E. Smith 2001; M. E. Smith and Montiel 2001; Stark 1990: 11–13, 32–14). In the early years, it was Emanuel Wallerstein's *The Modern World System* (1974) that seemed to offer a conceptual apparatus particularly germane to expansive imperial formations. With its focus on the interaction between cores and peripheries, unequal interregional exchange, and a single division of labor, world systems was more congenial to the study of empires than the prevalent cultural-ecological approaches to the state, which sought explanations for change within the self-contained bounds of comparably small-scale societies. Despite adjustments necessitated by the particular conditions that obtained in precapitalist systems (Algaze 1993; Edens 1992; Ekholm and Friedman 1979; Hall and Chase-Dunn 1993; Hall et al. 2011; Kepecs and Kohl 2003; Kohl 1979, 1987, 1989; Rowlands et al. 1987; Schneider 1977; Stein 1999), world systems brought anthropological archaeology for the first time into conversation with mainstream economic theories of imperialism.[3] Theoretical guidance on the specifically political characteristics of empires were sought elsewhere, primarily in the opening pages of international relations scholar Michael Doyle's oft-cited work, *Empires* (1986), a comparative history set in a nonsystemic framework that models the emergence and organization of empires according to the contingent conditions in both metropolitan centers and conquered territories. With its neat definitions and concise schematic formulations—e.g., empires exercise "formal" or "informal" control, and there are "metrocentric" and "pericentric" factors that account for their emergence—Doyle's work furnished the kind of classificatory vocabulary that was well suited to the requirements of socio-evolutionary typology. It also authorized an analytical optic locked on the strategic calculations of empires as real, agentive entities. Influential for much the same reason was American military strategist and foreign policy expert Edward Luttwak's *The Grand Strategy of the Roman Empire* (1976), a particularly peculiar source on which to build a foundational body of thought for archaeology given the controversy and critique it elicited among Roman historians (e.g. Isaac 1992). Archaeologists turned to Luttwak selectively and uncritically, drawing repeatedly on his distinction between "hegemonic" and "territorial" strategies of control. Ethnohistorian Ross Hassig's *Trade, Tribute, and Transportation: The Sixteenth-Century Political Economy of the Valley of Mexico* (1985) acquired similar prominence. While regional specialists lauded this macro-scale study of logistics and transport efficiency in the basin of

Mexico more for its thorough analysis and innovative propositions on the political economy of the region before and after Spanish conquest than for its somewhat eclectic theoretical framings, archaeologists latched onto Hassig's passing discussion of "hegemonic" and "territorial" modalities of rule (92–103) as the basis for modeling imperial strategies.

Other thinkers occasionally appeared in the early archives of the archaeology of empire (e.g. Eisenstadt 1963; Mann 1986), and out of this eclectic patchwork there emerged a suite of definitions and models that took for granted the ontologically solid imperial state—a formidable singular actor, relentlessly calculating, coordinated, and effective vis-à-vis the territories it ruled. It is fair to say that "strategy" became the buzzword in archaeologies of empire during the 1990s and into the new millennium, particularly, as we shall see below, with respect to economic control.[4] And while Luttwak's presumptuous modifier usually fell away (but see Earle 1994: 443; D'Altroy et al 2000: 22), the designs of ancient empires that archaeologists worked assiduously to reconstruct were nothing less than grand. We shall return below to the efforts of what might be called archaeology's "strategic thinkers."

In hindsight, empire's debut in archaeological thought rested on sources that were embedded in a pastiche of neo-Marxism, liberalism, and neocolonialism. Evaluated on its own terms, the classificatory procedure that had conjured the chiefdom and the state simply could not be replicated for empires. In virtually all cases (except e.g. the Wari Empire of the Andes), the entities in question were already constituted a priori as centuries-old discursive historical formations. Recalling the Latin derivation of the term "imperium," Kathleen Morrison (2001b: 2) has remarked that the comparative study of empires must grapple with this "difficulty of transforming a historically and culturally contingent term into a broader analytical category." A quality of circularity surrounded the very enterprise of definition, which made the low stakes of the effort all the more pronounced. Nor was archaeological inquiry particularly necessary to determine the adherence of a given imperial formation to one or another model of organization, since for almost every early empire this could be ascertained through the historical or ethnohistorical record.[5] Inadvertently, the taxonomic reasoning that had attended the forwarding of empire into the social evolutionary matrix effectively deprived archaeology of any truly constituting work vis-à-vis the unit of analysis. To be sure, these pioneering efforts were very important for augmenting historical reconstructions of early empires; but the teachings of Wallerstein, Doyle, Hassig, Luttwak, and others ultimately left to archaeology the somewhat marginal task of illustrating "on the ground" the strategies of imperial control undertaken across time and space, as these were already historically attested (Ohnersorgen 2006; Parker 2003; M. E. Smith 2001).

Yet what consigned this first wave in the study of empire to the periphery of archaeological thought was not the limited role that it assigned to itself, but rather the particular understanding of imperialism that underlay the preoccupation with economic strategies and grand designs. Even as archaeologists of empire were working to make innovative use of the writings of Wallerstein, Doyle, Mann, and others, their colleagues in sociocultural anthropology had already been looking, for a decade, beyond prevailing political economic approaches to work out a cultural reading of colonialism that turned away from both modernization theories and their Marxist alternatives. There have probably been few moments in the history of American anthropology when archaeologists and socioculturalists have been so out of sync on otherwise common ground, as the two fields pursued incompatible new directions in the study of empire. That would change in earnest in the new millennium, when a new set of priorities and principles shaped archaeological research on imperial colonies and provinces. Borrowing from seminal texts in the historical anthropology of colonialism (Comaroff and Comaroff 1991, 1997; Cooper and Stoler 1997b; Dirks 1992), talk of strategies, statecraft, political economy, and other governmental abstractions receded, as attention turned to culture, agency, the blurred and novel social categories to which colonial encounters give rise, the transformative effects of colonial life on all parties involved, the experience of domination and resistance and the heuristic limits of both, and the active and contingent processes of appropriation, negotiation, improvisation, and manipulation that reproduce colonial and imperial hegemonies in the practices of everyday life (e.g. Dietler 2010; Given 2004; Liebmann 2012; Lyons and Papadopoulos 2002; Mattingly 1997a; Voss 2008a, 2008b; Wernke 2013).

In the rest of this chapter, I develop a critical appraisal of "where things stand" in archaeology's accounts of imperial reproduction and the colonial encounter over the course of three and a half decades of sustained inquiry into the provinces and colonies of these expansive macropolities. My purpose is not a comprehensive literature review, but a selective examination of research on empires and colonialism that can be analyzed to effectively illustrate broad trends. The choice to fold the imperial and the colonial into a single diagnosis may jar some sensibilities, given the distinct conversations that have coalesced around each. The archaeology of empire conjures perhaps antiquated interests in conquest, political economy, infrastructure, and governmental strategies of control, while the archaeology of colonialism brings to mind cultural encounter and everyday forms of subjection, resistance, and negotiation. These distinctions, however, carry little relevance when inquiry pivots not on the fortunes of states, societies, and persons per se, but on figurations of things. Even as the foregoing exploration bridges the divide that separates the archaeologies of empire and colonialism, it delimits the scope of the investigation by focusing on ancient and modern imperial formations that are traditionally understood as agrarian macropolities—those amassed by empire-builders who perceived their provinces as vassals, and whose domination extended beyond the point of exchange to that of production. In excluding mercantile empires like the Dutch, British, and French, this assessment of the latent presumptions regarding imperial things sets to one side the workings of colonial objects in capitalist exchange economies, about which much has already been said (e.g. Thomas 1991).

As we move in this chapter broadly from problems of empire to colonialism, from the actions of imperial agents to the agency of imperial subjects, a range of perspectives on things will emerge that cast them variously as goods, symbols, artifacts, and media. Detailing these prevailing perspectives establishes a baseline from which an explicit theorization of the relations among humans, matter, and the layered sovereignties of imperialism can take shape in the next chapter. Yet in addition to defining the open spaces for new intervention, the appraisal offered in this chapter also brings forward the careful and concerted attention that archaeologists have long given to what Ann Stoler (2008, 2013) calls, with rather different intent, "imperial debris." The excerpt that opens this chapter registers the enduring political afterlife of structures of dominance, the postcolonial legacies of imperial projects that take material and metaphorical forms as ruins, residues, and remains "of matter and mind" (Stoler 2008: 203). "To think with ruins of empire," Stoler writes, "is to emphasize less the artifacts of empire as dead matter or remnants of a defunct regime than to attend to their reappropriations and strategic and active positioning within the politics of the present" (196). Without diminishing the importance of gauging the persistent psychic and material "aftershocks of empire" (194), it is worth pointing out a misleading dichotomy that lurks in Stoler's rhetoric of ruin and ruination. Juxtaposed against her provocative vision of ruins as vibrant and violent in the present, as actively engaged in "vital refiguration" (194), is a commonplace sense of ruins as objects of a "melancholic gaze" that looks with nostalgia on the likes of the Roman Coliseum or the Acropolis—"often enchanted, desolate spaces, large-scale monumental structures abandoned and grown over." Yet this "wistful gaze" of long-gone European poets on the "inert remains" of empire (194), which perhaps finds its contemporary echoes in the more sensational offerings of the Discovery Channel, is but one of many dispositions toward imperial ruins today. Between this popular melodrama of ruin and Stoler's evocative redeployment is a modern archaeological project that long ago displaced the colonial visions of bygone "rubble seekers" and archaeologists in the employ of European imperial powers (198). But what took their place? What does this archaeological gaze see when it looks both east and west on imperial ruins ancient and modern? How has it figured the political life of imperial things in their prime, before their senescence into imperial debris?

GOODS OF THE GOOD LABORER

In a certain sense, for the strategic thinkers of the mid-1980s and the 1990s, imperialism was about nothing if not things. In its genesis, the archaeology of empire as a self-conscious comparative enterprise was an avowedly materialist project that subsumed the political work of dominion under the technocratic organization of a political economy (Costin and Earle 1989; D'Altroy 1992; Earle 1994; Smith and Berdan 1996: 8). It thus envisioned imperial worlds as fundamentally dependent on the continuous production, aggregation, and circulation of things. In this view, empires were complex systems designed to enable the realization of such forms and flows through the capture and channeling of "energy" (D'Altroy 1992; D'Altroy and Earle 1985). Things in the guise of "goods" served as the repositories of such energy. Goods mattered not for their inherent material properties or transformative capacities, but for the values conferred on them by the judgment of imperial agents. Processual economic archaeology recognized the *goods* of empire as hard at work in imperial reproduction. "Surplus goods" fed armies, imperial personnel, the state labor force, and urban populations. "Craft goods" either enabled the production of surplus goods (utilitarian crafts) or, in the commodity state, fueled the "tournaments of value" (Appadurai 1986) that resulted in the adorned bodies and rarified rituals essential to sociopolitical reproduction (luxury crafts). Crafts were thus *managed* things that functioned to facilitate relations of exchange (Blanton and Feinman 1984: 676–677). Control of luxury goods, in particular, was necessary in order to restrict access to valuable raw materials, to ensure quality and homogeneity, to regulate output, and to limit distribution (Costin 1996: 212). The constraints on the "capture of energy" in the prevailing economic logic derived from factors that the steadfastly strategic imperial machine could anticipate: the social and economic organization of conquered communities, the availability of labor, and the natural environment (D'Altroy 1992: 5). Rarely was the *messiness* of imperial political economies brought into view (Sinopoli 1994b). The task of archaeology was rather to reveal the effective strategies that transformed matter into imperial goods—seed to staple, textile to tax—by searching for the long arm of the well-oiled imperial machine in all arenas of production, and tracing the circulation of such goods through systems of exchange.

This was fertile ground for world systems analysis. Interregional asymmetries, Wallersteinian theory held, largely depended for their reproduction on the continuous flows of matter, from the raw materials whose extraction constituted the basis of exploitation, to the finished products whose movement through networks of taxation, tribute, and exchange created incentives and obligations that preserved relations of dominance and subordination. Some of the earliest applications of world systems analysis in the study of early empires looked to Rome's northern provinces. To Richard Hingley (1982), for instance, Roman Britain was an imperial periphery in something of a Wallersteinian sense. Under a politically managed economy, towns (*civitates*) and other administrative institutions exploited provincial resources by taxing the countryside in agricultural goods and raw materials, and monopolistically controlled the exchange of luxury goods and other finished products. Colin Haselgrove (1987) likewise explained the emergence and reproduction of central Gaul as a Roman periphery. In this case, core–periphery dynamics led to the formation of local elites who were able to accumulate wealth in the form of Roman luxuries (wine amphorae, fine pottery, bronze and silver service), procured in exchange for slaves, raw materials (metal), agricultural products (wool and salt pork), and other commodities acquired from external trading partners.

In the final analysis, world systems proved to be an awkward fit for the Roman economy; in a significant deviation from Wallerstein's schema, the "cellular structure" of the Roman "world-empire" ensured that much consumption of extracted goods took place in the peripheries rather than the all-important core (Woolf 1990). Indeed, most efforts to contend with the utility of world systems for understanding precapitalist imperial economies entailed considerable theoretical contortions (Schneider 1977); even so, its functionalist form of reasoning provided a scaffolding that shaped early efforts to think systematically about flows of imperial things. In the Aztec Triple Alliance, it was the state's promotion or control of market flows in preciosities and raw materials (especially obsidian) that enabled the exchanges needed to reproduce social privilege and recruit and reward warriors and officials (Blanton and Feinman 1984; M. E. Smith 2001). In the Inca Empire, the mechanisms of resource extraction that worked to maintain imperial hegemony included taxation through labor allocation, the use of women as tribute, the storage of agricultural surplus, control over craft production, and the forced transformation from kin-based to tribute-based economies (Kuznar 1999; La Lone 1994). At a time when world systems was already démodé in the social sciences for, among several other reasons, its inability to incorporate human agency, Mitchell Allen (1997) forwarded Wallerstein's often neglected "semi-periphery" in his account of Assyrian rule over Levantine Philistia, a region well positioned to facilitate long-distance trade in preciosities. Evidence for intensified production of olive oil and textiles suggested to Allen that trade in these goods enabled Philistia to meet its tribute obligations.

In the world systems paradigm, the goods of empire lived perpetually itinerant lives. While familiar anthropological critiques of the theory centered less on its construal of things than on its neglect of cultures and societies, it is worth also noting that the goods of world systems were always in transit, never analytically "still" long enough to permit a close look at their material qualities and intimate human entanglements. It is little surprise that most efforts to grapple with imperial economies through a world systems lens were rather more historical or ethnohistorical than archaeological in their methods, insofar as archaeological evidence was ill suited to the enormous, systemic scale of the analysis. When archaeologists began to look closer at processes of production, the politico-economic lives of things destined for itinerancy appeared to slow down. Attention turned to regional landscapes, the economic engines that powered the transformation of things into goods. From the highlands of Peru to the lowlands of Mesopotamia, archaeological surveys told similar stories of agricultural intensification marked by the downward movement of settlement, from higher-elevation areas that hosted mixed agro-pastoral economies for local subsistence needs, to fertile cultivation zones where plants could be turned into surplus. In the Upper Mantaro Valley of the central Andes, just as in southern parts of the Inca Empire like the Calchaquí Valley, scholars looked for evidence of surplus extraction, and found it in the downward movement of settlements from high ridges toward fertile fields (better suited for maize, the valued crop used to produce *chicha* beer), in land improvement works like irrigation canals and terraced field systems, and in the building of large storage facilities (D'Altroy 1992, 1994: 183–195; D'Altroy and Earle 1985; D'Altroy et al. 2007: 114–116). On the far south coast of Peru, just as in the Titicaca basin, settlement patterns likewise pointed to resettlement efforts geared toward agricultural intensification (for maize) and resource extraction (Covey 2000; Stanish 1997). Other forms of evidence supported this general picture. Paleoethnobotanical remains collected from domestic compounds in the Upper Mantaro Valley indicated a shift in focus, after the Inca takeover, from potato to maize cultivation. This, along with an increase in the incidence of stone hoes and a decrease in household storage, together pointed to state strategies of agricultural intensification and surplus extraction that placed new burdens of labor on commoner households (Costin et al. 1989: 131–133; Hastorf 1990, 2001). Inca strategies of agricultural intensification, Katharina Schreiber's (1992, 2005a: 257) survey research showed, had their antecedents in the preceding Wari Empire of the Middle Horizon. Nor was it only in the Andes that these research concerns took hold. Comparable surveys in the Near East sought the traces of economic extraction in the landscapes of the Assyrian heartland and provinces. In the Upper Tigris River Valley, evidence for settlement intensification, the downward movement of occupation closer to fertile land, and imperial investment in administrative infrastructure suggested to Bradley Parker (2003) the presence of an Assyrian agricultural colony, possibly of resettled deportees, whose labor was directed toward the production of agricultural surplus destined for imperial storage facilities. In the Jazira, the northern Mesopotamian lands between the Tigris and the Euphrates, Tony Wilkinson and colleagues (2005) also saw signs of agricultural intensification and possibly surplus production attendant to the general expansion of settlement into formerly unoccupied lands. Using remotely sensed data, they detailed the Neo-Assyrian hydraulic and road networks that would have facilitated the production and transport of such surplus to feed sizable populations in the urban centers of the imperial heartland.

Apart from agricultural surplus, economic archaeology's goods-centered view of empire also directed much attention to the organization of craft production as a measure of the intensity and nature of imperial centralization and the success of the system of finance that expropriated wealth for the state (D'Altroy and Earle 1985; Earle 1994). Particularly in archaeologies of the Inca Empire—in many ways the laboratory for the anthropological archaeology of imperial economies—the long arm of the state, as a coordinated force engaged in the organization of labor and the control of craft goods, was sought in a wide range of technologies (Costin 1996; D'Altroy 1994: 195–204). Most significant of these, we know from ethnohistorical accounts, was cloth, a material of exceptional importance to the Inca for its symbolic and practical affordances in preserving and strengthening social standing and alliances (Lechtman 1993). "*Is this the stuff of which empires are built?*" Heather Lechtman (1993: 259, emphasis added) asks with no small dose of irony—for could it really be that mere matter, mere clothing, are protagonists in the theater of sociopolitical life? The Inca clearly thought so, and they are by no means alone (Miller 2010: 12–41). To D'Altroy and Earle (1985), Inca control over cloth production operated in a system of "wealth finance" that served to economically integrate subject territories by dictating the value of goods while also allowing for their distribution as prestige gifts. Spatial distributions and densities of spindle whorls and other weaving implements at sites in the Upper Mantaro Valley and elsewhere indicated imperial intervention in the organization of textile manufacture, both in households and through the creation of retainer workshops (Costin 1993, 1996).

Inca cloth represents just the tip of the iceberg. Other archaeologies of imperial craft production have looked to Inca intervention in the production of ceramics, particularly the canonical imperial-style vessels that carried maize beer, a key lubricant of Inca commensal politics (Costin 1996, 2001; D'Altroy and Bishop 1990; D'Altroy et al. 2007: 119; Hayashida 1999), or highly valued luxury metals (D'Altroy et al. 2000; D'Altroy, et al. 2007; Earle 1994; Lechtman 1993). Beyond the Andes, in the context of the decentralized Aztec Triple Alliance, craft production has emerged less as a proxy for state control than as an arena in which to explain the impact of an open commercialized market sector that existed alongside a politically controlled economy involving land, labor, and tribute. In the Basin of Mexico and beyond, industries ranging from pottery to lithics to figurines to weaving were dispersed, and carried out by independent and part-time specialists bound not to Aztec patrons but to channels of commercial exchange (Brumfiel 1987; Charlton 1994; Hodge and Smith 1994; Nichols 1994; M. E. Smith et al. 2003; Smith and Heath-Smith 1994). Beyond the Americas, archaeologies of Roman nonagricultural production have also probed the role of the state in the production and exploitation of stone and metals, textiles and ceramics (Mattingly and Salmon 2001). Only recently have such questions reached the archaeology of Near Eastern empires in a targeted fashion (e.g. Glatz 2012).

What this brief glance at the work of archaeology's "strategic thinkers" has hopefully made clear is that, in a certain sense, from the very start the archaeology of empire was an inquiry into the relationship between power and things. It could even be said that people, not things, were epiphenomenal to imperialism, insofar as it was things that were recognized as actively productive of political perdurance through their exchange and use. "In Mesoamerica," Richard Blanton and Gary Feinman (1984: 677) wrote, "the goal of political expansion was less the conquest and administration of large masses of people than an endeavor designed to regularize or increase the flow of luxury items, or the raw materials required in the manufacture of luxury items." Yet it is partly for this very disregard of the "masses of people" that the economic archaeology of imperialism provided a troublingly partial account of the relationship between imperial sovereignty and things. The approach rendered imperial worlds not so much unpopulated as populated by people whose social positions were exhausted by their productive capacities as peasant or specialist "labor." The imperial subject was a variable in the macro-systemic field of the political economy and, in many cases, could only be conjured either as an isolated being—a potter or a weaver—obediently and diligently crafting for the empire, or as an anonymous and phantasmal mass—an acquiescent labor class without interests, divisions, or dispositions toward community or crown. There was certainly never any question of alienation, of whether we can speak of people working as the instruments of their own subjection. In the early political economic frameworks, the "power" of the imperial state was thus something entirely implausible, a force unmediated by social relations, in part because the imperial subject was nothing but the apotheosis of the good laborer.

It did not take long for archaeologists to try to redress this problem and recalibrate their attentions toward the sociality of agricultural and craft production. In a characteristically precocious turn, Elizabeth Brumfiel (1991) forwarded the strategic efforts of producers themselves and the gender politics of production in the Aztec Triple Alliance, later to argue for the great range of social identities among Aztec specialists (Brumfiel 1998), some of whom clearly worked under conditions of coercion (Brumfiel 1997). Cathy Costin (1998) likewise tempered the language of strategic thinking in a reconsideration of Inca craft production, revealing the extractive economy of textile tribute as nothing less than a project of social reengineering that produced new social categories of cloth workers through manipulation of gender, class, and ethnic identities. Carla Sinopoli's (1998, 2003) analysis of craft production in the Vijayanagara Empire of South India also revealed a complex social world marked by individuals and groups of producers who were not only aware of their social positions but also in some cases able to change them through opportunities for upward mobility (particularly weavers and smiths). Sinopoli approached craft production as a social act that occurred in India in a political and economic field that was not regulated by a single monolithic institutional apparatus of production. For various reasons, these scholars relied heavily on documentary evidence to register the social logics of production in imperial economies. But scholars of the prehistoric Wari have shown that it is also possible to examine archaeologically the ways in which the production and flows of goods and resources among laborers and imperial agents are embedded in webs of sociopolitical relations (Nash and Williams 2009).

Less progress has been made on this score when it comes to landscapes and agricultural production. That is, few have followed Susan Alcock's (1993: 33–92) footsteps in her study of Roman Greece, and looked beyond evidence of intensification and exploitation to understand the wide range of economic factors associated with landscape reorganizations under empire, including changing agricultural regimes, landholding patterns, and demographic trends. And few archaeologists have attempted the kind of postcolonial archaeology of imperial economy that David Mattingly (1997b, 2011: 146–166, 167–199) has pursued in his survey work on Roman Africa and his study of Roman copper mining in Jordan. Mattingly has shown how interpretations centered on resource extraction and economic growth can recognize the high human and environmental costs of exploitation, and the opportunities for both resistance and local profit-taking, at the same time.

Thus, despite important exceptions, from an economic perspective archaeology has conjured imperial domination as a productive, mechanistic, and asocial process. Even as materialist approaches recognize that imperial political economies were variable and dynamic, they invariably constrict the field of action of the imperial subject to the realm of labor. This critique is a familiar one, since it is precisely this "personless," mechanical bearing that has historically separated accounts of the imperial from the colonial. And yet there is another kind of constriction that talk of imperial political economy enforces, one that has passed largely unnoticed. For it is not only human beings who are narrowly typecast in the laborious plot of imperial economics, but also the things of empire themselves. Just as the bounds of human efficacy are permitted to extend no further than the productive efficacy of the worker, so too things are ontologically restricted to their narrow roles as goods. The things that matter in economic archaeologies of empire are what Gluckman (1983) called "kingly things"—the stuff of taxes and tribute, usually destined to become "enclaved commodities" (Appadurai 1986: 22) that circulate in or, to expand Gluckman's formulation, get redistributed from, highly privileged and royal spheres. If, as Mauss (1990) maintained, the gift is infused with the spirit of reciprocity, and commodities, as Appadurai (1986) maintained, are infused with the spirit of exchange, then imperial goods are permeated with the forceful, nonnegotiable spirit of extraction. They are steeped in the vigor of coercion both before and after they enter the commodity or gift state, where they act as conspicuous symbolic participants in ritual or sumptuary regimes.

The great irony of the archaeological preoccupation with the production of imperial goods is that in most cases the things themselves lie beyond our grasp. Textiles, metal luxuries, and vessels brimming with maize beer are either scarce or nonexistent; they make up an infinitesimal fraction of the "imperial debris" that constitutes the archaeological record and indeed once populated past worlds. What then of the material and social lives of the great masses, the other "stuff of which empires are built," the buildings and landscapes, the everyday and ritual things that work collaboratively or recalcitrantly with humans to preserve or undermine satrapal conditions? Enslaved to the logic of rarified goods, in the economic archaeology of empire the great masses were left to serve as mere inert debris—as passive indices in the present for the making of past "kingly things."

SIGNIFIERS AND THE PLIANT SUBJECT

If, in the economic logic of empire, things were infused with the spirit of extraction, in the new millennium an emerging interest in the hegemonic face of imperial rule recast material culture as a world of signs. This shift represented, in many ways, a natural extension of "strategic thinking," now into the terrain of political persuasion (DeMarrais et al. 1996). Empires perdured not only through threats of force and the continuous flows of goods, but also through strategically designed forms of symbolic projection that affectively tapped into people's hearts and minds and, by communicating various meanings, created the conditions for pliant subjects who quietly submitted to their own subjection. Harnessed here was that most deeply rooted scholarly and popular view of things as symbols that signify or represent the claims and values of persons and collectives.

To greater or lesser degrees, this perspective on things, particularly state-sponsored built forms, as signifiers of political ideology and authority, underlies interpretation in virtually every empire that archaeologists study. In the provincial centers of ancient Assyria, it was the palaces and governors' residences of the eighth century B.C., with their modular replication of audience hall, other ceremonial areas, and residential quarters, that "stood as visual symbols that both manifested and reinforced the royal ideology of the Assyrian imperial program" (Harrison 2005: 29). The Achaemenids likewise projected "imperial power statements" through built forms at satrapal centers like Daskyleion, in Anatolia, where monumental structures adorned with elaborate Ionian architectural elements served to "reflect and reify imperial administrative authority" (Dusinberre 2013: 57). Archaeologists of Roman urbanism would have us believe that, by the turn of the first millennium, the use of built spaces as signifiers of imperial authority had reached a high art form, both literally and figuratively. In a synthesis that brought together established perspectives on Roman cities, Hingley (2005: 77–87) argued that urban built forms inculcated subjects through a panoply of universal symbols that communicated messages of unity and order. Particularly in the early centuries of imperial expansion, cities shaped by a Roman urban template, involving regular and systematic planning and standard public buildings at monumental scales (fora, theaters, amphitheaters, baths adorned with sculptures and inscriptions), were built in regions that lacked urban centers with the facilities necessary for Roman governance. Rome encouraged (but did not enforce) these building initiatives. "This new form of organization of space and life acted, in a highly symbolic manner, to project the character of the relationship of the individual urban community to the city of Rome" (77). Cities modeled on the Roman ideal, the thinking goes, expressed the religious and political ideology of the empire, hegemonically unifying its constituent parts through the collaboration of local ruling classes who reproduced their status through their involvement in the rituals of urban life. The material trappings of Roman urbanisms were also themselves generative, working to recreate imperial hegemony through their use as stages for routine activities.

No less immersed in the work of semiosis were the built landscapes of Andean empires. The Wari used a standard architectural form known as the D-shaped temple, found in heartland and provinces alike (Cook 2001), to materially manipulate the ritual experience of religious landscapes of conquered communities. As in the Sondondo Valley of Peru, these imposing structures were sometimes placed in proximity to a local shrine, in an effort to symbolically co-opt local beliefs and emit messages of power by virtue of formal affinity to the imperial architectural canon (Schreiber 2005b). Elsewhere, in Peru's upper Moquegua Valley, canonical Wari platform constructions served to "symbolize the elevated positions of presiding officials" and acted as "visual cues communicating the social order" (Nash and Williams 2009: 263).

The Inca further elaborated Wari strategies of religious appropriation. In the highland Collasuyu Province of the south-central Andes, on Lake Titicaca's long-sacred Islands of the Sun and the Moon, they co-opted and refashioned an existing sanctuary into a state-controlled pilgrimage complex that was visited by commoners and elites alike from across the empire. According to Charles Stanish and Brian Bauer (2007), such manipulation of natural and built space, a bold appropriation of a renowned shrine from the local population, served at once to assert the power of the Inca in this one province and to establish the legitimacy of the polity in a pan-Andean cosmological frame. Materially, the natural features, architecture, and assemblages of the shrine complex—sacred rock, metal altar, stone offering place, plaza—"combined into a comprehensive metaphor for transmitting the ideals of the state religion" (50) that were the basis of Inca political legitimacy. As a strategy of rule, Inca manipulations of sacred space could also take more subtle forms (e.g. Jennings 2003). In an analysis of architectonics at the palatial compound of La Centinela, the political and religious core of the coastal Chincha region both before and after Inca incorporation, Craig Morris and Julian Idilio Santillana (2007) detect a sophisticated, dual principle of governance, symbolically reflected in closely articulated spatial oppositions between Chincha and Inca architectural and institutional forms. The reorientation of an important

Chincha pyramid toward an Inca religio-political structure and the associated blending of vertical (i.e. Chincha) and horizontal (i.e. Inca) planning techniques, coupled with the juxtaposition of Chincha and Inca plaza and palaces, and the spatial forwarding of Chincha elites in spectacles of power, bespeaks Inca efforts to practically and symbolically incorporate local elites into a sociopolitical order staked on alliance. The built environment is here both deeply symbolic and banally functional, serving at once to encode structural positions that are at once aligned and distinguished, and to "provide settings" for the enactment of dual power (147). According to Morris (2004), La Centinela is but one example of a provincial Inca administrative center, along with Huánuco Pampa and Tambo Colorado, that served this dual function as "stage set" and symbolic "incarnation of authority" (see also DeMarrais 2005: 83–88; Morris 2004: 299, 321). As "essential vehicles of state creation" (Morris 2004: 321), these centers and the royal palaces within them provided "both the symbolic armature and the real architectural spaces and buildings that shaped the human interactions necessary for forging links between rulers and ruled" (311).

I have focused thus far on the abiding archaeological interest in the semiotics of built things, yet this disposition extends to other forms of "imperial debris," from Roman coins (Ando 2000) and Achaemenid seals (Dusinberre 2013) to Inca polychrome vessels (Bray 2003) and Aztec sculptures (Ohnersorgen 2006; Umberger 1996). All these things and more have been endowed with communicative capacities to dutifully express messages of social difference and imperial authority, and, through their symbolism, conscript subjects to the work of imperial hegemony. The view that monuments and materials associated with political practice and imperial style always worked effectively as materializations of ideology (DeMarrais et al. 1996) has come under scrutiny. But the focus of such scrutiny has been the all-too-tidy formulation of monolithic state power, rather than the limiting view on the capacities of things themselves. Claudia Glatz and Aimée Plourde (2011) have convincingly argued, for instance, that the "costly" stone monuments strewn across the Anatolian landscape during the period of Hittite hegemony reflect less the confident proclamations of kingly power, as has long been thought, than the competitive struggle among a range of elite actors to assert their prerogative over land and resources. Here, there is a shift in the sociopolitics of things, a change in the messages being transmitted; yet the things themselves remain consigned to the communicative work of signaling on behalf of a large cast of human characters.

The problem looks a bit different when the focus of scrutiny turns to the things themselves. Indeed, the prevailing semiotic view is in many ways the ultimate conceptual foil to the material turn, the clearest interpretive proxy for a stark and hierarchical distinction between humans and things, where the latter function as the nonverbal mouthpieces of human ideas, intentions, and meanings. To cast things as mere signs that convey meaning, Bruno Latour (2005b: 10) dissents, is to obscure their own capacities to act, to reduce them to "hapless bearers of symbolic projection." He prefers to see things "not only as full-blown actors, but also as what explains . . . the overarching powers of society, the huge asymmetries, the crushing exercise of power" (72). Things do not just exist at the margins of the social, able to "sometimes 'express' power relations, 'symbolize' social hierarchies, 'reinforce' social inequalities," but can be "at the origin of social activity" (72–73). Likewise, Daniel Miller's (2010: 10) work has pursued what he calls a "demolition" of the commonplace idea that things are mainly signs or symbols that represent humans, that their study should be like "a neglected adjunct to the study of language" (see also Gell 1998; Miller 2010: 11). Miller prefers to see a dialectically generative relationship between humans and things that closes the gap between them by bringing forward the productive capacities of both. To Webb Keane (2005: 183), the problem is not semiotics, but a Saussurian and poststructuralist lineage that seems to "render material forms into little more than transparent expression of meaning," with little care for actions and consequences. When he writes that "signs are not the garb of meaning," he means that things do not illustrate something else, like identity or, in our case, imperial power, but are themselves embedded in social life through the mediation of signs (184). In the next chapter, I explore alternatives to a semiotic perspective on "imperial debris," engaging more deeply with the interventions of the material turn. My purpose here is only to bring forward and begin to denormalize the deep-seated notion that the relation between imperial hegemony and things is played out only in the arena of signs and symbols.

ARTIFACTS, MEDIA, AND THE AGENTIVE SUBJECT

Thus far we have seen that things are accorded different kinds of capacities in different domains of imperial reproduction. Where stress is placed on the imperative of economic regeneration, the thing itself, in the guise of the *good,* occupies center stage, working vigorously to keep the machinery of empire in motion from the moment of its genesis at the hands of the overdetermined laborer to its circulation as wealth and symbolic media in the hands of imperial elites. Where attention shifts to the perdurance of power, things themselves recede somewhat, as their semiotic capacities as ideological instruments that legitimate, justify, and mask asymmetries wholly displace the material entanglements that surround their coming into being. To an extent, signification demotes substance, once the imperial subject begins to appear as a political being whose compliance can and must be secured not only in the theater of war but in the theater of signs. In this section we shall see that, until very recently, the demotion of the thing progressed still further with the advancement of the subject. That is, as the imperial subject acquired agency and the ability to negotiate, embrace, shape, resist, or opt out of hegemonic institutions, things often *lost* their capacities to affect the course of imperial reproduction and receded still further into the background. This is, to be sure, not a perfectly inverse relation, but a general trend, and one that Keane (2005: 183) has also noted in the social sciences more broadly: "The more social analysis stresses the intentions, agency, and self-understanding of humans . . . the more it tends to reproduce the very dichotomy between subject and object it might better be putting under scrutiny." As we shall see, when agentive subjects are endowed with the prerogative to make choices vis-à-vis their identities and their interactions with dominant groups and dominant ideologies, they do so either in relative autonomy from the world of things (once seen as complicit in the work of empire), or else by holding things captive to their agentive efforts. Humans are acting autonomously when things are seen primarily as proxies *in the present* for such actions in the past. Things in this guise we typically call artifacts or ruins; they are mere indices, traces, or "leftovers," as Mark Leone (2007: 206) aptly described them, of action that they played little or no role in enabling or constraining. Humans are holding things captive to their agentive efforts when the thing is seen primarily as a *medium,* or more precisely an *intermediary,* in Latour's (2000: 18) sense, through which subalterns and colonists alike negotiate their encounter. To Latour, an intermediary (as opposed to a mediator) is a thing "that does nothing in itself except carry, transport, shift, incarnate, express, reify, objectify, reflect" meaning. The thing as intermediary "confronts us only to serve as a mirror for social relations. . . . Of course, it carries meaning, it can receive it, but it does not fabricate it" (19). In the case of a mediator, a thing that figures more rarely in archaeologies of empire, meaning does not antecede matter. Meaning "is no longer simply transported by the medium but in part constituted, moved, recreated, modified, in short expressed and betrayed" (19). As we shall see, both artifacts and intermediaries entail a downgrading of the transformative capacities of things, entirely in the case of artifacts and substantially in the case of intermediaries. It will also become apparent in the discussion below that, in many accounts, things continued to act symbolically, signifying the sociopolitical dispositions of their creators. But the competing perspectives on things that reduced them to their indexical and intermediating properties result in a general sense of the dilution and diminution of thing efficacy in the emergence of the agentive subject.

It is at this point in our diagnosis of "where things stand" that we cross the experientially dubious but intellectually real boundary between imperialism and imperial colonialism. That is, the agentive imperial subject emerged in the first instance out of scholarly circles quite separate from those with which we have engaged thus far. In archaeologies of colonialism, agency was first accorded to the transformative indigenous female figure of the Spanish Americas. Knowledgeable social agents eventually took shape as a conspicuous force in the colonial endeavors of Rome, Egypt, and beyond. Indeed, even before processual archaeology's turn to empire, the pioneering research of Kathleen Deagan (1983) laid the groundwork for the figuration of the imperial subject as an active participant in imperial projects. By directing archaeological attention to the intimate spaces of the colonial home, Deagan's work endowed indigenous women with potent capacities to forge new "creole" or "mestizaje" identities in situations of imperial colonialism. At the same time, however, it set what we might call the "artifactual limits" of things. Deagan focused especially on ceramic styles and patterns in the distribution of local versus nonlocal forms in households at the Spanish colonial site of St. Augustine. These things served as *indices* of intermarriage between colonial men and indigenous women. They pointed to the retention of indigenous practices in the putatively private spaces of the home. The artifacts *reveal to us* the role of women as cultural brokers, who enabled the genesis of new social categories that forced "responsive adjustments" to grand imperial designs concerning the appropriate course of social integration (Deagan 2001: 181).

As Barbara Voss (2008b: 192) has already discussed, Deagan's approach reverberated across subsequent studies of colonial contact in the circum-Caribbean (Deagan 1995; Ewen 1991; South 1988) and elsewhere in the Americas. Its legacy is also felt in places as far from Spanish Florida in space and time as Egypt during the second millennium B.C. In his study of the frontier fortress of Askut, Stuart Tyson Smith (2003a, 2003b) has posited that the lives of Egyptian colonists and Nubian women became closely intertwined and mutually transformed. Smith's argument rests on the occurrence of mixed assemblages across a broad range of artifact classes—tools, adornments, seals, pottery, and so on—in both Nubian and Egyptian styles. Particularly notable is the presence of Nubian cookpots, which come to dominate the cooking assemblage and, taken together with residue analysis, suggest a shift over time to Nubian foodways. In their interactions with Nubian women at this colonial outpost—a kind of St. Augustine on the Nile—colonists crossed the very cultural boundaries that imperial ideology worked to maintain. The thing as artifact is here fully realized: fortress architecture *shows* fidelity to Egyptian technology, groundstone axes are *markers* of Nubian identity, pottery used in public and private contexts *reveals* different ethnic identities, and so on.

These efforts that have peered into the domestic spaces of colonialism and seen in their kitchens an agentive colonial subject powerfully shaping the course of imperialism from behind the scenes have gone a long way toward fracturing the dominant image of the passive colonial victim, and have also complicated the putatively neat distinctions long drawn between the social positions of colonizer and colonized. But they have also had the unintended consequence of "domesticating" imperialism, as Voss (2008b) has cogently noted. The focus on the home concomitantly seemed to cut out from analysis the coercive institutions of imperial governance, and rendered the imperial subject an excessively consensual participant (sexual and otherwise) in her or his own subjection. Moreover, overemphasis on the ability of colonial subjects to actively produce new identities that undermine imperial domination can obscure the ways in which instances of ethnogenesis in the colonies can, quite the contrary, stabilize colonial power and create a host of new social inequalities to the benefit of the empire (Voss 2008a: 289, 304). An unsettlingly ephemeral line is thus drawn between the agentive imperial subject and the subjugated imperial agent. To these critiques can be added the exile of things from colonial worlds, now crowded with active and interactive settlers and subalterns.

What is perhaps most striking is that the analytical banishment of things that attended the arrival of the agentive subject obtained even when things themselves were the galvanizing sources of subaltern agency. In an utter evaporation of the aforementioned fine line, several studies have framed the powerful capacities of those trapped in imperial snares in terms of *dependence*, in which the perdurance of hegemonic institutions hinges on the actions and abilities of the conquered. Often such dependence rests on the productive capacities of actors to feed the material needs of the imperial establishment, and thus this interpretive direction entails lifting the veil of passivity off the once quiescent laborer. Brumfiel (1991: 226), for instance, has stressed how women's reproductive work allowed the population growth that maintained the Aztec army and political economy (particularly labor-intensive *chinampa* agriculture), just as their household-based productive efforts in weaving ensured the flows of woven mantles, loincloths, blouses, and skirts through the market system, the tribute system, and the redistributive economy. Through their work in the home, women of the Aztec realm enabled the dependencies that linked polity to patio, just as did the "chosen women" of the Inca, who were brought to imperial palaces to produce the cloth and corn beer that "underwrote the imperial project" (Bray 2003: 132). To be sure, Brumfiel and Bray both fully recognize, indeed emphasize, the importance of the things themselves in the Aztec and Inca political economies. But empowering women appears to require the rhetorical displacement of the dependence from the thing to its human creator. Such displacement is also at work in less clearly extractive contexts. According to Peter Wells (1999a: 139–147), for example, soldiers of the Roman Empire stationed in frontier forts in the provinces of temperate Europe depended heavily on local communities in surrounding garrison settlements, who, judging by industrial debris excavated at several such sites, supplied the army with enormous quantities of manufactured goods like pottery, metalwork, leather, textiles, and even weapons that could be used against their very makers. "Without the constant cooperation of the local producers," Wells (1999b: 91) writes, "the Roman venture would have failed." Once again, the language of interpretation concentrates imperial dependence on the autonomously able subject. It is the *craftworkers* who shaped the identities of the troops at the imperial frontier (Wells 1999a: 147) and enabled the conditions of their own subjection. In no explicit way is it the crafted things themselves.

The analytic repression of the thing is pushed even further on the fullest realization of subaltern agency, when the conquered and colonized choose actively to opt out or even resist the hegemonic institutions of the dominant. As was so often the case, Brumfiel (1996) helped usher in this new direction in archaeological thought, to discern in the material record dispositions of noncompliance in early empires. Brumfiel quantified the shifting frequencies of females in ceramic figurine collections from hinterland sites of the Basin of Mexico before and after Aztec dominance. She also noted differences between androcentric state-sponsored representations of women and the popular images of female figurines that more often invoked reproduction. Brumfiel concluded that the commoners who made figurines in the hinterlands managed to refuse the dominant Aztec gender ideology. Women made choices through their craft and pursued alternative ideological formulations that left unrealized certain hegemonic tenets of the state (for a similar take on figurines from the Akkadian empire see Pollock 2011). The thing as artifact is here fully realized. The figurines serve *in the present* as a "gauge" of Aztec ideological penetration into households (Brumfiel 1996: 149). They "reflect" popular sentiments of resistance, but they played no role in the past in enabling, reproducing, or disseminating such dispositions. The Aztec world has in recent years emerged as far more differentiated and nuanced, as matters of imperial strategy and political economy are increasingly viewed in the context of complex social negotiations (Garraty and Ohnersorgen 2009), but the shift has come at the expense of a material world relegated to mere index.

In like fashion, landscapes also have at times slipped in status to passively indexical "ruins" of resistance. In Roman Africa, for instance, the nucleated villages that existed beyond the limits of the hinterland of Caesarea, and the settlements and hill forts of mountainous areas situated above and beyond the zone of wadi agriculture, differed in morphology from the large villas and Roman-style farms of the plains, and were thus taken by Mattingly (1997b, 2011: 159–160) as "indicative" of values and lifeways alternative to those that Roman provincial administration had put in place. Elsewhere in the Roman empire, when native groups in the provinces of temperate Europe actively chose to preserve Iron Age building techniques and architectural forms, pottery and fibula styles, and ritual deposits, they were asserting their adherence to traditional values and beliefs as an alternative to Roman lifeways (Wells 1999a). The work of resistance was performed not by the things themselves, but by the human "actions of production" of which the material results are potent "expressions" (170). Even the "high art" of insubordination, subtly pursued by imperial collaborators in vassal states, entails a paralysis in the material world. When the leaders of the Late Bronze Age kingdom of Ugarit, a subordinate polity of the Anatolian Hittite Empire, embraced the cultural production of the Hittite state's rival, Egypt, they were deliberately trying to negotiate their subjection by choosing non-Anatolian forms of royal representation. For Glatz (2013), the Egyptian statues and stone vases, just like the Egyptian-style ivory plaques and stone stele, were themselves little implicated in the work of resistance to Hittite royal culture, its realization or dissemination. Such things are rather a means for us *in the present* to infer or reconstruct human strategies and choices at Ugarit.

A second strand of reasoning in archaeologies of the active imperial subject—aware and at times defiant of her or his social position—relocates the signifying capacities of the thing from the present to the past, according the material world the same kinds of semiotic efficacy as we have already seen with respect to imperial power, but here deployed toward its gentle or strident subversion. For a particularly early example of this approach, we return once again to the northwestern limits of the Roman empire, where, Hingley (1997) tells us, native groups in Britain created distance between themselves and the institutional centers of imperial control through their use of built landscapes (see Schreiber 2005a for a Wari instance of a similar spatial practice of resistance). After the second century A.D., such groups built new towns in the style of pre-Roman settlements, dispersed around *civitas* capitals—former tribal centers that were transformed into seats of Roman control and run by native elites. To Hingley (1997: 92–93), this pattern reflects the decisions of the multitudes to use space as "subtle statements of resistance" to the tribal elite's extension of Roman control. So too does the continued construction of roundhouses in some areas of Britain—a house type characteristic of the pre-Roman Iron Age. By building roundhouses, subalterns put material culture into "active use" (88) as markers or statements that could "represent" their subtly defiant sociopolitical dispositions.[6]

In a sophisticated recent analysis of the Pueblo Revolt that takes its place in a long line of historical archaeologies of this extraordinary event (Preucel 2002), Matthew Liebmann (2012: 17) encapsulates this approach to colonial resistance as "the struggle over signs." Taking inspiration from Russian linguist Valentin Voloshin's opinion that "the struggle between colonizer and colonized 'is always carried out in an area of signs,'" Liebmann sees the material practices of the Jemez people of New Mexico during the Spanish interregnum of 1680–96 as tied up in just such a symbolic contest. To advance their clash against the Spanish, the Jemez *used* the material world in a number of ways that served to purge traces of Spanish influence and create new meanings. In keeping with the revivalist ethos of the revolt, they relocated their settlements (from mission villages to mesas), rearranged their built environments (from dispersed to aggregated forms), and changed ceramic styles (from Jemez black-on-white to pan-Pueblo motifs—see also Mills 2002), all in ways that broke with their recent lifeways under Spanish rule and referenced, embodied, and recreated a perceived ancestral past. This struggle through signs extended to acts of catachresis that created new "semiotic weapons," as through the fusion of Catholic icons with images of traditional Pueblo spirituality (Liebmann 2012: 142). The things of Liebmann's analysis are not only hard at work in signification. Architecture works indexically (signaling a dual social organization), as well as actively, in shaping daily practice, though it must be said that the latter is something of an afterthought (122–123; see also Ferguson 2002).

To recapitulate the terrain traversed thus far, the status of the thing in relation to the active subject is bound up with the work of signification, either as an index in the present or as a sign in the past. Between these two positions, the thing of the savvy subaltern at times also assumes yet a third bearing, as an *intermediary* in the struggle of intercultural negotiation and identity formation. The origins of this formulation once again trace to archaeology in the Americas. Deagan's interpretations of ceramics as indices of "creolization" brought about by the agentive capacities of the conquered contributed to the ensuing archaeological concentration on processes of creolization, crystalized by a number of later works mostly focused on the African-American experience (see reviews in Dawdy 2000; Liebmann 2013). These often framed material culture in colonial contexts as products of the recombination of shared lexical elements into an ambiguous cultural "grammar" that signaled the blending of lifeways and the genesis of new colonial societies out of contexts of asymmetrical power (Ferguson 1992: xlii). Creolization offered a very particular ontology of things, predetermined by a linguistic metaphor that assigned to the material world the intermediating qualities of language. This is particularly visible in the work of Jane Webster, perhaps the first to apply the concept of creolization to the things of Old World empires. The hybrid religious art produced in Roman Gaul, Webster (2001, 2003) argued, ought no longer be seen as testimony to submissive "Romanization" but as a medium for "resistant adaptation" and the forging of new social identities. The things of Webster's analysis—clay statuettes, stone reliefs, and so on—have little explicit effect on the world, semiotic or otherwise, yet nor are they mere indices for modern analysis. Rather, creole things, in this case those bearing the ambiguous iconography of various deities, are akin to the wooden dummies of the ventriloquist—a material intermediary through which the subalterns of Roman Gaul expressed and worked out their accommodation of Roman dominance. In an unfortunate simplification of both colonialism and things, Webster (2001: 218; 2003: 42) proffered that material culture as a medium of expression "encapsulates colonial experience."

Interestingly, the construal of things as intermediaries obtains across the otherwise stark divide in understandings of the social as constituted principally through signs or through practice. If the linguistic metaphor of material creolization cast the thing as a medium of expression, then the social logics of structuration theory cast the thing as the medium of daily practice. Thus, in her Giddensian study of public architecture in the towns of several Roman provinces, Louise Revell (2009: 3) views built space as "the medium and product of human action." The agency of Revell's Roman provincials is of the collaborative sort that we have already seen—a capacity directed toward the reproduction of the structures of imperial power (see also Gardner 2002). Imperial dependence on the efforts of subalterns is here played out though a variety of daily activities and interactions. The forums and basilicae of the provinces, with their porticoes, shops, council chambers, and tribunals, along with other built spaces of political activity and public spectacle, were the settings that framed and enabled the human practices essential to the maintenance of both local distinctions and the wider Roman ideology of urbanism. In the framework of practice theory, the intermediating work of things does produce social consequences; but this work is quite incidental to the compliant practices of agentive subjects. "Although the buildings form the primary evidence," Revell (2009: 23) writes, "they are not my primary research interest; rather it is the people who inhabited them, who moved through them and occupied them on a daily or routine basis."

Voss's (2008a) account of Californio ethnogenesis at the Spanish-colonial military post of El Presidio de San Francisco offers a more nuanced perspective on the intermediating work of material things in the practical enactment of colonial life. Like Revell, Voss takes seriously the "entanglement among social subjects and the materiality of the world" that works to "bind people, things, and places together" (22–23). Things, to Voss, are a "resource" with "dual properties," in that humans deploy them in their efforts either to transform or to stabilize social identities (23). She puts these views to work in her effort to explain how Californio identity emerged among a heterogeneous group of settlers of principally Mexican Indian and African heritage. To cite just one example from this wide-ranging work, in her examination of the architecture at El Presidio, Voss sees the construction, maintenance, and transformation of the main quadrangle as inextricably linked to the emergence of this new identity. The shift from mixed architectural materials and techniques toward uniform adobe construction was one means through which settlers effected their transformation from an ethnically heterogeneous group into a unified colonizing presence that was distinct from local Native Californians (190–191). The expansion of the quadrangle and the size of the central plaza allowed another kind of a shift, in this case in approaches to sexual surveillance that transferred the ethical responsibility for ensuring honorable sexual relations from the household to the military leadership (200). To Voss, architecture is neither a mere index of ethnogensis, nor a symbolic reservoir, but a practical affordance that "is produced through and simultaneously structures social relationships" (201). Extending this line of reasoning, Voss writes: "It is often argued that archaeological evidence is needed to compensate for the political biases found in documentary sources and to fill in evidentiary gaps in the historical record . . . however . . . a methodological focus on material practices contributes much more than a simple additive or corrective to archival documents. Material practices constitute the *interface* between institutional systems of power and the agency of social subjects. They are the *media* through which people navigate, respond to, and precipitate the historical events that constitute their lives" (302, emphases added). This is perhaps the clearest articulation of the intermediating logic of colonial things. It is also, it must be said, a forceful rebuke of anemic rationalizations for an archaeology of imperialism that hinge on the limitations of written sources.

Hints at an alternative view on colonial things that opens the possibility of a somewhat more prominent role for materials are to be found Steven Wernke's work in the southwestern Peruvian highlands. Drawing on William Sewell's (2005) reformulation of the Giddensian concept of structure, Wernke emphasizes the recursive relations between schemas (or rules) and resources, which include nonhuman materials. To Wernke (2013: 25), materialization entails not the use of the material world as intermediaries, but instead "the process by which schemas are constrained, maintained, and potentially destabilized." Schemas and material resources are mutually constituted, yet the material world not only reproduces the rules of social life, but can potentially exert limits on schemas and also give rise to new ones.

Such was the case with the built landscape in the Colca Valley of Peru. Franciscan friars involved in Spanish colonial evangelization built a number of doctrinal settlements in locations of former Inca administrative sites (Wernke 2007, 2013). At these doctrinas, the friars arranged their rustic chapels in spatial association with former areas of Inca ceremonial activity—great halls and plazas—and conducted Catholic rites such as catechisms outdoors, in spaces of Inca public ritual, as part of what Wernke calls an "analogical" approach to conversion. The impossibility of direct conversion necessitated that Christian doctrine be introduced in ways that would be locally intelligible, and the improvised incorporation of the local ritual landscapes was one such way. The paradox—indeed a clear example of the conditions of satrapalism discussed in chapter 1—is that spatial references to the places of Inca-era ritual activity preserved the very past that the friars were charged with eradicating (Wernke 2007, 2013). Over time, the friars shifted toward less accommodating, more coercive spatial practices, culminating in the 1570s in the resettlement of indigenous populations into European-style *reducción* villages. Through careful spatial analysis, Wernke (2013: 211) detects early signs of this shift at one doctrina in his study area, where changes in spatial organization over time enhanced possibilities for surveillance and directed foot traffic away from Inca ceremonial spaces and toward the colonial plaza and chapel complex. "The built spaces introduced in this case—chapel/atrium/plaza—and the rituals carried out there . . . must have (if they were to find cultural purchase) resonated with the analogous forms and practices from the Inkaic-era (the great hall-plaza couplet), even as the friars sought an eradicative strategy that routed traffic away from them" (211).

Wernke does not at any point cast the co-opting spatial manipulations of the friars as efforts to express, or reflect, or project, the authority of church and crown.

Rather, the forms and arrangements of the buildings and plazas worked to enable particular practices intended to produce Christian subjects. Nor does Wernke assume that the friars' strategies were effective. The enduring spatial association of the doctrina with Incaic buildings would have made this difficult: "Rather than conversion as the Spanish clergy understood it . . . the experience of building, dwelling in, and moving through the spaces of this doctrina must have produced . . . a hybrid, improvised arrangement that was neither conceived nor controlled by either the friars or their charges" (211). Inca buildings themselves in effect placed limits on colonial schemas and gave rise to unintended social practices that were neither wholly indigenous nor wholly colonial.

CONCLUSION

A degree of simplification is unavoidably entailed in any effort to bring forward the predominant dispositions toward imperial things that have emerged over the past three decades in the archaeology of empire. At higher resolutions, of course, a rather more granulated picture can come to the fore—one in which things take on (usually implicitly) a number of capacities simultaneously, whether indexical (in the present), semiotic (in the past), or mediating. Susan Alcock's (2001, 2002) work on social memory in Roman Greece exemplifies some of the complexity that I have filtered out in these pages for the sake of drawing forth discrete patterns. Sometimes, the temptation to pin *things* down is resisted in favor of more fluid narratives that open numerous interpretive possibilities. Thus, for example, the picture that Alcock paints of the Athenian agora in the centuries of Roman rule is materially alive. We learn of "itinerant temples" moved from countryside to agora, of building renovations and of new constructions—all part of a deliberate commemorative project on the part of imperial Roman and Athenian elites to reuse and reformulate the classical Athenian past in and for the Roman present. At times monuments and spaces appear to work as mediators or conduits, enabling elite solidarity, self-representation, and competition, facilitating Greek negotiation with Roman imperial authorities, and creating a demos complicit in the work of remembering (Alcock 2002: 41–42, 70). At other times the buildings recruited to these various efforts are taken to act symbolically and communicatively, for instance in asserting Roman authority or promoting the status of Greece's privileged elite (58–97). Sometimes monuments and spaces are cognitive conjurers that "summon up" or "provoke" social memories (Alcock 2001: 326–327). And at others still, materials are like imperial debris, markers or indexes that "testify" to past commemorative dispositions (327). Are all of these simultaneously possible? Are the capacities of the material world really this capacious? Perhaps. Indeed, Alcock makes a strong if unspoken case for it. The problem, I would submit, is that this is not a question to which archaeologists of empire have given sufficient thought.

The intent of this assessment of "where things stand" has been neither to reject altogether the varying perspectives on imperial things that have emerged over recent decades, nor to devalue the coexistence of a diversity of views. It is precisely this rich range of orientations that has helped establish problems of empire and colonialism as legitimate concerns of archaeological research. Rather, my purpose has been to make the case that in our efforts to refine our understanding of the social workings of imperialism—human strategies, intentions, practices, and experiences—things in themselves have received comparably short theoretical shrift. Both the evolutionary approaches of the 1990s and more recent archaeologies of colonialism have, I suggest, stopped short of fully realizing a distinctly archaeological epistemic of imperialism that is dedicated to understanding the work of things in reproducing the layered sovereignties of empire. Scholars of imperialism and colonialism have made an art form of surpassing untenable binaries, be it colonizer and colonized, domination and resistance, West and East, and so forth. Yet the subject/object, animate/inanimate dichotomy remains firmly in place. As archaeology grants conquered communities the capacity to engineer subtle forms of resistance, including opting out of dominant ideological, cultural, or political institutions, the human agent is endowed to control a world of things that has little control over it.

What might an alternative look like? Is it possible to preserve the agentive human colonial subject while at the same time according autonomous capacities to the vast assemblages of nonhuman matter that also populate imperial geographies? We turn in the next chapter to an exploration of the philosophical terrain out of which such an alternative might emerge.

3

Imperial Matter

Between 1801 and the 1890s, the production and consumption of soap in Britain increased exponentially, from barely 25,000 to as much as 260,000 tons per year. Manufacture and marketing of this everyday substance developed into an imperial commerce that pushed Victorian cleaning habits to the farthest colonized corners of the globe, just as it brought images of empire into the most intimate spaces of British homes (McClintock 1995: 209–210). In a wide-ranging study of gender, race, and class in imperial Britain, Anne McClintock has shown how advertising campaigns for the mass-produced Pears' soap (figure 11) contributed to a larger system of representation that unified the new commodity economy of nineteenth-century market capitalism under the "celebration of imperial spectacle" (1995: 219). Pears' soap was one of several domestic things at the vanguard of this "commodity spectacle," playing a leading role in the drama of colonialism alongside tobacco tins and whiskey bottles, biscuits and toothpaste, toffee boxes and baking powder. To McClintock, in the hands of Britain's advertisers and marketers, everyday things became intermediaries for semiotic manipulations that allegorically displayed jingoistic messages of imperial success. Soap in particular served as a "mediating form" (208) that embodied such middle-class values as monogamy ("clean" sex), industrial capital ("clean" money), and the civilizing mission (cleaning the savage). The industry surrounding this cheap and portable thing prospered in part because "it could persuasively mediate the Victorian poetics of racial hygiene and imperial progress" (209).

McClintock's telling of what she calls the "soap saga" has much to teach us about the ways in which imperial agents harness the material world to further projects of colonial rule. Her account is also, however, one that reduces imperial things

FIGURE 11. Advertisements for Pears' Soap (sources: left, *McClure's Magazine*, 1899, courtesy of the British Museum; right, http://3.bp.blogspot.com/-wP92yoMzqT4/Ua7hMG4-7SI/AAAAAAAAA4E/Juazav7N4WI/s1600/heathens.jpg).

themselves to a condition of bondage, in thrall to human intention and a tyranny of signs. A parallel analysis of soap in late-nineteenth-century Britain casts this mundane matter in a rather different guise. For Simon Schaffer (2008: 148), the story of soap is a story of science, and of the "eloquent objects" of soap physics, namely bubbles. To be sure, Shaffer also attends to soap's commodification and the combination of market forces that made it possible, from the accelerated production of alkali, to the extraction of palm oil and copra from colonial plantations in West Africa and the South Pacific. But his main concern is the project of Britain's classical physicists to establish and communicate the underlying laws of material science through work and play with bubbles. Britain's public scientists, intent on demonstrating to receptive popular audiences the achievements of physics in deriving general scientific principles pertaining to the structures of matter, looked as closely as was then conceivably possible at suds themselves. These evanescent things contributed to the development of microphysics, time-lapse photography, and cinematography, as scientists worked to describe the properties of bubbles (their dimensions, colors, formation, duration, oscillations, etc.) and to stabilize them despite their inherent transience.

I begin this chapter with these two contrasting stories of suds and spectacle in late-nineteenth-century Britain because, examined side by side, they bring to the fore the critical challenge that attends our understanding of the relation between imperial power and things. The two studies nicely illustrate what Lorraine Daston (2008: 16) has called the paradox of matter: "On the one side, there are the brute intransigence of matter, everywhere and always the same, and the positivist historiography of facts that goes with it; on the other side, there are the plasticity of meaning, bound to specific times and places, and the corresponding hermeneutic historiography of culture."

McClintock and Schaffer bring this paradox into high relief. On the one hand, following Marx on the mystique of the commodity fetish, McClintock (1995: 220) addresses not the "brute intransigence" of the thing itself, or even its use value, but only "its potency as a sign" that was open to manipulations of meanings tied to imperialism and domesticity. Schaffer, on the other hand, is more concerned with the sensible materiality of soap and the "positivist historiography of facts" that was built around it, directing far less attention to its interpretation in a cultural system of value centered on the civilizing mission. McClintock (1995: 220) gives little thought to humans' tactile confrontation with the thing itself, instead forwarding human contact with the abstraction of "commodity culture" embodied in the advertisement. In contrast, Schaffer's history leans in so closely to the encounter of London scientists with soapy suds that the wider political context of global soap consumption is lost.

Finally, the two accounts also part ways when it comes to the capacities that each accords to its nonhuman protagonists. To McClintock, it is not so much soap that has an autonomous effect on the world, but the commodity form that it takes. Soap is an "agent" in the civilizing mission only when it is "abstracted from social context and human labor" (1995: 221–222). Schaffer's bubbles are rather more powerful. Their very physical properties and the independent temporality of their lives impel scientists to devise instruments to suspend their movement. It is these same properties, according to Schaffer, that entice physicists and publics to apprehend and appreciate the very laws of nature. When Schaffer speaks of soap bubbles as "eloquent objects," he picks up on Daston's (2008: 12) idea that things do not merely repeat the human voice, but themselves "press their messages" on us. They too "have a say" (Olsen 2010: 31).

How, then, are we to discover a working analytic for imperial things that conjoins in equal measure the force of both matter and meaning in shaping satrapal conditions? How can archaeologies of empire discover the nodes of intersection between the physical properties that things possess and impose on us, and the politics in which we enlist them, individually and in assemblage? And how are we to do this analytically, in a way that rises above the limitless multitudes of things that abound in specific imperial times and places, while at the same time remaining beneath the soaring register of ontology, where the sociopolitical specificity of things is lost to the cause of philosophical abstraction? This question matters because things are not everywhere and always the same. It may be the case that their abilities emerge in part from the inherent physical properties that allow them to stand up to us, to make a difference in the world, to invite *some kind* of tactile encounter, to conjure *some kind* of affective response, and to compel *some kind* of dependence. But the forms of those encounters, the substance of those affects and differences, and the strength of those dependencies arise from the particular political and social constellations that humans and things together create. This is not to suggest a social "a priori" into which things enter (Olsen 2010: 36–37), but to accept that the collaborative work of humans and things can give rise to different kinds of nonrandom associations.

With five millennia of macropolitical power behind us, for example, students of empire have come to understand that the relations between humans and things recurrently produce a cluster of interlinked associations of coercion, violence, extraction, compromise, affiliation, mimicry, complicity, and revolt, played out across vast distances and across sundry social boundaries. Humanity's role in this bundle of associations that we have come to call imperialism is by now rather well documented. But in this chapter I want to make the case that we have yet to think concertedly about the collaborative capacities of nonsentient things in realizing the conditions and conditionals of empire. Humans alone are not the sole protectors of effective imperial sovereignty, any more than they are independent actors in their ambivalent attempts at bricolage or the determined exertions of dissent. Such efforts are made possible, encouraged, and at times undermined or enforced by decidedly nonhuman partners.

Three steps lead us in this chapter to a conceptualization of the things that work to produce satrapal conditions. The first section, by way of background, distills a selection of key interventions in post-phenomenological and post-Marxist philosophy, social theory, political theory, and archaeological thought that have made it possible to recognize confederacies of things as efficacious participants in social and political life. Several materialist perspectives emanating from a range of scholarly locations that have come to constitute the "material turn" have carefully diagnosed and contested the gradual exile of things from the humanistic and social sciences—how it happened that language, reason, and culture eclipsed matter, how we came to be so deeply distrustful and disdainful of things (Frow 2010; Olsen 2010; A. T. Smith 2015). I shall not retread the philosophical historiography that has long branded as "fetishistic" the supposedly misplaced gaze that rests too long on putatively passive and inert stuff, instead of hastening to discover the primary concerns that lie behind the "mere surface" of things (Olsen 2010: 25, 57, 64). Even if not yet back from banishment, things are nevertheless slowly making their return to philosophy and social theory. Thus, the question that I pose in the first section of this chapter is: How are we coming to terms with them? How are philosophy, social theory, and archaeology conceptualizing their capacities, affordances, and relations with humans? In this highly selective and abridged introduction to material theory, my concern is less to explore the most fundamental questions of the metaphysics of things (e.g. Harman 2002, 2010) than, rather more modestly, to broadly synthesize the terms now on hand to describe *what things are able to do* independent of the human-ascribed work of semiotic projection with which archaeologists, as we saw in the previous chapter, are already well familiar.

From this general background discussion of the material turn, I turn in the next two sections to the crux of the matter: a diagnosis of the conspicuous lacunae in material and colonial thought that has left us without an adequate account of imperial things. Several recent political theories of matter have heterodoxically asserted the determinative role of things in making political association possible. But at the same time, these bodies of thought have arguably set the limits of the political quite narrowly, in such a way as to exclude imperial polities from the reach of their concepts. Conversely, anthropologies of colonialism have placed at the center of their analyses precisely the unique relations of power that obtain in imperial formations. Yet like McClintock's soap saga, those historical ethnographies that cast things prominently in the theater of colonialism tend to leave unresolved Daston's paradox, short-changing things in their abilities to shape imperial projects, quite apart from the intentions of the humans who make them, use them, and conscript them to the work of signification.

To address these lacunae requires an analytic that is expressly centered on the politics of matter in imperial formations. Such is the extended focus of the final section of this chapter, which develops a schema for imperial things that pivots around the four material concepts that I call *delegates, proxies, captives,* and *affiliates.* As we shall see, each is distinctive for the different interventions of its constitutive matter in sociopolitical life, *as well as* for the nature of its relations to the others and to human makers and users, from the most privileged imperial agents to the subjugated whom they rule. Yet despite the varying ways in which delegates, proxies, captives, and affiliates make and modify imperial projects, they emerge analytically out of the well-founded postulate that virtually all things are bound up in human–thing assemblages that make some sort of difference in the world. Coming to grips with such capacities is a prerequisite for recognizing delegates, proxies, captives, and affiliates as serious matters of empire.

WHAT CAN THINGS DO?

At the heart of most efforts to reclaim a place for things in the commotion of existence is a withering critique of two intertwined orthodoxies: the distinction and centrality of the human in philosophy and social theory, and the tyranny of semiotics that long rendered things inert and passive receptacles for the imprint of culture and meaning. "Post-humanist" arguments that check the "long dictatorship of human beings in philosophy" (Harman 2010: 2) and the "narcissistic reflex of human language and thought" (Bennett 2010: xvi) have struggled to demolish the long-cherished view that intention and cognition warrant a hierarchical figuring of humans and nonhumans in their capacities to make a difference in the world (Harman 2002: 167). Things, these arguments hold, are not ontologically exhausted by the representational qualities of signification that we assign to them. As Olsen (2010: 10) aptly summarizes, things "do not just sit in silence waiting to be embodied with socially constructed meanings. Landscapes and things possess their own unique qualities and competencies that they bring to our cohabitation with them." It is through these unique capacities for action and their intrinsic material properties that things are able to commingle both productively and obstinately with humans to generate the associations that we call polities and societies. Yet how are we to characterize these actions? A highly abridged synthesis of four perspectives drawn from contemporary social, political, and archaeological thought provides a broad sense of both the emerging transdisciplinary consensus on the power of things, and the range of ways in which that power can be conceived.

"They have to be *actors* . . . and not simply the hapless bearers of symbolic projection" writes Bruno Latour (2005b: 10) in his polemical introduction to actor–network theory, a framework that forcefully forwards the unqualified agency of things in the associations that continuously gather together "the social." The key insight of actor–network theory is that social aggregates are not held up by "social forces," but endure because of a heterogeneous array of human *and* nonhuman actors that continuously associate in impermanent networks. What allows the various institutions that we conventionally understand as social or political to obtain with any degree of endurance is our interactions with things of different durability, which lend a quality of stability or security to such associations, without which the fleeting "social" could never be recognized as such, let alone reproduced (Callon and Latour 1981; Latour 2005b). The actions of such nonhuman things can be seen all around us: "kettles 'boil' water, knifes [*sic*] 'cut' meat, baskets 'hold' provisions, hammers 'hit' nails on the head," provided we accept that action may be linked not to intention but to the ability to alter a given state of affairs (Latour 2005b: 71). Things that make a difference are themselves actors, participants, or "actants," which describes "any entity that modifies another entity in a trial" (Latour 2004: 237). In their capacities as actors, things can "authorize, allow, afford, encourage, permit, suggest, influence, block, render possible, forbid, and so on" (Latour 2005b: 72). Not all things are equal in their agentive possibilities, being efficacious to different degrees. Nor are they fully autonomous, because every acting thing mobilizes a number of other things in its efforts. But agency is dispersed across the full range of entities that differentially intervene in the world (see also Gell 1998). Latour unequivocally divests agency of its traditional associations with human motivation, stripping it down to the most basic capacity to produce effects. It is a justifiable redefinition since, as others have noted, even cognitive capacities for symbolism and self-awareness, insofar as they inescapably emerge from human corporeality, are themselves "indelibly material in their provenance" (Coole and Frost 2010: 21), and thus provide something less than a primary, determinative basis for the allocation of agency. Yet Latour's democratic redistribution of what has long been regarded as the human being's most singularly distinctive quality, however expressly redefined, might still sit uncomfortably with those concerned to avoid any whiff of anthropomorphism in our efforts to make sense of nonhuman things on their own terms (e.g. A. T. Smith 2015).

As we saw in chapter 2, Latour also draws an important distinction between a thing as a *mediator* and as an *intermediary.* An intermediary does nothing more than convey or transport meaning without causing any change (2000: 18). It is a messenger that reflects, represents, expresses, or projects already existing meaning: "Defining its inputs is enough to define its outputs" (Latour 2005b: 39). Intermediaries are the stuff of "material culture," collections of things whose actions and influences amount to little more than the passive projection of society (84–85). Mediators, in contrast, do not singularly signify meanings assigned to them, but instead cause transformation: "Their input is never a good predictor of their output. . . . Mediators transform, translate, distort, and modify the meaning [of] the elements they are supposed to carry" (39). Reassembling the social requires bringing mediators out of the shadows and not mistaking them for mere faithful intermediaries. Intermediaries are rare exceptions in a world brimming with mediators. Mediators do not only symbolize relations, like "humble servants . . . on the margins of the social" (73), but productively generate social action. Things exist in at least these two modes, though more often as mediators. The challenge is to discern them (79–82).

Latour's formulations have reverberated across many fields in the humanistic social sciences and beyond, from archaeology (e.g. Knappett 2008; Webmoor 2007; Witmore 2007) to political theory (Bennett 2010). For Jane Bennett (2010: viii), materials enjoy a quality of "vitality," which refers to "the capacity of things—edibles, commodities, storms, metals—not only to impede or block the will and designs of humans but also to act as quasi agents or forces with trajectories, propensities, or tendencies of their own." These active powers of nonsubjects are intrinsic to matter itself, and not acquired through an external force that comes to inhabit any given body. Echoing and building on Latour, Bennett speaks of material agency, the effectivity of nonhumans, and most especially, of "thing power"—the tendencies of matter to persist, to issue calls, to provoke affects, to act, and to produce effects (2–6). Thing power is "an efficacy of objects in excess of the human meanings, designs, or purposes they express or serve" (20). In suppressing the determinative weight of human design, Bennett means not to deny the existence of intention, but to view it as "less definitive of outcomes" (32). Thing power stems from a vitality, a kind of life, that is inherent in all matter, and is marked by a propensity of things to "actively endeavor to express themselves" and their emergent qualities, which external forces like human artisans can only bring forward, but not endow (56; see also Ingold 2007: 12, and below). Importantly, Bennett speaks of *things* rather than *objects,* for the latter are in her view only partial things, insofar as they are products of human semiotics whose intrinsic existence is thus less than fully realized. Or, in Bill Brown's (2001: 4) words, an object is what we look *through* to see what it reveals about society, culture, and most of all about us, while a thing (at least in its nonambiguous sense) confronts us with its very own material presence. Like Latour, Bennett (2010: 5, 10) holds that objects ought to be philosophically forgotten, replaced instead by "actants" in all their thing power.

Yet thing power on its own is insufficient for grasping the agency of the material world, because it suggests an overly fixed and atomistic order of things. Following Deleuze (and earlier, Spinoza), Bennett (2010: 21, 23) insists that agency resides not in individual things, but in the "agentic assemblage" of ontologically diverse and vibrant entities that come together in ad hoc groupings. Things have a tendency to "conglomerate," to collaborate, to act in "confederations" of humans and nonhumans, which demands a "congregational understanding of agency" (xvii, 20–21, 23). In assemblages, effects result not from root causes residing in a subject, but in the vast "swarm of vitalities at play" (32). This emphasis on the tangle of the assemblage has been taken up and rethought by others concerned to move beyond the singular object to the coalescence of multiple thingly components (A. T. Smith 2015).

Like Latour, Bennett explodes the distinction between life and matter. In apprehending a kind of vitality in "inanimate" things she trespasses a most sacrosanct boundary of post-Enlightenment metaphysics. It is in much the same vein that Lorraine Daston radically redistributes the capacity for speech among organic and inorganic beings. To Daston, in their own nonverbal way, things can be said to talk. They do not only ventriloquize or project human speech, but themselves "press their messages on attentive auditors" (2008: 12). Daston works to check the "narcissism" of Cartesian anthropocentrism, which "asserts a monopoly on language for human beings" and "condemns things merely to echo what people say" (11). Things do not merely repeat. By virtue of their inherent material properties as well as their cultural significance, they have their own say. These ideas finds echoes in Walter Benjamin's (1996: 73, quoted in Olsen 2010: 2096) interest in "the material community of things in their communication," which makes it possible to attend to the ways things express themselves. Much like spoken speech, things talk by conjuring certain "ways of thinking, feeling, and acting" (Daston 2008: 20).

In contrast to Latour and Bennett, Daston here crosses over from a literal to a metaphorical analytic for things. When Latour and Bennett speak of material agency, they do not mean that things are active *in a manner akin to* humans, but that they manifest their own forms of action and livelihood. It is more difficult to get away from a metaphorical understanding of thingly loquaciousness (without doing considerable violence to the meaning of the word "talk"), and to look past Daston's flirtation with an anthropomorphizing of things, their colonization under the overbearing weight of the humanist discursive trope. But we can nevertheless observe across these thinkers a shared project to dismantle the old certainty that "subject" and "object" exist in stark opposition, and "acknowledge things not as a backdrop to, or embodiment of, remnants of societies and cultures, but as an inseparable part of their very constitution" (Olsen 2010: 149).

Social theory has thus largely propelled the "turn to things." And yet, as some archaeologists and anthropologists have been quick to note (e.g. Hodder 2012; Ingold 2007; Olsen 2010), ironically these bodies of thought have in many cases maintained a remove from actual things in themselves, rarely pausing long enough to undertake a sustained and serious examination of any particular thing—its material properties, intrinsic capabilities, and what Hodder calls "entanglements." As the discipline with the deepest expertise in the points of encounter between humans and things, archaeology has entered the conversation on matter in some instances with an eye to "theoretical repatriation, that is, reclaiming a concept" that has long occupied the center of the field's theories and methods (Olsen 2010: 152; but see Fowles in Alberti et al. 2011: 898).For Ian Hodder, a new way of thinking about things entails not necessarily a redistribution of agency, but a turn to how thingly and human existence evolves out of deeply mutual and multifaceted entanglements with one another. At the heart of Hodder's theory is the concept of dependence. Humans depend on things because they enable our existence through their affordances, and at the same time as we rely on them to secure life's routines, they can constrain us in less than productive ways (dependency—Hodder 2012: 17–18). Our existence as humans is irreducibly "thingly" (38). Yet at the same time as we rely on things, things rely on each other. "Things assemble" (8). They are connected, entwined with one another and engaged in collective work in a manner perhaps akin to Bennett's assemblage. Things also rely on humans. If we want them to persist in a particular state of being that is important to us, we must accord them our care, for things can break down if left unattended, given their own nonhuman temporalities. This dependence of things on humans "draws humans deeper into the orbit of things" and imposes on us a "double bind, depending on things that depend on humans" (Hodder 2012: 86, 88). It is this mutual, dialectical entrapment that Hodder means when he speaks of an "entanglement" between humans and things. In an important departure from Latour and others, Hodder maintains that to understand such entanglements requires a very close look at things in themselves, their physical properties and the "non-human ecologies in which they interact," as well as their fluctuating hold over humans (93–94). Hodder calls for a shift in focus from "how things make society possible to the thing in itself" (3), yet this cannot be realized if the social dominates our approaches to things, and if the boundaries between humans and things are relentlessly effaced to make way for dispersed networks of undifferentiated actants. Entanglements are physically as well as socially constructed, and archaeology is particularly well positioned to probe their relatively neglected former dimension (95).

These and other invitations to realize the existential autonomy of things, the compass of their abilities, and the tangles in which they and we are ensnarled, exhort us to utterly recondition both our innate sense and our analytical stance on the very nature of existence. They provide the primal resources of the new materialisms, the philosophical grist for deliberating their first principles and forward bearings. Yet there is also a quality of relative tranquility in the atmospheres of being that they call up, auras of thought that are free of struggle or contestation over the proper distributions of energies and effects. How, in other words, do such tranquil ontologies hold up against the agitations of political life?

THE POLITICS OF THINGS

It is perhaps a mark of a second wave in the material turn that things appear increasingly inseparable from matters of politics, forcing yet another reconditioning, this time of political philosophy. As "the victim of a strong object-avoidance tendency" (Latour 2005a: 15), traditions of political thought from Hobbes to Habermas have long written things out of the body politic, where only human participants assemble, authorize, and speak (see also A. T. Smith 2015). Yet in response to calls for a post-humanist political theory that addresses the material constitution of political association, things are increasingly being recast from outcasts to participants in the political arena. Such a turn to take seriously the "stuff" of politics (Braun and Whatmore 2010a: ix) would seem to open productive inroads into rethinking the matter of imperial formations. And yet, as we shall see, there is an emerging tendency to narrowly circumscribe the scope of either the material or the political in attempting to define the relations between them. The result is that recent materialist political thought, while offering critical insights on the thingly qualities of our political lives, nevertheless offers insufficient analytic purchase on the distinctive operations of materials caught up in the undemocratic politics of imperial formations.

For example, to some critical thinkers of the "new materialism" the politics of matter is quite exclusively a politics of the body. We learn from Coole and Frost (2010: 15–24), for instance, that the revolution in biomedicine and biotechnology has denormalized received wisdom on the proper subject of political action and the just locations of political culpability. They note that the deleterious health effects of environmental toxins raise new questions about how processes that impact the materiality of the body have consequential policy implications. Our bodily encounters with fertility and marriage, epidemics and food hygiene are the realization of state intervention (23). One limitation of this concern with "biomaterialism" is its exclusive focus on the body as the material site of the political (19), to the radical exclusion of the vast world of nonbiological matter that brings bodies into being. Such a politics that is centered wholly on the body, even in its most visceral, corporeal mode, appears rather less "post-humanist" than the "new materialisms," as Coole and Frost understand them, would seem to otherwise endorse.

Other renegade strands of political thought, which have allowed for a more capacious universe of material participants in public affairs, simultaneously advance a rather constricted sense of the political. Latour (2005a: 16), for example, calls for an "object-oriented democracy" that is alert to the long-neglected *res* of the *res publica,* or the "things" of the public. He puts into play an expansive world of things that moves far beyond the clearly delineated matter of traditional object ontology. The things of Latour's "*Dingpolitik*" range from the objects of the assembly and the instruments of a parliament, to the "matters-of-concern" that divide a public and the evidence that can settle or sharpen them. Such things join in a participatory public sphere that assembles humans and nonhumans "in hybrid forums and agoras"—the physical, institutional, and virtual arenas that are able to bring to life gatherings of various sorts (23). Of concern here is a sense of politics inextricably tied to the public assembly.

Yet, as Latour and Weibel (2005: 47) themselves note, this kind of politics is one that "entire empires have survived without." It is the politics of democracy in places like modern and contemporary Europe and America, where political representation is a "Western obsession" (Latour 2005a: 34). For Latour the only apparent alternative is the rejection of politics itself, which to him is equivalent to the rejection of political assembly. Such objections can be detected far and wide beyond the Western world, from the traditions of the Jivaros and Jihadists, to China and Japan. Can these traditions count as *political* traditions, Latour skeptically asks (35)? "Can we enlarge our definition of politics to the point where it accepts its own suspension?" Yet perhaps the more immediate question to ask is whether we should accept a definition of *Dingpolitik* that applies only to what Latour himself reckons to be a mere "fraction of humanity." In millennial terms, compared to democracy, imperialism has been the far more enduring form of association in humanity's (and indeed Europe's) political repertoires (Burbank and Cooper 2010), a coercive approach to aggregation that is premised not only on the rejection of assembly but on the denial of the very option to those thus amassed. Yet *Dingpolitik* admits of no such thing as the *res imperia.*

Latour is not alone in locating the matter of the political in the *res* of the *res publica.* In Bennett's telling too, "vibrant matter" appears to exist exclusively in the public sphere of the democracy. The capacities of nonhumans for political activity require our heightened attention only, it would seem, in the production of the pluralist demos (2010: 30). Bennett draws on the theories of democracy advanced by philosophers John Dewey and Jacques Rancière to locate the political materiality of things in their role as members of a public. Her appropriation of Dewey's formulations suffices to demonstrate the politically constricted pertinence of her vitalist materiality.

In *The Public and Its Problems,* Dewey defines a public as one of many coexisting, contingent, and temporary collectivities that arise in response to a shared experience of a harm that eventually turns into a problem (see Bennett 2010: 100). Such problems are the result of what Dewey calls "conjoint action," which involves initiatives undertaken alongside a swarm of countless other actions in a crowded field of human endeavor and consequence. Indeed, this constant fluxing of simultaneous acts and consequences that limits the possibility for full control is what, for Dewey, makes a political system akin to an ecology. As in a natural ecosystem, the inescapable interactions of overlapping initiatives mean that no conjoint action can be fully controlled by plans and intentions. Thus, in Dewey's theory, publics arise not out of will but out of consequences. While Dewey himself recognizes only human origins for these actions, it is in his focus on outcomes over intentions that Bennett sees the opportunity to admit all material bodies as members of a public. Publics of human and nonhuman members coalesce around the need to tend to a shared problem that results from conjoint action.

I have described Dewey's idea of a public because it provides one window onto the difficulty of extending Bennett's (2010: 106) "materialist theory of democracy" to contexts of macropolitical dominion. To make the case, let us continue with Bennett and Dewey's metaphor of the ecosystem. Imperial polities are made up of such staggering "ecological diversity" (which is to say, diversity of political systems) that it is impossible for a mass of humans and nonhumans existing in different ecosystems to be affected by, and respond to, a common harm. We may of course conceive of multiple publics within empires, just as Dewey allows for multiple publics within democracies. But the multiple publics of a democracy emerge out of a shared ecology and the conjoint actions of its multitudes. So while it might be possible to speak of the multiple publics *in* an empire, there can be no "imperial public." And to the extent that, for Bennett, political actions of nonhumans are effected through their participation in a public, we are once again left with no way to think about the actions of nonhumans in the production and reproduction of imperial sovereignty.

Perhaps the most developed alternative to date to a materialist theory of democratic politics hails from archaeology. In his "object-aware account of sovereignty," Adam T. Smith (2015) seeks to reground the polity writ large "in the machinery of sovereign reproduction." For Smith, the political machine invokes the "logics of material assemblages *in addition to* . . . the agency of humans" that together drive sociohistorical transformation. The conditions for such reproduction are three: a coherent public (in this case a human collective) defined by relations of inclusion and exclusion, the figure of a sovereign (or total sovereign establishment), and an apparatus capable of formalizing governance. All three of these conditions are materially produced through encounters of human-and-thing assemblies—encounters that are grounded in the material workings of "sense" (which concerns the evocative work of things), "sensibility" (which relates to the physicality of things), and "sentiment" (which pertains to the imagined capacities of things). There is no teleology underlying Smith's theory of sovereignty; but at least the first of his three conditions—a cohesive public—is quite clearly a precondition for the other two.

Smith provides a tight and elegant political theory of sovereignty as it obtains in the relatively small and nascent polities of prehistory (the focus of his case study) and, presumably, the nation-states of today. And yet the compelling suite of concepts in *Political Machine* are imperfectly suited to making sense of the political matter of empire. To the extent that Smith's three conditions obtain through accretion, he provides a robust analytical armature for tracing the work of things in the incipient formation of sovereignty within a relatively cohesive and emergent political community. Yet his emphasis on the necessity of a "coherent public" effectively excludes imperial polities from his theory of sovereignty. As we have already seen, there can be no cohesive "imperial public," no matter how efficacious is the world of matter in creating encounters of sense, sensibility, and sentiment. Smith leaves to others the question of the formation and reproduction of sovereignty when instantiated in an aggrandizing modality that inherently refuses the possibility of "a" public.

Traditionally, as Jennifer Pitts (2010: 212) has noted, "political theory has come slowly and late to the study of empire," and early signs suggest a similar inattention in its new materialist orientation. Latour, Bennett, Coole and Frost, Smith, and others certainly make it possible to imagine a kind of analysis that allows room for nonhumans as efficacious participants in the political affairs of imperial macropolities (see also Bennett and Joyce 2010; Braun and Whatmore 2010a: ix). But when it comes to rethinking in detail the work of political matter in the layered sovereignties of empires, these important perspectives provide inspiration more than an analytic schema. Political association is not exhausted by Western humanity's democratic projects, nor by other small-scale political projects grounded in the materially mediated relations between a contained public and a sovereign. The view of politics as a question of assembling is one shared by only a small slice of humanity. A "more fully materialist theory of politics" that recognizes the powers of nonhumans in political affairs (Braun and Whatmore 2010b: x) is perhaps best reformulated in the plural, to allow for multiple theories of the political that can account for the different ways in which humans and things come into association under different constellations of power.

COLONIALISM AND THE MEANING OF THINGS

If materialist political theories take us only part of the way toward a conceptual reckoning with imperial matter, can materialist theories of colonialism bring us any closer? While thus far the new materialisms have largely assumed the representational democracies of the present as their historical laboratory, their twentieth-century precursor, materiality studies, often centered precisely on the human–object encounters wrought by the nexus of European imperialism and colonial capitalism. It would therefore be a mistake to suggest that a concerted interest in the matter of empire is somehow new. In the 1990s, the meaning of things occupied a prominent place in several seminal historical anthropologies of colonialism, providing a critically important foundation for the present inquiry. And yet, as we shall see, these foundational efforts also left unresolved the problem of matter itself, the physical properties of things and their capacities to transform human users. A close look at three influential accounts suffices to acknowledge the important precursors to *Imperial Matter,* as well as to press the case that anthropologies of colonialism have taken the things of empire quite seriously, and at the same time not quite seriously enough.

One of the earliest extended efforts to contend expressly with the materiality of colonialism was Nicholas Thomas's *Entangled Objects* (1991), which afforded a penetrating view onto the ensnarement of things in regimes of exchange and commodification (see also Mintz 1985). Thomas's concern was to direct anthropology's attention concretely toward "the variety of liaisons men and women have with things in the conflicted, transhistorical history of colonialism" and away from the "abstracted domain of man, subject, and object" (1991: 26) that had preoccupied the revitalized material culture studies of the 1980s (Miller 1987). To Thomas, the diverse liaisons of humans and things involved mutual appropriations and crossing currents of two-way traffic. For example, in the nineteenth century, European commodities infiltrated indigenous societies of the Pacific islands, while indigenous objects found their way into the private and public collections of European travelers and institutions. What held Thomas's attention were the encounters with the unfamiliar entailed in these exchanges, and the incorporation of the exotic into new regimes of value. On the European side, collecting practices exposed the ambiguity of curiosity that surrounded European interests in, and apprehension of, indigenous artifacts and their makers. On distant colonial shores, the responses of Pacific islanders to the European objects brought by traders—iron axes, hatchets, muskets, gunpowder, whale teeth—revealed the ways in which a desire to acquire such goods arose not from "the irresistible magnetism of white commodities" (Thomas 1991: 87) but out of local political and cultural agendas.

Thomas's work introduces a style of engagement with objects that is common to the anthropology of colonialism: one that privileges meaning and its malleability over matter and its physicality (Daston 2008: 17). Like McClintock's study of soap and commodity spectacle in the British Empire, Thomas is quite deliberate in his inattention to the brute and durable physicality of things. His central purpose is precisely to counter the notion that a thing has a stable identity in its "fixed and founded material form," focusing instead on how "objects change in defiance of their material stability" (1991: 4, 125). Even so, despite their apparent prominence, it is fair to say that the things of Thomas's study are largely epiphenomenal. That is, indigenous objects matter only to the degree that their acquisition and representation illuminate the sentiments and ethnological inclinations of the explorers, missionaries, and settlers who collected them. For Thomas, the objects-turned-curios and artifacts are the passive casualties of colonialism, not quite accorded powers of their own to transform, but instead subject to the dispositions and desires of acquisitive colonizers. Powerless, too, are the European objects that enter indigenous worlds, which figure in Thomas's story only to illuminate their appropriation and recontextualization in Pacific exchange regimes. When Thomas writes evocatively of the "promiscuity of objects," (27) or of their inherent "mutability" (88), he is not referring to their own capacities for unpredictability, in a manner akin to Latour's "mediators." What mutate as objects cross cultural regimes are, rather, the values and meanings that human agents ascribe to them, and their standing in relations of exchange, variously as commodities, gifts, or prestige valuables. It is this act of crossing, "the movement and displacement of competing conceptions of things," that concerns Thomas, more than the things themselves (123). Thomas's "entangled objects" are thus ensnared not in immediate, human–object dependencies, but in the abstract transactional relations between givers and receivers. These are metaphorical entanglements of culture and meaning, of Western and non-Western peoples, in which objects are inextricably if collaterally swept up. As Hodder (2012: 90) notes, what is missing from Thomas's study is "an adequate engagement with the object nature of things. The focus is on relationships between people, how things connect opposed categories and allow for hybridity and transformation."[1]

Though foundational, *Entangled Objects* provides only a partial springboard toward the satrapal condition also because of Thomas's conspicuous silence on power. A contrasting yet complementary case is to be found in John and Jean Comaroff's (1997) telling of the nineteenth-century encounter between Britain's Nonconformist missionaries in Africa and the people of southern Tswana. The Comaroffs attend to the everyday forms of consumption in homes, fields, and missions that brought the Tswana into the global order of capitalism and contributed to the rise of modernity in Europe, Africa, and beyond. For their purposes, materiality means rather more than a concerted disposition toward things. The critical intervention that puts materiality into play is a rebuke of the approaches to colonialism centered on the "psychic forces" of "discourse and dialogics" (410) that cut colonialism off from the realities of social, economic, political, and cultural experience. No mere "cultural formation" or "discursive field," no mere problem of "consciousness, representation, subjectivity, textuality," colonialism is to the Comaroffs in large measure about "material production" (19–20). Their primary concern is the commodification of Tswana and its forced entry into the order of capitalist relations. "Material" is here a capacious idea that accepts in its broad folds all of colonialism's lived realities on the ground—mundane human practices, unequally distributed agencies, the tastes, styles, and gestures of quotidian life as it is actually lived, *as well as,* to be sure, material things of the most solid and chunky sort—cotton clothes and brass bedspreads, plows, cupboards, and windowpanes.

Such an expansive mandate does not necessarily call for close dissection of the affordances of things, assemblages, and their close-up encounters with their makers and users (though nor does it foreclose such engagement). What matters more is how objects are embedded and deployed in regimes of value and desire, in projects of commodification, consumption, and civility. Objects and architecture are very much present in this account. More often than not they figure as tools—powerful ones, to be sure—of human intention, particularly the intentions of the evangelists who worked to remake personhood, habits, and notions of virtue and value in southern Tswana through clothing and the design and trappings of the home. The instrumental and semiotic logic of the object is clear: "Western clothing, the social skin of civility, was to be both a *sign and instrument* of this metamorphosis" (227, emphasis added; see also 267). The evangelists were not the only ones who harnessed objects to their desired ends. The Tswana also used European clothes, house furnishings, and architecture, sometimes unconventionally, in acts of anachronism and bricolage that lay somewhere between rejection and acceptance, and served as "a riposte to the symbolic imperialism of the mission *tout court*" (241).

However unequally, the generative forces that changed the Tswana world emanated from humans, who wielded their power *through* European objects—paradigmatic "intermediaries" in the Latourian sense. It was the human colonialist who was in the business of "making subjects by means of objects" (218). Such asymmetry in the distribution of effort and effect lurks behind a language of subtle displacement that stops short of the emancipation of the thing from the over-determinacy of human agency and perception. Thus it is "style," not the cotton of cotton clothes, that fabricates "new Southern Tswana social cleavages and alliances" (255). It is "style," not the wool of woolen blankets, that was part of the "very making" of realities (273). One finds in this analysis a deliberate effort to provenience effects not in matter per se, but in the meanings that cloak objects and put them to work. To get this subtle nuance wrong requires correction: "African subjects were reoriented and reoriented themselves, in large part, through recommissioned European objects; *more accurately,* through *regimes* of such objects"

(12, first emphasis added). Precisely speaking, it is the systems of value in which objects are ensnared that made the African subject, not the objects themselves.[2]

A more recent effort to rethink the relation between colonialism and things represents the beginning of a significant shift toward according matter powerful capacities to shape colonial encounters. In *Archaeology and Colonialism* (2004), Chris Gosden defines colonialism as "a particular grip that material culture gets on the bodies and minds of people" (3) or "a process by which things shape people, rather than the reverse" (153). Of vital importance to Gosden is the production and transmission of value, which occurs through our somatic relations with material culture. It is the attachment of *human values* to things that empower material culture to "move people," to cast them in their "thrall" (5, 20, 41, 81). Thus, we are to understand that value-affixed things "grip" and "move" people in ways unique to colonialism (though precisely how they generate these affective states, and how they do so differently than in noncolonial contexts, is not quite clear).

Gosden's emphasis on the human-ascribed values attached to things means that they are not quite yet mediators, able to bring about effects independent of humanity's plans for them. Yet at the same time, he clearly empowers things sufficiently to suffer that most classic critique voiced by the material turn's skeptics: he has been said to fetishize material culture, to accord it too much determinancy at the expense of human agency, to confuse human relations as relations between humans and things (Dietler 2010: 20–21). Dietler urges us to resist the seductive trap of fetishism to which, in his view, Gosden has succumbed, instead preferring to return things to their proper place as "tools" and "symbolic markers" of control and cross-cultural engagement—important tools and signs to be sure, but instruments nevertheless, fettered to human choices and desires (20, 60, 63). But are not human relations both relations among humans *and* among humans and things? Far from over-empowering things, I would instead suggest that Gosden does not go quite far enough.

As others have noted, one of the main points of divergence between material culture studies and the turn to matter is the differential emphasis placed on consumption. Thomas's *Entangled Objects*, the Comaroffs' *Of Revelation and Revolution*, and Gosden's *Archaeology and Colonialism* vigorously push the material world to the front of their analyses of colonialism, but they do so only once objects, embedded in putatively pre-existing social relations, have been tagged with meanings and values that allow them to fashion subjectivities. They do so primarily at the point of consumption (see also Dietler 2010). These accounts "take as a starting point a world of objects that has, as it were, already crystallized out from the fluxes of materials and their transformation" (Ingold 2007: 9). They are concerned with objects that work instrumentally because they have been "turned into signs and consumed *as* signs" (Olsen 2010: 32), in the Tswana case under a close colonial gaze. Insofar as value and signification are what empower things, they serve as Latour's intermediaries, which cause the secondary occurrences put in motion by human cognition. To study satrapal conditions is by no means to turn a blind eye to consumption, use, and value, as we shall see in chapters 4–6. But it does entail allowing matter—its vitality, properties, and the dependencies in which it is entangled—to have a say in shaping imperial projects. Such is the work of delegates, proxies, captives, and affiliates.

DELEGATES

"I found Rome built of clay: I leave it to you in marble" (Dio 1987: 245). The famous boast of the emperor Augustus gives poetic voice to perhaps one of the most unmistakable constellations of delegates in imperial history, the iconic marble monuments of the Roman Empire. In the first several centuries A.D., the city of Rome and countless other urban communities across the Mediterranean became ensnared in a relationship with marble that was so ardent, it can fairly be described as enslaving. From civic architecture to sculptural arts—basilicae and temples, baths and theaters, fountains and statues—untold tons of this metamorphic rock of recrystallized carbonite minerals made possible the practical mediations of Roman authority. Marble permeated the public sphere, constituting the spaces of assembly, commerce, and ritual, defining the terms of political competition, leisure, and conspicuous consumption. Imperial agents came to rely on its affective and practical contribution to the reproduction of Roman imperium as ideology and practice. To feed the dependence on marble, Roman emperors expropriated and exploited marble quarries in conquered lands from Asia Minor to North Africa, from southern Spain to the French Pyrenees, sometimes transporting the stone on purpose-built carriers to reach the marble-yards of Rome. This in turn set in motion practices of patronage and emulation by civic elites across the Roman world, who refashioned their cities in Rome's image to win favor with citizens and sovereigns alike, fueling a complex commercial marble industry that extended beyond the control of the imperial center (Long 2012). Marbles of all sorts ensnared countless people in their use and care, from slave laborers to rural landowners, from artisans to architects, from contractors to patrons, from traders to pedestrians (4). The Roman Empire as we know it is simply unthinkable without marble, a powerful substance that palpably made its own difference in the perdurance of Roman sovereignty.[3] But the political fixation with marble came at a cost, fettering imperial agents to a material without which the total apparatus of imperial sovereignty could not be maintained in its desired form. Marble necessitated ever-expanding workforces and administrative resources. And at the expense of civic prosperity, it entailed exorbitant expenditures that may have led to stagnation in the growth of the Roman economy (284, 292).

Like the marble public buildings of the Roman Empire, delegates are things that take a share in the preservation of the very terms of imperial sovereignty through the force of both their material composition and the practical mediations they help afford. They are devilish things, however, for in return for their collaborations with the human agents of empire delegates in a certain sense come to govern the very entities that empower them. The effects of delegates are unattainable by humans alone, but this is not to deny a human role in their emergence and workings. Because imperial agents appoint delegates to assist in their plans, such things are kinds of representatives, conglomerating or standing in for the will and worldview of many. Yet delegates are delegates less because of the source than the outcomes of their actions, since their continuously unfolding effects are always in excess of their assignments.

The designation of a thing as a "delegate" has a well-known precedent in science and technology studies. Latour (1992) used the term to refer to a very particular class of things, namely technological mechanisms, like hydraulic door closers and automated turnspits, that are tasked into action by humans in order to make easier those functions that would require more effort if people had to carry them out on their own (a porter to close a door, or a cook to turn a skewer). This is not, however, what I mean by a delegate. Indeed, there is a curious elision in Latour's conception, a conspicuous silence on the political connotations of a word that is ultimately concerned with empowerment. The focus of his formulation is on the *replacement* of the human by the nonhuman, rather than on the element of designation or authorization entailed in this transference. Latour's (1992: 229) notion of delegation involves "shifting down" to nonhumans work that humans could also do if only they could be bothered or trusted. It is apparently an apolitical process of substitution. But of course, not all nonhuman things accomplish their work by standing in for us. Indeed, the vast majority of things that humans make and use act in ways that are wholly beyond autonomous human capacities.

In the sense forwarded here, delegates are less technological than political entities, and thus they produce political effects. To restore the political connotations of the term is to acknowledge three key qualities of delegates. First, since delegation always entails the ceding of the prerogative to bring about effects from one entity or assemblage to another, human or nonhuman, material delegates come to play a role in the forces of political transformation under empire. They do so by mediating, through direct somatic encounter, the practices that reproduce a sovereign's prerogative to rule. These nonhuman imperialists make their own difference in the routines and rituals that sustain the values and institutions of an imperial polity. As we shall see in chapters 4 and 5, it is not that delegates passively facilitate such practices in dutiful accordance with the intentions of their creators. Delegates are not intermediaries, obediently expressing or carrying out prescribed purposes. They instead bring about effects that emerge from their own physicality, which may block or facilitate, attract or deter, invite or impede, conjure or refuse, and thereby keep the machinery of empire in motion. Delegates attain such efficacy in imperial reproduction not through their singular operation, but in confederation with an extensive assemblage of other delegates, as well as privileged human agents, who together collaborate in ad hoc groupings.

Second, once empowered, delegates in some measure come to hold sway over those who entrust them. It is the *reliance* that imperial agents come to have on delegates, on both their physical materials and their political effects, for the preservation of the very terms of imperial sovereignty, that are most critical to their definition. Things of empire are delegates when the sovereign establishment is to some degree fettered by its own need for the materials out of which such things are made—the palm oil of British soap, the marble of imperial Rome, the alpaca wool of the Incas, the silver of Achaemenid Persia. In such cases, sovereignty comes to be contingent on the delegate materials on which it relies. The polity becomes unviable or inconceivable in their collective absence. Such "contingent reliance" on matter (Hodder 2012: 17–18) leads to a host of institutional effects—the extraction of materials, the regulation of flows, the imposition of standards, the specialization of skills—all vigorously ensured by the assemblages of violence. Importantly, when it comes to delegate matter, instrumental and affective dependences come to blur. Rome is no less conceivable without marble aqueducts than without marble statuary. In this sense, in certain modes delegates are akin to Heidegger's "gentle things"—things that bring forth the material itself, rather than dissolving substance into utilitarian purpose. Metals, once formed, come to glitter and shine; rocks once polished reveal their colors and patterns. Such gentle things are the work of *poiesis,* bringing forth the material and calling for its care (Olsen 2010: 83). It is when materials compel imperial agents not only to instrumentally use them but also to care for them through regimes of affect that the things forged of such materials can be said to be delegates. Delegates and human imperial agents are thus enmeshed in mutual dependence in Hodder's sense, the former dependent on the latter for their emergence, appointment, and care, the latter reliant on the former for the continuance of the social order that upholds their positions in the political community.

PROXIES

The allure and efficacy of delegates can paradoxically lead to the slow erosion of their own powers. Their desirable qualities and effects can trigger what Michael Taussig (1993: 2) has called the mimetic faculty, which by its very force "shares in or takes power from the represented." That is, delegates can give rise to what archaeologists and art historians of empire sometimes call "copies" or "imitations"—things conventionally taken as local emulations of imperial canons in alternative materials and modified forms. In contrast to delegates, such as the marble public buildings of ancient Rome, proxies defy singular exemplification, precisely because they are not exemplary but derivative. But terms like "copy" and "imitation" are unfortunate misnomers because they implicitly repress the properties and political potentialities of things under the replicative aspirations of their makers.

As their name implies, proxies, like delegates, are involved in the work of political representation. Like delegates, they also emerge out of assignments to act that derive from sources outside themselves. These sources are both human and nonhuman; mechanically speaking, proxies are made out of the conjuncture of human design and material affordance. Behind the human design are one or more material delegates that provide their templates for the proxy replacement that stands in its place. Delegates confer the prerogative to act down the line to their less authentic proxies, whose representations can attenuate or dilute the delegate's force. Proxies are in this sense at times rapscallion siblings of their delegates, whose political mischief can arise out of (at least) two possible opportunities for slippage.

The first opportunity can derive from their material properties. Unlike delegates, proxy matter does not entrap the most privileged human agents of empire into relations of dependence, any more than proxy matter requires their care and attention. The viability of imperial sovereignty is not necessarily contingent on its extraction, regulation, policing, and concern. The differing relational properties of delegates and proxies between their chemical composition and the humans groups they ensnare give rise to a constitutional potentiality for proxies to bend the rules. This possibility begins at the very point of production. As Timothy Ingold (2000: 60) has argued, all material production takes place through a process of interaction between material properties and a "field of forces" from the environment to the human artisan. Human-made things are never merely the successful outputs of the transcription of preconceived form onto raw material. The template of the craftsperson does no more than set the parameters of the process that gives rise to a thing, but does not exhaustively foreshadow the resulting form, because form "is not imposed upon the material but arises through the work itself" (61). As Ingold notes, materials engage their makers as much as the makers ply their materials (see also Malafouris 2008). In this mutual engagement, "the properties of materials are directly implicated in the form-generating process" (Ingold 2000: 61).

Since proxies can be made up of different materials than delegates, their properties can press themselves on their makers during the form-generating process in different ways than delegate matter, in turn producing forms that may differ, to greater or lesser degrees, regardless of the precision of the craftsperson's template. The maker of the proxy has in mind a design, but the material does not follow blueprints or dictates, governed as it is by its own movements and tolerances. It is thus both the properties of the materials and the designs of the makers that can account for the formal variance between delegates and proxies, whether significant or slight. Proxies are never really copies after all, or at least not "faithful" copies (Taussig 1993: 52). The dissimilitude between delegates and proxies that results from this work is in part what invites the possibility of roguery. It precludes the possibility of successful emulation and, as we shall see, it can support efforts at mimicry and bricolage, or makeshift creativity.

A second opportunity for unruliness can stem from the company that proxies keep, which is to say the immediate assemblage of humans and things with which they collaborate in the production of social life. Proxies make a difference in the world through their cooperation in assemblages usually made up primarily of other nondelegates. The dutiful mediation of proxies in the practical reproduction of rule can be attenuated if delegates reside at the peripheries of the assemblages in which proxies mingle. I noted above that delegates are most efficacious in supporting the institutions of imperial sovereignty when they work in confederation with other delegate partners. Proxies are more shallowly entangled in the work of effective sovereignty because they act in relative isolation from a broader world of nonhuman imperial agents.

To be sure, human intention plays an important part in the work of unruly emulation. Proxies can provoke dilutions of the values and ways of doing promulgated by their material masters when human users deliberately harness them to such unruly ends. Since the mid-1980s, social theory and postcolonial thought have provided a well-worn vocabulary to capture this kind of human unruliness. From Homi Bhabha's (1997) concept of mimicry, to Michel de Certeau's (1984: xviii) analysis of the everyday tactical acts of "artisan-like inventiveness," it is by now clear that, operating within the bounds of dominant orders, humans can "make do" through minor and creative appropriations and disruptions that "lend a political dimension to everyday practices" (xvii). De Certeau and Bhabha alert us to the unanticipated effects attendant on the replication of established logics of practice, and thus fracture the metaphorical mirror that putatively represents imperial values in the enamored consuming subject.

But human intention alone cannot possibly realize the unanticipated effects of bricolage and making do. What is left unsaid in these accounts is how matter participates in the acts of mockery and play that Bhabha's "mimic men" and de Certeau's "users" undertake (Khatchadourian, forthcoming). In the case of mimicry, while it may be tempting to simply *add* materiality to its conceptual force field (Fahlander 2007: 27), Bhabha's own formulation simply does not permit this. His mimicry is analytically limited by the denial of its practical operation beyond the discursive field. Mimicry, to Bhabha, is not an agentive capacity of a colonial subject (much less of matter), not a strategy of practice, but a pathology imposed on the subject by the authoritative voice of colonial power in a space of discourse that is, even if ambivalent, nevertheless closed (Aching 2002: 32–38). De Certeau may offer more scope for the admission of matter into the tactical art of imitation by the consuming masses. In a certain sense, however, he observes the tactical practices of subjects whose capacities for creativity emerge *in spite of* a backdrop of constraining objects. Thus bricolage operates in the ways that a given text is read, or a planned city is walked, such that tactics become tactics only when the subject escapes or subverts the prescriptions of the object.

A consideration of the unruliness of proxies shifts the analytical emphasis from the craftiness of users to the craftiness of the craft itself, and explores how material things can be accomplices in human acts, not impediments or passive props. Due to the ways in which they deviate from delegates in their material properties and in the company they keep, proxies encourage and invite human efforts at gentle play in the arts of production and consumption. Proxies themselves can help diffuse the hegemonic force of that which the dominant make available. It is in the material and contextual distance between delegates and proxies that things can go wrong (or go right, depending on one's vantage), that the practices and principles of an empire can be dulled by what are, in effect, material malcontents. The challenge is to distinguish between poor and proper proxies, between those things that act in accordance with the delegates that authorize them, and those that may help their makers and users tinker with, poach from, or evade the expectations that their delegate assemblages recommend or impose.

CAPTIVES

If proxies originate from the centrifugal flows of delegates that stream outward, however periphrastically, from centers of imperial cultural production, captives are displaced things moving in reverse, deported along centripetal routes that lead on a straight course toward imperial centers. Captives are political things compelled to collaborate with the sovereign in reproducing the terms of authority and subjection. We need look no further than the idols of the conquered in the Inca Empire, in many ways consummate material captives, to appreciate the role that captivation can play in the making of satrapal conditions. According to the Spanish Jesuit missionary Bernabé Cobo (1990: 3–4), the Incas purloined the idols of subject lands and brought them to the imperial capital of Cuzco as hostages:

> When some provinces rebelled against them, the Incas ordered the protective native gods of the rebellious province to be brought out and put in public, where they were whipped ignominiously every day until such province was made to serve the Incas again. After the rebels were subdued, their gods were restored to their places and honored with sacrifices. At this time the Incas would say that the province had been subdued through the power of the rebels' gods, who wanted to avoid being insulted. And it is even said that the majority of the rebels surrendered just because they heard that their idols were exposed to public insults.

Material captives are the consequences of theft that come to assume a share in the work of political and cultural domination. They are the casualties of what

John MacKenzie (1995: 53) has called "that ultimate imperial act," and they can take several forms. Captives were the spoils marched through the streets of Rome during triumphal processions, eventually to adorn public buildings and private homes alike as constant reminders of conquest and as a continuing "incentive to glory" (Beard 2007: 30). Captives are the "curiosities" from colonized lands that British explorers, missionaries, officials, and ethnologists, with the approval of the state, the navy, and the Royal Society, acquired and subsumed under the authority of disinterested science, or harnessed to the emerging imperialist narratives of evolutionary hierarchies, or destroyed in the name of idolatry, or objectified in the name of colonial knowledge and control (Thomas 1991: 138–139, 153, 175). Captives too were the countless antiquities that British and French scholars and bureaucrats took from their colonial possessions in order to fill private collections and museums in Europe with artifacts that affirmed the manifest destiny of Western civilization (e.g. Bahrani 2003; Cohn 1996: 76–105). Finally, no less captive are those provincial things that become targets for innovative replication and co-optation in the imperial metropole—the weak prey in the theft of ideas on materials, their forms, and forces. Redeployed to metropolitan ends, these borrowings too are things of imperial appropriation, from the imitation orientalia of nineteenth-century Europe's world exhibitions (Mitchell 1988) to, as we shall see in the next chapter, the co-opted and adapted architectural canons of ancient Persia's urban landscapes.

Captives, then, are things in states of displacement and dislocation, things wrested from their embedded dependencies in now subjugated communities and thrown into new entanglements. Conscripted into the work of imperial reproduction, captives often undergo a modal shift, transmogrifying from captives to delegates. Captives, in other words, are liminal, chameleonic things, irreducible to the cultural property of either sovereigns or subjects. They are, like proxies, things that disrupt those very social categories, things that—through their crossing—blur the boundaries between conquerors and conquered and make possible the willing or unwilling incorporation of the latter into the work of imperial hegemony (Gramsci 1971).

AFFILIATES

"Missing masses" is what Latour (1992) called the overlooked, mundane, nonhuman mechanisms that hold societies together, a term that also best describes imperialism's unnoticed affiliates. By affiliates I mean the great throngs of inconspicuous things that reproduce social life under empire, even as they preserve an inviolable space of experience within it. I am speaking of local habitats and habiliments, apparatuses and adornments, foods and furnishings that bind people under empire into distinct collectivities. Unlike delegates, proxies, and captives, affiliates become imperial things by sheer happenstance, carried along by the human and nonhuman forces that brought them under the net of empire. Whereas delegates, proxies, and captives come to directly mold and modify the logics of imperial sovereignty, stimulating new practices, affects, values, and dependencies among imperial agents in metropoles and provinces alike, affiliates stand at a considerable remove from the human agents and centers of state power, falling beyond the gaze of sovereigns and satraps, and instead bound in mutual dependencies with commoners in homes, villages, towns, and cities.

The forms and effects of affiliates are pervasive and varied, but nevertheless unified by the way in which such things maintain, deepen, and impel affective and practical ties to place and to the community of human agents who collectively depend on them. Affiliates are the things that make it possible to preserve difference among the disparate groups that imperial formations envelop into their folds—the distinctive forms of dress or dwelling, the tools of subsistence and the paraphernalia of ritual, the things of leisure and luxury that to some degree retain an existence despite or alongside imperialism's new "gifts." While, through movement and display, delegates, proxies, and captives variously traffic in the spread of practices and principles across social boundaries, to the point where they become unequivocally imperial things, affiliates mark the limits of such diffusion and the unmitigated imperial conquest over the material world. Such armies of things, the immense masses with which most imperial subjects daily interact, keep their distance and hold their ground, passively affiliating with empire only by virtue of their existence within imperialized social worlds that had no direct part in their genesis.

In this way, the work of affiliates is ambiguous, on the one hand affording the practices of everyday life that make possible the exploitation of resources and bodies, and on the other hand preserving the possibility of imagining a social existence once again unanswerable to distant sovereigns. This work is accomplished through the material properties of affiliates themselves, and the "local" entanglements and webs of dependency in which they and their human users are mutually enmeshed.

CONCLUSION

The schema of delegates, proxies, captives, and affiliates does not aspire to comprehensively envelop all the molecularly or ethereally constituted entities contained by the concept "thing." Nor does this conceptual apparatus attempt to do work at the fuzzy boundaries where organic and inorganic, human animal and nonhuman animal, blur—where "the us and the it slip-slide into each other" (Bennett 2010: 4; see also Latour 2000; Stengers 2010). This framework does not invest heavily in policing what does and does not count as matter, nor does it utterly transcend old dualisms, as the "new materialisms" espouse (Coole and Frost 2010). It is possible to recognize the vitality of matter in the imperial enterprise, decentering the human as the locus of all agency, without refusing the different forms that such vitalism can take as a matter of degree and not kind. Human and nonhuman organic bodies of course belong to the universe of matter, and themselves have fluid existential boundaries. And while all material beings may be mutually generative in their emergence, a fully "monological account" (Coole and Frost 2010: 8) of existence runs the risk of effacing the "presumption of difference" to which different kinds of beings are entitled (A. T. Smith 2015: 20; see also Olsen 2010: 96). To build a theory of imperial things around the ordinary things that humans experience in everyday life and suspend judgment on living, highly transitory, incorporeal, or marginal phenomena is not to deny them materiality. Nor is it to fall into the trap of Cartesian oppositions, since all matter is here accorded some efficacy, and humans are deprived of the fiction that "'we' really are in charge of all those 'its'" (Bennett 2010: x). But the approach advanced, which readily curtails the human monopoly on "agentic efficacy" (Coole and Frost 2010: 14), takes as a starting point the nonsentient but by no means inert materials that can perhaps be said to have come to occupy the center of thing ontology, or the space where ontological debates on things today hold the lowest stakes. We have yet to come to grips with how the solid, chunky, bounded objects of traditional ontologies inflict "some kind of blow" on imperial realities, to paraphrase Graham Harman (2010: 20), much less living species and microorganisms, bodily reactions, and other natural or transitory forces. One way or another, if inquiry centered on things is to move beyond problems of ontology to politics or society, it becomes necessary to somehow heuristically segment the mind-bogglingly infinite world of nonequivalent matter, and to focus on certain things—things that may possess certain degrees of nonsentience—embedded in the relational webs that link them with others.

In chapter 1 we saw that the satrapal condition registers two dialectically related phenomena, on the one hand conjuring the experience of subjection, as it is generated through human encounters with the material world, and on the other hand recognizing the limits of imperial sovereignty, as these are produced in the relations of humans and matter. In the latter sense the satrapal condition acknowledges the potential attenuation of imperial rule as a very consequence of its extensive reach. I suggested that such limitations, restrictions, or modifications arise from the inevitable dependencies of imperial agents on the practical actions and material entanglement of their subjects. We can now be more specific in naming some of the material actants responsible for such conditions of effective and attenuated sovereignty. The reproduction and attenuation of imperial sovereignty depends in part on the variable roles played by delegates, proxies, captives, and affiliates in social and political life. These material participants are by no means predestined to create particular satrapal conditions, but they do exhibit predilections or tendencies depending on their relations, properties, and mediations, as well as on the confederacies of humans and other things with which they assemble. On a heuristic continuum, taut entanglements with assemblages dense in delegates, captives, and proxies will be efficacious in the reproduction of conditions of imperial subjection, while tight mutual dependencies between humans and confederacies of affiliates and proxies will generate the conditionals of imperial rule, opening the possibilities for autonomous action, deviation and deviance, indifference, or the imagination of alternative futures. In reality, of course, there are limitless permutations between these poles, and it is hardly the point to advance a cookie-cutter model of the relations between sovereigns, subjects, and things that obscures the untidy contingencies of imperial histories. Indeed, as we now turn in part 2 to the Achaemenid Empire, precisely such complexities and ambiguities will come to the fore. Yet we approach the expanse stretching from the windswept mountains of the Caucasus and the Armenian highland to the plains of southwest Iran now equipped with the analytical tools for conceptualizing the variegated work of things in the making and experience of satrapal conditions.

PART TWO

4

From Captives to Delegates

Among the earliest extant documents in the archive of ancient Persia is an astonishing disclosure on the acquisition of material captives and their transformation into dutiful delegates. The text is the work of the charismatic king Darius, who, soon after assuming the throne in the year 521 B.C., saw to the distribution of a number of inscriptions across the buildings of Susa, an imperial center that covers approximately one square kilometer in the lowland plains of southwestern Iran's Khuzistan Province (figure 12). Some of the texts were written on clay tablets and likely buried in the foundations, others were stamped on glazed bricks and placed in building walls, and still others were etched on stone. Such ritual gestures of founding, marking, and sanctifying the built environment had a long history in the ancient world (Ellis 1968). This particular collection of closely related documents, the so-called Susa Foundation Charters, enumerates in striking detail the mass accumulation of matter from the far reaches of the imperial realm for the purpose of building the king's palace (Grillot 1990; Henkelman 2003a; Root 2010: 178–186). After an encomium for the god Ahuramazda and a description of preliminary work ("the earth was dug deep until it went through to the bedrock"[1]), the texts proclaim that Darius arranged for the transfer of all and sundry things from far and wide: from Lebanon, Ghandara, and Carmania came exotic timbers; from Lydia and Bactria came gold; from Sogdia, lapis lazuli and carnelian; Chorasmia sent turquoise, while Egypt sent silver and ebony; from Nubia, India, and Arachosia came ivory; the stone for columns arrived from nearby Elam, while Ionia provided assorted ornaments (map 1).[2] Accompanying this migration of disparate matter were human laborers, likely indentured to the court and skilled in the corresponding crafts: stonemasons from Ionia and Sardis, goldsmiths from Media

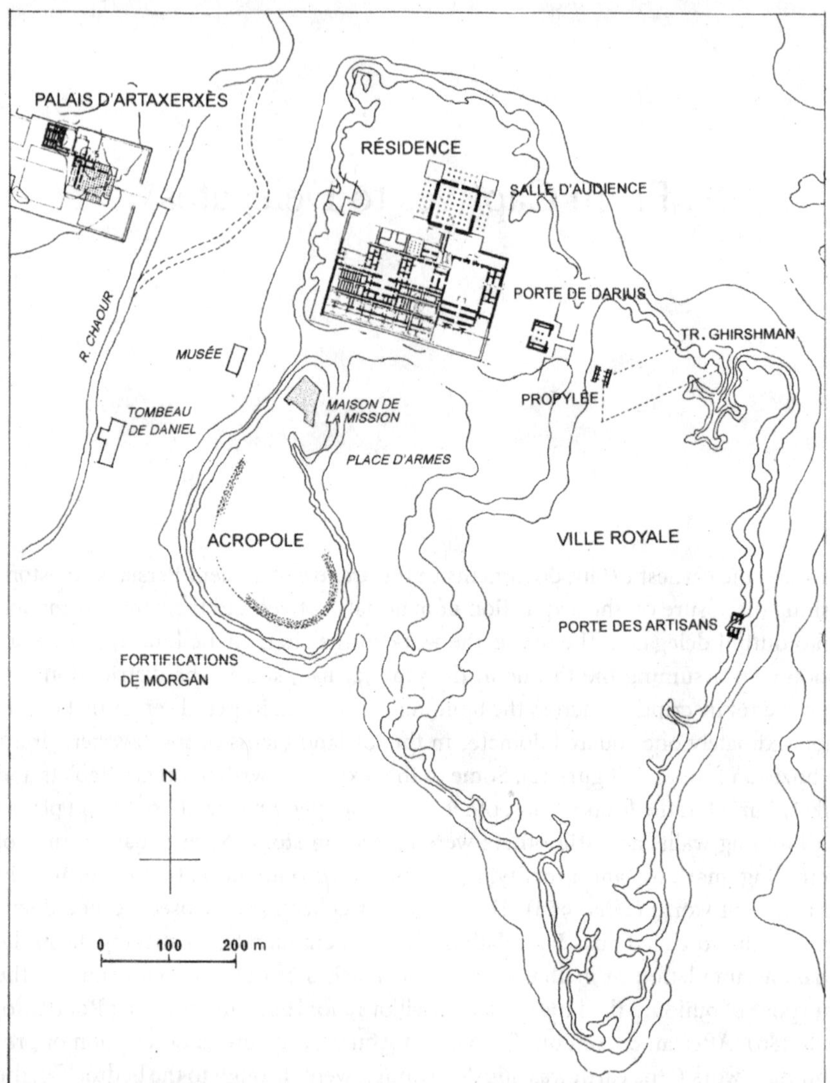

FIGURE 12. Plan of Susa (courtesy of Mission archéologique de Suse).

and Egypt, woodworkers from Sardis and Egypt, bricklayers from Babylon, and so forth. In a boast of veiled appropriation, on one of the tablets Darius reports, "With the protection of Ahuramazda, the materials of the decoration of the palace [at Susa] were brought from far away and I organized it."[3] The result was a monumental complex dominated by an enormous columned hall with soaring gray

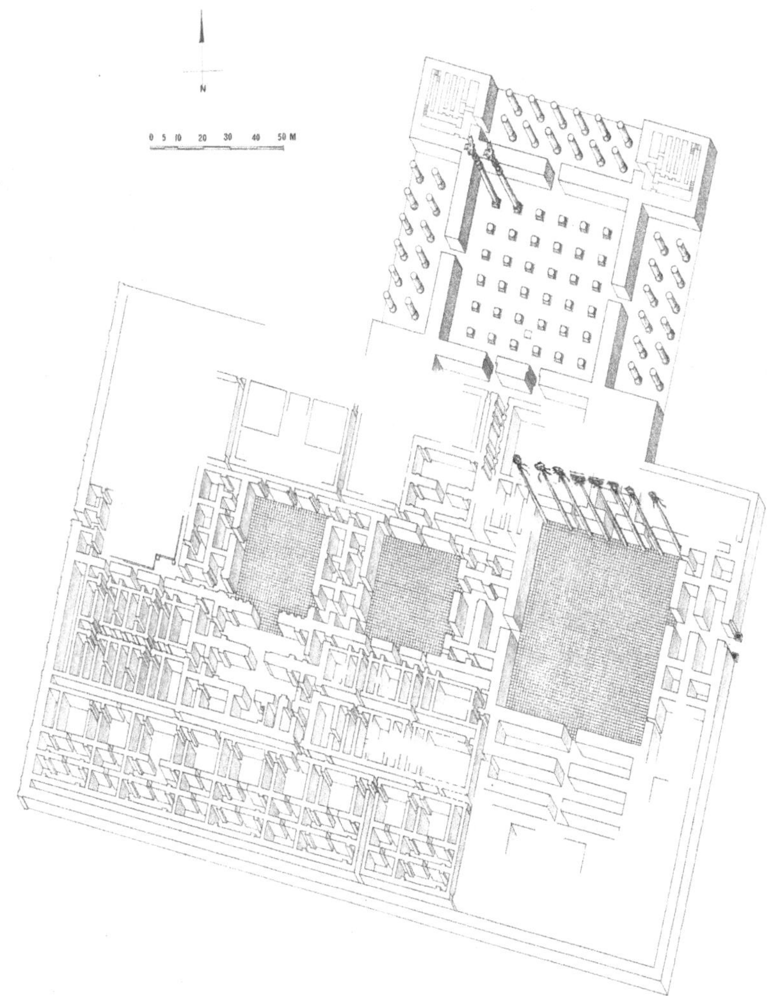

FIGURE 13. Axonometric view of the Susa Palace (courtesy of French-Iranian Mission at Susa, Archives de la Maison Archéologie & Ethnologie, René Ginouvès, cote JP_V03_37, illustration by Anne Ladiray).

limestone columns that reached 20 meters to the sky, backed by palatial quarters disposed around three courtyards (figure 13).[4] In its scale, splendor, and abundant use of fluted, painted columns arrayed with exacting symmetry, the hall was like no building ever built before in Persia or neighboring lands.

It is perhaps tempting to read the Susa Charters as, above all else, the self-assured representation of a sovereign's authority to extract and displace resources and bodies from subject populations (e.g. Allen 2005: 68). To Root (2010: 186), the charter operates metaphorically, relating the foundation of a building to the foundation of the empire itself. It is equally possible to recognize in these texts yet another instantiation of the recurrent Achaemenid ideological trope, already encountered in the throne-bearing scenes discussed in chapter 1, of inclusive, aggregative empire in which everyone everywhere participates in its realization, in this case through the contribution of both labor and matter. Thus Lincoln (2012: 373) writes that the Charters render the complex at Susa "a microscopic representation of the empire as a whole, each part of which contributed to its construction." But I would like to suggest that these texts do not speak only to the confident demonstration of sovereign power. Self-evident, if only implicit, is equally a subtle profession of reliance, whether metaphorical or actual, on the part of the sovereign on substances and knowledges purloined from subjugated lands. This dependence was not merely one of instrumental necessity, a practical requirement in constructing the pivot of the empire's political infrastructure. Rather more profoundly, it was a dependence on which hinged nothing less than humanity's eventual return to the state of cosmic perfection that obtained before the forces of evil contaminated Ahuramazda's original creation (see chapter 1). Testimony to this taut bond among pilfered substances, sovereignty, and salvation is a single word with which Darius describes the building that resulted from his capture of such diverse and distant things. He called his new palace a "wonder,"[5] using the very same term invoked elsewhere to describe Ahuramazda's original cosmological works. As Lincoln (2012: 374) notes, "Calling this place a 'wonder' equated it with the first 'wonder' created by the Wise Lord, i.e. heaven and earth in their pristine state, before the Lie's assault introduced some admixture of evil. The palace thus reproduces the primordial cosmos on a microscopic scale, while also anticipating the day when the empire encompasses the earth and the perfection of the latter is restored." Cosmic renewal and the Achaemenid obligation to see to its realization rested on the capture of materials and their proper redeployment.

The Susa Foundation Charters are irreducible to either literal records of extraction or purely ideological representations, but probably occupy the tantalizing gray zone of discourse in which representation acquires plausibility and actuality stretches the imagination. In any case, there can be little doubt that material captives were assembled for the building of one of the empire's most effective delegates: an immense building complex, designed and tasked by the sovereign to reproduce the most elemental values and political practices of the Achaemenid imperial project. In turn, however, the delegate exerted its own autonomous power over its creators, holding the Achaemenid kings and court to so tight a dependence on its materials, forms, and effects that, as we shall see, Darius and his successors replicated many of the basic principles of the architectural complex at Susa with relentless consistency for decades to come. In creating the columned hall and associated palace, Darius ceded to built matter the prerogative to preserve the lofty imperial promise of cosmic restoration, through the practical affordances that made the structure efficacious in the day-to-day work of governance. As we shall see, Achaemenid columned halls would come to pledge the Achaemenid sovereigns to compulsory routines of maintenance, care, and sustained use, through their effective mediation of the practice and spectacle of governance. In some measure, the columned halls came to govern the very sovereigns who empowered them.

In this chapter I explore how the Achaemenid imperial project was maintained in part thanks to the work of delegates like the columned hall at Susa: built things that came into being through acts of material capture, but that ultimately also captured the capacities of sovereign authority. In particular, I focus on captives that involved the empire's northern highlands, a term I use to describe the broad territory that arcs east-southeastward from southern Caucasia to the central Zagros Mountains—what would roughly become the Achaemenid *dahyāva,* or lands, of Armenia and neighboring Media (map 2). The instances of captivity examined in this chapter are concerned with the matter of built space—the building materials and resulting spatial forms that mediate human encounters with one another and with the myriad things that surround us. In turning attention to columned halls such as the one at Susa, I am unconcerned to preserve a distinction between the putatively fixed matter of lived landscapes (themselves made up of an array of elements in motion) and the portable matter we conventionally call "objects," seeing no meaningful ontological distinction between these material categories. In addition, the acts of material capture under scrutiny involve not principally the literal transference of matter to the imperial heartland, but the more subtle capture of *ideas about* material forms and their effects. I will further examine how such architectural captives-turned-delegates in turn locked imperial agents into relations of dependence on such buildings, and the practices of political reproduction that they afforded.

To speak of captives in relation to Persian cultural production may seem to undermine the decades-long project in Achaemenid history and archaeology intent on firmly establishing the originality and creativity of an empire once dismissed as aesthetically derivative of its predecessors and contemporaries in Greece, Mesopotamia, and Egypt. The study of the Achaemenid Empire began to coalesce two and a half decades ago, in large measure around an emancipatory project to release Persia from its own captivity, as it were, confined to the margins of both Classical and Near Eastern studies and trapped in bygone orientalist discourses (Briant 2005, 2010; Harrison 2010; Sancisi-Weerdenburg 1987a). Attendant on this process of disciplinary "self-legitimation" (Giddens 1995) has been a latent celebratory rhetoric, not uncommon in the study of a great many ancient civilizations, that lauds the eclecticism of the Achaemenid sovereigns and turns a blind eye to

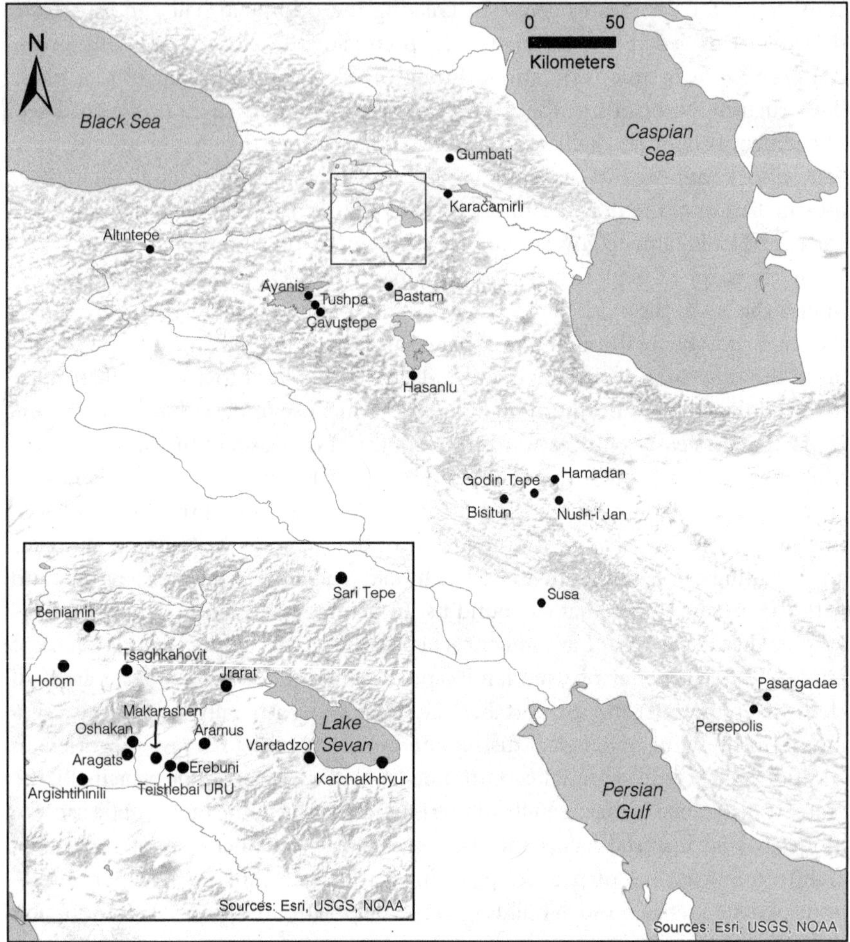

MAP 2. Map showing sites mentioned in the text (created by Lori Khatchadourian and Adam T. Smith).

the forms of cultural and physical violence that all imperial polities leave in their wake—even one that may have been relatively tolerant compared to empires since (Pollock 2006; but see Lincoln 2007). Scholars of Achaemenid architecture and visual culture are accustomed to speaking in terms of "influence," "borrowing," and "synthesis" to describe the inventive reformulations of Achaemenid architecture and visual culture. While these may be apt art-historical descriptors, from the vantage of political anthropology they are diffuse, benign, and sociologically vacant, purifying imperial aesthetics from the contexts of political asymmetry in which they are embedded. Such asocial terms, at least in their typical deployment with respect to the Achaemenids, inadvertently run the risk of keeping intact a perverse illusion of dignified domination. The terms ultimately obscure the politics of co-optation that led to the taking of what I am calling material captives. Some may find that talk of captivity pushes too far in the opposite direction, imputing violent and wrongful taking in a mosaicked cultural milieu with porous boundaries. But it must fairly be admitted that, among conquered groups whose cultural production came to be "captured" or "emulated," the evidence that such reformulations were perceived as benign is no stronger than the evidence for discontent. I thus favor a terminology whose inflection keeps us mindful of the political inequalities entailed in the emergence of an imperial aesthetic. Achaemenid cultural production was not unimaginatively derivative, nor is it best understood as the impressive result of creative borrowings. It was instead the consequence of a mutual dependence between sovereigns and material delegates, many of which came into existence through direct and indirect acts of captivation.

THE PREHISTORY OF AN ACHAEMENID CAPTIVE

For all the detail that Darius provided in the Susa Charters concerning the captives purportedly acquired for the building of his palace complex, he is surprisingly silent on the resulting "wonder" itself. The texts withhold much. They do not reveal that, quite apart from its component material parts, the overall *form* of the building also entailed a capture of sorts, in this case of an architectural approach that originated outside the imperial heartland of Fars and Khuzistan, where no precedents are to be found in the architectural canons of the preceding centuries. It is the empire's northern highlands of Media and Armenia that offer the most likely source for the notion of a large, undivided space, marked by a forest of symmetrically ordered columns.[6] What is the political significance of an act of captivation centered on a built form such as this? How did the "capture" of the columned hall contribute to the making of satrapal conditions? The answers to these questions pivot on the underlying logic of the building's origins in the preceding centuries, and thus the first part of this chapter provides an extended prehistory of the Achaemenid Empire's most notable architectural captive. In the century before Persia's rise to power, the hypostyle buildings that would later provide a template for Achaemenid architectural delegates contributed significantly, I shall argue, to a fundamental transformation of political practice in parts of southwest Asia that would come to make possible certain key routines and rituals of Achaemenid governance.

History at a Glance: The Seventh-Century Crises

The second half of the seventh century marked a major watershed in the political history of the ancient world. The Neo-Assyrian Empire, a dominant hegemon centered in northern Mesopotamia that had held sway over much of southwest Asia since the ninth century, experienced a precipitous decline from the apex of its power in 640 B.C., when imperial control stretched from western Iran to Egypt, to the fateful year of 612 B.C., when the capital at Nineveh was sacked by an insurrectionary coalition of Babylonians and Medes. The first of these antagonists, the Babylonians, consisted of disparate urban and rural peoples of southern Mesopotamia who fashioned themselves the cultural inheritors of the ancient Sumerian tradition. Their involvement in the demise of Assyria comes as little surprise, given the prolonged, if not unbroken, history of hostility, resistance, and intermittent war between the two players following the Assyrian conquest of the south in 747 B.C. Rather more enigmatic are their co-conspirators, the "Medes," who, having opted out of literacy, are known to us mostly from the variously terse, creative, and stereotypical writings of outside observers in Assyria, Babylonia, Persia, and Greece. It is therefore uncertain to what extent the etic classification "Mede" describes a meaningful social collective. By all accounts the term embraces a heterogeneous group of Indo-Iranian peoples of the central Zagros Mountains, an area where the Assyrians had established provinces in the late eighth century, perhaps to secure a steady supply of horses, to prevent allegiances with other regional foes (Lanfranchi 2003), and/or to command the primary overland trade route leading from the lowlands of Mesopotamia to the uplands of the Zagros and beyond (Radner 2003).

In keeping with the enduring Mesopotamian suspicion of mountain peoples, Assyria's settled, urban agriculturalists regarded the pastoral, tribal groups of the Zagros as intractable and barbarous, if at times useful, adversaries (Lanfranchi 2003). It appears that the peoples of the mountains were spared or, in the protective cover of the mountains, were able to evade the harshest tactics of Assyrian rule (e.g. deportations). And in certain periods Median leaders coexisted profitably with their overlords. But the events of 612 B.C. make plain that animosity toward the Assyrians was nevertheless acute, at least by the late seventh century (but see Lanfranchi 2003: 117). There is a tendency to reduce the Median assault on the Assyrian heartland to either the opportunistic ransacking of disgruntled mercenaries or the reckless raiding of mountain brigands. Neither account allows for the possibility that such insubordinate acts were undertaken in the name of a calculated political project. Some scholars have suggested that in the attack on Nineveh, coalition forces undertook carefully targeted acts of revenge for past abuses, suggesting no mere looting expedition.[7] For their part, the Babylonians returned from the battles in northern Mesopotamia with some of Nineveh's ashes in hand, as retribution for the Assyrian destruction of Babylon in 689 B.C. These acts of desecration notwithstanding, Median and Babylonian motivations in the invasion cannot be equated, for while the Babylonian dynasty would go on to forge an imperial polity modeled in large measure on its Assyrian predecessor, there is no evidence that the Medes sought to claim Assyrian territories or appropriate and replicate the empire's political traditions, premised on vertical political authority. Indeed, as we shall see in due course, Median architecture suggests a rather different approach to political association. Whatever their respective goals, the Medes and Babylonians jointly seized on a period of vulnerability at the Assyrian court, recently mired in a series of particularly severe succession struggles, to lay waste to the imperial heartland. All evidence suggests that by around 610 B.C. the Assyrian polity had entirely disappeared from the geopolitical landscape.

Assyria was not the only political power to disintegrate during the tumultuous years of the second half of the seventh century. So too did the kingdom of Urartu, Assyria's northern neighbor and formidable foe, a kingdom whose heartland lay on the eastern shores of Lake Van. Beginning in the late ninth century B.C., Urartu had built a regional empire encompassing eastern Anatolia, the South Caucasus, and northern Iran. As the polity expanded, it developed into one of Assyria's major adversaries, and the two were embroiled in constant skirmishes. Accounts of Urartu's demise differ depending on the weight accorded to varying sources of evidence, but the most satisfactory telling holds that the polity had collapsed somewhat earlier than Assyria, by around 640 B.C., in large measure due to internal political fragmentation that prevented Urartu from responding effectively to incursions by external groups like the Scythians, long seen as the primary culprit behind the polity's demise (Çilingiroğlu 2002; Hellwag 2012; Kroll 1984; Smith 2003; Zimansky 1995: 253–254).[8]

As with the case of the Medes, in which aversion to the Assyrian political tradition might explain the apparent disinterest in appropriating Assyria's institutions of rule, so too in the aftermath of Urartu's demise did political actors on the Armenian highland reject the forms of authority that had obtained across eastern Anatolia and southern Caucasia during the preceding centuries. Most notable in this regard is the abandonment of virtually all hilltop fortresses, once the distinctive hallmark of the Urartian regime. Urartu's ashlar masonry fortresses had hosted a multifaceted imperial apparatus designed to organize the empire's political, economic, religious, and military affairs. The citadels of the regime mediated relations between people and that most prominent of structural positions, the imperial administration, collecting taxes, organizing labor, constraining peoples' choices and actions. In other words, the fortress anchored a network of powerful institutions that articulated peoples with one another as subjects of an authoritative imperial regime. By the early seventh century, the fortress appeared to have been firmly rooted as *the* place for the reproduction of order and authority throughout Urartu's territories. The widespread rejection of these well-built sites of political privilege following Urartu's collapse—sites that in almost all cases offered still-standing remains—speaks to the repudiation of the rules and schemas that had defined the Urartian imperial project for centuries. The pattern is unmistakable. From imperial centers to more minor outposts, from eastern Anatolia to the Ararat plain—Tushpa and Ayanis, Bastam and Teishebai URU, Oshakan and Aragats, Argishtihinili and Çavuştepe, Anzaf and Horom—nearly all Urartian fortresses fell into disuse as sites for the promulgation of political authority.[9] The few important exceptions to this pattern (see chapter 5) would become critical to the Achaemenid political project.[10]

In sum, the specific catalysts behind the demise of Assyria and Urartu, two antagonistic but closely linked polities, differ (and scholars rarely narrate them as related events). My purpose in this historical synopsis has not been to conflate the particular circumstances surrounding the decline and disavowal of Neo-Assyrian and Urartian political life. But the near simultaneity of their disintegration, in the span of one generation, and the common disinterest in appropriating, adapting, and reestablishing the forms of authority and political association that both polities had pursued, ultimately indicate something more than mere coincidental occurrences in the inevitable vicissitudes of dynastic power and in the ubiquitous devilry of history's raiding marauders. Instead, I suggest, the circumstances of their demise and its aftermath point to a mounting disaffection during the mid-to-late seventh century—concentrated in the mountainous regions of the Zagros and southern Caucasia—with the forms of political complexity that had become firmly rooted in Mesopotamia and eastern Anatolia over the course of the preceding millennia. In their own respective regions, both imperial polities emerged out of political traditions fiercely premised on steep sociopolitical hierarchies, extractive economies, and the institutionalized use of violence—classic instances of political organization determined by what Pierre Clastres (1987), citing Lapierre, has called the relation of "command-obedience."[11] From their own royal archives and other contemporary sources, it is clear that both imperial formations developed out of similarly draconian tactics of rule, including population movements, overbearing tax and tributary regimes, and aggressive visual, spatial, and discursive rhetoric designed to control those whom they conquered and thwart dissent. It was these trappings of political complexity that mountain groups appear to have challenged in the second half of the seventh century B.C. That is, the decline of Assyria and Urartu do not constitute merely typical transitional moments in southwest Asia's long political history, in which one dynastic polity rises to preeminence in the shadows of another. More profoundly, these processes signal the culmination of an attempted transformation in the history of political association itself, at least in the region's mountainous uplands, where, as we shall see, the earliest signs of experimentation toward such a shift can be detected during the eighth century B.C.

The Matter of Congregational Politics

In his classic account of political power in the absence of the State, Clastres (1987) identifies a profound conceptual poverty in scholarly reckonings with societies that seem not to adhere to our expectations regarding the proper constitution of political life. Can we speak of political life where coercion and violence, subordination and authoritarianism—in short, where relations of command and obedience—appear not to obtain? But what kind of perversion is this? How misplaced a question to pose of the mid-first millennium, by which time "proper" States—literate, urban, hierarchical—have risen and fallen in neat succession for centuries with little interruption? And so the Near Eastern highlands after the fall of Urartu and Assyria leave us flummoxed because we are unable to discover what our civilizational narratives require, what even Herodotus felt compelled to insert—a "phantom empire," in Van De Mieroop's (2011: 275) words. This "phantom empire" was a supposedly expansionary Median polity with its own capital, Hagmatana (Greek: Ecbatana), neatly fitted in time between the Neo-Assyrian/Urartian and Achaemenid empires, whose reconstruction leaves undisturbed what John Agnew and Stuart Corbridge (1995) call the "apostolic succession of Great Powers" cherished by various teleological histories. For in regions already familiar with the traditional playbook of political complexity (its pages well tattered by the first millennium B.C.), this is no longer the age for egalitarianism, tribalism, pastoralism, subsistence economies, and the "barbaric" refusal of the State.

Until quite recently, historians have tended to accept the Herodotean account of a Median empire in the century before the ascendancy of Achaemenid Persia, though it is supported by virtually no other sources of evidence, written or archaeological.[12] The efforts of the last few decades to grapple with the enigmatic Median phenomenon have confronted the limitations of Herodotus' literary account as a reliable historical source and its conspicuous incommensurability with the archaeological and epigraphic record (Liverani 2003; Rollinger 2003; Sancisi-Weerdenburg 1988). From the highlands of the central Zagros, where the "empire" was purportedly centered, and northwestward across its once-conjectured territories in the South Caucasus and the eastern Anatolian plateau, archaeological remains suggestive of an empire as it is customarily understood are close to nonexistent. The few Assyrian texts of the ninth through seventh centuries B.C. that bear on the Medes provide no indication of a centralized authority, no singular sovereign who could have cemented power to forge a unified and expansive polity.[13] Thus, the latest studies regard the Medes as a collection of tribes sharing common ties (whether linguistic, religious, economic, etc., is unknown) that developed into "chiefdoms" and then, by the seventh century, into a "secondary state" to Assyria (Liverani 2003), or alternatively, and less formally, the leaders of a loose coalition of Iranian peoples from across northern Iran who joined forces solely to defeat Assyria, and thereafter disbanded (Waters 2014: 34).

What followed, so the standard narrative now goes, was a decades-long political vacuum across the northern highlands, a veritable "dark age" (Kroll 2003: 282;

Liverani 2003: 7; Roaf 2003), until an ascendant Persia emerged on the world stage in the mid-sixth century B.C. under the leadership of Cyrus and engulfed these apolitical reaches back into the fold of the State. In sum, in relinquishing Herodotus's strong statist interpretation of the Medes, the question of political practice in this period of "transition" is taken off the table, too difficult to square with history's prevailing concepts of political life. We are left to conjure the quintessential visions of the stateless society, either romantically unencumbered by the shackles of political power—"bands of nomads roaming freely over an extensive area" (Sancisi-Weerdenburg 1988: 198), or else lapsing, evolutionarily, into primitivism—"the Zagros area under Median hegemony reverted to a stage of tribal chiefdoms" (Liverani 2003: 11). The Medes became "some kind of 'tribal' entity without political stability" (Rollinger 2003: 290). They become defined by the ways in which their traditions do not measure up to engrained expectations concerning what constitutes political life: "mountaineers lacking urban centers, centralized states, bureaucratic statecraft, or literacy. Well able to destroy, they were less able to reconstruct" (Liverani 2001: 390).

But what if formalized political association in the late seventh and early sixth centuries is not so much absent as difficult for us to recognize and understand, precisely because it is not premised on coercion, a kind of power that exists "totally separate from violence and apart from any hierarchy" (Clastres 1987: 22)?[14] What if such forms of political association are forged through consortia of humans and material things that concertedly insist on the refusal of the State? What would such a consortium look like? The answer, I suggest, is to be found in the building form known as the columned hall that, by the late seventh century, had become firmly established in the political landscapes of the northern highlands, from southern Caucasia to the Zagros, leading to the production of a common sensibility among mountain communities regarding what constitutes the proper schema of political order. On current evidence, that shared sensibility took shape during the eighth and seventh centuries B.C. in the central Zagros of western Iran and the southern Caucasus, at places like Godin Tepe, Tepe Nush-i Jan, and Erebuni, each of which is briefly described below.[15]

Godin Tepe. Godin Tepe is strategically perched atop a mound in west-central Iran's Kangavar Valley of mountainous Luristan. Excavations conducted at the site under the auspices of the Royal Ontario Museum between 1965 and 1973 uncovered four millennia of near-continuous occupation, beginning in roughly the late sixth millennium B.C. A devastating earthquake in the second millennium B.C. initiated a prolonged hiatus in settlement activity, which endured until around 750 B.C., when social life returned to Godin at a scale never before seen on the mound. The new inhabitants built a complex measuring approximately

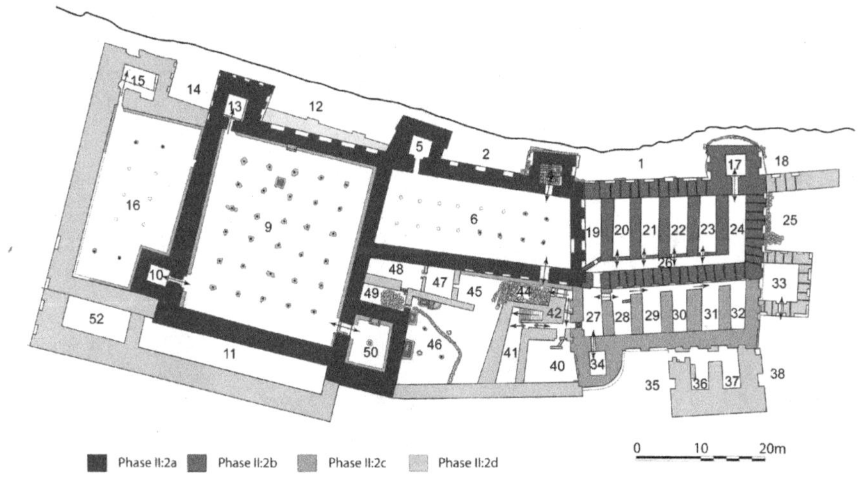

FIGURE 14. Plan of Godin Tepe II.2 (courtesy of Hilary Gopnik).

120 by 50 meters and surrounded by 3-meter-thick fortification walls that were pierced with arrow slots; these fell into disuse during the use of the complex (Gopnik 2011; figure 14). The mud-brick buildings were built in stages, at indeterminate intervals, and included rooms for food preparation, storage, and gatherings in columned halls. There is no evidence for residential quarters at Godin Tepe, although some have supposed that dwelling space may have occupied a second story above the storerooms.

The largest columned hall, which Hilary Gopnik (2011: 306) has described as the "*raison d'être* of the Godin citadel," was the first building to be built at the site during the first millennium B.C. occupation horizon. The building measures approximately 24 by 28 meters in its interior dimensions. Thirty wooden columns, arrayed in five rows of six, supported the hall's roof of wooden beams, reed matting, and mud plaster. The wooden columns were possibly coated in red and white lime plaster, judging by traces of similar surfacing on a narrow bench that runs along three of the four interior walls. The bench along the northwest wall was interrupted by a conspicuously off-centered, slightly raised area that is fronted by a footrest—what Stronach and Roaf (2007: 156) called a "throne-seat" but Gopnik (2011: 306) more soberly designates a "seat of honour." Roughly 5 meters in front of this seat was a brick hearth, built three courses high, showing evidence of recurrent replastering to cover ash buildup. Three rooms (possibly towers) abut the hall at its corners, one of which contained a single column, benches on all four sides of

FIGURE 15. Reconstruction of the interior of the Godin II: 2 columned hall (courtesy of Hilary Gopnik).

the room, and another "seat of honour." The terminus for the main occupation of the Godin II complex is uncertain.[16]

The excavators of Godin Tepe anachronistically referred to the building as a "manor house" (Gopnik 2003), a feudal term that has recently given way to "palace-citadel" (Gopnik 2011: 290). In the latest and most comprehensive reassessment of the settlement, Gopnik holds the view that Godin Tepe was the seat of a singular ruler, a "family mansion" (306) of a Median *bēl āli*, as the Assyrians called such local leaders. Its imposing buttressed walls and conjectured towers notwithstanding, Gopnik (336) reasonably maintains that Godin was not primarily designed as a military outpost (guards' quarters, barracks, weapon rooms, and weapons are absent, and there is ample evidence that the arrow slots were filled in during the use of the complex). It was in her view instead a palace, centered on the main columned hall. Here the *bēl āli* of Godin "held court," controlled large herds of livestock that could be used or consumed once tributary obligations were met, and generally enjoyed "dominance over the surrounding countryside" (297–298, 336). The columned hall itself (figure 15) was "used as an assembly room for a single, powerful figure to receive his subjects," suppliants who waited on the hall's benches to be received (338–339). A close look at two other highland halls provides key grounds for an alternative explanation.

Nush-i Jan. Just over 50 kilometers to the east-southeast of Godin Tepe as the crow flies is the site of Tepe Nush-i Jan, on the fertile uplands of the Malayer plain. At the summit of Tepe Nush-i Jan, a steep-sided outcrop that rises above

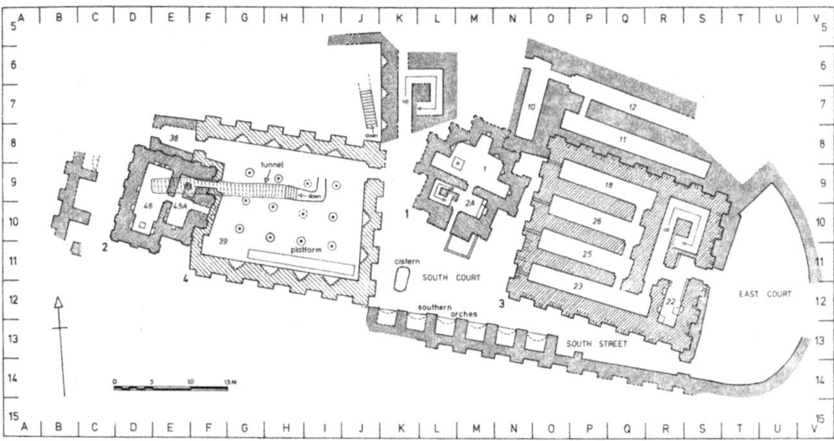

FIGURE 16. Plan of Nush-i Jan (courtesy of David Stronach, after Stronach and Roaf 2007, fig. 1.9).

the surrounding valley floor, excavations conducted between 1967 and 1977 by the British Institute of Persian Studies uncovered a complex of four mud-brick structures enclosed by an oval circuit wall (Stronach and Roaf 2007). A temple structure dominated the site from its inception in the eight century B.C., around which were built another building of presumed religious function in the west and, in the east, a "fort," used principally for storage (Stronach and Roaf 2007: 129). Likely the last edifice built at Tepe Nush-i Jan during the seventh century B.C. was a columned hall, built atop a mud-brick platform and measuring roughly 20 by 15 meters in its interior. Supporting the flat roof were twelve wooden columns arranged in three rows of four (figure 16). The overall effect is one of unbroken symmetry, apart from the distortion of the western wall, where the hall was built to accommodate the eastern facade of an earlier building, as well as a very low brick platform running off-center along the southern wall. Due to a subsequent "squatter" occupation inside the hall during the sixth century, no artifacts associated with the primary use of the hall could be recovered.

The excavators surmised that Tepe Nush-i Jan's hall "was principally erected to support the religious functions of the adjoining temple, not least in order to provide shelter for worshipers" who, they suppose, would have slept on the low brick platform along the southern wall (Stronach and Roaf 2007: 200). This is an understandable attempt to explain the conspicuous absence of residential quarters, but it stretches the imagination to suppose that a single narrow, elongated feature of 14 by 1.3 meters served as a bed for multiple visitors, just as it does to imagine that an undifferentiated internal space of the hall's scale would have been required for such a restricted sleeping space. To conclude this snapshot of Tepe Nush-i Jan, it is important to note that unlike other buildings at the site, all of which were at some point filled in with layers of shale and mud, the columned hall was never shuttered and thus could have remained in use without interruption through to the "squatter" occupation of the sixth century.[17]

Erebuni. The third columned hall under view in this prehistory of Achaemenid captives is situated at a considerable distance from Nush-i Jan and Godin Tepe, on the Ararat plain of the Armenian highland.[18] The site of Erebuni sits atop a steep hill, which rises up at the eastern end of the fertile valley, on the outskirts of modern Armenia's capital, Yerevan. This is the most challenging of the sites under examination in terms of its chronology. Excavations at Erebuni began in the late nineteenth century, but systematic efforts got underway only in the 1950s under the joint sponsorship of the State Pushkin Museum in Moscow and the Academy of Sciences of the Armenian SSR (Hovhannisyan 1961). Beginning in 2008, Armenian and French teams revived excavations at the site in an effort to refine our understanding of the history of occupation.

Urartian royal inscriptions at Erebuni securely date the first significant occupation of the hill to the first half of the eighth century B.C., when the king Argishti I built the fortress (in approximately 782 B.C.) to serve as a political center for the Ararat plain. Within a buttressed fortification wall were several densely packed buildings whose arrangement, as Smith's (2003: 247) spatial analysis has shown, favors isolation over integration of activities (compared to the nearby Urartian fortress at Argishtihinili, though not compared to the later fortress of Teishebai URU) and the regulation of movement through the use of multiple access points (figure 17). The Urartian complex included a reception area, storage facilities, residential quarters, and temple contained within a sacred precinct. There is evidence for one or more significant later building phases at the site, marked most notably by the expansion of a preexisting court or portico into a columned hall (apparent by, among other indicators, the mixed masonry of the final structure). Some of the original Urartian constructions may have been reused during subsequent centuries (the nature of the original excavations prohibit conclusive claims on this point), and the fortification wall underwent minor renovation. In its final iteration, the later-phase columned hall at Erebuni measured approximately 29 by 33 meters (figure 18). The walls consisted of stone foundations of andesite blocks with a mud-brick superstructure, and contained five rows of six wooden columns that rested on tuff column bases (figure 19). From the main hall, there was one doorway leading to an ancillary room in the west, but the only point of egress into and out of the complex as a whole was on the east.[19] The Erebuni hall was colorfully ornamented with wall paintings depicting multiple registers of vegetal motifs, animals, griffins, and geometric patterns, judging by the extant fresco fragments

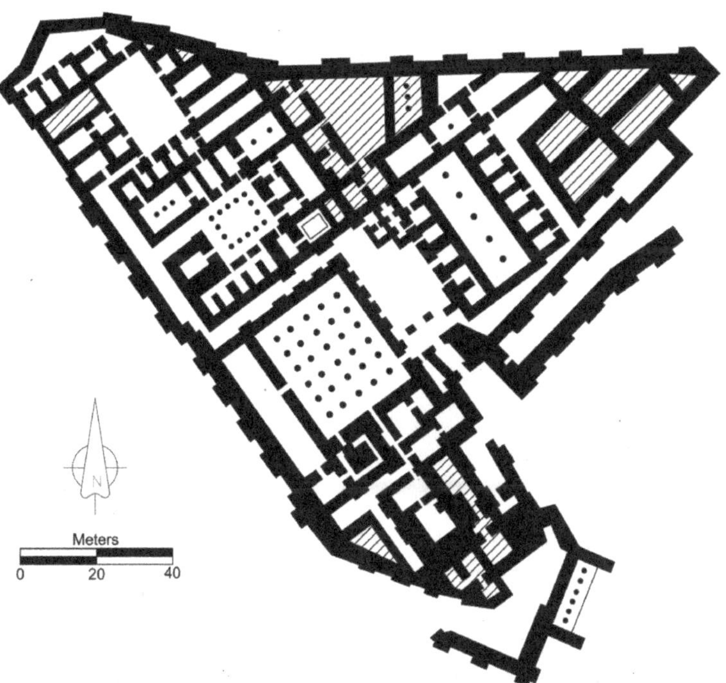

FIGURE 17. Plan of Erebuni (courtesy of Adam T. Smith).

(Hovhannisyan 1973; Ter-Martirosov 2005a). There were two fixed features inside Erebuni's columned hall: a low, packed-clay bench running along the walls and a three-stepped clay altar built against the southwestern wall; traces of ash and charcoal were found on this feature and on the wall behind it (Hovhannisyan 1961: figs. 43, 44; Stronach et al. 2010: 119).

Until very recently, the prevailing view on the basis of the early work at the site held that the hypostyle hall was built during the period of Achaemenid rule and represented an Apadana-like structure intended for Armenia's satrap and modeled on the elaborate halls at Susa and Persepolis—see below (Hovhannisyan 1961; Summers 1993; Ter-Martirosov 2001, 2005b; Tiratsyan 1960, 1988: 24–27). But the recently revived excavations at Erebuni have cast doubt on this established dating and instead assign the construction of the hall to the closing decades (or even years) of the seventh century (de Clairfontaine and Deschamps 2012; Deschamps et al. 2011; Stronach et al. 2009; Stronach et al. 2010).[20] The excavators have yet to define a terminus for the reoccupation, but as we shall see in the next chapter, there is reason to believe that Erebuni remained in use into subsequent centuries,

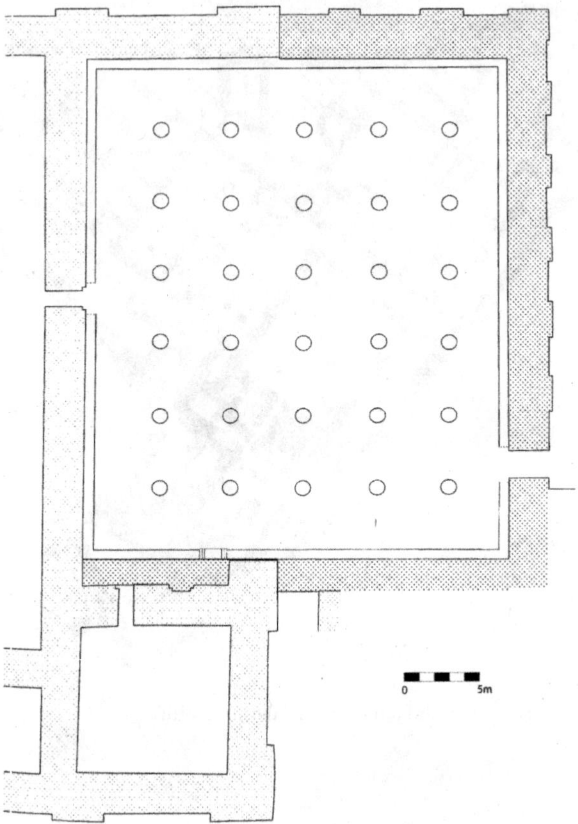

FIGURE 18. Plan of the columned hall at Erebuni. Dark-stippled walls belong to the later building phase. Above-floor brick-and-mortar surrounds are conjectural (courtesy of David Stronach, after Stronach et al. 2010, fig. 10).

FIGURE 19. Reconstruction of the Erebuni hall (after Hovhannisyan 1961, fig. 27, courtesy of the Institute of Archaeology and Ethnography, Republic of Armenia).

now as an Achaemenid installation. The foregoing interpretations thus proceed on the basis of the revised dating. The recent excavations at Erebuni have been of critical importance to our understanding of Erebuni's chronology and periodization, yet the question of the sociopolitical significance of the space in the context of a late-seventh- or early-sixth-century construction date remains to be rethought.

* * *

What then are we to make of these enigmatic many-columned constructions that recur across the Near Eastern highlands? What kinds of politics did they afford for the pastoralists and mixed agro-pastoralists of the Zagros and southern Caucasus? Addressing these questions is key to understanding why the columned hall became an Achaemenid captive, and the significance of its transformation into an imperial delegate. And yet there are no ready answers, nor has the question been given much consideration. This is in part due to what Smith (2003: 59) has called a kind of "romantic subjectivism" vis-à-vis built space, in which form is overly aestheticized as culturally expressive at the expense of a concern for practices and actions. The scholarly silence on the active work of the halls in political reproduction also stems from a romance of a different sort, a deep sentiment of attachment among scholars of the first millennium B.C. to a politics of *rule,* which sees at every turn the material indices of authority and domination. Yet a close look at the evidence suggests that the halls themselves played a critical role in mediating political interaction at these sites, and that the politics at hand was not one of control, coercion, and supremacy.

Before returning to the halls, it is worth first recalling that in these centuries communities across the highlands elected to utterly disavow technologies of administration, materialized ideologies of social asymmetry, and unequal distributions of wealth. After centuries of archaeological research in the highlands, it is insufficient to attribute the paucity of prestige goods, the absence of archives, and the virtual lack of symbolic media to scholarly neglect, peaceable site abandonments, settlement reuse, unidentified mortuary landscapes, or an archaeologically recalcitrant capital city.[21] Some of these factors no doubt contribute to a thin archaeological record for the seventh and sixth centuries B.C. on the Iranian highland and the post-Urartian period on the Armenian highland, but they do not tell the whole story. To a considerable degree, mountain communities in these periods must also have been opting out, per Clastres, of the classic material trappings of sociopolitical complexity, political practices of which they were no doubt well aware. It is for this reason that terms like "manor" or "palace-citadel" or even *bēl āli* obscure more than they reveal, for they conjure senses of grandeur, rulership, and official residence, none of which are borne out by the evidence. It must again be emphasized that excavations exposed virtually no signs of dwelling quarters (or, in the case of Erebuni, of the reuse of possible Urartian residences) and no prestige objects in the period under consideration.[22]

It is in this context that the active interventions of the highland halls in political life at Godin Tepe, Nush-i Jan, and Erebuni come into stark relief, for all three structures share in common an emphatic refusal to sanction the human prerogative to command. They are in a sense, to adapt Clastres's formulation, political matter against the State.[23] The forests of wooden columns, standing in rigidly symmetrical formation, insist on the denial of any frontal orientation that might encourage steeply hierarchical sociopolitical interaction (Khatchadourian 2008: 420; 2013: 132). The columns "draw attention to themselves instead of to the space around them or toward a particular focal point such as an altar or throne" (Gopnik 2011: 342). In their multiplicity, these same columns worked in collaboration with one another and the wooden beams that spanned the walls to create enclosed spaces of unprecedented scale, affording indoor congregation in large numbers for the first time in the history of southwest Asia (Khatchadourian 2008: 419; 2013: 132). At the same time, in the cases of Godin Tepe and Erebuni, mud-brick benches surrounding the walls of the halls supported the columns in conjoint defiance of directionality. So too did the hearths at Erebuni and Godin Tepe, which conspicuously occupy offset rather than central locations. Gopnik (2010: 203) has aptly described the overall architectural solution as one directed toward the "negation of axiality to create commonality." This would indeed be an "odd choice for a throneroom" (Gopnik 2011: 342), thus begging the realization that the highland halls are not throne rooms at all.

The repertoire of political architecture does not provide a ready explanation for the kinds of political association that such buildings might make possible. Gopnik (2010: 198) has looked to the religious architecture of early congregational mosques, with their evenly spaced, multiple rows of columns, an appropriate architectural comparison that nevertheless leaves unanswered the question of political interaction at sites otherwise recognized as "centers of power." In her view, the halls speak to a new kind of relationship between leaders and "followers," one focused on "many-to-one" encounters that allow "large public displays of strength in numbers" (Gopnik 2011: 342). They do so both through their architectonics and, she proposes, semiotically, through the metaphorical substitution of subjects for upright supports: "In the Iron Age multi-rowed columns, the columns themselves may have been visual referents for the subordinates to the figure of power" (Gopnik 2010: 205). It would certainly appear that one of the innovations of the highland halls is the invitation to gather people in large numbers (Khatchadourian 2008), but it is less clear that the halls also afford hierarchical relations as would obtain between leaders and followers, rulers and subordinates. The halls are open spaces that architectonically provide for the undirected movement of traffic, the shifting orientation of gaze, and the distributed, unfixed patterns of interaction. I thus suggest that the columned halls at Erebuni, Godin Tepe, and Nush-i Jan are best understood as sites of congregational politics for leaders of disparate groups inhabiting the northern highlands—agriculturalists and pastoralists alike—who were empowered and obliged not to hold the reins of institutionalized violence but instead, to quote Clastres (1987: 218), "to speak." Such leaders periodically gathered to deliberate on collective actions, resolve disputes, store surplus, engage in commensal consumption,[24] and indeed cooperate in the very upkeep of the built structures (especially the high-maintenance mud-brick) that helped establish and enforce the terms of their relations.[25] The assemblage of columns—multiple, uniform, insistently present at every turn—worked to reinforce a politics of assembly constituted by the many and the same.

Such cooperative effort might explain two particularities observed at Godin Tepe, the site from which we have the most evidence with which to work. Gopnik (2011: 315–316) has noted a surprising variability in the size of the mold-made bricks used to build the complex, explaining it as "probably a reflection of the Godin builders' decidedly improvisational attitude toward construction." Certain walls combined bricks of a range of dimensions, a "construction flaw" that one of the original excavators, Cuyler Young, is said to have attributed to a "gang of drunken bricklayers,"[26] leaving spaces to be filled in with plaster before the surfaces were coated with lime plaster and the variability was concealed.[27] A second, comparable idiosyncrasy in the Godin assemblage is the tremendous variety of ceramic types recovered at the site. A scrupulous analysis identified more than 1,600 types among only 2,312 sherds, meaning that on average fewer than two sherds represented each type (Gopnik 2011: 330). This is a highly abnormal ceramic pattern for an archaeological horizon (Godin II) lasting less than three centuries. When compounded with the fact that excavations at Godin revealed no evidence of either pottery or brick production, it would seem that both pots and bricks were reaching the site from a considerable number of distinct workshops.[28] Both at the point of construction and through ongoing use, large numbers of people entangled in different canons of brick and pottery production came together to make Godin possible. Moreover, not only did the architectural composition of the halls in itself call for congregational political practices at all three sites, but, at least in the case of Godin Tepe, the basic building blocks and the paraphernalia of consumption collaborated with the architectural form to press forward a collective political project. The confederation of columns, walls, benches, bricks, and pots imposed—perhaps even in excess of their human creators—a formidable challenge to any claims to despotic power.[29] They offered an approach to politics that averted the exclusionary spatial technologies and steep political hierarchies of the State—producing less a "secondary state" in the conventional sense (Brown 1986; Liverani 2003: 9), and less a shadow state (Barfield 2001), than an anti-state.[30] What made such buildings susceptible to capture? How would their appropriation and transformation into delegates shape the contours of imperial sovereignty, and to what new entanglements did they give rise?

FROM CAPTIVES TO DELEGATES

Over the course of the next two hundred years, roughly 550–330 B.C., the Achaemenid king and court built, by a most conservative estimate, no less than seventeen multi-rowed columned halls, amounting to a staggering 655 stone and wood columns stretching over 22,000 square meters of interior, symmetrically ordered space with virtually no architecturally defined axial definition.[31] For centuries, scholars have noted this distinctive characteristic of Achaemenid architecture, long heralded as the defining feature of the imperial aesthetic. Much ink has been spilled in describing the structures, the techniques used in their construction, the ethnic origins of their workmen, their decorative elements, and the sources of inspiration that gave rise to them, which the scholarly consensus now firmly locates in the highlands of the Zagros (e.g. Boucharlat 2013b: 417; Curtis and Razmjou 2005: 50; Gopnik 2011: 339; Roaf 2010; Young 1994).[32] And yet there is a conspicuous silence on the question of how we are to account for this apparent compulsion for, indeed infatuation with, an imperial landscape that is premised on expansive, unyieldingly symmetrical, non-partitive, and insistently colonnaded buildings. What was the political impetus for such an appropriative imperial act involving the comparably modest highland halls, and what effects did such captives-turned-delegates come to press on the polity and its sovereigns?

In chapter 3 I argued that delegates produce nonhuman effects in ways that are distinctly political, that the work of delegates sustains and defines the practices and values critical to the reproduction of imperial sovereignty, and that delegation entails the ceding of the prerogative to make a difference in the world from one entity or assemblage to another, thus allowing for the possibility that materials can shape the world in excess of their assignments. Captives become delegates not only when human agents of empire reappoint them to assist in their plans, but equally importantly, when such imperial agents come to rely on delegate matter for the preservation of the terms of imperial sovereignty. In the pages that follow, each of the major hypostyle halls of the Achaemenid heartland is introduced in turn, unavoidably recounted as a kind of "great man" history of Achaemenid public architecture. My purpose in this descriptive review is to establish that, notwithstanding considerable diversity among the sites in question, the Achaemenid sovereigns who took captive, redesigned, and maintained the columned halls shared an astounding commitment to, captivation with, and dependency on this building style. It is only then that we can understand how the buildings operated as material delegates.

Achaemenid Columned Halls

The formative act of captivation traces to the first king of the empire, Cyrus, who campaigned northward from a small polity in southwestern Iran to suppress the lands of Media and Armenia in the middle of the sixth century B.C.[33] Soon thereafter, he built the first of the empire's architectural delegates—an open, unfortified royal settlement known as Pasargadae (figure 20) that, in its openness, was designed "in defiance of every existing canon for the construction of either a local or an imperial capital" (Stronach 2001: 96).[34] Pasargadae covers some 300 hectares of the Dasht-e Moghrab plain. The site includes Cyrus's tomb, a 12-meter tower called the Zendan-i Sulaiman, a hilltop platform called the Tall-i Tahkt Sulaiman (with mud-brick structures, including courtyards, storerooms, and a columned hall built by Darius), a sprawling complex of stone and mud-brick buildings on the plain below—all set around a defined garden space that was likely but one part of a large parkland—and nearby gardens and agricultural production areas in the Tang-i Bulaghi valley to the south (Boucharlat 2008, 2013b, 2014; Stronach 1978).[35]

It is here that Cyrus designed a many-columned hall (Palace P, figure 21), adding to the highland form of the structure two lines of porticoes on either side.[36] A stone platform on the southern portico that projects beyond the surrounding bench (not unlike the mud-brick prominence in the bench at Godin) has led some to suppose the existence of a "throne seat" (Stronach 1978: 89), which if correct, is notably located outside the hall itself, facing toward the garden. The hall contains five rows of six columns, which for the first time were made of stone—a cream-white limestone or sandstone and a black limestone (Nylander 2006). In certain respects the building is quite similar to those at Godin Tepe and Erebuni: all three structures are rectangular and contain the same columniation, and all are broadly comparable in scale. But the inclination for fine masonry—"stone wall surfaces, stone wall-socles, stone doorframes, stone antae and . . . stone columns and capitals" (Stronach 2001: 98)—forced the designers to confront the unfamiliar requirements of their building materials. Stone masonry was entirely new to southwestern Iran. The choice to build with it in turn pressed on Cyrus a need to recruit craftsmen from Asia Minor, judging by the masons' marks, anathyrosis joins, and dovetail clamps observed at Pasargadae (Nylander 1970). Stone thus set in motion a relation of reliance on distant people and new technologies that would extend to many subsequent sovereigns, beginning it seems with Cyrus's son, Cambyses.

At the site of Dasht-i Gohar, on the fertile Marv Dasht plain 3 km north of what would later be Persepolis, archaeologists in the early 1970s identified the remains of two unfortified and possibly unfinished monuments, one of which was a hypostyle hall measuring approximately 21 by 32 meters and containing five rows of

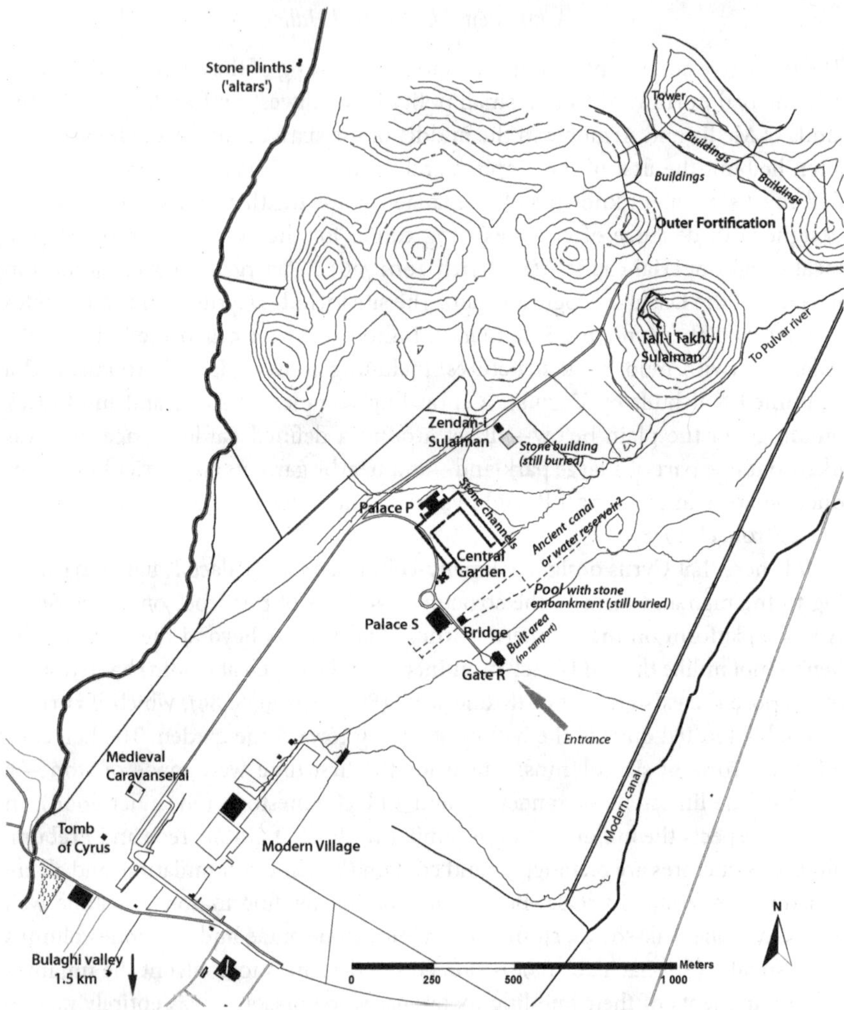

FIGURE 20. Site plan of Pasargadae (courtesy of Rémy Boucharlat and the Iranian-French Mission at Pasargadae).

eight columns (figure 22). The dating of the structure is uncertain, but it is generally thought to be the work of the empire's second king, Cambyses. The poorly preserved hall at Dasht-i Gohar is at the same scale as the Godin Tepe hall (and similar in plan to Palace S at Pasargadae), but with a considerably denser array of columns than any of the previous structures (Kleiss 1980; Stronach 2001: 100–101; Tilia 1978). It appears that the king who designed the building to some degree resisted the

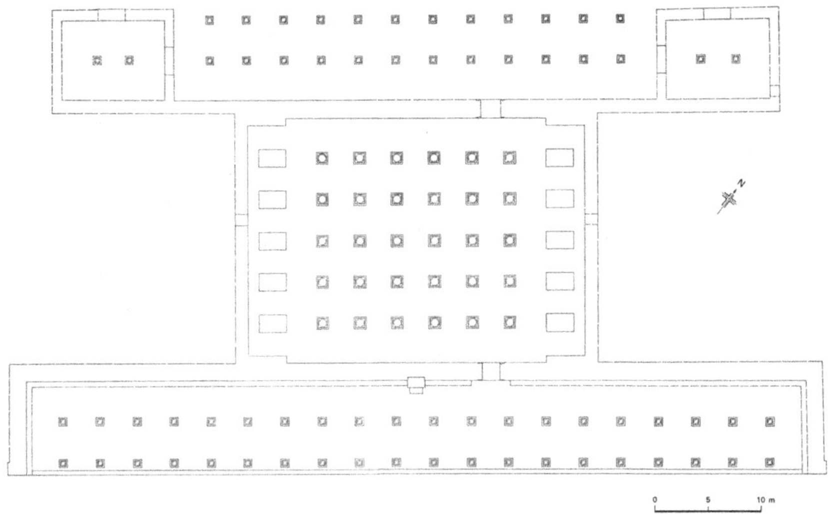

FIGURE 21. Plan of Palace P at Pasargadae (courtesy of David Stronach, after Stronach 1978, fig. 41)

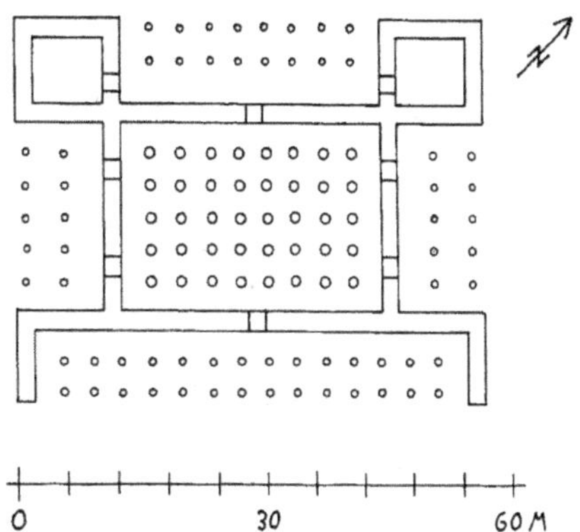

FIGURE 22. Plan of the hypostyle hall at Dasht-i Gohar (source: Kleiss 1980, fig. 3).

demands of stone as a building material, likely using wood columns and opting for simpler limestone column bases that probably did not require foreign craftsmen.

The reign of Darius heralded an architectural tipping point for the hypostyle hall. Planning simultaneously at multiple centers, Darius engaged an enormous workforce in the construction of at least two major halls, at Susa and Persepolis. These concurrent building projects required a tremendous investment of labor, materials, and other resources, amassed from all corners of the empire. We have already seen the "palace" at Susa, whose three main elements included a monumental gate, the hypostyle hall, and a large mud-brick compound of three courtyards connected by gated passages and surrounded by a multitude of rooms (figures 12, p. 82, and 13, p.83). John Curtis (2013: xix) has written that Susa produces "a neat fusion of highland and lowland," insofar as the hall was built "in the Iranian style," while the adjacent compound recalls Assyro-Babylonian or Elamite architecture (Amiet 1973, 2010; Gasche 2013; Henkelman 2013; Roaf 1973: 952). The hall at Susa introduces for the first time a square ground plan, measuring 58 by 58 meters in its internal dimensions, well over three times as large as any previous columned hall. This shift from rectangular to square—to ever more symmetry—would obtain in almost all subsequent multi-rowed columned halls. The hall at Susa contains six rows of six fluted limestone columns—each at least 1.6 meters in diameter—paired with elaborate bases and bull-headed column capitals, for a combined height of approximately 20 meters (Ladiray 2013: 186). The building has corner towers, and is surrounded with porticoes on three sides, while the fourth side provides access to a passageway leading to the residential and administrative compound. As defined by the Susa Charters, the stone for the columns and column capitals had to be imported (the geology of the region suggests from a distance of at least 50 km), and brick masons and stoneworkers were likewise brought from the western provinces—a detail of the Susa Charters that is corroborated by the discovery of masons' marks in the hall that match marks known from Ionia (Perrot 2013c). For years, speculation has surrounded a square stone slab at the south end of the central aisle, near the entrance to the compound. Though its location is well suited for a throne, as many have noted, the meagerness of the evidence has been rightful cause for hesitancy (Ladiray 2013: 148; but see Perrot 2013b: 226), not least since none of the other Achaemenid halls contained interior thrones.

As the work at Susa got underway, Darius initiated a second major construction project at Persepolis, over the southern Zagros mountains, on the Marv Dasht plain.[37] Persepolis would eventually consist of a 12-hectare terrace, and a second compound to the south, as well as a fortified ridge to the east that towered over both lower-lying complexes (figure 23). The complexes were set in an open agrarian plain that hosted royal residences and, it is often supposed, tent installations. By all accounts, it was an imperial center in every respect—ideological, spiritual, military, geographic, and administrative (Root 2015). By the time of his death in 486 B.C. Darius had seen to the construction of only a handful of structures (perhaps because of the time it took to build the terrace, foundations, and drainage system), the most predominant among them being the hypostyle hall, conventionally called the Apadana, which stood on a platform that rose an additional 2.5 meters above the surrounding terrace (figure 24; see also figure 7, p. 17).[38] The hall boasted perfectly square interior dimensions of 53 by 53 meters, and was

FIGURE 23. Site plan of Persepolis (source: Kleiss 1992, fig. 1).

surrounded by four corner towers and porticoes on three sides, the fourth side reserved as storerooms and staging areas for the activities that took place in the hall (Root 2015: 26). In the extension off the west portico are traces of what may be the footing for a throne, which would have provided the king with a panoptic vista onto the outstretched plain below and a reciprocal view of royal spectacle (Root 2015). Estimates hold that the hall could accommodate up to 10,000 people at ground level (Curtis and Razmjou 2005: 54). It contained six rows of six bluish-gray limestone columns, quarried from the Kuh-e Rahmat mountains (Nylander 2006), which are thought to have reached a height of 21 meters (slightly taller than the hall at Susa). The columned building dwarfed a small adjacent structure offset to the south, usually referred to as Darius's Palace.[39]

The Apadana at Persepolis, along with some of the other buildings that Darius started, could not be completed in his lifetime. His successor, Xerxes, continued his father's work, in addition to designing new constructions. Despite Xerxes's additions, Rémy Boucharlat (2013b: 419) notes that Persepolis in the time of these two kings was not a compact landscape cluttered with buildings but likely planned with "open spaces . . . developed as gardens or large courtyards," such as

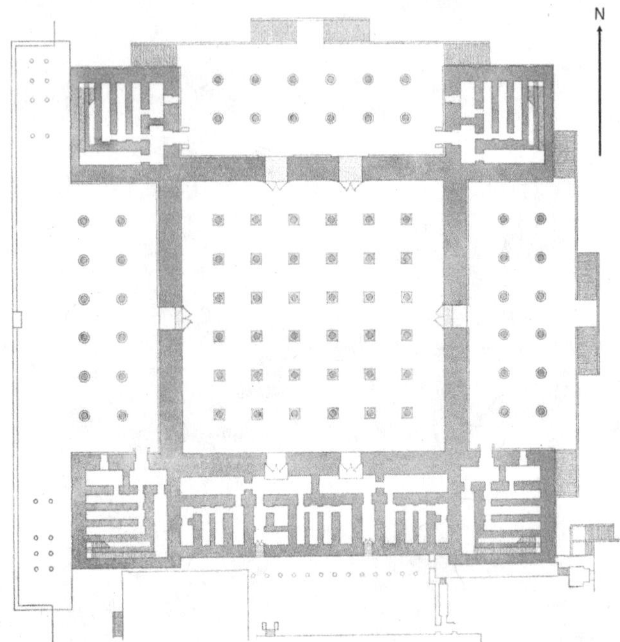

FIGURE 24. Plan of the Apadana at Persepolis (source: Schmidt 1953, fig. 30, courtesy of the Oriental Institute of the University of Chicago).

an open-air courtyard to the south of the columned hall. Successive kings would gradually extend the site (until it reached an estimated size of 20 km^2) and fill in much of the unobstructed space in the settled areas, ultimately creating a veritable forest of columns across the terrace and on the plain to the south, where a small columned hall of approximately 20 by 20 meters, possibly initiated by Xerxes, stands amidst other buildings (figure 23). In its final iteration the terrace itself had no less than eleven covered hypostyle halls of more than two rows of columns, amounting to 473 columns of stone and wood. Two of these contained as many as 100 columns each (a third came close, with 99 columns), the more elaborate being Xerxes and his son's stone-columned Hall of 100 Columns which, at 68.5 by 68.5 meters, exceeded Darius's main hall in its interior dimensions (figure 25).

The hall at Susa likely remained in use even after the building at Persepolis was complete; indeed, the terrace on which it stood would have required annual maintenance (Perrot 2013a: 464). But during the reign of his grandson Artaxerxes I (465–425 B.C.) the building was partially destroyed in a fire, and it remained in this damaged state for at least a quarter of a century, when Artaxerxes II (405–359 B.C.) saw to its restoration.[40] Among other improvements, cracks in the stones

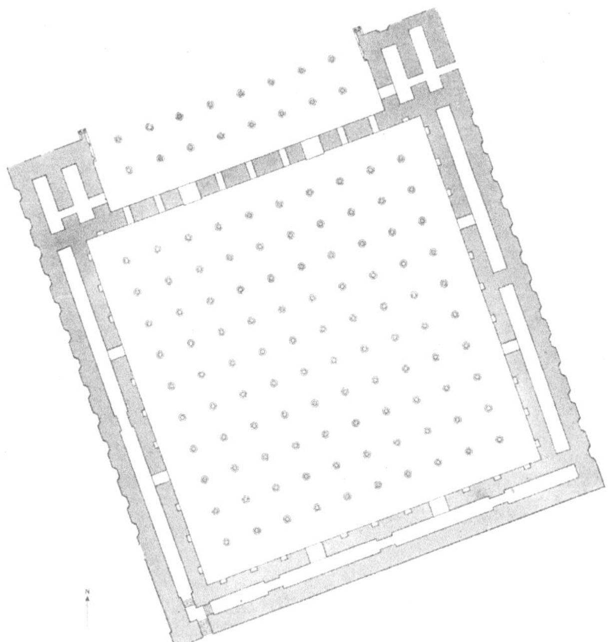

FIGURE 25. Plan of the Hall of 100 Columns at Persepolis (source: Schmidt 1953, fig. 59, courtesy of the Oriental Institute of the University of Chicago).

of the columns were repaired with metal staples (Perrot 2013c: 189). Beyond this restorative work, and in keeping with his predecessors, Artaxerxes II also arranged for the building of a new hall at Susa within the so-called Shaur Palace (see figure 12, p. 82; Boucharlat 2013a: 372–395). Situated on a flat expanse to the east of the base of the mound where Darius's complex stood, Artaxerxes II's building project included, as at Pasargadae, a probable garden, situated amidst six or more (poorly preserved) plastered mud-brick buildings with shingle and gravel foundations, several of which were identified only through geophysical survey (figure 26). Overall, the Shaur Palace was an open rather than densely constructed compound.

The hypostyle hall appears to have been the largest structure of the complex, both in floor plan and in height. The hall itself measures a "modest" 38 by 35 meters, not including the corner rooms and porticoes. The porticoes of the Shaur Palace surround the hall on all four sides, marking a certain independence from the associated buildings, with which, in any event, it does not share the kind of adjacency as seen with the other halls at Susa and Persepolis. The Shaur hall contained eight rows of eight wooden column shafts (92 cm in diameter) resting atop gray limestone bases. There is evidence for a certain effort to economize, not only in the use of

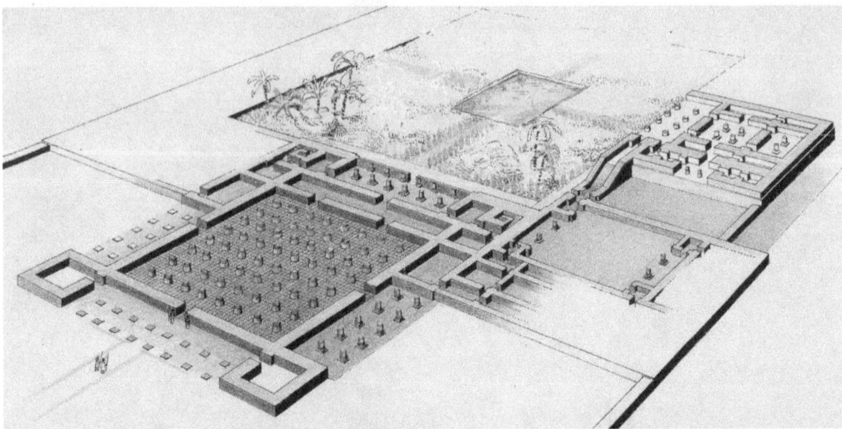

FIGURE 26. Axonometric view of the Shaur Palace (courtesy of French-Iranian Mission at Susa, Archives de la Maison Archéologie & Ethnologie, René Ginouvès, cote JP_V03_37, illustration by Daniel Ladiray).

wooden columns (which perhaps accounts for the reduced projected overall height of the hall, only half that of Darius's hall at Susa) but also in the occasional use of two drums, rather than one large one, to form the bases (Boucharlat 2013a: 380). Notably, Boucharlat's findings also suggest ongoing care and maintenance of the building: steel staples used to mend cracks, carefully carved replacement pieces to fill breaks, and gray cement used to conceal these repairs. Overall, the modest scale of the Shaur Palace (approximately 3 hectares) and its siting on the low-lying area beyond the official complex on the mound has led Boucharlat (393) to view it less as an official administrative center than as the personal residence or pavilion of Artaxerxes II. But there is reason to believe that this hall complex, with its central garden set amid the likely lush, well-watered surroundings of a riverbank, was more than just a pleasant retreat for a long-reigning king. In the one inscription found at the Shaur Palace we encounter a word used to describe all or part of the complex (or possible surrounding parkland) that, as we shall soon see, is of paramount significance for an understanding of the Achaemenid halls as material delegates; the word translates, as most scholars now agree, as "paradise."[41]

Captivation, Delegation, and Dependence

To the many people recruited in the transformation of highland captives into imperial delegates, the columned halls and associated buildings must at times have seemed like the furthest things from paradise. Thousands of laborers, from quarry miners and masons, to bricklayers and other supporting personnel, along

FIGURE 27. Unfinished bull capital at a Persepolis quarry (source: Nylander 2006, fig. 5, courtesy of Carl Nylander).

with their families, may have experienced the halls as little more than a cause of hardship.[42] Building called up tremendous numbers of displaced and recruited persons, most conscripted to do heavy, menial work on rations of little more than flour and wine. Stones were quarried from the surfaces of steep mountainsides or through laboriously cut trenches in horizontal rock formations, and sometimes defects in the stone were discovered only after the tedious work of carving had begun (figure 27; Nylander 2006: 124–126). It is estimated that, for the Susa hall alone, workers transported 4,000 tons of stone, likely using "wooden rollers, ropes, and much manpower" (Nylander 2006: 126), over a distance of 50 km for the columns and the stone supports for the door sockets (Perrot 2013a: 455). Just one of the bell-shaped stone bases from the Hall of 100 Columns at Persepolis weighs approximately 4 tons (Curtis and Razmjou 2005: 50, cat. 59). Others transported long cedar trees from regions rich in forests to form the wooden columns and the countless beams needed to span the rooms of these spacious buildings. Jean Perrot (2013a: 455–456) estimates that, for the main beams of the hall at Susa, laborers transported approximately 800 trunks over a distance of more than 1,500 km. He also estimates approximately 200,000 baked bricks for the wall courses of the Susa hall. At Pasargadae, Persepolis, and Susa, several hundred masons' marks, some of which match marks known from Ionia, indicate that many individuals were quite far from home (Nylander 1974, 1975; Perrot 2013c: 190; Stronach 1978: 21–23). The halls and their physical properties locked countless people into their care, not only at the time of initial construction (which often lasted decades) but throughout the active lives of the buildings, during which their mud-brick and stone features, as we have already seen in the case of the Shaur Palace, required constant upkeep.

In their own way, the buildings also imposed demands on the Achaemenid kings, who appear to have been enmeshed in an ineluctable pressure to build bigger with nearly each successive hall, directing ever more materials and manpower (and the resources needed to feed such a dependent workforce) to both the building of new constructions and the maintenance of the old ones. The buildings required more and more of the sovereign establishment, just as they did of the laborers, particularly as long as new structures continued to be built. Such was the case for at least the first six decades of the empire's existence, from Cyrus's relatively modest Palace P at Pasargadae to Xerxes's large Hall of 100 Columns. Certainly, the considerably smaller Shaur hall attests to an effort to scale back. In his discussion of dependence (see chapter 3), Hodder (2012: 18) distinguishes between forms of dependence that are enabling—that is, those that allow humans to accomplish desired goals—and those forms that become constraining, limiting the abilities of societies to develop (what he calls "dependency"). The architectural delegates that came to exert a hold on the sovereigns, that came to shape their choices and actions, that contributed to limiting their human insularity, in time may have constrained as much as they enabled, exhausting resources and energies that could have been directed toward the numerous crises of imperial history, from revolts in Egypt and Babylonia, to the unsuccessful invasion of Greece, to the civil war of the late fifth century B.C.

How did this happen? How did stone and mud-brick walls, stone and wood columns, and stone capitals and bases come to govern the dispensation of resources and the exercise of design choices? What made the columned halls so enabling, at least for the first century or so of the empire's history? How, in other words, did the columned halls work as effective material delegates? I suggest that the highland halls and the politics of congregation that they afforded provoked Cyrus and his circle of advisors to design a political experiment that would conjoin the participatory politics of assembly with a new approach to the practice of kingship. There is ample reason to suppose that the early imperial elite in southwest Iran would have been sympathetic to the premises of highland politics, with its repudiation of the steeply hierarchical Mesopotamian and Urartian models of complexity and its commitment to a distributed interactional space. Emerging as he likely did from an Elamite milieu (Henkelman 2003b), Cyrus may have shared the sensibility of antagonism toward an Assyrian past that groups in Iran, from the central Zagros to the southwestern lowlands, had contested during centuries of Assyrian hegemony.[43] The highland hall assemblages that the sovereign would have known from northern conquests may have been one of a number of impetuses behind the emergence of an alternative exemplar of monarchy that attempted to selectively couple the well-worn prerogatives of sovereignty as developed in Mesopotamia with the principle of (limited? privileged?) participation among the Persian groups whose tents may have come and gone across the plains of Fars.[44] Pasargadae's

Palace P and the unprecedented openness of the royal structures arrayed around the garden—unfortified, accessible[45]—provide compelling evidence for such an unusual political project.[46]

The entanglements of humans and built matter that made possible what we might call, for lack of a better term, participatory monarchy were sufficiently taut to endure and even intensify over subsequent decades, as the scale and quantity of the Achaemenid highland halls grew. And yet there was a significant metamorphosis, or even perversion, of the original schema. As much as the halls built by Darius and his successors retained an architectonic that insisted on strict symmetry, that refused segmentation, exclusion, and frontal orientation, their tremendous size is ill suited to the discursive and embodied practices of congregational politics. And indeed, it is of no small significance that from the time of Darius onward, unlike Palace P at Pasargadae, the halls come into close spatial association with buildings linked to imperial administration and control, such that ideas of cooperative, collective decision making are rendered deeply contradictory in the context of the wider political landscape. It is this incorporation of the halls in landscapes of bureaucracy, kingship, and extraction that lends support to the conventional, indeed ubiquitous designation of the most discussed of these halls—Darius's buildings at Susa and Persepolis—as ceremonial spaces and, to invoke the most common term, "audience halls," in which the king held court.[47] Thus Perrot (2013b: 226) writes that "the Hypostyle Hall [at Susa] is a place of assembly, reception, an audience hall or, if one so wishes, the throne room. . . . The central hall . . . could accommodate over 1,000 people. . . . Inside, we can picture the king enthroned in a ray of light, surrounded by his entourage against a sparkling backdrop of accumulated treasures. . . . The hypostyle halls were very symbolic of royal establishments; they appear to have been indispensable to the exercise of power."

It is hard to imagine an interpretation of the hypostyle hall that is further from the one I have been developing until now. Equally incongruous are the prevailing understandings of the Apadana at Persepolis as a space for ritual, ceremony, and audience, on which Root has recently given fresh perspectives. Through an integrated analysis of the hall that takes account of its siting on the surrounding landscape as well as the staircase reliefs that adorn it, Root (2015: 22, 30) has suggested that the actual activities that took place in the hall are "metaphorically mirrored" in the reliefs, the latter being not "mere illustrations of an actuality" but "visual hypertexts of ritualized court performances" set within the context of a "cult of hegemonic kingship."

It would seem, in other words, that by the time of Darius the captive of empire is all but dead; the king has replaced the congregation, imperial sovereignty has silenced "speech" (Clastres 1987: 218), and from Cyrus's novel and short-lived spatio-political experiment that conjoined kingship with assembly, only the monarchical component has emerged victorious.[48] Where Perrot's reading falls short is less in its politics than in its implicit theory of the material, which renders the hypostyle hall at worst a mere backdrop for the theater of kingship, and at best, to quote Latour (2005b: 10) once more, "a hapless bearer of symbolic projection"—a symbolic and practical *intermediary* in the realization of royal power (see chapter 3). Root (2015: 2) figures the materiality of the Apadana at Persepolis somewhat differently, according it the status of "active agent," even if still one primarily involved in expressing meaning. I would like to suggest that the columned halls themselves were not only instrumentally "indispensable to the exercise of power" (i.e. the space in which practices of the powerful could take place), or agentive as communicative things that conveyed intended meanings, but materially critical to the metamorphosis discussed above, that is to say, beginning with Darius, to the production and reproduction of the underlying premises of Achaemenid power as a hierarchically ordered project.

In chapter 1, I discussed at length the stone sculptural reliefs found on the tomb of Darius (and subsequent kings) and the door-jambs of the Hall of 100 Columns, with their so-called "throne-bearing" scene, in which subject populations stand in registers, their upright arms supporting the edifice of empire. There I noted, following Root, that the scene entailed a quasi-secularization of an earlier Mesopotamian visual trope that transferred the burden of imperial reproduction from deities onto political subjects. We might now discern wherefrom Darius conceived such a shift (the motif does not appear to have existed before his reign). The dominant component of the halls, which is to say their columns, may have provided a template for the throne-bearing scene (alongside earlier Mesopotamian models), each stone-and-wood support reconceived as a human participant in the body politic holding up the edifice of sovereignty and subjection. The columns of Pasargadae may have pressed their message (see chapter 3) on the sovereign, insisting on the presence of the many and the same to upraise and sustain the Achaemenid polity as a new kind of political "agreement" between sovereign and subject. Darius's response to this material provocation to set the terms of political association was to deftly manipulate what had originally been a message of congregation with limited hierarchy into a visual rhetoric of voluntary subordination and collusion.

I am suggesting that the column halls helped make possible the fullest elaboration of a fundamental tenet of Achaemenid ideology as it came to be developed in Darius's throne-bearing scene. We can at the very least recognize in the conceptual and material parallels between the columns and the stone-carved atlas figures an instance of what Hodder (2012: 125–126) calls "resonance," whereby people get entangled in their thinking about things, and abstractions cross material domains to achieve nondiscursive coherence. It is this co-constitutive connection between the material presence of the columns in the halls and one of the most salient arguments of Achaemenid political philosophy that could explain the multiplication and amplification of the halls and their numbers of columns from Cyrus to Darius to Xerxes. The amplification is quite staggering. For example, the increase *in area* from the Apadana (interior) to Xerxes's Hall of 100 Columns was 67 percent, but the *number of columns* nearly triples, with an increase of 178 percent. The expansion in the number of columns was far more important than the growth of the hall itself. In light of the regime's eschatologically charged political thought under Darius and his successors, it is as though the proliferation of columns was tantamount to the growth of the political community that was coming within the empire's (and, it follows, Ahuramazda's) embrace, thanks to the salvific work of the kings. The columns were thus contributing to the final restoration of cosmic perfection, the paradise of original creation (see chapter 1).[49] The columns did not *symbolize* that expansion, standing in for a growing body politic (for the empire does not expand under Xerxes or Artaxerxes I); rather, the columns *were themselves* a material instantiation of the Achaemenids' success in the tellurian struggle against the Lie.

We may approach this realization from another direction as well, and I see little reason to view the two as mutually exclusive. Elsewhere I have suggested that the Achaemenid halls may have borne some relation to the Achaemenid concept of the "paradise," a term that may have signified a number of kinds of gardens and parks (Boucharlat 2008: 557) but would have included enclosed, lush gardens containing a great variety of plantings and sometimes animals for hunting that provided idyllic spaces for leisure (Lincoln 2012: 5). Lincoln has made the case that the Achaemenid kings regarded these contained outdoor environments of vegetative and zoological abundance and perfection "not only as ideal spaces of repose, but also as models of the empire they were more actively laboring to create and prefigurations of what the world would be when their work was fully accomplished" (Lincoln 2007: 1; see also Lincoln 2012: 3–19). That is, the concept of the paradise was, to the Achaemenids, inseparable from their cosmogony, and their eschatological concern to see to the return to the state of primordial creation—beautiful, benevolent, pleasurable (Lincoln 2012: 77)—that obtained before the fall caused by the arrival of the Lie (see chapter 1). In Lincoln's (2012: 19) words, "The Persian paradise was a complex image: simultaneously a memory (better, a recollection) of the world as originally intended by the Creator and a promise that its perfection would be restored. . . . Within this ideological program, the construction of a paradise appears as the prefiguration of the world's ultimate salvation" (19).

Lincoln (2007: 1) describes what these venerated spaces of practice and fantasy were (or were imagined to be) like: "Plantings were arranged in geometric patterns to create a sense of perfect order and exquisite beauty."[50] This resolute commitment to pattern and order executed through the planting of trees in the gardens is mirrored by the meticulous arrangement of soaring columns in the columned halls. Moreover, many of the column elements, for instance at Pasargadae, Susa, and Persepolis, were adorned with vegetative and zoomorphic motifs, such as leaves, palms, and double-bull, griffin, lion, and horse protomes. I have previously argued that the zoologically animated forests in these spaces rendered the Achaemenid halls into built metaphors for the politico-religious paradises (Khatchadourian 2013: 133), a suggestion further supported by the spatial association between hypostyle halls and garden spaces at Pasargadae, the Shaur Palace at Susa, and perhaps at Persepolis (Boucharlat 2008; 2013b: 419; Root 2015: 24). It would, however, be more precise to recognize the halls less as iconic referents than as material instantiations of paradisiacal preserves on earth, much as Darius understood his "wonder" at Susa to be.

CONCLUSION

As effective delegates, for over two centuries the Achaemenid halls not only enabled the reproduction of political practice through their architectonics, but also helped realize the growth of the body politic and the just expansion of paradise on earth through their material properties. A recognition of their work as mediators in the deeply salvific Achaemenid imperial project allows us to finally confront the fairly obvious but unstated fact that the large columned halls are ill suited to a great many imaginable forms of social interaction; they are acoustically challenging in their scale and, thanks to the relentless obstruction of so very many columns that insistently stand in the way of free movement and clear viewshed, they also throw up obstacles to the practices of collective ritual, observance, and performance. The utilitarian "function" of these halls as places for assembly, procession, audience, storage, or display was a derivative result of their primary importance as political actants in the realization of the fundamental purpose of Achaemenid sovereignty. It is thus possible to understand how the once-captive columned halls, turned delegates, came to captivate the Achaemenid sovereigns—that is, to hold a firm grip on their attention and interest: they had acquired the prerogative to bring about political effects that the human sovereigns alone could not accomplish. The halls helped define and sustain those practices of governance that required collective assembly and, even more fundamentally, the values that made the polity appear morally upright in the eyes of the sovereigns and subjects. The main "cost," or unintended effect, of this process of delegation to a material thing was the sovereigns' own autonomy, as they became fettered to the physical materials—stone, wood, and mud brick—of which the halls were made.

The halls surely brought about other unintended effects as well, in excess of their assignments. Could such large, open, architecturally unregulated spaces offer venues for unsanctioned speech, subversive encounters, intrigue, and bricolage? Could they, in all their grandeur, monumentality, and fixity, expose the frailty of sovereignty's comparably diminutive mortal delegates? Could resentment over the Persian capture and the willful reformulation of the halls in a politics of coercion and control account, in some small measure, for the sustained revolts that the *dahyāva* of Media and Armenia—quite possibly in some kind of confederation with one another—fiercely mounted against the empire in the years before Darius's ascension to the throne?[51] We can only speculate, of course. But it is only by turning our gaze back to the mountains that we can begin to grasp the efficacy and the limitations of these and other Achaemenid delegates in the production of an imperial province. For, as we shall see, delegates were not alone in making satrapal conditions on the Armenian highland, a land, or *dahyu,* that the Persians called Armenia; they existed side by side with a populous material universe of proxies and affiliates that, along with their human makers and users, set the terms of limitation on imperial sovereignty.

5

Delegates and Proxies in the *Dahyu* of Armenia

The mountains are full of free and ungoverned people, where renegades can always find refuge under the cover of laws which are contrary to our interests.
—GENERAL ALEXEI PETROVICH ERMOLOV (1820)[1]

Alexei Ermolov, the infamous Russian general who ruthlessly brought the Caucasus to heel in the early nineteenth century, understood all too well that peoples of the mountains can at times be rather proficient at what James Scott (2009) has called "the art of not being governed." From the days of Pushkin to the era of Putin, Russia's conquest of the Caucasus takes its place in the annals of imperialism as an exceptionally protracted affair. It provides but one example of how expansionary projects of rule sometimes stumble in their attempts to subdue and make legible geographically difficult zones in the face of efforts to protect relative autonomy and self-governance. What is particularly illuminating about Ermolov's stereotypical figuring of the unruly mountain brigand is, first, an unexpected rhetorical turn that locates the subversion of imperial power not explicitly in the fixities of nature, but in the vicissitudes of culture: the mountain renegade takes refuge not literally in the craggy folds and long shadows of the Caucasus, as Ermolov might at first seem to suggest, but instead finds metaphorical cover under the protection of highland institutions of law. Mountains are here not determinative in undermining Russian sovereignty; and yet, in lending to law the material metaphor of cover, perceptibly they loom, a forceful presence that enables its continual corrosion. Second, there is the conspicuous contradiction at the heart of Ermolov's contemplation, whereby the peoples of the mountains are both lawless and law-bound at one and the same time. How can the mountaineers be ungoverned when it is precisely the legitimacy of Caucasian principles and regulations of collective association that makes imperial governance less than fully attainable?

This chapter provides our first foray into satrapal conditions in the *dahyu* of Armenia—both the conditions of subjection imposed by the conjoint efforts of imperial people and things (governance, in Ermolov's sense), and at the same time the conditionals or limitations, borne of local social logics, that human–thing collaborations in the mountains may have placed on sovereign prerogative. The essentializing trope of the timeless mountain brigand has no place in this story. And yet it remains the case that evidence for governance in the sense that imperialists like Ermolov have in mind is difficult for us to see among the Achaemenid Empire's "peoples of the hills" (Burney and Lang 1971). Across the region, delegates and proxies appear to have been in exceedingly short supply. It is an open question whether the empire's northern highlands were passively "left behind by civilization" (Scott 2009: 9)—a land seen by the Persians as "little more than a wild, inhospitable area of comparatively little value" (Summers 1993: 86) and best suited to deportees and exiles (Briant 2002: 179, 320)—or whether the scarcity of imperial things attests to lifeways that, under the cover of *both* mountains and customs, were deliberately orchestrated "as adaptations designed to evade both state capture and state formation" (Scott 2009: 9). The question at the heart of this chapter is not one of submission or resistance, compliance or defiance, consensual embrace or contentious refusal. At issue instead is the conjunction of human intentions and object efficacies that can collaborate to create what Scott (2009: 7) calls the "intermediate zone," neither fully within nor outside the empire, in which lifeways both alternative to and consistent with the principles of imperial sovereignty ambiguously coexist.

In an evidentiary sense, what obtains in this region during the mid-first millennium B.C. is that difficult conjuncture of lives lived lightly on the landscape and lives at the periphery of archaeology's vision, traditionally fixed on the lowland centers of "civilization." This chapter is therefore, it must be said at the outset, a study in fragments. I mean this in more than the general sense that holds true of all archaeological inquiry. In this case, the lacunae are truly gaping, for across the approximately 400,000 km^2 that made up the *dahyu* of Armenia, targeted archaeological research into the Iron 3 period (ca. 600–300 B.C.) has been virtually nonexistent.[2] The reasons for this are broadly twofold. The first is a long-standing privilege accorded to the region's prehistory, and the attendant preoccupation with phenomena that relate to the emergence of the *first* villages, the *first* signs of social hierarchy, or the *first* complex polities. Compounding this tenacious legacy of the social evolutionary paradigm is the equally powerful allure of "civilization," which persistently draws archaeology's attention to apical phases of complexity on the highland (best represented by periods of Urartian, Seleucid, Artaxiad, and Roman dominance), when technologies of writing, the arts, urbanism, monumental architecture, and the like serve to emplace the region, however peripherally, in familiar tropes and trajectories of momentous human achievement. The Iron 3 period, a time of neither pristine innovation in the structure of societies nor of autonomous state power, falls between the cracks of these hegemonic archaeological dispositions. As a result, the fragments available are virtually all the result of happenstance—unsought findings from surveys and excavations designed to investigate earlier periods, chance discoveries from construction or agricultural work, isolated and unscientific acquisitions of the art market.[3] Despite this state of affairs, it is nevertheless possible to sketch the broad contours of satrapal conditions across the highland, and the workings of a small but compelling collection of delegates and proxies. It is hoped that the necessarily tentative conclusions drawn from such an effort provide the stimulus for future research that might support or force reconsideration of the arguments advanced in these pages.

BORDERS AND FRONTIERS

Rarely have imperial formations sought to create fixed, territorially exclusive borders. For all the color-coded maps that purport the organization of political space to be neatly bounded, more often than not empires "have been unwilling or unable to close their frontiers" (Colás 2007: 19), ever intent on bringing new populations of the known world into their universal embrace. "Agents of imperial rule," Stoler and McGranahan (2007: 10) note, have often "invested in, exploited, and demonstrated strong stakes in the proliferation of geopolitical ambiguities." Missions to civilize the benighted or to faithfully deliver on divine will are ill served by hard internal edges and inflexible frontiers.

To the best of our knowledge, the Achaemenids never produced something like a two-dimensional imperial map. Instead, as many scholars have observed (Briant 2002: 180; Herrenschmidt 1976; Lincoln 2012: 43–46; Tourovets 2001: 252; Vogelsang 1992: 96), they rendered their cartographic imaginary through the directional ordering of toponyms or ethnonyms or visual depictions of peoples in various representations of the empire's territorial possessions. Such "lists," which varied somewhat from one to the next, would "plot spatial, ethnic, and political relations as a set of concentric circles surrounding a privileged center" (Lincoln 2012: 43). Thus, for instance, the earliest such list appearing on the Bisitun inscription plots Persia in its permanent place at the center, then an inner circle of privileged near neighbors and former great powers, then an outer ring of more distant entities ordered according to cardinal directions, and finally two more remote peoples in the far north and far south. Since later lists included peoples not yet conquered, we may suppose that the Achaemenids produced a cartography of imperial space that was a "model for, rather than model of, what they purported to represent" (Winichakul 1994: 130). In this they were hardly unique. According to Carl Schmitt (2003: 281), "Every true empire around the world has claimed . . . a sphere of spatial sovereignty beyond its borders."

In virtually every royal representation of the imperial expanse, the *dahyu* of Armenia is claimed self-assuredly and unequivocally to fall squarely within the imperial embrace. We have already seen the Armenian delegation on the east staircase façade of the Apadana at Persepolis (figures 9, p. 18, and 10, p. 20), bringing as gifts before the king an amphora (likely of silver) and a horse.[4] Armenia is here but one participant in an elaborate metaphor of imperial collaboration. Indeed, in this studied visual contemplation of the empire's cultural and political geography, Armenia occupies a prominent place as the leading delegation in its row, and thus in close proximity to the king. Root (forthcoming) has suggested that the conspicuous forward positioning of the Armenian delegation, coupled with its clustering with two other groups with which the Armenian delegates share sartorial traits (Medes and Elamites), may signal the region's constitutive place in an emerging imaginary of a pan-Iranian identity. That is, the Armenians are not only included in the imperial vision, but in this one instance they are symbolically accorded cultural prominence. Greek sources, for their part, would appear to attest to the governmental and economic institutions that bound the region to the empire in practical terms. It is from these sources that we learn of powerful satraps with close ties to the crown, and of the *dahyu*'s tributary obligations, which may have taken the form of both silver and horses.[5]

Yet Schmitt's cautionary comment on the imperial habit of laying sovereign claim to territories in excess of effective sovereign control haunts any effort to reckon with the exercise of Achaemenid power in this supposedly constituent subject realm. As we shall see in this chapter, there are awkward silences that tell a different story about the efficacy of rule in this region, silences that press us to ask whether the Achaemenids artfully claimed to fully possess what they never fully mastered. It is noteworthy, for instance, that the Bisitun inscription (see chapter 1) is conspicuously inconclusive with respect to the reconquest of Armenia, leaving open the possibility of less-than-decisive military gains.[6] Not unlike Ermolov, it appears that Darius too had known his share of recalcitrance in the upland plateau of southern Caucasia. And while written sources tell of no other rebellions in the region, there is a curious instability in the figuring of Armenia in the imperial imaginary. In contrast to the prominent placement of the delegation on the Apadana relief, Darius's tomb façade (figure 6, p. 8) places the personification of Armenia in the bottom register of "throne-bearers," rather far from the Medes and Elamites, who continue to occupy the first and second positions (Root forthcoming). Such visual inconstancy may point to an underlying anxiety surrounding the status and integrity of Armenia within the imperial whole, at least during Darius's reign.

It is in this context that the boundaries of the *dahyu* refuse neat delineation. Broadly speaking, falling within the compass of this chapter is the highland region that spans west to east, from the northern Euphrates to the Lesser Caucasus, and north to south, from the southern shore of the Black Sea and the low-lying Kura River valley to the western shores of Lake Urmia (map 2).[7] This region, densely crisscrossed with a nearly unbroken web of formidable mountains, is the highest upland zone of southwest Asia. Geographically and environmentally, it is host to considerable variability. Immediately south of the Great Caucasus mountains are three orographic and vegetative zones: in the west, the low-lying Colchian Plain; in the center, the higher-elevation hills and temperate grasslands of the Iberian Plain; and in the east, the lowland semidesert of the Shirvan steppe. The Kura River provides a southern limit to these low-elevation regimes, running west to east, parallel to the Caucasus Mountains, until it drains into the Caspian Sea. The Kura and its drainages water this central belt of the South Caucasus, except in the far west, near the Black Sea, where the Rioni (Phasis) River dominates. Proceeding further south, in all but the far east, elevations rise once again as the various mountain chains that make up the Lesser Caucasus transition into the highland zone that stretches in a single orographic province as far west as the Anti-Taurus Range. This highland plateau is drained by several major river systems, including the eastward-flowing Araks River and the southward-flowing Tigris and Euphrates. I shall call this rugged, high-altitude plateau variously the *dahyu* of Armenia or the Armenian highland.[8]

In nearly all directions, other imperial lands neighbored the *dahyu*, with Achaemenid Cappadocia and Cilicia lying to the west, Mesopotamia and Syria to the south and southwest, and Media to the east/southeast. But the Achaemenid cartographic imaginary suggests that the fuzzy northern frontier of Armenia, conventionally demarcated along the southern edge of Great Caucasus Mountains that bisects the isthmus separating the Caspian from the Black Sea, loosely delimited not only Armenia but also the empire itself. The mountain chain and the lands just beyond, where the Caucasus gives way to the Eurasian Steppe, was no imperial *dahyu* at all, its inhabitants thus unbeholden to the Achaemenid sovereigns. Armenia was, in other words, a northern bridgehead in the unfinished advance against the Lie (see chapter 1, p. 4).

LANDSCAPES OF AMBIVALENCE AND EVASION: SETTLEMENT PATTERNS

We left the Armenian highland in chapter 4 with an account of the seventh-century B.C. renovation at Erebuni, which entailed the transformation of a typical Urartian fortress complex, characterized by labyrinthine spatial arrangements and correspondingly segmented, regulated activity areas, into a space of congregational politics enabled by the material properties and architectonics of the columned hall. This was, as we saw, an unusual revitalization; the demise of the Urartian Empire is otherwise associated with the repudiation of virtually all of that regime's most important delegates, namely, the hilltop fortresses that dotted the highland from the plains of Erzurum to Ararat. During the centuries of Urartian control, the fortresses connected people across vast stretches through shared understandings of how certain topographies and spaces must play a role in the organization of political association. As both a topographic and an architectural monolith, the fortress became the material and symbolic fulcrum of what was, by all accounts, a heavy-handed political apparatus that severely impinged on the social lives of its subjects—at least those in the vicinities of the hilltop citadels. Indeed, the Urartian kings successfully established the fortress as the location *par excellence* of political power on the highland, standardizing both its operation in built form and its resonance in diverse media (A. T. Smith 2003). Their dependence on the fortress was particularly intense through the period of imperial formation and initial consolidation, when it tightly pulled together bureaucratic, religious, and distributive functions. Fortresses were effective structuring institutions; the practices that took place within and around them reproduced the conditions of possibility that ordered social life. Fortresses worked to make alternative practices unthinkable.

A comparative analysis of surveys conducted across the highland suggests that an ambivalence surrounding the fortress as an indispensable material pivot of social and political life may have extended beyond the most privileged centers of authority during the centuries that followed the unraveling of the Urartian polity.[9] To the extent possible, this analysis tracks the fate of the fortress and other patterns of settlement during the sixth through fourth centuries B.C. by examining the topographic position of sites, or their relative siting vertically, on the variegated terrain of the highland, as well as patterns of settlement continuity or change, which can measure the degree to which groups of people went on the move as the political fortunes of the region changed from Urartian to Achaemenid hegemony.[10] The analysis draws on eight survey projects (map 3), each having varying strengths and weaknesses in terms of methodology and data publication: the systematic Tsaghkahovit Plain survey, located in the small mountain depression north of Mt. Aragats, and organized under the auspices of Project ArAGATS (Smith, Badalyan, and Avetisyan 2009); the University of Melbourne's systematic Bayburt Plain survey in the Çoruh River drainage of the northwestern highland (Sagona and Sagona 2004); the unsystematic Ijevan reconnaissance survey, in northeast Armenia's Kura River drainage, organized by Stepan Esayan under the auspices of Armenia's Institute of Archaeology and Ethnography (Esayan 1976); the extensive and unsystematic Doğubeyazıt and Erciş surveys of the Araks River drainage and wider environs, conducted by Catherine Marro and Aynur Özfirat (Marro and Özfirat 2003, 2004, 2005); the unsystematic southern Lake Sevan Basin survey, organized by Italian and Armenian teams (Biscione et al. 2002); the unsystematic surveys in the Lake Urmia region conducted by German and Italian teams (Belgiorno 1984; Kleiss 1973: 83–89; 1974: 80–82; 1975: 58–60; 1979: 290–298; Kleiss and Kroll 1976: 108–113; 1979: 213; Kroll 1976: 166–170); and the unsystematic Muş Plain survey,

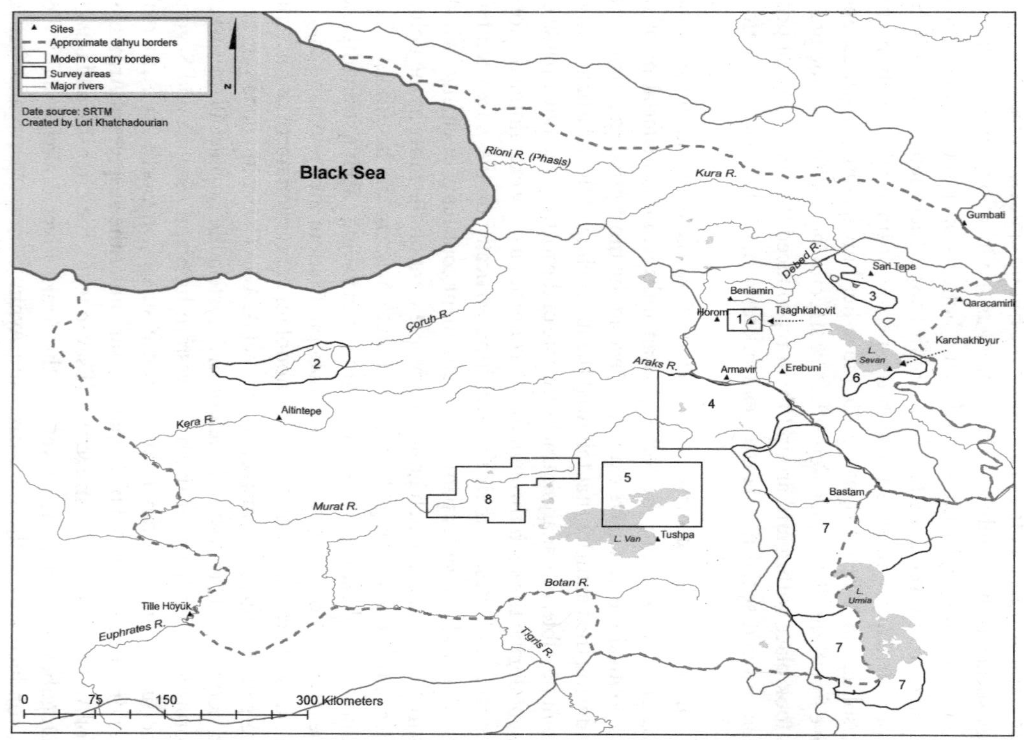

MAP 3. The Armenian *dahyu* with survey regions indicated: 1. Tsaghkahovit Plain survey; 2. Bayburt Plain survey; 3. Ijevan survey; 4. Doğubeyazıt survey; 5. Erciş survey; 6. Lake Sevan survey; 7. Lake Urmia surveys; 8. Muş Plain survey (Lori Khatchadourian).

a salvage effort led by American, Canadian, and Turkish researchers (Rothman 1992, 2004; Rothman and Gülriz 1997).[11]

A comparison of the findings from these efforts tentatively suggests that the broad contours of collective life on the highland changed radically during the Iron 3 period. Several regions that were either in the heartland of the Urartian Empire and inscribed with numerous fortress constructions (such as Doğubeyazıt and Erciş), or that hosted a major Urartian fortress (such as the Lake Urmia region, with Bastam), were substantially vacated by the time the Achaemenid Empire was ascendant.[12] Nor is there concomitant evidence for new, large settlements in these regions that might have hinted at settlement reorganization rather than regional abandonment. Bearing all caveats of survey methodologies in mind, it is as though there was an exodus from regions that were dense with fortresses occupied during the centuries of Urartian rule, particularly near the major fortresses of the Urartian governmental apparatus.[13] It is reasonable to ask whether the collapse of Urartu created the possibility of social disruption amongst groups in the vicinity of the Urartian fortresses that served to dissociate them from the weakened authorities of the dying regime and relocate elsewhere. Even as several regions that were near Urartu's political establishment witnessed a severe out-migration, some locales that had, as it seems, remained largely beyond the sphere of Urartian control, and had been scarcely occupied during Urartu's ascendancy, came to be settled in the subsequent centuries. In the Tsaghkahovit Plain and in the mountains of Ijevan, for example, social life returned or intensified during the sixth through fourth centuries.

Given that the clearest evidence for out-migration is in the more southern of the surveyed regions on the highland (Doğubeyazıt, Erciş, and Urmia) and that the evidence for in-migration is in the more northern of the surveyed regions (Tsaghkahovit and Ijevan), it is possible that, at a general scale, people were moving northward, perhaps following the removal of Urartian controls that concentrated labor and resources near royal fortresses. A northward movement would also amount to a flow of people further from the Achaemenid centers of power in Iran and Mesopotamia—a spatial separation that may well signal a tactic of evasion from the long arm of the imperial state.

At the same time, the comparison of surveys also suggests that communities were changing their practices and breaking from some of the rules of the past, once promulgated by the fortress. This is apparent not only through departures from once heavily fortressed regions, but also through changes in site location *within regions,* from higher to lower ground. In those regions that were largely abandoned, there is evidence that groups who continued to inhabit these substantially vacated areas regarded fortresses with some ambivalence. Thus, in the Erciş region, lower-lying sites were favored. In the Doğubeyazıt region, the numbers of fortress sites and open settlements are equal (in both regions, the numbers of sites are very low, only four in each). In Urmia, however, the fortress remained an important locale of habitation. Turning to places that evince possible constant levels of settlement intensity—namely Muş, the southern Lake Sevan area, and maybe Bayburt—there may be a trend toward lower-lying sites.[14]

Not only were people possibly moving away from fortress locations in the Iron 3 period, they were generally moving away from sites with strong associations with the preceding centuries. Several new sites in the southern Lake Sevan region were established, while most of the Iron 2 (Urartian) sites that were abandoned had not been active in the Iron 1 period. Moreover, most of the sites that were continuously occupied had been loci of activity in the Iron 1 period. Similarly, in the Muş region, several new sites were founded in the Iron 3 period. Most of the continuously occupied sites evince deep histories of occupation, reaching back into Iron 1 and the Late Bronze Age. In contrast, the majority of the abandoned Iron 2 sites had been newly founded in the Iron 2 period, and thus these sites were less rooted in local settlement histories.

The pattern in regions that were previously unsettled is particularly interesting. In the Tsaghkahovit and Ijevan regions, there was a strong preference for habitation near or in fortified locales. This may have been a defensive choice, as communities sought protection from threats beyond the *dahyu*'s frontiers. Apart from such strategic considerations, putting down new roots without building (or rebuilding) a fortress may have been regarded as a radical violation of the basic principles of social order, as they had come to be defined by the end of the Iron 2 period. Yet, as we shall see in the next chapter, even in such northern regions, the proclivity toward fortified, elevated dwelling was tempered by a countervailing effort to redefine and reduce the importance of the fortress in sociopolitical life. In sum, despite a tendency toward survey methods that give preference to likely fortress locations, the emerging picture from comparative survey analysis suggests that the role of the fortress changed during the centuries of Achaemenid dominion—perhaps not decisively and perhaps not universally, but nevertheless palpably. It could be said that the entanglements with the fortress began to loosen.

In chapter 4 I suggested that the appearance of the columned hall in various parts of the highland emerged out of a disaffection with the technologies of the complex polity. The coarse-grained picture that side-by-side survey affords adds some weight to this view. I am inclined to attribute (a) the movement away from areas of former Urartian power, and (b) the northward movement away from the core interior zones of the Achaemenid Empire, coupled with (c) the general ambivalence surrounding the fortress, to the very same turn away from the overbearing practices of state control. That is, I associate these settlement patterns with the rejection of institutions of administration and materialized ideologies of social asymmetry. In the next chapter we shall observe, at higher resolution than comparative survey can provide, the ways in which agro-pastoral communities and the material affiliates with which they were bound collaboratively developed the arts of not being governed. Yet at the regional scale of the *dahyu,* it is nevertheless possible to point to signs of disengagement, evasion, and ambivalence vis-à-vis the spaces of the complex polity. In terms of interregional politics, mountaineers and mountain landscapes partnered in placing limits on the possibility of effective Achaemenid sovereignty in the *dahyu,* while local considerations put into question the entanglements with the fortress institution that had previously encouraged a politics of hierarchically regulated political association. It was against this arguably inhospitable backdrop that the empire's material delegates worked to enforce the terms of subjection.

SILVER DELEGATES

Paramount among these delegates were the precious metal drinking paraphernalia of the feast, an apparatus whose vitality the Persians appear to have well understood. Consider this seal impression (figure 28) from a Persian-era coffin at the Mesopotamian city of Ur (Collon 1996: 74, pl. 20, fig. 10g; Curtis and Tallis 2005: no. 124). Prominently positioned in the center of the scene is a fluted, horn-shaped drinking vessel (known as a rhyton)[15] that terminates in a plastic rendering of the foreparts of a winged sphinx. In the field above the rhyton floats a fluted, one-handled jug of the type used to pour wine into the horn. Below is a flexed arm, which holds the rhyton as though preparing to raise it to a mouth. The arm is a body fragment, a human sherd, whose disarticulation from the body of the reveler contrasts with the integrity of the unbroken vessels that are the focal point of the image. The rhyton, disproportionately large in relation to the arm, is the most assertive participant in this unusual communion of a human part and object wholes.

This unusual glyptic scene unsettles ontological boundaries in more ways than one. For, can the human arm fragment be said to be any more fully human than the human-headed sphinx vessel? And what entity brings vitality to the encounter? Is it the personless arm that holds the vessel, or is it the vessel itself, which dictates the terms of the arm's exertion? Entirely cleaved from body and mind, the "human" brings to the action no more intention than the vessel, which I suggest plays the determinative role not only by virtue of its centrality in the scene but in the requirements for use that it imposes on the disjoined limb. As we turn to the making of satrapal conditions in Armenia, it is the efficacies of just such vessels of commensal consumption and their conjoint actions with human revelers that come to the fore. In what follows, I examine how a corpus of silver drinking vessels worked to extend into the mountains the material entanglements and sociopolitical values of the imperial court by virtue of both their physical properties and the practical mediations they afforded.

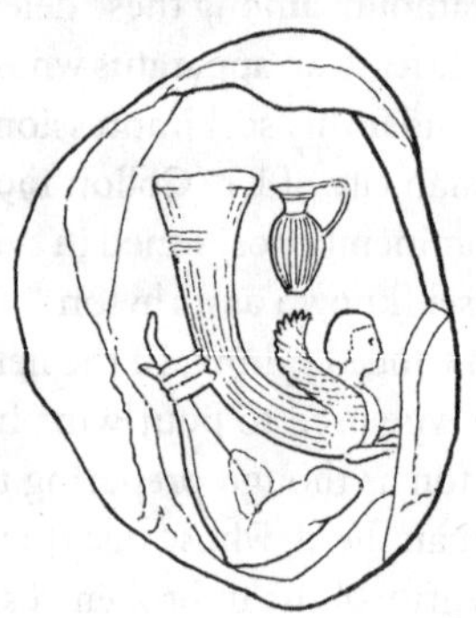

FIGURE 28. Photo (above) and illustration (below) of a seal impression from Ur (source: Curtis and Tallis 2005, fig. 124, courtesy of Dominique Collon).

Approaching the Corpus

The silver rhyton, a drinking vessel of thin sheet metal with animal foreparts and horn, is a quintessential hallmark of the imperial repertoire of fine consumption vessels. The Achaemenid rhyton takes its place in a long line of metal vessels that played an important part in elite commensality and gift exchange in the Near East since at least the early second millennium B.C. It is likewise but one instantiation of the widespread and exuberant use of various kinds of metal drinking paraphernalia in ritualized feasting events across much of the Mediterranean, Eurasia, and southwest Asia during the first millennium B.C. Allowing for variability in styles, methods of production, and rituals of use across such vast extents, it is nevertheless fair to say that by the mid-first millennium B.C. metal drinking vessels afforded a common sensibility of elite identity, as well as, it must be supposed, an interconnected world of shared metallurgical know-how, unprecedented in their geographic scope. It is in the context of this enduring and widespread field of praxis that the rhyton with animal terminal emerged out of metal workshops during the early decades of Achaemenid rule.

Approaches to these materials can take multiple forms. There are compelling grounds, for example, to blur the boundaries among distinct spheres of metallurgical production and consumption in order to trace the connections that forged a shared Eurasian affection for alcohol imbibed from containers of precious metal. In the interconnected world of the first millennium B.C., there is every reason to suppose that users understood metal drinking vessels as objects of desire and distinction well beyond the bounds of their own social or political communities. And yet, my interest here is to attend precisely to the kinds of work such things did in a particular imperial polity that placed extraordinary, even unprecedented, emphasis on the importance of metal vessels in reproducing the terms of political association, as we have already seen from the Apadana relief discussed in chapter 1. It was in that chapter too that I pressed the case for a prescient recognition in ancient Persian religio-political philosophy of the indivisibility of sovereignty and matter/metal. It is for these reasons that the analysis advanced here examines the role of silver vessels as delegates operating within the broad Achaemenid ecumene, setting to one side the transcontinental connections in which they were also imbricated. Silver vessels either *known* to be from the *dahyu* of Armenia or unprovenienced vessels *thought* to be from Armenia focus these discussions. We begin with the evidence that is less fraught.

In 1968, in the course of construction activities at the foothill of Erebuni (see chapter 4), workers chanced on an astounding discovery: a hoard of five silver vessels, *deliberately flattened,* and inserted into a "big jug" (*bol'shoi kuvshin*—Arakelyan 1971: 143). The buried group of smashed objects contained three rhyta in the shape of horns with animal terminals and one goblet-rhyton with a hole in the base, as well as a fifth vessel now lost (figure 29).[16] The goblet-rhyton has a smooth-surfaced neck and shoulder, a body with narrow vertical grooves, and a hole in its base through which drink could pass.[17] One of the rhyta takes the form of a calf's head, the upper part of the horn adorned with a relief frieze likely depicting a symposium among four figures rendered in repoussé: a man (perhaps Asclepius) seated on a throne, with one hand positioned in a gesture that anticipates the imminent receipt of a drinking bowl, or *phiale;* a woman who approaches him with just such a bowl; another woman playing double pipes; and a third woman seated on a throne or stool playing a cithara (or lyre).[18] The remaining two rhyta depict recumbent horses, in one case with a straddling rider. They provide further evidence for the close association between Armenia and the horse (figure 9, p. 18). Indeed, if the testimony of the Greek written sources is taken at face value, the horse rhtya from Erebuni would seem to symbolically conjoin into singular objects the *dahyu*'s twin tributary obligations of silver and horses.[19]

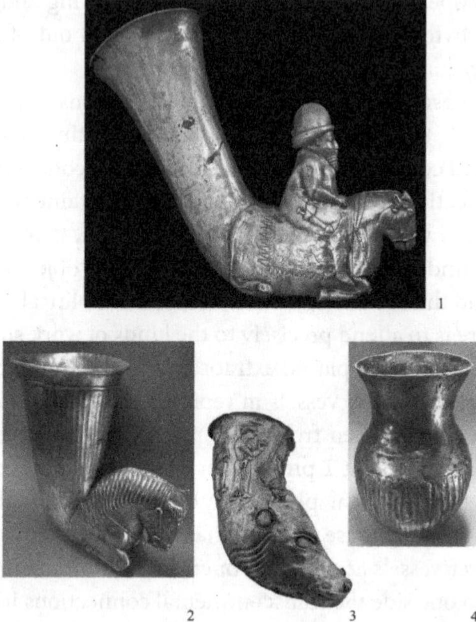

FIGURE 29. Erebuni silver vessels, shown at comparable scale. 1. Horse-with-rider rhyton; 2. horse rhyton; 3. calf-head rhyton; 4. goblet rhyton. (Photographs 1 and 3 courtesy of David Stronach, 2 and 4 courtesy of Mikhail Treister. Source: Treister 2015, fig. 1.)

The horse-with-rider rhyton is particularly interesting as a virtually unique example of the form. Whether it depicts a specific individual, as is often proposed,[20] or an archetypal, pan-Iranian horseman,[21] David Stronach (2011: 263) is surely correct in suggesting that the vessel betrays "barely concealed hints of high political ambition."[22] The Erebuni cache is among the few assemblages of precious metal in the territory of the Achaemenid Empire to be securely associated with an excavated site, although precise archaeological provenience is lacking.

In contrast, woefully problematic are the unprovenienced silver vessels that have come to be associated with Armenia despite unreliable post-depositional biographies involving uncontrolled excavations, art dealers, private collectors, and museum bequests. These materials, which include rhyta, bowls, and amphorae, simply cannot be accorded the weight of reliable evidence, and yet to ignore them would be to dismiss more than half a century of serious scholarship that has tried to come to terms with them. Two silver rhyta of uncertain provenience have been linked to Armenia. The Louvre bought one in 1897 from a dealer, who said it came from Erzerum, in today's eastern Turkey. This bent rhyton (with no pour hole) has a horizontally fluted horn that terminates in a recumbent gazelle.[23] The second was

FIGURE 30. Selection of vessels from the Franks bequest to the British Museum, said to be from "near Erzincan" (© The Trustees of the British Museum).

acquired by the British Museum in that same year as part of the Franks bequest, which included the notoriously dubious "Oxus Treasure," though the rhyton and associated silver artifacts were separate, and said to be from "near Erzincan" (not far from Erzurum). The vessel (figure 30) is once again horn-shaped, with partial gilding, and depicts a horned winged griffin with outstretched lion paws and a pour hole in the chest (Dalton 1964). It was with this same bequest that the British Museum acquired three deep silver bowls with rounded bottoms and carinated rims (a form so closely tied to imperial canons of taste that it has come to be known as the "Achaemenid bowl") and a silver bowl (figure 30) with embossed decoration of lotus flowers, also known as a *phiale* (another quintessential Achaemenid form).[24] Summers (1993: 96) has conjectured that the "Erzincan" objects were originally found as a set, possibly in a burial. Some have rightly urged caution with respect to the integrity of such sets when they occur on the art market, since they may speak more to the cunning of forgers and the tricks of antiquities traders than to ancient practices of consumption and deposition (Gunter and Root 1998: 11; Muscarella 1977: 165–166).[25] Finally, two additional silver vessels said to be from the *dahyu* of Armenia take the form of amphorae with zoomorphic handles. The silver gilt animal-handled amphora in the Rothschild collection is vertically fluted, with two spouts at the base, its handles taking the shape of leaping ibexes

(Amandry 1959: Pl. 24). Likewise there are two matching ibex handles from a single lost amphora, one now in Berlin and the other in the Louvre.[26]

To the best of my knowledge, none of these vessels has been deemed a forgery (Muscarella 2000). Moreover, the purported derivations, while entirely unsupported, are nevertheless not implausible. The Erebuni hoard provides direct evidence that silver rhyta were in circulation in the *dahyu.* While the zoomorphic amphora carried by the Armenian delegation on the Apadana does not offer direct support for the provenience claims of the two amphorae, it does point to an association between the region and the form (even if not an exclusive one).[27] As for the Achaemenid bowls, their ubiquity across the empire and beyond precludes any assessment of the strength of the provenience claim to Erzincan. What we are left with, then, is the recognition that sound and independent evidence makes the provenience claims on the rhyta and amphorae credible, but still unverifiable. By the most conservative logic, the foregoing discussion, which rests on the assumption that the unprovenienced vessels were deposited *somewhere* in the *dahyu,* and possibly in the purported vicinities, might be considered a thought experiment on how interpretation could proceed if such vessels were to emerge from secure contexts.[28]

Delegate Matter

How did the material properties of the Erebuni rhyta and the unprovenienced vessels work to conscript users on the highland into relationships that bound the *dahyu* to the empire and compromised regional sovereignty? Phrased another way, what role did silver play in the Achaemenid project of rule? The answer defies a simple brief, but a striking discovery from the excavations of Babylon in 1883 provides an intriguing point of entry into the complexities of the question. Uncovered in that year was a hoard of silver things existent in what can only be called advanced biographical states. There were broken fragments of coins that traced to mints across the eastern Mediterranean. There were melted lumps or sheets of silver in various unshapely states. Most striking of all were the broken pieces of fine jars and bowls in Achaemenid styles: a jar handle in the shape of a winged bull that had been hacked off the rim of the vessel with a chisel (and then further destroyed with blows to the head that left the bull nearly decapitated); a single embossed gadroon from a *phiale;* the right eye and curled forelocks of a bull's-head vessel—all flattened, crumpled, and twisted, in some cases nearly beyond recognition (Reade 1986; Robinson 1950).

The hoard from Babylon nicely attests to the commingling of two distinct monetary standards in the Achaemenid world, one based on a currency in coinage and the other an unminted currency in weighed silver. While the precise find spot of the Babylon hoard is not known, and thus we cannot pinpoint its location in the circulatory flows of silver into and out of imperial centers such as Babylon, its composition mirrors what is understood from written sources concerning the payment of taxes and tribute. By all accounts, the already monetized Greek cities of Asia Minor paid their debts in coin, but all tribute-paying lands contributed part of their obligation to the crown in the form of weighed silver. Importantly, only a minimal percentage of the annual silver tribute would be transformed into regal coinage (Briant 2002: 408; Zournatzi 2000). The life cycle of silver payment could in fact take a variety of forms. On clear view in the Babylon hoard is a currency in what is called hacksilver, fragments cut from finished silver objects that, as bullion, could serve monetary functions.[29] Tribute (and a parallel economy in the form of a "voluntary" tax in "gifts" to the crown) often took the shape of silver vessels, assessed by weight, which were used or stockpiled in their given finished forms.[30] There is less evidence for the melting and manufacture of ingots by royal workshops, although that possibility cannot be excluded, and certainly some inflows of silver scrap would find their way to metallurgists in the service of the court, to be assayed and refined (Zournatzi 2000), and then crafted into an array of luxury items that, as we shall see, fueled the empire's "tournaments of value" (Appadurai 1986). The administration may well have devised an imperial silver quality standard, regulated if not according to a specified purity of silver then to a percentage of copper alloy (Zournatzi 2000).

Textual evidence, both Greek and Persian, make plain that weighed silver also flowed out of imperial coffers in a complex system of redistribution (Sancisi-Weerdenburg 1989). Silver was one of the main media of royal benefaction. Rations to workers were sometimes disbursed in silver (Briant 2002: 422), as were gifts to valued individuals who, in one way or another, earned the king's favor through good deeds (305, 313). The testimony of Greek writers leaves little doubt that the Achaemenid kings also gave gifts of metal to visiting dignitaries and privileged subjects in the form of finished products like jewelry and silver and gold vessels, whose values were assessed by weight, in addition to their symbolic worth (Briant 2002: 307; Gunter and Root 1998: 23; Sancisi-Weerdenburg 1989; Simpson 2005: 104). Such material gifts were often given on the occasion of a royal banquet. Giving was, as Sancisi-Weerdenburg (1989: 140) notes, the king's "most important duty," the mark of good, benevolent, and just kingship. It also of course created reciprocal obligations of loyalty.

Much has been written on silver in the Achaemenid Empire, and it is not my purpose here to survey that field. Before returning to the Armenian highland, what I wish to bring forward from this brief sketch is the ontological implications of a silver economy in which matter and object, substance and form, instrumental and social value are indivisible. Even as some silver things may have enjoyed a long shelf life, they belonged to a system of metal flows in which silver was recurrently transfiguring from the liquid to the solid state, from monetary instrument to iconic enabler of the feast, from wrought spectacle to hacked fragments of crumpled, folded, twisted metal, from larger to ever-smaller bits of hacksilver, then back into the furnace and on to another finished form. Repeated over and over in unscripted cycles, each material state was liminal, unfixed—an ephemeral repository of what once was and a harbinger of what could come next. It is the elemental properties of silver that make this chameleonic circulation possible, a matter always and ever in a "vital state" (Deleuze and Guattari 1987; see also chapter 1), a nonhuman protagonist that can be fairly said to have kept the imperial machinery in motion no less efficaciously than the imperial agents who were beholden to it.

Silver, in other words, acquired the prerogative to bring about political effects in the Achaemenid world. It took a share in the forces of political reproduction and transformation. As the medium of tribute, it determined the grounds of compliance and noncompliance, of economic viability and vulnerability. As a medium of royal prestige goods and royal gifting, silver also became a "matter" of imperial dependence, a locus of autonomous power, whose continuous and regulated flows were critical to sustaining the sovereign's prerogative. In chapter 3 I argued that, among other requirements, things of empire are delegates when the imperial establishment is fettered by its own need for the physical substances out of which they are made, such that the polity becomes unviable or inconceivable in the collective absence of such matter. Such delegates sometimes take the form of things whose material substance itself brings about affective responses in their users rather than working only instrumentally to enable practical solutions to everyday requirements. The Achaemenid silver vessels (and other luxury items of silver) were just such "gentle things" (see p. 70).

Let us now return to the material states of the silver vessels from Erebuni and elsewhere in the *dahyu*. The flattened condition of the Erebuni vessels now invites interpretation as things in arrested transition between utensil and bullion, between whole and fragment. Babken Arakelyan (1971: 154), the first to publish the Erebuni hoard, suggested that the vessels were flattened and stuffed into the ceramic jar in haste, in a moment of crisis—an impending raid, perhaps, in the heady closing years of the empire. Close chronological analysis in recent studies has left open this possibility, and has occasioned comparison to a hoard deposited in a ceramic jug at Pasargadae (Treister 2013, 2015).[31] While I do not dispute that a crisis may account for the abandonment of the jug, the flattened condition of the vessels (given what is known of hacksilver) suggests less a scramble to sequester than the deliberate removal of silver from contexts of consumption and its forced entry into a "new" phase as monetary instruments. A number of factors not born of imminent threat could have provoked such a need to liquidize assets and store them as uncoined silver. Given that, by all accounts, tribute in the form of silver was customarily rendered in finished goods, it is probable that the hoard was not being held in reserve for the crown but was removed from such flows (in which one or more of the pieces very plausibly once circulated) and made available for smaller economic transactions regulated by weight in silver.[32] In any case, this much is clear: the vessels' silver properties thrust users at Erebuni into the same dependencies, material flows, and regulatory mechanisms that bound imperial agents elsewhere.[33]

It is of course more difficult to comment on the silver of the unprovenienced vessels. I wish to go no further than to address the co-occurrence of the three deep carinated bowls said to be from "near Erzincan." Studies have shown that Achaemenid silver vessels, specifically the distinctive *phialai,* often occurred in sets, with their combined weights in grams corresponding in round-number equivalence to the Achaemenid coin type known as the *sigloi* (Vickers 2002). A well-known example is the likely set of silver *phialai* associated with the Persian king Artaxerxes I (Gunter and Root 1998). Other supporting evidence for such sets includes the Parthenon inventories, where Achaemenid silver *phialai* are always counted in sets, with their combined weights indicated (9–10), as well as the so-called Darius Vase, which depicts a seated treasurer who is approached from one side by a man carrying as tribute a stack of three *phialai,* while from the other side there approaches an individual presenting his taxes in the form of a sack of coins (figure 31). The combined weight of the three silver deep Achaemenid bowls does indeed correspond to a coin standard, in this case 300 *drachmai,* a Greek currency minted not only on the mainland but also in the Greek regions of Asia Minor, like Lycia, that were a part of the Achaemenid Empire (Carradice 1987).[34] Meanwhile, the *phiale,* at 541.3 g, corresponds to 100 *sigloi.* The privileged actors of the Armenian highland who may have acquired and used these vessels were ensnarled in regimes of value that shaped the Achaemenid economy and were based in large measure on the affordances of silver.

It is impossible to say at what point in their biographies the unprovenienced silver vessels were removed from circulation. But if they were deposited in burials or hoards it would seem once again that, as at Erebuni, highlanders interrupted a possible centrifugal destiny of silver as tribute or gift to the center. It is worth noting in this regard that several delegations on the Apadana relief bear as gifts before the king the deep, so-called Achaemenid bowls like those from "near Erzincan" (Calmeyer 1993; Walser 1966).[35] And indeed, the one "Achaemenid bowl" in the collection for which chemical composition is known contains a percentage-copper alloy that is consistent with the values Zournatzi (2000) has proposed as a possible Achaemenid standard, suggesting yet again that the vessels tied their users to imperial systems of value and practice.[36] The vessels from the highland helped make possible the multidirectional silver flows that powered the material and symbolic economy of the empire. They imbricated their users in the cycles of tribute, gifting, royal redistribution, and imperial dependency on silver that materially reproduced the Achaemenid Empire.

FIGURE 31. Detail of the Darius Vase (source: Furtwängler 1909, plate 88).

Feasting with Delegates

The status of a thing as a delegate hinges on not its material properties alone, but also the practical mediations that such imperial things afford. In what way did silver vessels, like those from Erebuni and possibly elsewhere across the highland, also mediate, through direct somatic encounter, the practices that reproduced the sovereign prerogative to rule? It was through the institution of the feast that these nonhuman things made their own difference to the routines and rituals that sustained the Achaemenid polity. As with Achaemenid silver, much too has been written on the importance of the banquet in the practices and principles of Achaemenid kingship (e.g. Briant 1989; 2002: 286–297; Dusinberre 2013: 114–140; Gunter 1988: 22–30; Henkelman 2010)—ritual events involving the communal consumption of food and drink that conform in various respects to what Dietler (2001) has called "patron-role" and "diacritical" feasts. Like both modes of feasting, the Achaemenid royal banquet entailed "the maintenance of existing inequalities in power relations" (76). Royal feasts always involved the legitimation of the monarchic institution and attendant asymmetries in social and political relations. Such feasts, in accordance with the "patron-role feast," entailed excessive quantities of food and drink, and were premised not on equal reciprocation but on the reproduction of unequal patterns of hospitality. Consistent with the expectation of generosity that marked the "patron-role" feast, Achaemenid royal banquets entailed royal gifting to guests (nobles, foreign dignitaries, etc.) in the form of metal vessels (among other things) by "the king as omnipotent gift-giver," the consummate *magister* of Mauss's potlatch (Gunter and Root

1998; Sancisi-Weerdenburg 1989: 139). At the same time, the emphasis on style, through both differential cuisine and the use of luxury drinking vessels, more closely recalls Dietler's (2001: 85) "diacritical" feasts, in which styles of consumption serve as "a diacritical symbolic device to naturalize and reify concepts of ranked differences in the status of social orders or classes." As implements for the serving and consumption of wine—that most seminal lubricant of Achaemenid "commensal politics" (Dietler 2001)—vessels of gold and silver, including rhyta, *phialai,* amphorae, and deep bowls, were of such critical importance to enabling Achaemenid feasts and the sociopolitical relations they forged that, among Greek authors at least, "by the mid-fifth century the association of precious-metal wine-drinking vessels with the Persian elite had practically become a literary trope" (Dusinberre 2013: 118).

Also in keeping with Dietler's description of "diacritical" feasts, Achaemenid royal feasts were subject to emulation by those who "attempted elevation of status through representational means" (Dietler 2001: 86). Dusinberre (2013: 140) has especially focused on how privileged regional actors in Asia Minor replicated Achaemenid practices of commensality at the local level through both styles of action and the use of metal vessels that worked, in her view, to signify membership in the Achaemenid elite and thereby participate in "establishing, legitimating, and perpetuating imperial authority" (on Thrace, see Ebbinghaus 1999). It is indeed in Asia Minor that we find some of the best evidence for the styles of commensal politics established by the royal court and emulated by regional elites. Controlled and illicit tomb excavations in that region have yielded silver drinking bowls (both *phialai* and the deep variety), while visual depictions such as the relief frieze on the Nereid monument at Xanthos (figure 32), which shows a reclining banqueter at a drinking party holding a rhyton in one hand and a bowl in the other, inform the embodied performance of the feast (Ebbinghaus 2000). In Dusinberre's view (2013: 128 and passim), these practices were taken up in Asia Minor through deliberate manipulation on the part of imperial authorities. Mimetic feasting with glass and ceramic "copies" of the silver vessels (or what I discuss at length in chapter 6 as ceramic "proxies") occurred at a greater social remove from state actors.

To return, then, to the *dahyu* of Armenia, it is now clear that the silver bowls, rhyta, and amphorae from (or possibly from) the highland constitute imperial delegates on account of their material properties and the practical mediations they would have afforded in the conduct of elite feasting. The vessels would have enabled collective repasts that enforced modes of consumption in accordance with the norms of the Achaemenid banquet. The rhyta in particular imposed demands on their users that forced compliance with imperial practice. We have already seen how the rhyton called for a very particular manner of drinking: the spout at the front required a reveler to pour wine into a bowl or drink directly until the horn was empty, or else perhaps block the orifice with a finger until ready to serve. This

FIGURE 32. The Nereid Monument (© The Trustees of the British Museum).

unique kind of vessel placed unusual stipulations on its users, compelling them to continuously abide somatically by the requirements of the form (putting the vessel down when it was full would cause the liquid to spill out of the pouring hole). Rhyta allow little room for bricolage, for artful manipulations of use, but instead entrap users into prescribed embodied practices and enlist in this effort a wider assemblage of things, like jugs and bowls. The ritual meals in which these vessels were used presumably worked to define and naturalize privileged status and the exclusivity of the imperial elite, as well as to channel competition within such rarified circles on the Armenian highland (Dietler 2001: 86). In other words, to some extent, satrapal conditions of subjection were imposed through the work of these delegates, which conscripted highland actors to engage in Persian practices that reproduced their own subordination.

Silver Delegates and Imperial Ideology

Compared to their decisive role as mediators in the routines of Achaemenid commensal politics, less can be said at present concerning the work of silver vessels in sustaining the core principles that underlay Achaemenid sovereignty, another quality that determines a thing's status as a delegate. Gunter and Root (1998: 26–28) have made the point that dining and wine drinking in the Achaemenid court context would have incorporated cultic dimensions, and while the specifics elude us, they have suggested that the *phiale* in particular, with its floral forms, may in some way be connected with the realm of the paradise. Drawing on the work of Herbert Hoffmann (1989), Niccolò Manassero (2010: 247–250) has likewise probed the religious, specifically Zoroastrian, significance of the rhyton, in terms of the vessel's symbolic relation to kingship, libation, cosmic order, flowing liquids, fertility, and purity.

Here I suggest that the animal-handled amphorae may offer greater purchase on the links between Achaemenid feasting and the fundamental tenets of the

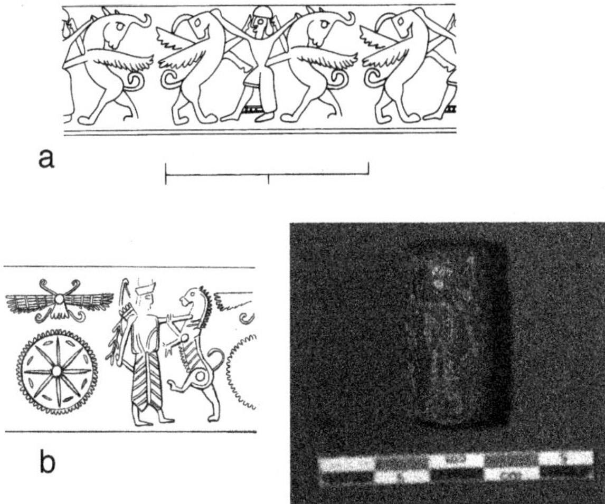

FIGURE 33. a. Collated line drawing of PFS 778 from the Persepolis Fortification Archive (source: Gunter and Root 2001, courtesy the Persepolis Seal Project and the Persepolis Fortification Archive Project); b. author's photograph of Horom seal and line drawing of sealing (courtesy of Stephan Kroll, drawing by Cornelie Wolff).

imperial politico-religious worldview. My interest here is in the tactile requirements of the two-handled silver vessel, the movements and muscle senses entailed in its use, which I propose may inform its capacity to intervene in forging dispositions of responsibility or affection toward the underlying political values that attached subjects to sovereigns. I arrive at this suggestion by way of Achaemenid glyptics, and one particularly prevalent theme within its iconographic repertoire, that of the "heroic encounter" (figure 33). Against the backdrop of its long and shifting life in western Asiatic glyptic, Mark Garrison and Margaret Root (2001) have carefully discerned the motif's social significance in the Achaemenid context. They define the heroic encounter as a scene in which "a protagonist exerts power or control over animals or creatures in a manner that explicitly transcends the plausible" (42). In one of its compositional formats (figure 33a), the motif entails a central male figure in direct physical engagement with animals on two sides, often through the seizure of the beasts' necks, heads or limbs.

The identity of the hero is, as Garrison and Root convincingly argue, deliberately ambiguous—only sometimes marked as royal, but more often intelligible generically as the "Persian Man" conjured in royal inscriptions (Root 1979: 305). The "Persian Man" was a potent and potentially inclusive ideological construct that cued a masculine ideal to which many males could likely relate, given the antiquity and wide distribution of the heroic-encounter theme. It was thus also one to which they could (or should) aspire (Garrison and Root 2001: 57). It is the

"Persian Man" who bears the burden of assisting the kings in their struggle to constitute proper sovereignty, as we learn from the poetic metaphor of a warrior on Darius's tomb at Naqsh-i Rustam: "the spear of a Persian man has gone forth far." Indeed, it is with spear in hand that we see one such "Persian Man" on a cylinder seal recovered near the Iron 2–3 site of Horom, to the west of Tsaghkahovit (figure 33b). Although the compositional format of the heroic-encounter theme in this instance differs from the image of heroic control that is of most relevance to the present discussion (figure 33a), this seal from Armenia, very likely a delegate in its own right, would have done its part in extending the ideals behind the "Persian Man" into the Caucasus.[37] Familiarity with the heroic encounter imagery as well as, likely, its sociopolitical associations is also indicated by a seal of similar composition from nearby Vardadzor, on the southwest shore of Lake Sevan (Karapetyan 2003: fig. 54.53).

The gesture entailed in the images of heroic control depicted on a seal like the one in figure 33a is consonant with that afforded by the animal-handled amphora, whose use demands the single-handed grasp of one or both sides of a leaping beastly body. Across these two thingly domains of image and object there is a "coherence" that reinforces and perhaps co-constitutes their mutual conceptual and practical entanglements (Hodder 2012). The violation of natural scale (that is, the diminutive size of the animal relative to the human who grips it) is inconsequential for this interpretation, for both the seals and the vessels portray or require a gesture of physical engagement with the beasts that transcends the plausible. Taken on their own, then, the vessels may be seen to invoke an immanence just before the domination of prey—an anticipatory moment that can be played out again and again before each seizure of the handles to pour the next round. Through the practice of conspicuous consumption, the vessels could have allowed the individual's transfiguration into the "Persian Man," an identity that takes hold as he takes hold of the handles that provide for his metamorphosis into the hero of a dangerous encounter, and the ideal male subject.

Insofar as the heroism of the hunt is what brings the zoological abundance of the paradise into being, it is tempting to speculate that the "vessels of heroic encounter" once again cohere with the themes of the paradise, though this is conjectural. We might also suppose that attendant to the privilege of becoming a "Persian Man" was an obligation in turn *to protect* the abundance that the wine-filled amphora embodies, just as scenes of hero-encounter in other media (seals and monumental sculpture) are tied in various ways to protection, whether of commodities or spaces (Garrison and Root 2001: 58). The "Persian Man" who comes into being in the grasping of the vessel assumes in return the responsibility to safeguard its contents from danger or unauthorized use and, by extension, perhaps to safeguard the cosmological project in whose name the bounty of the grape has been harvested. Users on the highlands who engaged with the silver zoomorphic amphorae were, I suggest, bound up in reproducing affects of care toward the core imperial values that orbited around the "Persian Man."

ARCHITECTURAL PROXIES

Two seemingly incompatible interpretations emerge from the comparative survey analysis and the silver delegates. The former, I suggested above, points to the repudiation of the complex polity at the regional scale, a turning away from both the spatial technologies of the fallen Urartian kingdom and the long arm of the contemporary Achaemenid Empire. The latter, I have just concluded, worked effectively to create a class of regional elites who in some measure complied with the norms of Achaemenid political culture. It may be tempting to hypothesize, on the basis of these seemingly opposed phenomena, a deep sociological division, whereby a privileged few—the paradigmatic local collaborators on which so many empires have relied—opted in, while the highland public tried to opt out. But a return to the columned halls of the *dahyu* suggests that architectural proxies do not permit such a comfortable resolution.

It is no coincidence that at least one of the sites to which we now turn is spatially associated with the silver delegates. The fortress of Erebuni, discussed at length in the previous chapter, came to host a columned hall sometime in the late seventh century or soon thereafter. Along with the halls at Nush-i Jan and Godin Tepe, the Erebuni hall would be taken captive by the Achaemenids and provide the rudimentary template for the empire's most salient architectural delegates (figure 18, p. 98). A reasonable *terminus post quem* for the abandonment of Erebuni would correlate with the latest vessel in the silver hoard discussed above, which is to say the third quarter of the fourth century B.C.[38]

The second site relevant to this discussion is the small hilltop fortress of Altıntepe, located on the Erzincan Plain (map 2, p. 86). It lies approximately 100 km south of the Bayburt Plain, discussed in the comparative survey analysis as an area of active settlement during the Iron 3 period, and possibly a destination for groups migrating into the area (Khatchadourian 2008: 360–364). Altıntepe sits atop a steep, conical mound that rises up at the eastern end of the plain (Özgüç 1966, 1969). During the Iron Age, it hosted three periods of occupation. After an initial Urartian phase, the site was reconstructed in a second Urartian phase, which is marked by a temple surrounded by colonnades, a temenos wall and ancillary storerooms, a structure to the south (perhaps a hall of two rows of columns), tombs, and a buttressed fortification wall. During the third phase, a columned hall was built atop the earlier structure to the south of the temenos (figure 34). The hall was made of thick mud-brick walls stacked atop a stone socle. Eighteen wooden beams set on poorly finished round stone bases supported the structure's roof. Access to this space (44 × 25.30 m) was afforded through an entrance in the

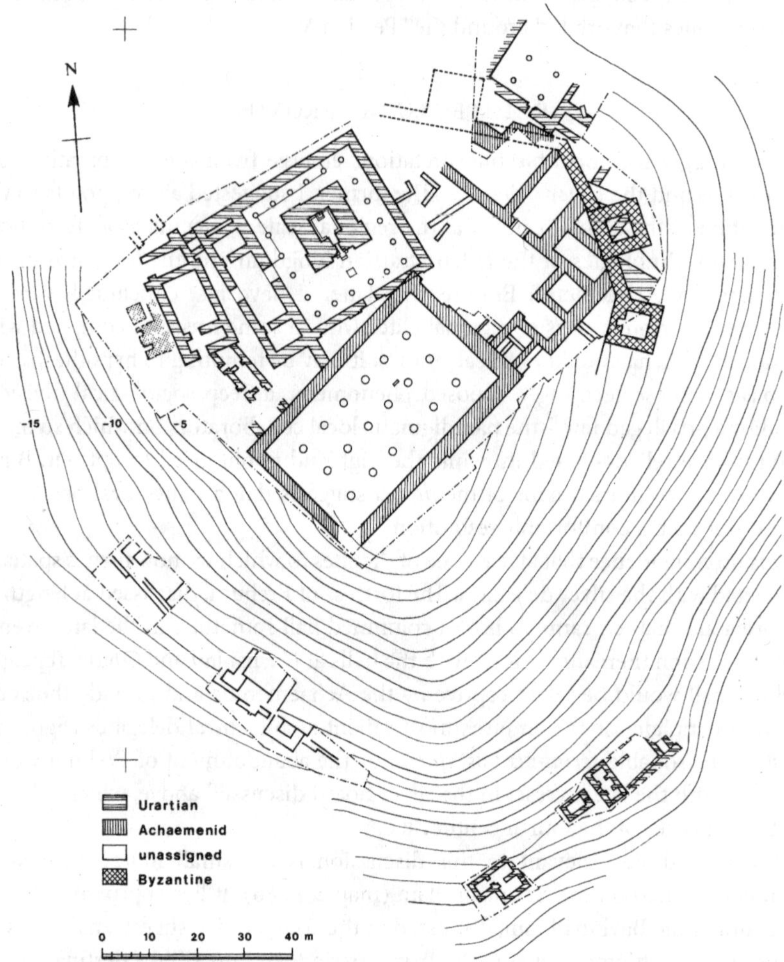

FIGURE 34. Site plan of Altıntepe (courtesy of Geoff Summers; source: Summers 1993, fig. 2, redrawn from Özgüç 1966, pl. VI).

east. Apart from a hearth in the hall's northeastern quadrant, there were no preserved fixed architectural features; however, fresco fragments were found on the floor of the hall (Özgüç 1966: 47–58). The dating of this third phase is a matter of debate in the specialist literature; for the time being, I regard the hall at Altıntepe as one built only after the Achaemenids had already taken captive this highland architectural innovation and transformed it into a delegate of paramount efficacy in the reproduction of imperial sovereignty (see chapter 4).[39] Some have suggested a possible linkage between the hall at Altıntepe and the silver vessels said to be from "near Erzincan" (Simpson et al. 2010: 438; Summers 1993: 93). While this is of course only speculation, the two forms of evidence do point to different patterns of sociopolitical activity that would seem to be reserved for the *dahyu*'s more privileged actors.

By the late sixth century B.C. the columned halls at Erebuni and Altıntepe would have shared a definite affiliation with the political landscapes of the Achaemenid heartland (see chapter 4).[40] After being taken captive in the early decades of the Achaemenid project, the highland halls were invariably repositioned within the universe of the empire's nonhuman architectural participants. Now analogous to a distinctly imperial built form, halls such as those at Erebuni and Altıntepe took on the role of representatives of the material delegates in Persepolis and Susa.[41] Indeed, it is the very architectonic analogy between the halls of Fars and Khuzistan and the *dahyu* that long led scholars to typologically and chronologically situate the latter in an Achaemenid frame of reference.

In chapter 3 we learned that proxies are involved in the work of political representation, and that such work emerges out of assignments to act that derive from both human and nonhuman sources. Rather than standing in for a person, a material proxy stands in for one or more things, and if "loyal" in its effects, it faithfully reproduces the practical affordances and semiotic mediations of the delegate for which it substitutes. In the case of Erebuni and Altıntepe, viewing the halls as dutiful proxies would mean understanding them as locales for the efficacious replication, on a more modest scale, of the political routines and religio-political claims linked to the delegate halls of the heartland. We would speak of the halls as venues for audience, for hierarchical relations between superiors and inferiors, for (as some have) the activities of ruling satraps of the *dahyu* (Sagona 2004: 313; Summers 1993: 96; Ter-Martirosov 2001: 160; 2005a: 50). Yet when conceptualizing imperial matter, I argued that proxies invariably "share in or take power from the represented" (Taussig 1993: 2), potentially leading to the slow erosion of those powers. And they can go even further than this, becoming unruly vis-à-vis the material delegates they represent. I discussed three opportunities for slippage that inform whether proxies can be said to be rapscallion siblings to their delegate partners. One of these pertained to the company that proxies keep, or the immediate assemblage of humans and things with which they collaborate in the production of social life. Site formation processes coupled with the methods of excavation at both Erebuni and Altıntepe prohibit a consideration of this factor, as we remain in the dark about the object assemblages once associated with these buildings. Yet it is nevertheless possible to assess the opportunities for roguery on the basis of the halls' material properties and the human designs that may have surrounded their construction and use. Doing so will cast doubt on the interpretation of these halls as effective representatives of their distant delegates.

The Erebuni and Altıntepe halls entangled their builders and users in rather different material webs than did their counterparts in Fars and Khuzistan. For instance, the socles of both buildings were made of local andesite blocks, a volcanic rock with a deep history of use as a building material on the highland, and one quite different from the gravel-and-shingle foundations and the gigantic limestone slabs that underlay the mud-brick walls of Susa and Pasargadae, respectively. A further deviation at both sites is the stone used for the bases. In the case of Erebuni, the bases were made of thick slabs of tuff, a type of rock, formed from volcanic ash, that is readily available in southern Caucasia, while at Altıntepe, andesite bases from the earlier Urartian constructions were reused.[42] Neither of these materials, andesite or tuff, figures in the columned halls of the heartland. These are not materials that entrapped the most privileged agents of empire into relations of dependence, and the viability of imperial sovereignty was in no way contingent on their extraction and regulation. While the halls of both regions required the regular maintenance of mud-brick superstructures and wooden beams, these two materials were long in use on the highland, and thus imposed no new dependencies, just as the stones used in the halls of the *dahyu* merely resituated users within continuing relations of reliance on local masons already skilled at working the locally available materials. As I argued in chapter 3, the differing relational properties of delegates and proxies between their chemical composition and the human groups they entrap give rise to a potential for proxies to bend the rules, by virtue of their very material constitution.

For the case at hand, perhaps the most compelling evidence for the roguery of the highland proxies relates to the human designs that account for their built forms. We may note, for instance, the numerous formal and architectonic deviations from the major columned halls of the imperial heartland: their occurrence in rectangular versus square plans (not seen in any of the major halls of Fars after Cyrus and perhaps Cambyses), the absence of porticoes and corner towers, the limited number of points of entry, the significantly diminished scale, the use of roughly finished columned bases, and, not least, the siting of the halls atop fortified hills rather than on open plains. At Erebuni, users during the Achaemenid era maintained the original seventh-century form that is best associated with the halls at Godin and Nush-i Jan. Even more notably, at Altıntepe, builders and users replicated the more "archaic," distinctly highland features of hypostyle construction. In both cases, there are few indications of earnest efforts at imperial emulation, but instead an allegiance to the hypostyle hall as originally instantiated in the highland during the eighth and seventh centuries B.C.

Ambiguity remains, however, for we cannot speak here of a politics of resistance or rejection. In light of early Achaemenid acts of captivation, the materiality of the halls and the practices they afforded could have been consonant with both highland and heartland political values, even despite differences in material, design, and the topographic siting of the buildings. That is, the very same features that had once, during earlier centuries, enabled practices of political association conjured as an alternative to political complexity—namely, the denial of frontal orientation through a relentlessly symmetrical forest of columns and the affordance of participatory indoor congregation, undirected movement of traffic, and unfixed patterns of interaction—were now also compatible with an Achaemenid worldview. That worldview had transformed the columned hall into a venue for the performance of monarchical authority and a material instantiation of the hierarchical compact between sovereigns and subjects (see chapter 4).

What I would like to suggest, then, is that the ambiguity surrounding the highland halls during the mid-first millennium B.C. may be less (or at least not only) a function of a fragmentary archaeological record than the very work of crafty "secondary consumption" and the tactical arts of "making do" that make for unruly proxies (Certeau 1984). The users of the halls could have preserved the distinctly highland political practices that first took shape in the pre-Achaemenid period, in just the same way as the buildings preserved highland materials and architectural forms. Indeed, in this work the halls themselves were material accomplices, inviting human efforts at gentle play in the arts of consumption. Yet at the same time users to some degree remained within bounds, conforming to expected norms of political association by operating within a built landscape that had become, by this time, quintessential to the Achaemenid political project. The latter they did not only by adopting a spatial idiom that would have been deemed highly appropriate to imperial agents, but also by partaking, with silver bowls, rhyta and the like, in empire-wide elite institutions of commensality. Greater clarity is not to be had here, *in part,* I suggest, because clarity was not on offer in the interior of an imperial province that increasingly appears to exemplify what Scott (2009: 7) called an "intermediate zone," neither fully within nor outside the empire, a zone in which a sociopolitics of conformity and autonomy could coexist. The question that inevitably arises from the recognition of the fragility of sovereignty in the *dahyu* is: What might an imperial response to such conditions of ambiguity look like? That is, what architectural delegates could be tasked to more effectively advance the making of acquiescent subjects?

ARCHITECTURAL DELEGATES

It is at the northern frontier of the *dahyu* that we see the clearest evidence for an imperial response to the frailty of sovereignty on the highland. In turning in this last section to today's northwestern Azerbaijan, it would seem, according to the discursive tropes of the Achaemenid cartographic imaginary, that we are approaching the edges of their known world. And yet, it turns out that these edges were in fact remarkably porous boundaries. Archaeological evidence indicates in no uncertain terms that communities of the mountains and the temperate grasslands residing beyond the Kura River valley engaged with the imperial polity to their south through the regular traffic of things and associated aesthetic sensibilities. From the Dnieper basin in the west to the Altai region in the east—and with a particular concentration in the south Urals—excavated burial mounds have revealed objects that Mikhail Treister has termed "Achaemenid," "Achaemenid-inspired," or in the "Achaemenid style": seals and sealings, elaborate silver and gold vessels (e.g. rhyta and bowls), jewelry (e.g. torques and bracelets), and weapons (e.g. a knife and sword—Fedoseev 1997; Treister 2010, 2014; Treister and Yablonsky 2012). Closer to the presumed frontier itself, in regions of modern Georgia north of the Kura River, researchers have uncovered wealthy burials (in most cases postdating the Iron 3 period), including the well-known Akhalgori and Kazbegi hoards, containing heirloomed Achaemenid silver vessels as well as other local finery of gold, glass, and pottery in distinctively Achaemenid styles (Knauss 2005, 2006). The northward flows of objects across the mountains and into the steppe thus plainly point to a permeable frontier, routinely penetrated through patterns of interaction that likely included a combination of gift exchanges, trades, and raids. Indeed, the possibility of lucrative interactions across this frontier may partly explain the hypothesized northern movement of settlement activity in the highland during the mid-first millennium B.C. Ijevan and Tsaghkahovit are the two surveyed regions that lie closest to the northern frontier, and it is in these regions where we saw the arrival or intensification of settlement activity.

It is also in these northeasterly regions of southern Caucasia, at the edges of the *dahyu* of Armenia or of Media, that we find the clearest case of an Achaemenid architectural delegate anywhere outside the imperial heartland, at the site of Karačamirli.[43] The recently discovered settlement is located in the Šamkir District of modern northwestern Azerbaijan, at the confluence of the Kura River and its southern tributary, the Shamkirchay (Babaev et al. 2007; Babaev and Knauss 2010; Babaev et al. 2009; Knauss et al. 2010, 2013). Ongoing investigations have uncovered a spacious compound consisting of a large rectangular enclosure (450 × 425 m) detected through geophysical survey. At the center of the enclosure, on the level hill of Gurban Tepe, are the remains of a large plastered mud-brick building (65.50 × 62.90 m) marked by a columned hall (figure 35). The hall was entered though a portico in the east and surrounded on the remaining three sides with subsidiary columned rooms (Knauss et al. 2013). The building's mud-brick walls, whose component blocks conformed in their dimensions to Achaemenid standards (14), rested atop a gravel foundation. At 27 by 27 meters, the columned hall at Karačamirli is just under half the size of Darius's hall at Susa. The hall's roof was supported by six rows of six wooden columns, which rested on limestone bases in the form of a circular torus on a square doubled-stepped plinth. In addition

FIGURE 35. Columned hall, Gurban Tepe complex, Karačamirli (created by Matthias Guette and Florian Knauss, courtesy of Florian Knauss).

to these bases, which are formally comparable to limestone column bases from Persepolis and Susa, found in situ in two rooms of the west wing were bell-shaped bases that also mirror bases from the heartland sites and happen to measure 52 cm in diameter, a Persian royal cubit (15). Notably, the interval between the rows of

FIGURE 36. Reconstruction of Karačamirli (created by Tobias Bitterer, Ferdinand Haschner, and Florian Knauss, courtesy of Florian Knauss).

columns in the hall is not uniform, such that there exists a slightly pronounced central aisle that leads from the doorway to a platform against the western wall. On the whole, the structure on the central hill of Guban Tepe resembles in plan the Palace of Xerxes at Persepolis, with its central hall, single portico, and surrounding colonnaded rooms. According to Knauss and colleagues, the building is best understood as a palatial complex that conjoined activities of residence, administration, and audience, overseen by a Persian official appointed to these northern limits of the empire.

In direct alignment with Gurban Tepe, atop a small mound that falls along the course of the eastern perimeter wall, excavations have revealed a large mud-brick building (figure 36) measuring 22 by 23 meters and consisting of three columned areas (two porticoes and a central hall), flanked symmetrically on the north and south by long and narrow rooms (Babaev et al. 2007; Knauss et al. 2010). The bell-shaped limestone column bases carried wooden columns and capitals that supported a flat roof estimated to have reached a height of around 6 meters. The overall architectural design suggests that the structure was a gate, or *propyleion,* and its closest formal parallel is the tripylon gate at Persepolis. Between the *propyleion* and Gurban Tepe, and indeed in most of the area surrounding the central mound, the apparent absence of built remains suggests to the excavators an open, garden space or "paradise" akin to the one at Pasargadae and, perhaps at one time, Persepolis (see chapter 4; Knauss et al. 2013: 19).

The details of the stonework, the dimensions and regularity of the mud bricks, the use of gravel foundations, the square plan of the hall, the overall plan of the gate, and the possible presence of an expansive garden suggest that Karačamirli was the work of designers and craftspersons deeply familiar with architectural canons and techniques elaborated at the imperial centers in the heartland. Corroborating this view is the utter absence of comparable traditions in the Kura River region prior to the sixth century B.C. Based on ceramics as well as architectural parallels with Persepolis, the investigators date the founding of Karačamirli to the reign of Xerxes or his successor, Artaxerxes I, which is to say, some time during the fifth century B.C., after 486.

What makes the complex at Karačamirli a delegate? With regard to its material properties, the columned hall (and associated buildings) reproduced the same dependencies as those that ensnared imperial agents in Khuzistan and Fars. The hall's users and builders at Karačamirli, just like those at Susa and Persepolis, shared a common reliance on gravel, limestone, timber, and mud brick—and on craftspersons with the skills necessary to acquire and work them in accordance with imperial measures and formal templates. The maintenance of the hall at Karačamirli, just as at the heartland sites, would therefore have imposed the same obligations of care. In its material constitution, the columned hall on Karačamirli's Gurban Tepe is the clearest conceivable case of an architectural delegate outside of the imperial heartland.

In terms of its mediating role in the practices of political association, the hall enabled collective gathering less in the tradition of the congregation (as at Erebuni and Altıntepe) and more in accordance with the sovereign's requirements for audience and ceremonial reception, as had been the case for the columned halls of the heartland since Darius. It is in this regard that the defined central aisle inside the hall, which is oriented toward the raised platform in the western wall, is particularly notable. Also in keeping with the halls of Pasargadae, Susa, and Persepolis, the Karačamirli hall's columns worked, in assemblage with the probable surrounding garden, to realize the exalted cosmological aspirations of the Achaemenid establishment that I discussed in the previous chapter. That is, the columns here collaborated with those of southwestern Iran to uphold the edifice of empire and recreate a small refuge where Ahuramazda's original creation could endure, uncorrupted by the pernicious Lie. Significantly, the columned hall at Karačamirli produced these effects on an imperial frontier, where it was poised as the material vanguard against the unknown world that lay beyond the Achaemenid dynasty's (and hence Ahuramazda's) putatively just embrace.

The excavators of Karačamirli have described the site as a case of "imitatio regis" (Knauss et al. 2013: 26). But its buildings are in no way mimetic, least of all the columned hall. Rather, by virtue of the material dependencies it put in place, the practical affordances of its use, and its complicity in sustaining the political and cosmological values critical to Achaemenid imperial sovereignty, the Karačamirli hall is in every respect an archetypical delegate that shared in the prerogatives of imperial sovereignty with its human creators and architectural partners in southwestern Iran. The hall and associated complex no doubt created conditions of compromised sovereignty among communities in the Kura River basin and surrounding regions. The building would have required the conscription of local labor and the exploitation of local resources for its construction and maintenance. It quite possibly facilitated the collection of taxes.[44] And it undoubtedly transformed the lived experience of a landscape that had never before witnessed such monumentality or participated in the attendant institutions of power.[45]

CONCLUSION

Let us now return to where this chapter began, to questions of evasion in the mountains in response to the designs of distant imperial sovereigns. Rephrased in terms of the logics of satrapal conditions, we return to assessing the role of things in forging both the experience and the limits of imperial sovereignty in this *dahyu.* In chapter 1, I explained that, in one of two senses, an inquiry into satrapal conditions fixes its gaze on the interventions of *things* as efficacious participants in the distributed work of aspirational sovereignty. In this sense, the satrapal condition is concerned with the ongoing, everyday making of acquiescent subjects who, like the atlas figures on the Achaemenid reliefs, "uphold" the imperial project through imposed, encouraged, or even chosen entanglements with things that, to varying degrees, transform habits, persons, and political and social lives. The delegate silver vessels entangled their users in empire-wide material dependencies of the Achaemenid elite, and afforded practices surrounding the consumption of food and drink that were inextricably tied to the royal court. They worked to produce privileged actors with sufficient commitment to the imperial project to ensure that the *dahyu* met the crown's annual tribute obligations. Likewise, the columned hall at Karačamirli extended into the Caucasus political practices of public gatherings that brought sovereigns and subjects face to face, and the associated principles of collaborative hegemony. This architectural delegate would have, through its own material capacities, transformed the lived experience of the Kura region, calling on local communities to work, gather, and contribute in the name of the crown.

However, the satrapal condition is not exhausted by experiences of subjection, but refers as well to the inherent limitations on imperial sovereignty that arise from the inevitable dependencies on the practical action and material entanglements of its subjects. The evidence may be threadbare, but it is sufficient to discern that the "people of the hills" also had their say in establishing the limits of sovereign prerogative in the *dahyu* even after the Achaemenid "enclosure movement" (Scott 2009: 4) to integrate and control the Armenian highland was underway. The tentative picture that emerged from the analysis of regional settlement patterns suggested a movement away from the spaces of former Urartian power and possibly a northward movement away from the reach of imperial controls. Consistent with these efforts were those of the proxy halls at Erebuni and Altıntepe, which, in their conformity to the seventh-century buildings of the highlands, worked together with their human users to uphold local political values developed in the preconquest period that were premised on the repudiation of strictly hierarchical figurations of political authority. They helped forge a *dahyu* that was, judging by all available archaeological evidence, uninterested in, if not averse to, the technologies of imperial governance. The proxy halls enabled local leaders to act differently, but within bounds, to incorporate old ways of being and governing into the new. Analogies between highland and heartland spatial practices could have allowed the subtle attenuation of effective imperial rule, as the halls enabled everyday forms of semi-autonomous action that were most immediately consistent with the "localized forms of sovereignty" (Humphrey 2004: 420, 435) of the recent past. The halls played a part in the workings of regulated autonomy on the highland, in negotiating the quiet bargains that made Achaemenid imperial hegemony possible and fragile at one and the same time.

There is reason to think the Achaemenid sovereigns were uncertain whether they would get the better end of those bargains. In the fifth century B.C., king Xerxes ordered that an inscription be placed high on a rock cliff on the southern façade of the fortress at Tushpa, former capital of the Urartian kingdom, on the eastern shore of Lake Van (figure 37). The text was carved on a blank niche chiseled into the precipice by his father, Darius. It reads:

> *A great god is Ahuramazda, the greatest of the gods, who created this earth, who created yonder sky, who created man, created happiness for man, who made Xerxes king, one king of many, one lord of many.*
>
> *I (am) Xerxes, the great king, king of kings, king of all kinds of people, king on this earth far and wide, the son of Darius the king, the Achaemenid.*
>
> *Xerxes the great king proclaims: King Darius, my father, by the favour of Ahuramazda, made much that is good, and this niche*[46] *he ordered to be cut; as he did not have an inscription written, then I ordered that this inscription be written.*
>
> *Me may Ahuramazda protect, together with the gods, and my kingdom and what I have done.* (Kuhrt 2007: 301)

In political terms, the Tushpa inscription served to "rebrand" Tushpa's mountain bluff as a landscape of submission to a foreign power. In carving the niche and inscription at this fortress, the heart of the former Urartian Empire, Darius and Xerxes were making a claim on the foundations of authority that had long prevailed in the region, now remade as a *dahyu* of empire. But there can be little doubt, this was not a monument meant for mere mortals. Its location on the high craggy tor made it difficult to see, and in a region with virtually no trace of literacy, it would have, in any event, been unintelligible to most observers.[47] What calls for

FIGURE 37. Xerxes inscription at Tushpa (courtesy of Paul Zimansky).

our attention, therefore, is the cosmological connotation of the text. Why would the kings have placed such an encomium to Ahuramazda—surely the intended audience of the inscription—in *this* of all *dahyāva?* This chapter's account of the major delegates and proxies from Armenia helps explain Xerxes's pious entreaty for divine support. For it suggests that the mountainous *dahyu*—a land that substantially constituted the imperial interior even as it marked the empire's porous northern frontier—was, at least in the time of Xerxes, a place where Ahuramazda's protection in realizing the aspirations of Achaemenid sovereignty *was still very much in need.*

6

Going Underground

Affiliates, Proxies, and Delegates at Tsaghkahovit

As the British archaeologist and diplomat Austin Henry Layard observed during his journey through Ottoman Anatolia in 1849, even the most ordinary constituents of the material world can play a part in the making of satrapal conditions. While passing through the governorate of Erzurum on his overland travels from the Black Sea port of Trebizond to Mosul (where he would resume his famed excavations at Nineveh), Layard encountered a number of humble mountain villages whose peculiar style of vernacular architecture caught his attention. He described the dwellings as "low hovels, mere holes in the hill-side, and the common refuge of man, poultry, and cattle" (Layard 1859: 12). Later European travelers also remarked on these curious abodes that dotted the landscape in villages across the Armenian highland. The distinctive houses were often likened to "ant-hills" or "small mud volcanoes" (Lynch 1901: 165; Tozer 1881: 287) because of their characteristic earthen domed roofs, left open at the top for light and ventilation (figure 38). Layard was particularly attuned to the political significance of these humble, semi-subterranean human and animal havens. They "cannot be seen from any distance," he noted, so thoroughly were they concealed in the natural landscape. And not only did the "hovels" provide natural camouflage, they were also "purposely built away from the road to escape the unwelcome visits of traveling government officers and marching troops" (Layard 1859: 12). The "ant-hills" were also like pitfalls that could snare unsuspecting outsiders: "It is not uncommon," Layard wrote, "for a traveller to receive the first intimation of his approach to a village by finding his horse's fore feet down a chimney, and himself taking his place unexpectedly in the family circle through the roof." In this remote corner of the Ottoman Empire, the people of the villages conspired with the earth itself to impose limits on the reach

FIGURE 38. Houses with lantern roofs, Hasköy, Muş, in 1980 (courtesy of Akın Günkut).

of imperial surveillance and control. Later ethnographies of Armenian village life also give voice to the sociopolitics of the semi-subterranean habitats that, however modestly, afforded a measure of community protection and enabled a politics of evasion (Lisitsyan 1955; Villa and Matossian 1982).

This chapter charts the conditions and conditionals of empire in a single mountain village of the Armenian *dahyu,* and the differential and intertwined work of both humans and things in their production. The resolution of the analysis is higher than in the previous two chapters, as we home in on human–material confederacies at work in semi-subterranean domestic spaces at the settlement of Tsaghkahovit in north-central Armenia. The earth-sheltered dwellings that Layard and others encountered on their travels through what were—over two millennia before—the lands of Achaemenid Armenia represent a remarkably enduring human–material entanglement in a highland region long swept up in vicissitudes of imperial power. The great antiquity of such lantern-roof houses, as they are sometimes called, has long been known, thanks to a terse ethnographic description of highland vernacular architecture by the Greek historian Xenophon, who passed through the region on his long march through the Achaemenid Empire at the end of the fifth century B.C.[1] But nine seasons of systematic excavation conducted at Tsaghkahovit between 1998 and 2013 have exposed for the first time, and in considerable detail, the practices that such underground havens made possible in the northern reaches of the *dahyu.* The findings from Tsaghkahovit provide a rare glimpse into the everyday work of affiliates, proxies, and delegates in a single village of Achaemenid Armenia.[2] They offer a much-needed corrective to the constricted vision of Achaemenid archaeology, long focused narrowly on prominent royal centers, urban settlements, and elite residences and palaces (Khatchadourian 2012). The first section of this chapter provides an orientation to the site, reviewing matters of chronology, economy, and daily life in order to establish a context for the analysis of satrapal conditions.

ORIENTATION TO TSAGHKAHOVIT

In the analysis of highland settlement patterns discussed in the previous chapter, we saw that the Tsaghkahovit Plain—a small, high-elevation plateau bounded on the south by the soaring peaks of Mt. Aragats (4,090 m above sea level), on the west by Mt. Kolgat (2,474 m above sea level), and on the northeast by the slopes of the Pambak Range—was one of the few regions in the *dahyu* with clear evidence for newly arriving populations during the mid-first millennium B.C. (map 4).[3] The return of settled life on a substantial scale took place after a prolonged period of abandonment, initiated by the violent destruction during the twelfth century B.C. of a number of Late Bronze Age (LBA) fortresses that had been built atop the lofty summits of the plain.[4] The demise of the LBA fortresses marked the end of the earliest iteration of political complexity on the highland, in which the fortress had stood as an iconic settlement form.[5] For at least five hundred years, the Tsaghkahovit Plain appears to have lain vacant. When new populations returned, sometime during the late seventh century B.C., they gravitated with unmistakable regularity to the dilapidated remains of the LBA fortresses. To varying degrees, regional survey conducted in 1998 and 2000 revealed evidence for Iron 3 activity in or near at least seven (if not eight) of the ten documented LBA fortresses, while turning up no evidence for Iron 3 settlement in dissociation from an earlier fortress site (Smith et al. 2009). The firm predisposition toward these LBA fortresses signals the traces of enduring, preexisting highland traditions that preserved certain spatial practices as essential to the putting down of new roots (Khatchadourian 2008).

However, the relationship between an LBA past and an Iron Age present is not reducible to a mere mimicking of old traditions. Simultaneous with the revitalization of the fortress was a refiguring of the spatial logics of social life, judging by the evidence from at least two of the sites, Tsaghkahovit and Hnaberd, where surface architecture (dated on the basis of both survey materials and excavation) attests to Iron 3 settlements that fanned out from the base of the fortresses into the surrounding foothills (figure 39). Nestled amid undulating terrain on a spur of Mt. Aragats, Tsaghkahovit is the largest and best-preserved fortress site that boasts both LBA and Iron 3 occupations, and therefore has been the main target of excavations to date. Dominating the site is an imposing fortress, which sits atop a conical volcanic outcrop (2,183 m above sea level) that rises 80 meters above the surrounding plain (figure 40). The Iron 3 settlement spreads out from the base of the outcrop to the south and east, while further to the east is a substantial LBA

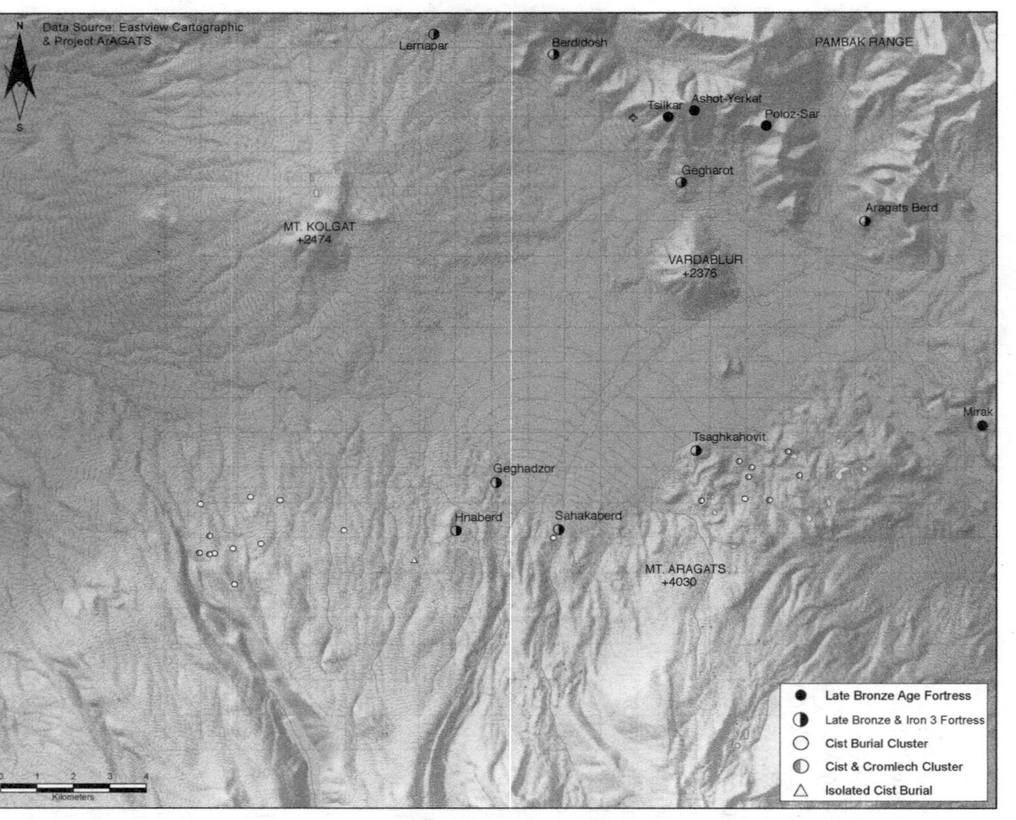

MAP 4. The Tsaghkahovit Plain, showing results of regional survey (Adam T. Smith and Lori Khatchadourian).

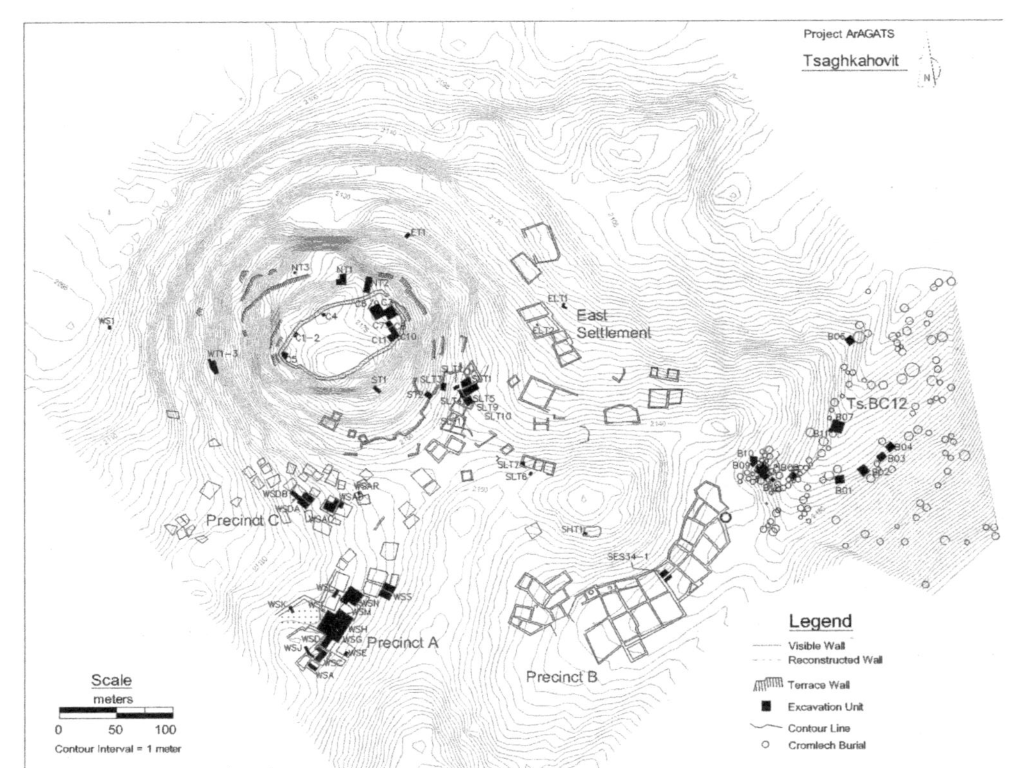

FIGURE 39. Site plan of Tsaghkahovit (courtesy of Project ArAGATS, created by Adam T. Smith).

FIGURE 40. A view of the Tsaghkahovit fortress from the plain below (author's photograph).

cemetery of "cromlech" burials. It is at this site that we have the clearest understanding of the timing and nature of an architectural reformulation that appears to have inverted the ordering of social life from fortress summits, the central pivot of social life during the LBA, to semi-subterranean shelters.

Excavations across Tsaghkahovit testify to a substantial reoccupation in most areas of the site, likely in the last third of the seventh century B.C.[6] The LBA citadel itself was reused, yet the nature of this reuse suggests that the fortress lost the status it had once held as the prime spatial location for practices of political authority. The reoccupation is marked by the reconstruction of the fortress wall, albeit using a more modest masonry style than the prior LBA wall, with its massive cyclopean blocks. Internally, the Iron 3 inhabitants evinced a thoroughgoing disinterest in the monumental space created by the ruins of a large LBA building in favor of a disarticulated internal arrangement of rooms (figure 41).[7] The opportunistic partitioning of the pre-existing, readily available monumental structure, and the general absence of a new kind of large-scale architecture within the citadel during the Iron 3 period, conspire to cast doubt on the capacity of the fortress to have served as an effective base from which to project authority, cultivate awe, or naturalize a right to rule.[8]

Beyond the fortress, surface architecture of the lower settlement points to two neatly clustered complexes, each made up of a compact nucleation of rooms,

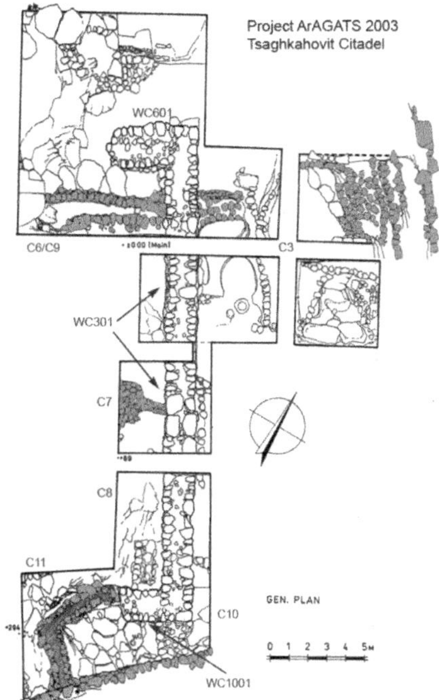

FIGURE 41. Plan of the Tsaghkahovit citadel showing architecture of the Late Bronze Age and (in gray) Iron 3 (courtesy of Project ArAGATS, drawing by Hasmik Sargsyan).

situated at some distance from the base of the fortress to the south and southeast (Precinct A and Precinct B). A third area is marked by the disarticulated array of room blocks that immediately hug the base of the fortress in an arc from the east to the southwest (Precinct C). It is only in the area to the east of the fortress that investigations have exposed the remains of substantial LBA activity outside the confines of the citadel (Badalyan et al. forthcoming; Badalyan et al. 2008; Lindsay 2006), yet parts of this area were repurposed into domestic spaces during the Iron 3 period.

Targeted research into the Iron 3 period at Tsaghkahovit has centered on Precinct A and the room blocks of Precinct C that lie due south of the citadel (figure 42).[9] Stratigraphy and radiocarbon dates indicate that both areas were occupied without discernable hiatuses after their initial establishment, until the site's abandonment. The date of abandonment is uncertain, but may provisionally be estimated as the late fifth or early fourth century B.C.[10] Precinct A is a well-preserved, agglutinative structure of interconnected rooms whose spatial regularity and integrated architectonics give the impression of purposeful planning (figure 43).[11] In contrast, spatial arrangements in Precinct C appear comparably haphazard, with little apparent investment in creating a homogeneous arrangement of structures.[12] The units here either stand alone, or cluster in pairs of two

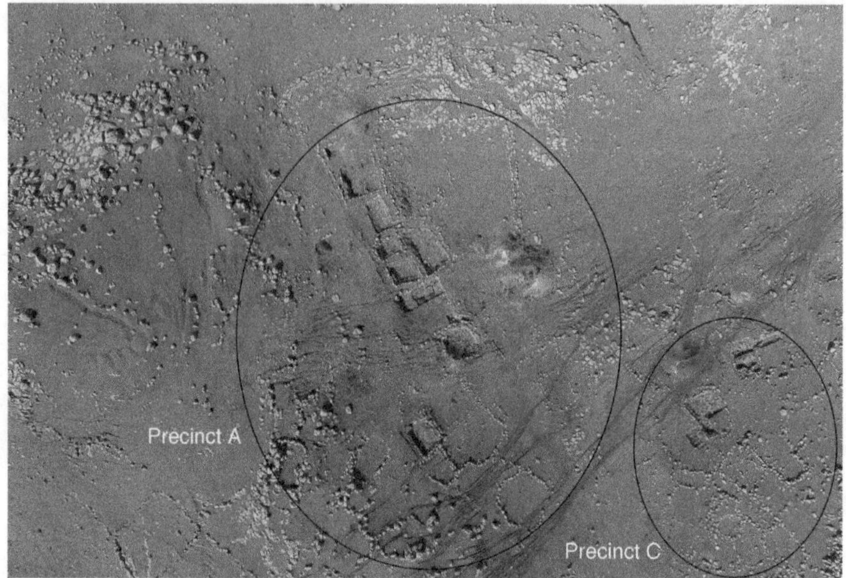

FIGURE 42. Aerial view of the Tsaghkahovit Iron 3 settlement (photograph by Ian Lindsay, courtesy of Project ArAGATS).

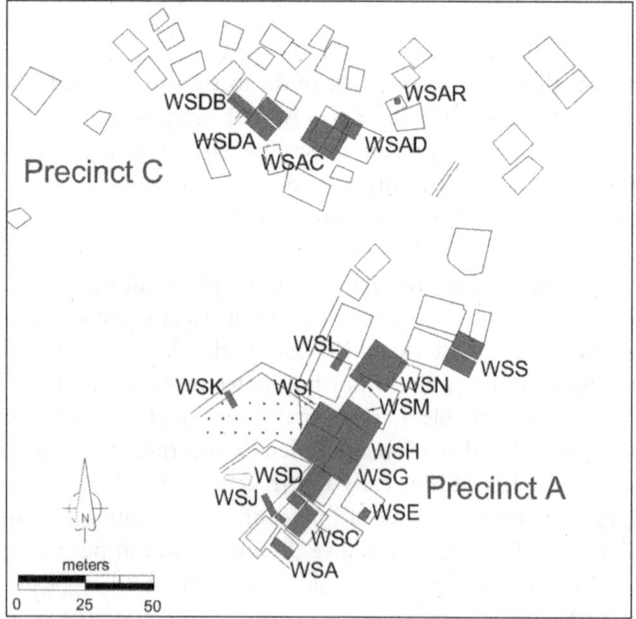

FIGURE 43. Detail of Precincts A and C showing surface architecture and excavated units. The WS prefix stands for West Settlement. (Courtesy of Project ArAGATS, created by Adam T. Smith and Lori Khatchadourian.)

or three, rarely more. In both areas, rooms were built against natural slopes and ridges and were thus substantially subterranean. The walls were not freestanding but instead lined the surrounding earth, functioning as retaining walls.[13] On present evidence, Precinct A appears to have been the residence of a leading family in the community and a locus of sociopolitical privilege.[14] Apart from the scale and regularity of the structure, this interpretation is based on the mounting evidence that it constituted not an agglomeration of equivalent household units but, at least at first, a single and functionally differentiated complex whose users commanded considerable productive capacities as well as wealth in the form of large herds. Functional nonequivalency among the rooms in the complex is supported by the fact that few rooms excavated to date in Precinct A are the same in their dimensions or internal features (figures 44 and 45). Variability is particularly marked among Rooms I, N, S, H, and G, whose internal installations point to different kinds and degrees of food processing, production, and storage activities. These five unique rooms in a unified architectonic environment support the case for a single complex in which a variety of productive, consumptive, and ritual activities took place. Locations of doorways further suggest that this was a unified architectonic environment, primary entry into which was afforded through Room I, from where traffic flowed deeper into the cavernous complex.[15] And yet several doors were clearly blocked over the course of the complex's use, an enigmatic aspect of the site's phasing.[16]

Alongside this evidence for variability, some rooms in the complex, namely C, D, and M, are quite similar to one another; these are also the rooms that collectively hint at large-scale herd management in the precinct. Rooms C, D, and M, the largest of the complex, contain the lowest densities of small finds and ceramics (predominately coarse-wares). The rooms have in common elongated flagstone floors running northeast to southwest and associated receptacles,[17] but no evidence for hearths or workstations (figure 46). It is probable that the receptacles functioned as troughs, and that the rooms were primarily mangers. But in the subterranean houses recorded by ethnographers of twentieth-century Armenia, a room in the dwelling complex known as the *gomi oda,* or cattleshed, also served during winter months as lounging or sleeping quarters for humans who, separated from the animals by a partition, nevertheless benefited from their body heat (Marutyan 2001: 95). Notably, it is specifically the doors of *these* rooms where excavations uncovered robust closures (as between D and G, and M and N). The reasons for the blockages can only be conjectured. Seasonal variations may have occasioned efforts to maximize or reduce cohabitation with livestock. Alternatively, inheritance practices may have led to the parceling of a once large complex into segmented units, each containing its own stable.[18] Finally, changes in the organization of animal husbandry—an expansion in herd size or a change in management structures—could have necessitated the stricter containment of

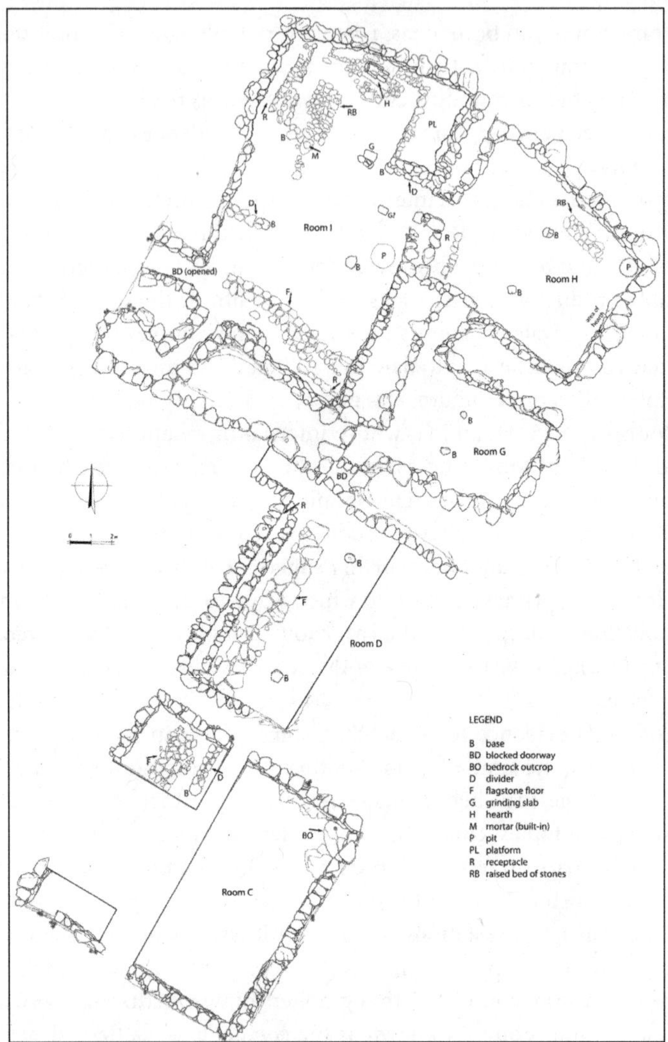

FIGURE 44. Drawing of Precinct A, Rooms C, D, G, H, and I (courtesy of Project ArAGATS, created by Hasmik Sargsyan, Lilit Ter-Minasyan, and Lori Khatchadourian).

livestock from the working quarters of the complex.[19] In any case, the existence of at least three such large mangers suggests that those who inhabited Precinct A enjoyed considerable command over one of the most important resources of the community.

The scale of exposures in Precinct C does not yet provide a clear understanding of the relationship between room blocks, though excavations to date lend support

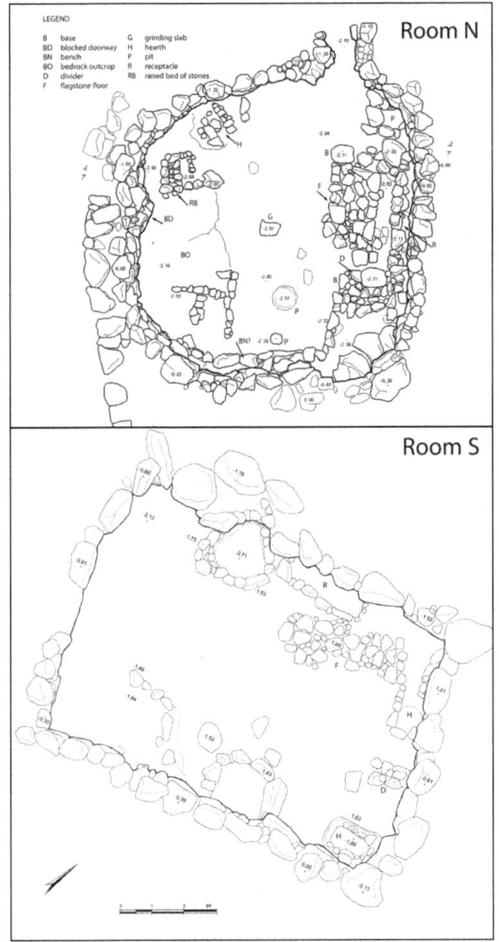

FIGURE 45. Drawing of Rooms N and S (courtesy of Project ArAGATS, created by Lilit Ter-Minasyan and Lori Khatchadourian).

to the picture of disarticulated structures gleaned from surface architecture. Thus far, two pairs of interconnected rooms are clear: AC and AD, and DA and DB (figure 47).[20] Until broader exposures are undertaken in Precinct C, conclusions concerning social differences between the two precincts must remain tentative. It is nevertheless notable that Room AC is comparable in scale to the larger rooms of Precinct A, and shares some features with them (flagstone floor and "receptacle"). But it differs from these rooms in a number of respects, including the presence of a grain-processing station in the center of the room and a flagstone floor that covers much of the interior. Moreover, the density and diversity of materials in Room AC were far greater than in the large rooms of Precinct A. It is possible that day-to-day activities that were otherwise segregated in the more privileged social space of Precinct A were combined in the tighter quarters of a two-or-three-room house.

FIGURE 46. Photograph of the northwest half of Room D (author's photograph).

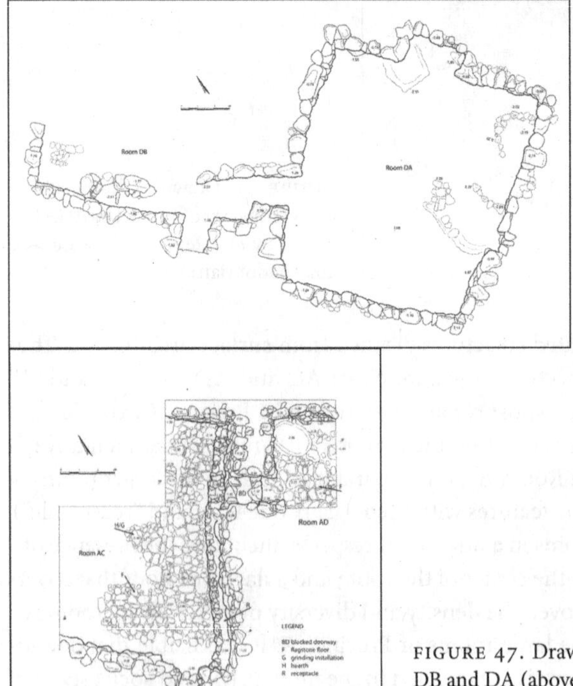

FIGURE 47. Drawing of Precinct C, Rooms DB and DA (above), and AC and AD (below) (courtesy of Project ArAGATS, created by Lilit Ter-Minasyan and Lori Khatchadourian).

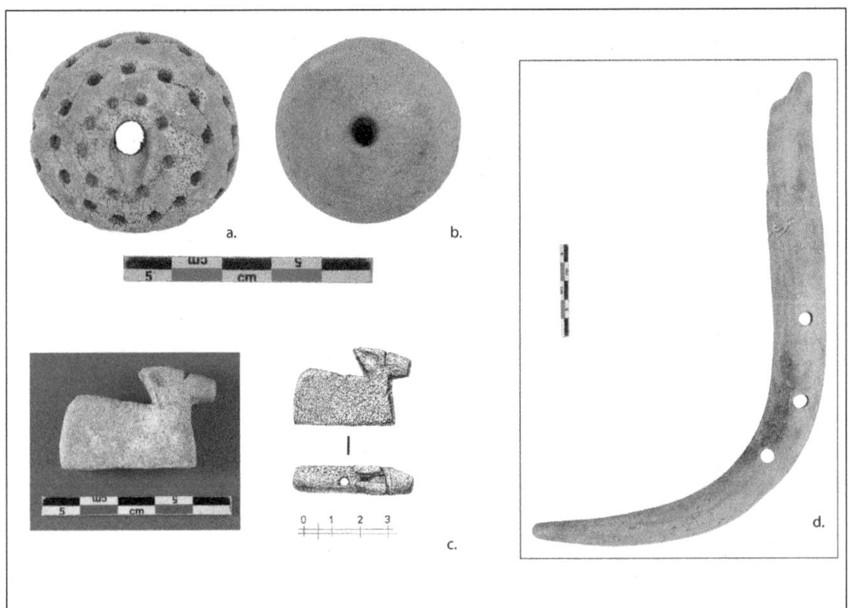

FIGURE 48. Selection of bone artifacts from Iron 3 Tsaghkahovit: a, b. spindle whorls (WSAD.18.B.01, WSH.11.B.01); c. statuette of a stylized horse with vertical perforation, perhaps to secure an attachment of a rider now lost (WSI.09.B.01); d. *psalia* or cheek piece (WSN.65.B.02). (Courtesy of Project ArAGATS. Horse photograph by author, drawing by Hasmik Sargsyan. All other photographs by Vram Hakobyan.)

Working and living in such close quarters, in clear view of a more spacious complex to the south, would have reproduced on a daily basis the social boundaries of the community. The Iron 3 settlement at Tsaghkahovit was abandoned peaceably, without any trace of conflagration. There is no evidence of substantial subsequent occupation.

The Tsaghkahovit community was organized around a mixed, agro-pastoral productive economy that took advantage of the ideal pasturage on the north slope of Mt. Aragats and the open plain that extends west to east from the southern slope of Mt. Kolgat to the Kasakh River drainage.[21] Tending to sheep, goat, cattle, pigs and horses (including domesticated taxon, *Equus caballus*), was an essential part of daily life.[22] The nature of the faunal assemblage indicates a pastoral economy focused on meat consumption, as well as secondary products like milk and wool (figure 48a, b).[23] The role of the horse in the Tsaghkahovit economy is particularly important given historical reports that Armenia met its tributary obligations with horses (see note 5 in chapter 5). It is possible that the village economy was partially structured around the rearing of horses (figure 48c).[24] Notably, a worked-antler industry may have centered on the production of *psalia,* or cheek pieces

FIGURE 49. Hearths in a. Room I, b. Room N, c. Room S (author photographs).

(figure 48d).[25] There is a higher concentration of equids in Precinct C than in A, pointing to some marked difference of use for this particularly important animal. In contrast, faunal evidence of hunting (of bear, fox, and deer, for example) centers on Precinct A. Augmenting a diet of sheep, goat, cattle, and other animal products was a range of cultivated grains.[26] Evidence of cereal processing in the form of basalt grindstones is abundant, and correlated with locales dense in macrobotanical remains, inbuilt grinding stations, and hearths, such as Rooms I, N, S, and AC (figure 49).

ARCHITECTURAL AFFILIATES

The subterranean interior spaces and material assemblages at Tsaghkahovit sustained a community that dwelled, on a day-to-day basis, in the folds of the earth itself. The rectilinear dugouts built into natural slopes were likely roofed through a corbelling technique that would have entailed an alternation between short beams placed diagonally across corners and beams laid parallel to the walls, in multiple levels, until the roof narrowed to an opening that provided light and ventilation. The resulting polygonal dome was then likely covered with reeds or straw and plastered with clay and earth, creating a heavy superstructure that was supported on the interior by wooden pillars (roughly hewn stone bases are extant in many rooms). Whether grown over with grass or laden with snow, from any distance the houses of Tsaghkahovit would have appeared like little hillocks. As Layard's observations make clear, variants of this form of vernacular architecture endured into the twentieth century (figure 38, p. 154), from the foothills and plains of Muş, Erzurum, and Sivas, to the mountains of the South Caucasus, with modern names like "head house" (*glkhatun* in Armenian) or "smoke-hole house" (*tüteklikli ev* in Turkish) that allude its distinctive features (Akın 1996; Marutyan 2001).

Earth-sheltered habitats exist worldwide, in numerous ecological zones (Boyer and Grondzik 1987). In upland environments marked by dramatic fluctuations of climate, the protected and long-lasting edifices of semi-subterranean housing can maintain relatively stable interior temperatures due to the thermal "flywheel" effect: the soil and stone surrounding the lived space absorb and release the sun's energy at a relatively slow rate, thus tempering the effect of dramatic temperature change (5). As thermally rechargeable materials, the basalt blocks that lined Tsaghkahovit's earthen dugouts were continuously at work, intercepting and storing solar energy and returning that heat to their surroundings at cooler times thanks to their vibrant mineralogies, densities, and emissivities (Rempel and Rempel 2013). In general, underground living underscores the ways in which humans habituate to the challenges of extreme mountain zones, and explanations for the unique semi-subterranean houses of the Armenian highland often rest on the affordances of their thermal properties (e.g. Akın 1996).

But climatic factors alone cannot explain what is manifestly a built vernacular designed to enshroud. Centuries of occupation on the Tsaghkahovit Plain during the Early and Late Bronze Ages entailed the very opposite of underground living; communities of these periods favored above-ground constructions on mountain perches rather than subterranean shelters. Likewise, across the highland, there are no known antecedents to Tsaghkahovit's semi-subterranean dwellings of comparable scale and architectural sophistication. The closest comparanda may be the nearby and contemporaneous site of Beniamin, on the Shirak Plain, where limited excavations have exposed two rooms of a semi-subterranean complex that may also have resembled the modern lantern-roof houses (Ter-Martirosov et al. 2012: 201).[27] At Tsaghkahovit, it is possible that the adoption of semi-subterranean stone dwellings emerged in the first instance out of a practical necessity to accommodate a changing subsistence economy that placed greater emphasis on pigs than had earlier societies. But this seems unlikely. Even though represented in higher proportions than during the Early and Late Bronze Ages, pigs make up too small a proportion of the faunal assemblage (7 percent) to be viewed as the driving factor behind greater sedentism and a style of permanent architecture that could both shelter humans and fodder livestock during the winter months. Ultimately, since Bronze Age and earlier Iron Age populations were able to weather the highland's severe winters without resorting to such elaborate underground dwellings, determinative weight in explaining this building practice cannot be placed only on its environmental advantages.

In the last two chapters I developed the argument that communities of the highland during the late seventh century B.C. repudiated the technologies of the complex polity, or more specifically the draconian institutions of authority that the Urartian regime promulgated through its commanding and extractive hilltop fortresses. We saw this first with the introduction of the columned hall at Erebuni and the associated shift from vertical institutions of rule toward what I called congregational politics (chapter 4), and second with the distancing of settlements from locales once central to the Urartian political apparatus (chapter 5). It is in this context that we may understand the refounding of Tsaghkahovit in the late seventh century under new spatial logics, and the sociopolitics of the village's underground dwellings. The decision to settle permanently in the mountains and submit to the challenges of severe winters and high-altitude agriculture was born, I submit, of an escape from the designs of sovereign states and the attendant institutions of surveillance and rule. It is noteworthy, in this regard, that the general location of the Tsaghkahovit settlement in the undulating terrain north of Mt. Aragats would have hidden it from view of north–south passing traffic across the plain. Seen in this context, the semi-subterranean complexes take on new meaning, as a kind of camouflage architecture that offered a solution to a collective concern for concealment. I am suggesting that the people of Tsaghkahovit, who came to the region at a time roughly coincident with the demise of Urartu, and there fashioned an underground lifeway in the protective embrace of the earth, did so, at least in part, to take shelter from the overbearing contrivances of extractive governments. It is not the case that the community cultivated a strict sense of isolation from the wider ecumene; too many artifacts point to Tsaghkahovit's engagement with the cultural currencies of the mid-first millennium B.C.—a bronze snake-head bracelet, a

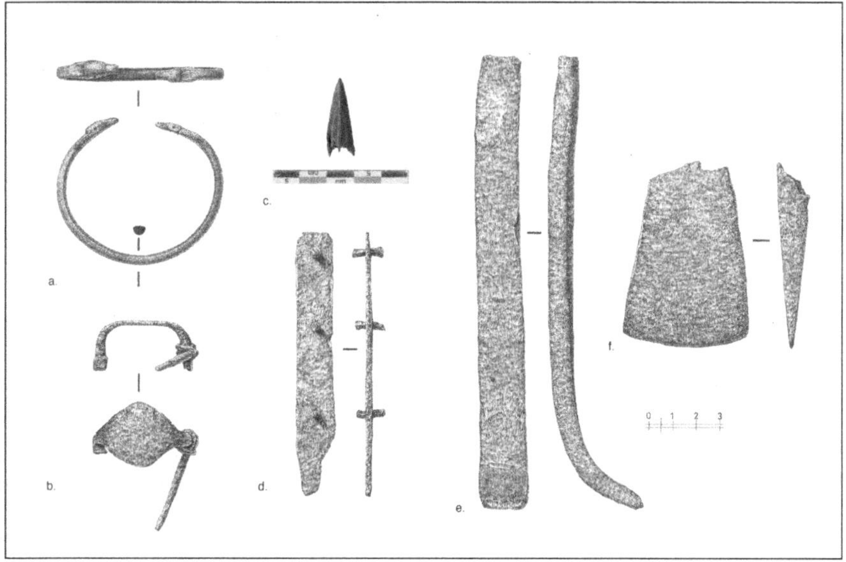

FIGURE 50. Iron and bronze artifacts from Iron 3 Tsaghkahovit: a. bronze bracelet with snakehead terminals (SLT6.04.M.01); b. iron hinged fibula (WSI.12.M.01); c. bronze trilobed point (WSS1.04.M.01); d. iron knife tang (WSI.19.M.01); e. iron chisel (WSG.18.M.02); f. iron axe head (WSG.18.M.01). (Courtesy of Project ArAGATS. Drawings by Hasmik Sargsyan, arrowhead photograph by Vram Hakobyan.)

hinged iron fibula, the tang of an iron knife hilt, a bronze socketed trilobed point, and the proxies and delegate discussed below (figure 50a–d).[28] But metaphorically and literally, the semi-subterranean architecture afforded the people of the village the opportunity to try to absent themselves from the reach of the state.

In so doing, they become beholden to new masters. What enabled a life of semi-subterranean living was a host of mundane but demanding material things. Building rooms required extensive earth removal and the quarrying, transportation, working, and stacking of large basalt blocks. Judging by our experience excavating these rooms, the mortarless stone walls would have required relentless attention, especially the retaining walls that were built against the hillsides. Retaining walls prevented down-slope movement and erosion, and depended on the weight of their mass to counter the lateral earth pressure imposed by the ridges into which they were built. They appear to be the most susceptible to caving and collapse. Building and maintaining the walls would have in turn required regular access to stonemason's tools, such as the iron chisel and axe head buried under the floor of Room G (figure 50e–f), and the continuous transmission of specialized skills. Similarly, roofs would have called for regular, perhaps even annual, upkeep, as heavy winter snows would take their toll on the earth, clay, and plaster materials, and eventually on the timber beams as well. In Hodder's (2012: 17–18) terms (see chapter 3), semi-subterranean dwellings would have created constraining dependencies for those who came to live in them, locking people into regular and high-stake regimens of care. Given such dependency, it is little surprise that the Tsaghkahovit community continued to live in semi-subterranean shelters for centuries, well after Cyrus's conquest of the highland in the mid-sixth century B.C. The day-to-day routine of going underground would have reproduced a sense of communal privacy and thus reinforced the very need to preserve such seclusion.

As a material apparatus of political evasion, Tsaghkahovit's underground dwellings are consummate affiliates. As defined in chapter 3, affiliates are quotidian, inconspicuous things that reproduce social life under empire even as they preserve an inviolable space of experience within it. Affiliates fall beyond the gaze of sovereigns and satraps, and instead are bound in mutual dependencies with commoners caught up in imperial snares. Affiliates also maintain, deepen, and impel affective and practical ties to place, and to the community of human agents who collectively depend on them. As such, they make it possible to preserve difference, to retain an existence despite or alongside imperialism's new "gifts." Yet the work of affiliates is ambiguous. On the one hand they afford the practices of everyday life that make possible the exploitations of empire; on the other hand they preserve the possibility of a social existence once again unanswerable to distant sovereigns.

The assemblages of things that make up the earth-sheltered dwellings at Tsaghkahovit provide a clear instance of the work of affiliates in the making of satrapal conditions. Such things enabled a mode of life that had no bearing on the dependencies and concerns that preoccupied the sovereign establishment. These affiliates would have worked contrarily to preserve communal ties to the hills north of Mt. Aragats, and to retain a distinctive and autonomous existence. To the extent that this mode of life obtained in other regions of the *dahyu,* as the excavations at Beniamin and Xenophon's account make plain, semi-subterranean affiliates may have created common affects of attachment to mountainous lifeways that could have cross-cut immediate group allegiances. Yet at the same time, Tsaghkahovit's affiliate architecture sustained a community that was unmistakably bound to the institutions of empire, thanks to a diverse array of ceramic proxies and one very significant stone delegate. It is to these imperial things that we now turn.

PROXY POTS

In the archaeology of the Achaemenid Empire and Classical Greece, relationships between prototype and likeness, model and mimic have long revolved around pottery "imitations" of imperial metalwares. Three of the vessels that we encountered in chapter 5 have come to occupy the center of these discussions, namely, the *phiale*, the deep "Achaemenid bowl," and the rhyton (figures 29, p. 130, and 30, p. 131). These metal delegates generated ceramic translations across the empire and beyond, from Attic Greece, to Asia Minor, to South Asia (Dusinberre 1999, 2003, 2013; Hoffmann 1961; Miller 1993; Petrie et al. 2008). As substitutes, it is tempting to view such "copies" (or, as conceptualized here, *proxies*), as unproblematic enablers of the kinds of consumption practices for which the metal delegates are well known, albeit reproduced with greater modesty. Elsewhere I have called this the "emulation hypothesis" (Khatchadourian forthcoming), which holds that objects of formal resemblance separated by the sociopolitical inequities of their users index particular affective dispositions toward a polity. Held in the grip of these affects of desire are political subjects, intent to preserve or enhance their relative power through reference to the aesthetics and practices of the sovereign establishment. The axiom assumes voluntary compliance, acquiescence, and an earnest ambition of the subjugated to replicate material forms, because of both their inherent capacities to project fixed social values (that is, a capacity that resides in the symbol-laden object) and their capacities to enable imitative practices as symbolic devices.

At first glance, a corpus of pottery recovered from across the underground havens of Tsaghkahovit would seem to fit neatly into this prevailing perspective. However, as we shall see, when the materials are approached through the logics of the proxy as developed in chapter 3, an alternative to the emulation hypothesis emerges that recognizes the potential for proxies to erode the power of their delegates. To the best of my knowledge, while the size of the Tsaghkahovit collection is modest, the corpus is nevertheless unprecedented in the diversity of Achaemenid metal feasting paraphernalia on which it is modeled (extending beyond bowls and rhyta to include amphorae and other jars), in addition to the secure and detailed contextual information on each and every vessel in the assemblage. The Tsaghkahovit materials are thus well suited for a reevaluation of the doxic view on ceramic "copies."

In general, ceramic production in the Iron 3 period at Tsaghkahovit was primarily a local enterprise. Instrumental neutron activation analysis (INAA) of 250 sherds covering all the major ceramic types from Iron 3 Tsaghkahovit has made it possible to identify the general location of clay sources that were exploited in the production of the pottery from the site.[29] Seventy-nine percent of the sampled sherds trace to clay sources on the north slope of Mt. Aragats, while the clays of 7.2 percent of the sample match deposits in the vicinity of Gegharot or in the wider Pambak range, on the north side of the Tsaghkahovit Plain. Only 4.8 percent of the sample has chemical signatures that differ appreciably from those known from the Tsaghkahovit Plain, and these vessels are most probably foreign to the region. Caution is required when attempting to infer ceramic production technology from

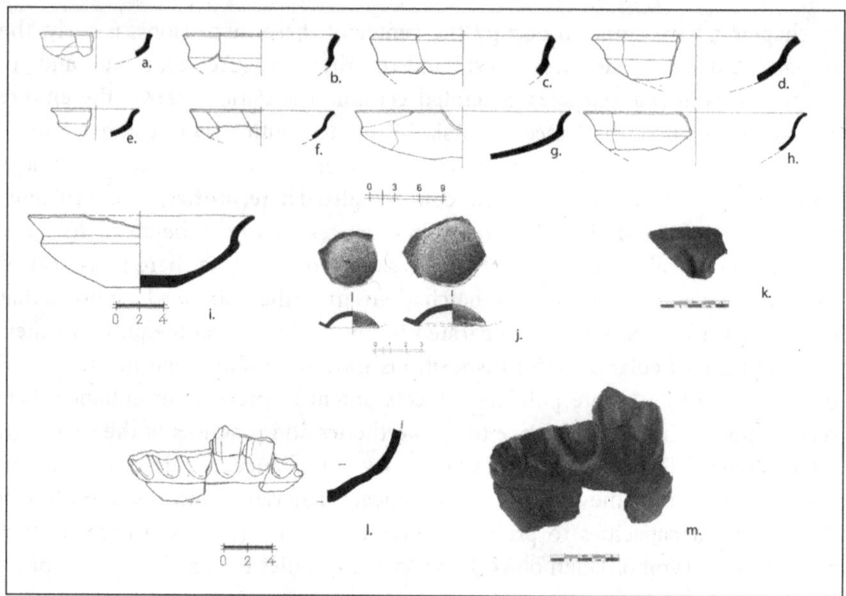

FIGURE 51. Ceramic bowls from Iron 3 Tsaghkahovit (courtesy of Project ArAGATS, drawings by Hasmik Sargsyan and Narine Mkhitaryan, photographs by Vram Hakobyan and Catherine Kearns).

visual and tactile examination of sherds alone (Roux and Courty 1995); however, several factors point to an "individual workshop" ceramic industry (Rice 2005: 184).[30] Let us now turn to brief descriptions of the proxies in question.[31]

Bowls

Red- and black-burnished bowls with everted concave rims are extremely common in the Tsaghkahovit corpus. Many are quite shallow (and thus belong to a wider Iron Age tradition—figure 51a–h), but some exhibit the depth of the typical "Achaemenid bowl" (figure 51i), also known from other sites in Armenia, like the collective tomb at Jrarart, in the Hrazdan valley (Tiratsyan 1964: fig. 5). A variety of Achaemenid metal bowl prototypes are recalled in the form of two black-burnished *omphaloi* recovered from the floor of Room H and a buried cache of Room G (figure 51j), as well as a black-burnished bowl with petals or lotus buds from Room I (figure 51k).[32] Despite its *phiale*-like petals, this latter bowl departs from the standard metal *phiale* in that the rim is not everted and concave, but tapers continuously off the axis of the body, a form for which, to my knowledge, there are few metal examples (Abka'i-Khavari 1988: fig. 1). Another black-burnished bowl, this one from the floor in Room AC, is distinguished for the incised parallel vertical grooves (rounded in cross section) that surround the body (figure 51m). INAA indicates that the chemical composition of the fabric matches ceramic reference groups of the Tsaghkahovit Plain (Minc 2009), and is thus the product of a local workshop. The vessel can be compared to numerous Attic black-gloss wares, themselves modeled on Achaemenid metal bowls (Abka'i-Khavari 1988; Miller 1993; Simpson 2005: fig. 97; Treister 2010: fig. 7).

Animal-Handled Amphorae

Near a hearth in the northern corner of Room I, excavations uncovered fragments of two amphorae with leaping quadrupeds rendered in relief on the handles (figure 52). One (figure 52a) is sufficiently preserved to discern an overall quality of axial symmetry created by the correspondence between the height of the neck and its base diameter (both 10 cm). A narrow relief rib marks the transition between the neck and shoulder. A bowed handle, circular in section, joins the vessel at the top of the rim and the top of the shoulder. The vessel's orange-red exterior is slipped and burnished. Prolonged firing in a an oxidizing atmosphere, high temperatures, and fine grain size account for the striking hardness of the fabric. Adorning the one preserved handle in low relief are three highly stylized anatomical elements of a four-legged mammal likely created during the leather-hard state through either a process of clay surface displacement, like planorelief carving, or applique surface addition joined by a fluid clay slurry or slip (Rice 2005: 146–148). The animal is depicted in profile. The lowest of the three linear components extends down the handle toward the shoulder and represents the beast's hind limbs, whose terminus is either fragmented or abraded to a lower plane, and may have consisted of a hoof-like element. Attached to the hind leg is a second straight element that stands in for the beast's minimal, diagrammatic body. This element is fragmented at the top, as is the third and shortest element, which parallels the second and appears to represent the beast's flexed forelimb, tucked tightly beneath the body. The knee joint meets the vessel at the rim. The animal is, in other words, facing the vessel in mid-leap. The vessel likely had a second symmetrical zoomorphic handle, now lost. INAA indicates that the chemical composition of the fabric does not match any of the ceramic reference groups of the Tsaghkahovit Plain (Minc 2009). The vessel is statistically an outlier, and thus an import, though its place of origin remains unknown.

In the case of the second zoomorphic amphora (figure 52b), preserved after restoration are parts of the rim and thin-walled neck, as well as the upper part of a spouted (or "beaked") handle, which is hollow and circular in section. The spout's opening is fragmented, but the orientation of the orifice in relation to the horizontal plane of the top of the handle suggests that it extended outward, perpendicular to the axis of the vessel. Projecting vertically off the rim of the

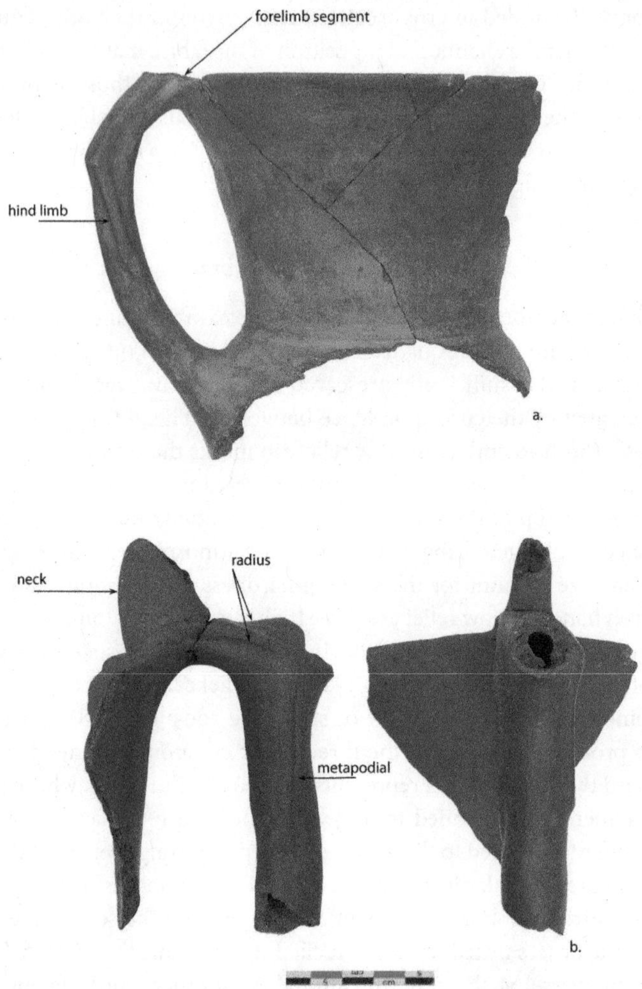

FIGURE 52. Ceramic amphorae with zoomorphic handles from Room I (courtesy of Project ArAGATS, created by Vram Hakobyan and Lori Khatchadourian).

vessel where it meets the handle is a protrusion, semi-triangular in profile, which tapers toward the vessel's interior. Surfaces are slipped and burnished red on both exterior and interior. Straddling both sides of the spouted handle are linear relief elements that depict, once again, the legs of a leaping quadruped, created with the same technique of either displacement or applique. The limbs terminate through a gradual lowering of the plane of relief, without any apparent delineation of

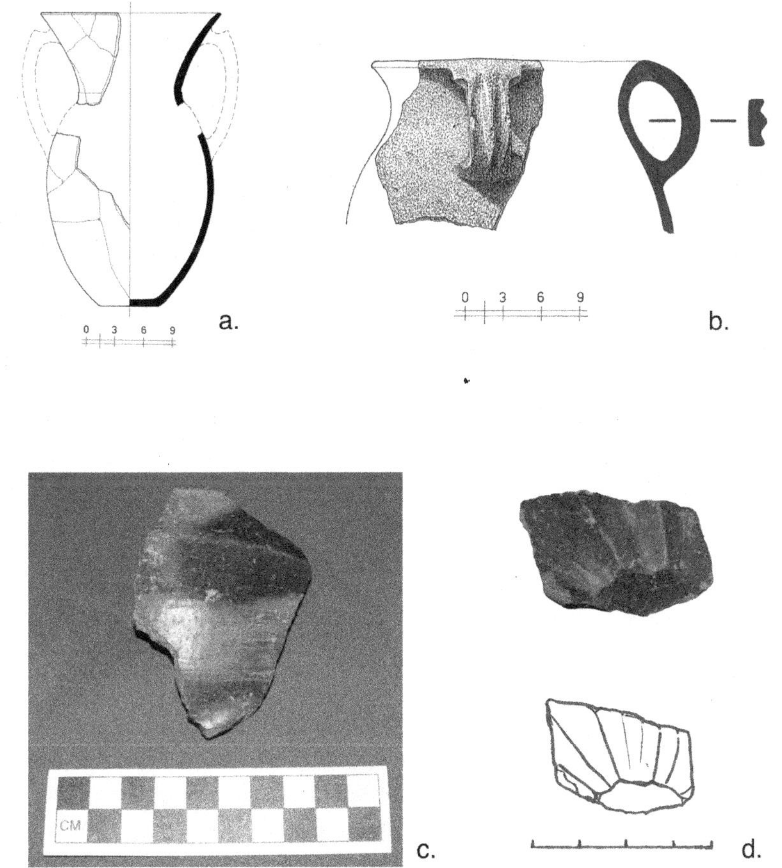

FIGURE 53. Ceramic jars from Iron 3 Tsaghkahovit (courtesy of Project ArAGATS, drawings by Hasmik Sargsyan, photographs by Catherine Kearns and Lori Khatchadourian).

hoofs. They appear to be the beast's forelimbs (radii and metapodials), and the vertical projection on the rim its neck, providing the overall impression that the animal is meant to be leaping out of the vessel. The vessel's second handle (likely not spouted, but also zoomorphic) is not preserved. The similarities in technical execution of the relief decoration, overall vessel morphology, and surface treatment suggest that the two pots were made by the same workshop or potting community, if not the same hand. Indeed, INAA indicates that the fabric of this amphora chemically matches that of the previous vessel. It is thus also an import from the same unidentified source. The overall body form of both animal-handled vessels likely resembled the vessel from neighboring Room H (figure 53a). A third spouted amphora with zoomorphic handles is strongly suggested by the

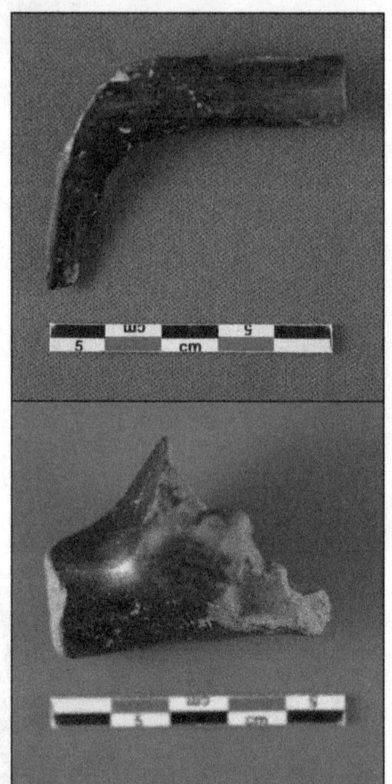

FIGURE 54. Black-burnished sherds of a perpendicular spout and zoomorphic element, likely belonging to an amphora, from Room H (author photographs).

elongated tubular black-burnished spout and fragmentary zoomorphic sherd with the same fabric and surface treatments, both found together in Room H (figure 54). These vessels are similar in form and concept to the provenanced and unprovenanced silver zoomorphic amphorae discussed in the previous chapter as active participants at the Achaemenid royal table (see p. 131). The most securely dated objects of comparison are the amphorae that the Armenian and Lydian delegates carry on the eastern staircase façade of the Apadana (figure 10, p. 20), with composite animals on their handles, rendered through a combination of low relief and modeling. The relief elements include the bodies, wings, and extended hind legs of the beasts, while the tightly tucked forelegs are formed as if in three dimensions, in such a way that the joints of the bent legs meet the vessel rim. Rising above the top of the vessel are the rear-facing heads of griffins (in the case of the Armenian's vessel) and bulls (in the case of the Lydian's two vessels). Projecting perpendicularly from one of the handles of each vessel is a spout. The Tsaghkahovit ceramic variants of course differ in their material composition and the highly minimal anatomical elaboration of the animals.[33] But there can be little doubt that the potters who made these vessels had the metal vessels in mind.[34]

Also belonging to the category of zoomorphic-handled pitchers (possible amphorae) is a collection of five handle fragments, three from the floors in Rooms G, H, and S, and two from above the floors in Rooms AC and H (figure 55). The

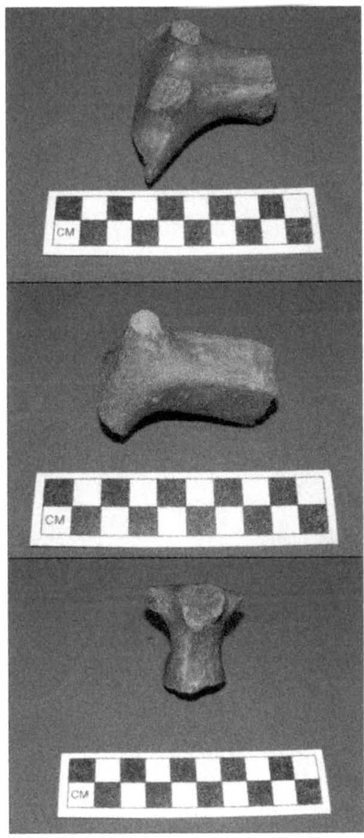

FIGURE 55. Ceramic protomes from Rooms H, AC, and G (courtesy of Project ArAGATS, photographs by Catherine Kearns).

most striking example is an animal-spout that takes the form of a bull's head (figure 56). This black-burnished fragment (its surface treatment no doubt meant to invoke the sheen of silver) belonged to a ceramic jar. The animal has two flaring nostrils on the muzzle, and two incised arcs above the eyes. These few details suffice to recognize the direct iconographic parallels with stylized bull imagery from the Achaemenid heartland, most notably the double-bull's-head capitals that supported the roof beams of the columned halls (figure 57). As Root (2002: 197–198) has noted, bulls figure prominently in Achaemenid art, not only as symbols of royal power, strength, and fertility (as they do in the art of earlier Near Eastern polities—figure 2, p. xxiv), but also as symbols of purity linked to Mazdean belief, in which the bovines held pride of place as the first animals of creation (see p. 12). Apart from the bull spout, the remaining zoomorphic handle fragments are more stylized, appearing to depict the face or head of an animal, in one case with possible horns. Trace-element analyses on these other examples suggest that none are clear imports.[35] To my knowledge, there are few if any ceramic parallels for the zoomorphic amphorae from Tsaghkahovit.[36]

Moving to other jar forms, five vessels from various rooms of the settlement (in both Precincts A and C) have circumferential vertical fluting that creates a series of alternating protrusions and depressions. Three of the examples have

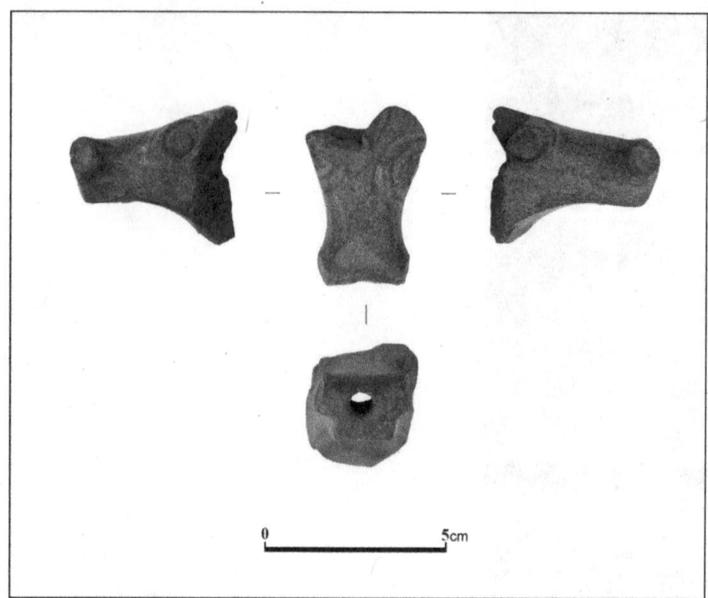

FIGURE 56. Black-burnished bull-spout protome from Room S (courtesy of Project ArAGATS, photograph by Vram Hakobyan).

lustrous black or dark-gray burnished exterior surfaces (figure 53c–d, p. 175). Three of the five are definite products of local workshops, firmly linked to the clay sources on the northern slope of Mt. Aragats (the remaining two have not been analyzed). Dark-burnished vertically fluted vessels like those from Tsaghkahovit find few ceramic parallels (Carter 1994: fig. 14.14), but are similar to the vessels carried by the Apadana's Lydian delegation, as well as provenanced and unprovenanced silver amphorae and goblets (e.g. Amandry 1959; Özgen and Öztürk 1996: fig. 65–66; Treister 2007, 2010), including the Erebuni goblet rhyton (figures 10, p. 20, and 29, p. 130).

One last jar or amphora sherd is worthy of note (figure 58). The vessel was found on the floor of Room AC. Its surfaces are modeled with several distinctive decorative attributes. Horizontal fluting encircles the vessel's neck, of which two thin arrises and one and a half individual flutes are preserved. A series of petals or lotus buds bulge on the shoulder, forged through a combination of grooving and pressure on the vessel interior. The adjacency of the petals is interrupted at one point where a handle would have joined the shoulder, suggested by the circular spall (another non-joining sherd is similarly spalled, where a second handle was affixed). And finally, widely spaced on the vessel body are a number of slightly arced, nearly vertical, elongated relief lobes created as if through the upward stroke

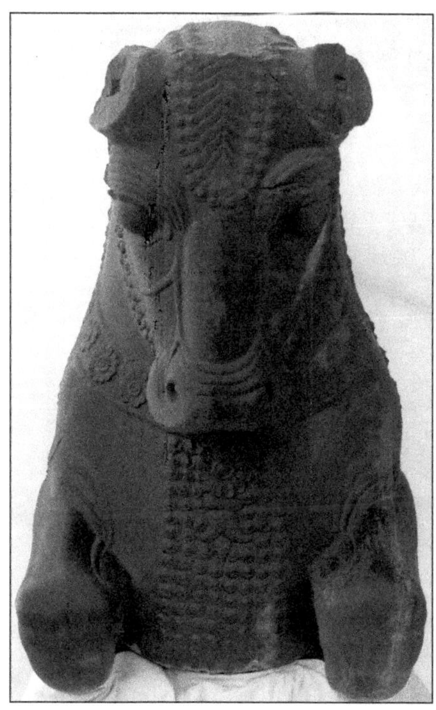

FIGURE 57. Restored bull capital from Persepolis (courtesy of the Oriental Institute of the University of Chicago).

FIGURE 58. Ceramic two-handled vessel from Room AC with horizontally fluted neck, petaled shoulder, and vertical lobes on body (courtesy of Project ArAGATS, photography by Vram Hakobyan).

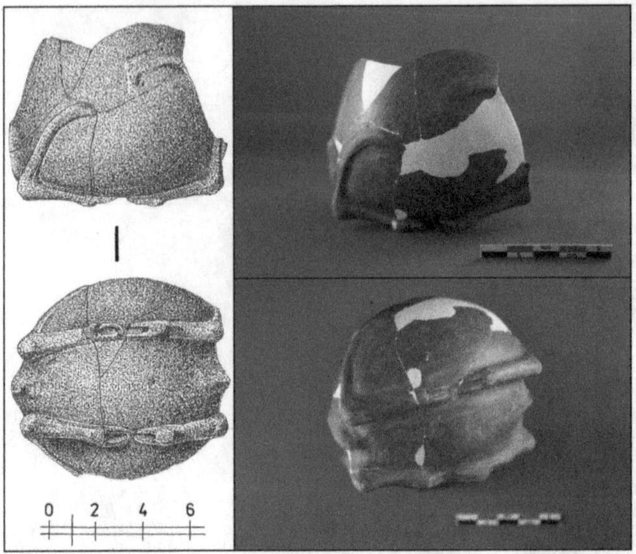

FIGURE 59. Red-burnished ceramic rhyton in the shape of a goat, gazelle, or ibex from Room H (courtesy of Project ArAGATS, drawing by Hasmik Sargsyan, author's photographs).

of a thumb on the vessel's interior.[37] Each of these features occurs separately on Achaemenid metal bowls and jars, but to my knowledge they do not co-occur on any individual vessel in the known delegate assemblage. INAA results are inconclusive, providing a *possible* link to the northern Aragats clay sources.

Zoomorphic Rhyta

Two red-burnished vessels of this type have been recovered to date, one from the southern quadrant of the floor in Room H and the other in an alluvial deposit of Room N (figure 59). The former, substantially restored, reveals the rear, body, legs, and horn of a recumbent animal whose portly body bears down on its legs, each with precisely rendered joints and hoofs. The horn arcs across part of the animal's upper body, marking it as a goat or ibex. The vessel's overall form is uncertain, but the positioning of a recumbent animal at the base of a restricted vessel base is immediately reminiscent of the metal rhyton, even as certain details of the vessel make it quite unlike any specific metal delegate.[38] INAA results on the fragmentary, unrestored specimen are inconclusive, providing a *possible* link to the northern Aragats clay sources.

* * *

Like all proxies, the Tsaghkahovit vessels reviewed above are things that palpably stand in for other things, specifically some of the most distinctive and powerful Achaemenid delegates, the indispensable objects of the feast. And as with all acts of mimesis, the sharing in the power of the represented also results in its dilution. Such dilution emerges specifically from the opportunities for slippage that I defined in chapter 3 as conditions for the realization of unruly or rogue proxies. These opportunities derive from the material properties of the proxies and the broader assemblages with which they commingle, each of which is now addressed in turn.

Proxy Matter

Unlike the silver of the delegate vessels, clay was not a substance that imperial agents cared for or regulated on an empire-wide scale as a necessity of political reproduction. Indeed, while it may well be apocryphal, the Greek historian Ctesias reports that the Persian king reserved clay vessels for those who did not merit his high regard (Ath. XI.464a, cited in Sancisi-Weerdenburg 1989: 133). The clay of the Tsaghkahovit vessels was in almost all cases locally extracted and worked, with the exception of the zoomorphic-handled amphorae, whose place of manufacture is unknown. Entailed in their production were local webs of extraction and relations of human–material reliance.

The differing relational properties of delegates and proxies between their chemical composition and the human groups they entrap gives rise to a constitutional potentiality for proxies to bend the rules. This possibility begins at the very point of production. In chapter 3 I discussed Ingold's suggestion that materials engage their makers, a refutation of the notion that human artisans autonomously control the outputs of their craft, without any "say" on the part of the materials themselves. Since the ceramic proxies are made up of different materials from their delegates, their properties press themselves on their makers during the form-generating process in different ways, in turn producing forms that will differ, to greater or lesser degrees, regardless of the precision of the craftsperson's template. The maker of the proxy has in mind a design, but the clay material does not follow blueprints or dictates, governed as it is by its own movements and tolerances. It is thus both the properties of the materials and the designs of the makers that account for the formal variance between delegates and proxies. Proxies are very rarely really copies after all, or at least not "faithful" copies (Taussig 1993: 52). The formal dissimilitude between delegates and proxies that can result from working with materials with significantly differing characteristics is in part what invites the possibility for roguery. It precludes the possibility of successful emulation, and, as we shall see, it can support efforts at makeshift creativity.

The clay medium of the vessels from Tsaghkahovit both forced and invited various departures in the form-generating process from the delegate template.

In the case of the zoomorphic amphorae, I have already noted the conspicuously minimalist rendering of the leaping animals, in contrast to the detailed renditions found on the metal vessels. To be sure, the use of relief rather than incision or paint to render the beasts' bodies on the proxies bespeaks an effort to attain the modeled dimensionality of the toreutics, while the thin walls and red-burnished surfaces afford a delicacy and luster akin to the metal variants. But the plastic medium of clay simply would not permit the modeling of anatomical precision similar to what can be achieved with metal.

It is perhaps this unavoidable deviation from the metal delegate form, occasioned by the material medium itself, that opened the possibility for other forms of experimentation. With regard to the zoomorphic amphorae, for instance, the spouted vessel is most peculiar in the way the beast's forelegs, loosely flexed at the knee, clearly face outward from the vessel. This is a complete reversal of the delegate's form, in which tightly tucked forelegs always face the vessel, the knee joining at the rim. I suggest that the potter was here deliberately taking liberties, for which the clay itself created the conditions of possibility.

Other examples of experimentation that "play" on metal delegates include the "composite" jar from the floor of Room AC (figure 58, p. 179), with its horizontal flutes, petaled shoulder, and haphazard vertical lobes on the body. The vessel brings together a number of elements from Achaemenid metalware to ultimately novel effect. In making such a composite, the potter once again appears to have been exercising creativity that the commonplace, unregulated, plastic material of clay made possible. We might also see experimentation at work in the unusual Tsaghkahovit rhyton (figure 59, p. 182), for which close metal or ceramic parallels have also yet to be found (but see Moorey 1980: 24.568). A fourth and final example of "play" is the bull's-head animal spout (figure 56, p. 178). Spouted bulls' heads do not occur on Achaemenid zoomorphic metal jars, whose spouts are always simple linear projections that emerge horizontally from the animal's body (figures 10, p. 20, and 54, p. 176). In this way the Tsaghkahovit vessel is at once both derivative and deviant. In concept and color, it clearly stood in for the classic metal animal-handled amphorae, and drew on Achaemenid bull imagery. And yet, measured against the corpus of delegates, the bull-spouted jar likely also would have appeared aberrant, anomalous, out of step.

To be sure, the divergences from Achaemenid metal delegates in part emerge from the creative intentions of the potters (in almost all cases local inhabitants of the plain) to, quite literally, take matter into their own hands and explore, through the medium of clay, subtle twists that nevertheless kept their craft within the bounds of Achaemenid styles. But I am also suggesting that the clay itself invited such manipulations, that the material opened the possibility of stretching the rules of the canon, and doing so at very low stakes, given the ubiquity of the material and its triviality compared to the strictly regulated silver. It is in this regard particularly notable how casually, if not carelessly, some of the proxies appear to have been produced, against the standards of Tsaghkahovit's own finewares. For example, apart from the bull protome, the other protomes are featureless in their execution; the grooved bowl (figure 51m, p. 172) is thick-walled and poorly polished compared to other serving and consumption vessels from the site; and the broadly spaced groves of the "composite" vessel (figure 58, p. 179) appear hastily rendered with the stroke of a finger or tool, resulting in slightly arced elements, rather than the tightly adjacent linear grooves that would be expected of a metal delegate's proper proxy. In terms of their formal properties, then, some of the proxies are products of an artisan-like inventiveness that stems in part from their material constitution. In some cases they conform to the basic form-concept of the delegates but dispense with those essential qualities of exactitude and elegance that make the latter objects of social distinction and the political sublime. In other cases, the proxies poach on the delegate through inversion, recombination, selective conformity—all of which can signal and enable the "plays," "ruses," or "ironies" of Certeauean tactics (see chapter 3, p. 72).

Proxy Assemblage

A second opportunity for unruliness defined in chapter 3 can stem from the company that proxies keep, which is to say the immediate assemblage of things with which they collaborate in the production of social life. Proxies make a difference in the world through their cooperation in object assemblies usually made up primarily of other nondelegates. All of the ceramic proxies from the modest underground havens at Tsaghkahovit mingled with a vast array of mundane affiliates—animal troughs and hearths, grindstones and cooking pots, bone and obsidian tools. Taking only the example of the amphorae, these most intriguing of the Tsaghkahovit proxies were recovered from one of the more clearly work-a-day spaces of Precinct A. Room I is a particularly prominent room in the complex. It is centrally located, afforded direct access to the outdoor courtyard (Area K), and contained a number of features indicative of large-scale food processing and preparation, from multiple grinding stations to a distinctive large hearth (figures 49, p. 166). While many other features in this room are functionally uncertain, they point to an area of intensive activity with high traffic flows, likely including livestock. This is a room whose faunal and botanical remains provide no compelling evidence for feasting, no evidence for marked consumption that would suggest the practices with which the silver delegates are associated. We are of course dealing with the partial evidence from a peaceably abandoned complex. But the spatial context, internal features, and extant remains nevertheless produced a rather unmistakably quotidian workspace of which the ceramic proxy amphorae were just one part.

FIGURE 60. View of the northeastern half of Room I (courtesy of Project ArAGATS, photograph by Elizabeth Fagan).

By virtue of the wider assemblage to which they (and other ceramic proxies) belonged, these vessels were invariably more shallowly entangled in the work of safeguarding the Achaemenid project than their delegate partners. That is, against the context of Tsaghkahovit's underground dwellings, it is rather unlikely that the user who seized the handles of the zoomorphic amphorae partook of the semiotic transfigurations that, as discussed in the previous chapter, rendered him a "Persian Man" (see p. 140). Instead, I propose that proxies such as these invited the playful manipulation of Achaemenid concepts and the loosening of the conventions of use that otherwise surrounded the metal delegates. The kind of imperial subject that such proxies helped forge was an ambiguous one—enlisted to have a hand in the practical affordances and symbolic resonances of the empire, and at the same time, under pressure from a host of relentlessly banal objects and spaces, provoked to redefine intended purposes and meanings. While the proxy amphorae represent their delegate partners, they also diminish their powers through the ordinary company they keep.

The possibility for earnest efforts at emulation cannot, of course, be entirely foreclosed. But close contextual and material analysis of the Tsaghkahovit proxies instead points to a field of human–thing interaction geared toward the minuscule procedures of "making do," whose effects, as Certeau realized, dilute in small measure the solidity of the dominant social order. The efforts that concern proxies are reducible to neither resistance nor conformity. Rather, they amount to what Alexei Yurchak (2006: 28), writing in a very different context, has called "minute internal displacements and mutations" that "do not have to contradict the political and ethical parameters of the system and, importantly, may even allow one to preserve the possibilities, promises, positive ideals, and ethical values of the system while avoiding the negative . . . constraints within which these are articulated." The proxies at Tsaghkahovit were not contrarian, not discernibly defiant of, say, onerous demands for tribute or troops. And they may well have held open the possibility of preserving the promises and values of their delegates. On present evidence, however, their efficacy in creating imperial subjectivities can best be described as partial, as they, along with their makers and users, sometimes worked tactically as bricoleurs to allow conformity that evades, escape without leaving. Such are the workings of the conditionals of sovereignty that define the satrapal condition.

A STONE DELEGATE AND THE DIVINE

And yet imperial matter is not to be underestimated, for sometimes delegates insinuate themselves into the most unlikely places. Room G in Precinct A is an exceptionally unique space. In this small room there is no flagstone floor, no storage receptacle, no hearth or any other of the internal features found elsewhere across the settlement (figure 44, p. 162). In the northwestern side of the room, approximately two meters from the threshold, a large jar was deposited beneath the floor, its dark gray ashy contents suggestive of a cremation burial. In the southern corner, also buried under the floor in an otherwise sterile clay matrix, was a collection of iron stonemason's tools—chisel and axe head (figure 50e–f, p. 169)—accompanied by a set of matching painted bowls and the black-polished *omphalos* (figure 51j, p. 172)—perhaps the curated objects from a work feast. This room, a repository of cached memories, is located relatively deep in the Precinct A complex, accessible only by passing through two other rooms.

In situ on the floor of Room G was an unusual assemblage of objects (figure 61). Half of a smashed footless green stone plate lay centimeters away from a ceramic, hourglass-shaped stand, whose diameter is only one centimeter larger than the diameter of the base of the plate (figures 62 and 63). The plate, as we shall see, has secure and well-known comparanda, but the matching ceramic stand is, to the best of my knowledge, without known parallels. A small fragment of a second stone vessel appears to be an open spout decorated with a linear incision. The possible spout is too small to definitively associate with any known vessel forms, but the very presence of an incised stone vessel in the same context as the serpentine plate is itself notable given that no other certain stone vessels have been found at the site to date. Just centimeters away from the ceramic stand lay a basalt mortar,

FIGURE 61. Artifacts on the floor of Room G (author's photographs).

while a second, unusually well-made mortar was recovered from elsewhere in the same room (figure 64). Relatively small mortars such as these are exceptionally rare in the Tsaghkahovit lithic corpus (n = 4), compared to other types of grindstones (n = 47), and thus the presence of two in the same small room is noteworthy. Strewn amid these artifacts were fragments of large storage jars, and carinated and uncarinated bowls, along with a fine red-polished jug (figure 53b, p. 175) with a one-of-a-kind ornamented handle.

It is the stone plate (figure 62) that calls for sustained attention. The plate has a slightly protruding base in the shape of a flat disk, and a shallow, convex body leading continuously to a square rim. The vessel's highly polished surfaces have the characteristic greenish mottled appearance of some serpentines, and indeed, mineralogical, chemical, and petrographic analysis conducted by Arkadi Karakhanyan and colleagues, of Armenia's Institute of Geological Sciences, confirmed this attribution. Serpentine deposits exist in the South Caucasus, in the Shahdag or Sevan mountain range (northeast of Lake Sevan), as well as in the Zagros and Elbrus ranges. The specific mineralogical composition of the Tsaghkahovit plate, which is chrysotile with enstatite-pyroxene inclusions, points most probably to a source in the Zagros Mountains of western Iran.

FIGURE 62. Serpentine plate from Room G (courtesy of Project ArAGATS, photograph by Vram Hakobyan).

FIGURE 63. Ceramic stand from Room G (courtesy of Project ArAGATS, author's photograph, drawing by Hasmik Sargsyan).

FIGURE 64. Mortars from Room G (author's photographs).

The closest parallels for the Tsaghkahovit serpentine plate are to be found in the abundant corpus of green stone plates discovered in the Treasury at Persepolis (Schmidt 1957: 53–59, 89). The comparable Persepolis plates are made of green stone—veined chert or green-and-black mottled serpentine. Nearly 300 chert and serpentine footless plates were found scattered in the northern halls of the Treasury

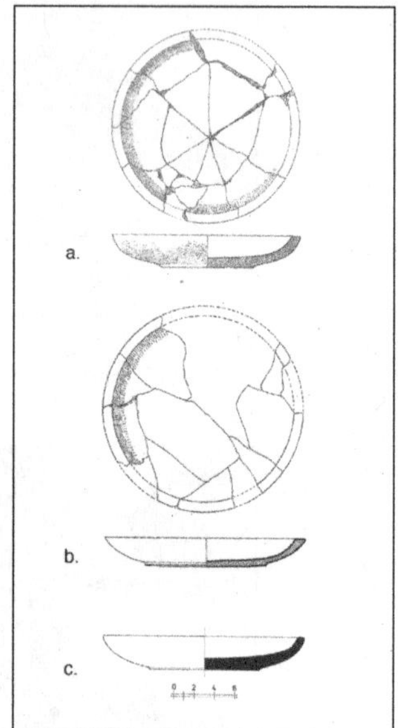

FIGURE 65. Chert and serpentine footless plates: a. chert plate from Treasury at Persepolis, diameter 20.4 cm (Schmidt 1957: Pl. 24.23); b. serpentine plate from Treasury at Persepolis, diameter 21.6 cm (Schmidt 1957: Pl. 59.57); c. serpentine plate from Tsaghkahovit, diameter 20.5 cm.

(particularly Halls 38 and 41), and of these, 263 have plain square rims that make them morphologically nearly identical to the Tsaghkahovit plate (figure 65). All of the plates vary only slightly in size, and the Tsaghkahovit plate fits within the standard diameter range. The majority of the chert plates from Persepolis were ink-inscribed on the base exterior in Aramaic (Schmidt 1957: 55). Only one of the 270 serpentine specimens carries an inscription (91, table VIII).[39] Until now, sourcing analysis has not been performed on the serpentine plates from Persepolis.[40] Nevertheless, the Tsaghkahovit plate is quite clearly an import, likely from the imperial heartland, which probably reached the village through a number of down-the-line exchanges that at one point involved privileged imperial actors.

It is possible to propose an approximate date for the serpentine plate from Tsaghkahovit based on the dating of the inscribed vessels at the Treasury at Persepolis that co-occur with the comparable vessels. The inscriptions point to a pattern of activity surrounding these plates occurring especially during the reign of Xerxes (486–465 B.C.) and Artaxerxes I (465–424/3 B.C.).[41] I thus propose that the Tsaghkahovit plate was made no earlier than the reign of Xerxes. Therefore, the activity implied by the complex of in situ artifacts on the floor of Room G occurred some time after 486 B.C. This is the most conservative estimate.[42] The Tsaghkahovit plate is among the few serpentine vessels directly comparable to those found in the Treasury at Persepolis that archaeologists have uncovered through systematic excavations.[43] It is also a rare example (if not the first) of a footless serpentine plate excavated outside the imperial heartland and found on a floor, in a use context with associated artifacts.[44]

The serpentine plate is the only delegate thus far discovered at Tsaghkahovit, and the objects with which it occurs combine to suggest a rather effective assemblage that helped to create satrapal conditions of subjection in this semi-subterranean village. It will be recalled that imperial things are delegates with "thing power" (Bennett 2010) when imperial agents are dependent on the physical materials from which they are made, and when such "contingent reliance" on matter (Hodder 2012: 17–18) leads to the control over extraction, or the regulation of flows, or the imposition of standards, or the specialization of skills (chapter 3). We have already seen that the Achaemenid court coveted and cared for vessels of green stone, particularly serpentine, and while it is unclear how the Achaemenids regulated the flows of this particular material and the labor that surrounded green-stone manufacturing, the accumulation and sequestering of chert and serpentine vessels in the Treasury and their comparability of form suggest considerable investment in controlling the transfers of the green-stone materials and the skills entailed in working them.

The plate is also a delegate because it afforded, through direct somatic encounter, a practice that was relevant to the underlying values of the Achaemenid politico-religious project, and thus to the reproduction of the sovereign's prerogative to rule. The plate did this in partnership with the other things found alongside it on the floor of Room G, and indeed in collaboration with the wider assemblage of green plates and associated objects in Persepolis. The case to be made here is complicated, and rests on the existence of an enigmatic concentration of 97 green chert mortars and 80 pestles alongside the chert and serpentine plates in the Treasury (Schmidt 1957: 55). The plates, mortars, and pestles were likely used in sets (Cahill 1985: 382), making the presence of mortars in the Room G assemblage no mere coincidence. The sets appear to have been involved in a religious rite that entailed crushing a plant with a mortar and pestle and the consumption of the resulting substance with a footless plate. A number of seals and seal impressions depict mortars and pestles in association with a fire altar.[45] In one instance, the mortar and pestle are held in a figure's hands (Curtis and Tallis 2005: no. 200), while in two other cases the objects are shown on a low stand placed beneath the god Ahuramazda in a winged disk (figure 66). At least two, and possibly three, of these glyptic examples also show a flat plate in the hand of one of the figures (figure 67; Boardman 2000: fig. 5.31; Moorey 1979: fig. 3A). It is generally accepted that the seals with mortars and pestles depict a ritual ceremony linked to fire and the patron deity of the empire; the presence of the plates on the Gordion seal, coupled with the physical association of plates with mortars and pestles in the Treasury, gives good grounds to argue that the footless plates also figured in this rite.

FIGURE 66. Impression of a seal from Persepolis (no. 20) showing two figures on either side of a fire altar (holding sticks, possibly *haoma* twigs) and a stand on which rests a mortar and pestle (source: Schmidt 1957: pl. 7, courtesy of the Oriental Institute of the University of Chicago).

The precise nature of the rite remains uncertain. Many scholars agree that it likely involved the crushing of a hallucinogenic plant or flower, called *haoma* (Bowman 1970: 6–15; Cahill 1985: 382; Razmjou 2005: 153; Root 2015: 26; Schmidt 1957: 55).[46] Complications arise, however, because the details of the ceremony are known to us from later, codified Avestan religion (and Vedic materials), in which the *haoma* (or *soma*) ritual involves the crushing of a plant and the combination of the resulting juices with another liquid to create a sacred drink with psychotropic effects (Malandra 1983: 150–158). The Avestan rite required plates, mortars, and pestles, and the stems or stalks of an unknown plant. With regard to the latter, it is notable that on at least two of the Achaemenid seal impressions a figure appears to be carrying a twig or twigs.

The parallels between the rite known from Avestan religion and the combination of implements found in the Treasury and depicted on the seals are unmistakable. It

FIGURE 67. Drawing of a seal impression from Gordion showing two figures on either side of a fire altar carrying twigs and flat plates (source: Dusinberre 2005: 52, courtesy of Elspeth Dusineberre).

is of further significance that the vessels, both chert and serpentine, are green, and the word for "green" is linguistically linked in Iranian languages to Vedic *soma* and Avestan *haoma* (Rossi 2006: 462, cited in Root 2015: 2026).[47] Moreover, it is quite clear that the word *hauma* (as it appears in Old Persian) was already in use in the fifth century B.C., and it may have had religious connotations even then.[48] However, the details of the rite and indeed its very name are provided by later sources. It would be anachronistic to assume that the ceremony occurred in the same way, and with the same meanings, during the period of the Achaemenids as it did in later times. And it would be contrary to reason to entirely dismiss the correspondences that would suggest that the chert plates, mortars, and pestles were used in a religious rite, perhaps involving the juices of a plant. To date, no alternative interpretation for the practice involving these objects has been put forward.

Let us return, then, to Room G at Tsaghkahovit, with its serpentine plate, basalt mortars, ceramic stand, stone vessel fragment, and ceramics. I have already noted the rarity of mortars at Tsaghkahovit, and while one of those recovered from Room G is unremarkable, the other is strikingly well made compared to all other grindstones from the site, suggesting that it served a special purpose. As to the one-of-a-kind stand, its association with the plate is beyond doubt. Morphologically, the stand does not correspond with any other stands in earlier phases of the archaeology of the Caucasus. I note only in passing that the symmetrical hourglass profile of the stand, with squared-off top and bottom surfaces, broadly mirrors that of the altars with stepped top and base that are depicted on some Achaemenid seals and on the royal tomb facades at Naqsh-i Rustam (figure 6, p. 8), one of which was recovered in fragments at Pasargadae (Stronach 1978: 141). In sum, the Achaemenid religious rite involving footless plates, mortars, and altars and/or stands that would have taken place in the imperial heartland also appears to have taken place at Tsaghkahovit.[49] Given the apparently primary deposition of the plate, stand, and mortar on the floor of Room G, it is possible that we are seeing the remains of a final enactment of the ritual before the site's abandonment.[50]

Whether observed by many at Tsaghkahovit or restricted to a privileged few, the serpentine plate and associated objects would have reaffirmed the social status of the actors involved in this rarified rite. The delegate and associated things (like the basalt mortar proxy) may have conferred legitimacy on the local leaders in Precinct A, a legitimacy perhaps derived in part from religious authority. The precise social position of the celebrants eludes us. While the *haoma*-crushing ceremony is usually associated with priestly individuals (the Median *maji*), Boyce (1982: 147) and Bowman (1970: 7, 15) have suggested that laymen or military commanders belonging to a warrior class could have conducted the rite. It is possible that social boundaries between political, military, and priestly roles were blurred at Tsaghkahovit, precisely through practices like the religious ritual implied by the artifacts in Room G. The combination of artifacts on the floor on this room suggests that certain individuals at Tsaghkahovit had privileged access to what may have been rather esoteric kinds of knowledge. In reinforcing that privileged access by conducting the ritual, these actors would have reproduced their positions as political/religious leaders in their community.

At the same time, the serpentine delegate and its human users would also have reproduced, in small measure, the prescribed rules of a single religious and political institution of the empire. While the specific meaning of the ritual in the Achaemenid context remains uncertain, the link between the green-stone vessels (especially those of chert, but I have suggested those of serpentine as well) and Ahuramazda, the divine guarantor of the Persian realm, is not, judging by the glyptic evidence. The delegate at Tsaghkahovit made its own difference in this community. It called for a ritual stand; it called for a mortar (and a pestle now lost); and it called things into a new entanglement that was closely bound up in the metaphysics of imperial sovereignty.

CONCLUSION

In this chapter I have argued that in one mountain village of the Achaemenid highland, architectural affiliates and ceramic proxies established the limits of subjectivization, working with human users to define and preserve an autonomous existence under empire. And yet, I concluded with a material delegate and associated things from Room G that pointed to the very opposite phenomenon—an assemblage that helped create satrapal conditions of subjection even in this remote corner of the realm. In this way, the findings from Tsaghkahovit speak directly to the paradox at the heart of imperial sovereignty: that it is only possible if it is partial; that it is grounded in an irreconcilable tension between practices that at once erode and buttress a sovereign's prerogative. We saw in chapter 5 that the Achaemenid kings were nothing but self-assured in their claims to hold sway over Armenia. And while several lines of evidence from Tsaghkahovit and the wider highland have revealed the frailty of those royal assertions, the delegate assemblage belonging to an occult imperial practice that took place in a dark semi-subterranean room of a secluded mountain village forces the recognition that the only folly as great as accepting the truth of the stories sovereigns tell about themselves is dismissing those stories as false.

Conclusion

This book began with the observation that contemporary geopolitics has given rise to forms of expansionary power that seem to elude conventional analytics, but that concepts of empire derived from ancient Persia can provide more than the satirical insinuation of hauntingly resurgent "oriental" approaches from the hoary past. An in-depth examination of the sematic field surrounding a millennia-old word that has come down to us as "satrapy" revealed an early material theory of imperial sovereignty, tantalizingly discernable across a range of ancient Persian cultural production. This was intended less as an exercise in historical ethnography, than an effort to investigate an untapped reservoir for contemporary political and material thought that lies beyond the Western philosophical canon. My intention was in no way to diminish the importance of contextualized historical and philological research on ancient Persian concepts, but to take an admittedly atypical approach to these materials in order to discover their pertinence to the disciplinarily diffuse study of imperialism writ large.

If ancient Persia provided the deep foundation for the analytic that lies at the heart of this book, the full elaboration of the "satrapal condition"—which is to say, a workable framework for imperial analysis that centers on the material constitution of aspirational sovereignty—could only come about in conversation with the contemporary material turn, out of which the schema of *delegates, proxies, captives,* and *affiliates* emerged. To the extent that interpreting antiquity through the lens of modern social thought runs the risk of anachronistic readings on the past, the evidence that ancient Persian thinkers (from kings to scholar-priests) gave concerted thought to the relations between imperial power and the material world mitigates powerfully against such risk. Nevertheless, the four-part schema laid out in this book is only a heuristic, and one not meant to be exhaustively embracing, for the forms and capacities of things will always differ across time and space. It *is* meant, however, to reshuffle archaeology's conventional typologies of the material world, organized according to scale or form (e.g., architecture, artifacts, landscapes), in favor of an alternative ordering, premised on political efforts and effects, that focuses our attention on the power of things working in complex confederations alongside the long-privileged human entities of social analysis.

When put to work in part 2 of this book, these concepts brought to the fore the ways in which columned halls, semi-subterranean houses, and silver, ceramic, and stone vessels shaped the Achaemenid project. In the heartland, hypostyle halls that developed out of highland captives came to be imbricated in mutual dependencies with imperial agents, while also enabling and cultivating the practices and principles of Achaemenid kingship. In the mountains of the Armenian *dahyu*, the extant evidence points to opposing currents. Delegates like silver vessels, the buildings of Karačamirli, and the serpentine plate from Tsaghkahovit worked to create conditions of compromised sovereignty in the *dahyu* by enlisting people in imperial practices and new material dependencies. At the same time, modest, highland-style columned halls at Erebuni and Altıntepe, coupled with underground mountain dwellings and ceramic proxies at Tsaghkahovit, worked to place limits on the reach of imperial power. My main concern in these investigations was not specifically to demonstrate that such conflicting sociopolitical tensions of empire obtained, for both Achaemenid studies as well as decades of postcolonial scholarship have already taught us to expect as much; rather, operating under the premises of the satrapal condition, this book scrutinized the active role of the material world in partnering with imperial subjects to put such tensions into play. The things that this study brought under view produced multifarious effects that depended on both their material properties and practical entailments, on both the designs of their human makers and users as well as their own affordances. There is no archaeological scale that can weigh these various effects in the balance and offer some definitive synthesis on the experience of Achaemenid rule over the course of over two centuries and across such a large geographic expanse. But Scott's (2009: 7) notion of the "intermediate zone", that ambiguous space in which the practices of everyday life fall within and beyond sovereign reach, does, to my mind, offer real purchase (see chapter 5, p. 119). In a prosaic sense, it is the case that greater clarity will be hard to come by without targeted and sustained excavations at other Iron 3 settlements, coupled with systematic surveys that attend seriously to the early historic periods on the highland.

In bringing this book to a close, I would like to touch on two themes that have heretofore remained unaddressed, yet are critical to any claim that a distinctly archaeological approach to problems of empire should be a matter of concern.

TOWARD A SELF-GOVERNING ARCHAEOLOGY OF EMPIRES

At least since the new millennium, historical archaeology in its most expansive sense seems to have arrived at a comfortable resolution to the dilemma of how to navigate the evidentiary pastiche—material and discursive—that provides its *raison d'être.* In a study of imperial craft production, Carla Sinopoli (2003: 7) succinctly captured this sense that a period of disciplinary soul-searching has run its course, when writing, "What I do not wish to rehearse is a formulaic discussion of the advantages and disadvantages of historical versus archaeological data. Both are valuable; both are problematic." This is, to be sure, an eminently sober and unassailable appraisal, which neatly sums up what is surely the consensus view to have emerged from recent reassessments of archaeology and history's relative strengths. And yet, at the risk of seeming disputatious, I would like to suggest that, despite having the merits of harmony and balance, the middle-ground perspective that underscores the symbiotic relationship between archaeological and textual analysis is not as unproblematic as it may seem.

It is worth briefly revisiting the rationales that have until now worked to clear a space for an archaeological approach to problems of empire and colonialism. The prevailing views coalesce into what can be called corrective, emancipatory, and cooperative logics, each of which construes archaeology's prerogative in the study of imperial phenomena differently, but all of which are in one way or another tethered to textual production. The corrective rationale has deep and enduring roots in archaeological thought, tracing at least as far back as the fifteenth century, when the Italian antiquarian Cyriac of Ancona dubbed monuments and other material remains the "seals of history" (*sigilla historiarum*) that serve to challenge the veracity of textual sources (Schnapp 1997: 110). From Peru to Persia, the Anconian rationale can still be heard. For example, nearly a century after Max Uhle tasked archaeology to set right the errata of the documentary sources on the Inca, Alan Covey (2008: 809–813) has recently reasserted the verificative project, noting discrepancies between the written and material records with respect to such things as Inca origin myths and state formation (see also Malpass 1993). Leading scholars of the Achaemenid Empire have called this archaeology's "rôle correcteur" (Briant and Boucharlat 2005: 22). American historical archaeology, drawing on traditions of postcolonial thought, has adopted this foundational logic in more political terms, with calls to critically expose discrepancies between archaeological and documentary sources as part of an effort to break free from the hegemony of imperial discourse and expose the biases of master narratives, as Lisa Overholtzer (2013) has recently done for Aztec Xaltocan and Matthew Liebmann (2012: 8) for the Pueblo Revolt.

Anconian reasoning, particularly in its postcolonial reformulation, is a compelling justification for the archaeology of empires. It recognizes archaeology's prerogative not only to set the skewed record of history straight, but also to bring political awareness to the causes and consequences of such bias. Endowed with the ability to fact-check the imaginings of the chroniclers, archaeology would thus seem to enjoy a kind of disciplinary autonomy. But in fact, Anconian logics imply the very opposite, shackling archaeology to history as its appointed auditor. To say this is not to trivialize an important role that archaeology can indeed play vis-à-vis history, but to recognize the insufficiency of staking a guiding principle for one discipline on the limitations of another.

Alternatively, under the auspices of an emancipatory rationale, historical archaeology is fashioned as the champion of the proverbial "people without history" (Wolf 1982). The purpose of the subfield is to open a window onto the "lives of nonelites," the "men and especially women who formed the bulk" of ancient empires, about whom texts are usually silent (Sinopoli 2001: 440; S. T. Smith 2003b: 189). Archaeology alone can make up for "elite bias" in colonial histories (Given 2004: 4), can allow those written out of history to "speak" for themselves (Wells 1999a), to have their "voice" be heard (Hingley 1997: 82; Lyons and Papadopoulos 2002: 11; Morrison 2001a: 253), to tell their untold stories (Liebmann 2012: 13). "Because of the nature of written texts," Kathleen Deagan (2001: 181) has written with respect to the study of Spanish America, "it is only through material expression that action and agency are implied for all actors in the past, that is, not only those who produced written or iconographic accounts." The argument is compelling not only because a vigorous emancipatory stance appeals to the political sensibilities of the left-leaning academy, but also because, as both Morrison and Deagan note, the lived experiences of the "silent majority" (Alcock 1993: 3) that archaeology brings into view substantially shaped processes of imperial reproduction.

Be this as it may, the emancipatory logic is nevertheless a defense of historical archaeology premised on its ability to "fill in the blanks" (Liebmann 2012: 83) that history leaves behind. Lurking beneath this argument is the troubling notion, also concerning to John Moreland (2001: 21), that "the value of archaeology is inversely proportional to the quality and quantity of written sources." It forces the enfeebling conclusion that if the kinds of archives on which social historians rely were to become available, archaeology's redundancy would be laid bare. It should be stressed that, like the corrective rationale, an emancipatory logic is neither incorrect nor unimportant; it is simply thin, less concerned to define a robust archaeological role in the study of empires and colonies than to provide a defense construed in relation to textual production.

Lastly, what of the ecumenical appeal to collaborative inquiry—to the integration and interplay of all possible lines of evidence in the daunting project of making sense of early imperial formations? The phenomena under our gaze are so tremendously unwieldy and the datasets each so threadbare on their own, the cooperative logic goes, that archaeology must do its part in the effort to amass evidence and participate in "interdisciplinary cooperation" (Morrison 2001b: 6). "In many ways we are worse off than the proverbial blind man and the elephant," writes D'Altroy (2001: 127), in a metaphor for the study of early empires. "Instead of a firm grip on a tail, a trunk, an ear, too often we have a few broken ribs in a bag, some fossilized dropping in a vial, and a corner of a circus poster under plastic." It follows that "our analyses depend on intersecting lines of evidence from different sources—historical, monumental, dynastic, numismatic, archaeological."

Interdisciplinary cooperation is, of course, a cardinal virtue in the academy and one that would seem exempt from questioning. And yet it arguably provides an anemic rationale for archaeologies of empire. For one, it creates a false sense of equivalence among the disciplines, as if archaeology and history have become equal partners in the effort to reconstruct the historical past. But have we really achieved such disciplinary parity? The research carried out in the writing of chapter 2 of this book would suggest otherwise, instead pointing generally (though of course not universally) to the authoritative, indeed foundational influence of written sources in the design of archaeological research questions pertaining to problems of empire and imperial colonialism. It might fairly be asked why this should be cause for concern. If nothing else, a position of disciplinary subordination does not provide a strong footing from which to advocate for the reproduction of the field. More troublingly, calls for interdisciplinary cooperation presume the existence of a fundamentally common set of research questions, to which different approaches and kinds of evidence can be put. Archaeology is here reduced to a *method*, rather than a branch of study devoted to the production of knowledge pertaining to the workings of the material world broadly construed, and thus one irreducible to the logics of history. My contention is that cooperative, multidisciplinary inquiry with respect to imperial politics and societies is most vigorous when it is based not on the aggregation of different forms of data, but on the encounter of independent modes of reasoning.

Archaeological reasoning centers on the relational webs that link humans with other animate and inanimate things, as such things exist in and through space, as they are discursively represented on the "page," as they are visually represented in media, or in any other condition. A self-governing archaeology of empires and colonialism is one that rests its epistemological prerogative in the expansive study of imperial things in all their multifarious states of being, animate and inanimate, real and virtual, vibrant and vestigial. It takes responsibility for explaining the varying powers of things to mold our politics, our passions, and our planet, and to register our imperial pasts and present. Such a position finds close affinity with recent views that archaeology's strength in the study of colonialism is its ability to attend to human practice (e.g. Dietler 2010; Voss and Vasella 2010; Wernke 2013), but forwards a more explicit role for things in affording these practical entanglements by virtue of their substantive and relational qualities. On these grounds, it is possible to envision a revived comparative archaeological project that differs in important respects from approaches we have seen thus far. To be sure, a concerted turn to the variegated work of matter in imperial and colonial worlds provides an alternative to the asocial classificatory concepts that originally gave shape to the comparative enterprise in the 1990s (see chapter 2). In remaining attuned to the question "What do imperial things do?" there is no presumption of cross-cultural uniformity, no fixed models into which contingent historical phenomena are to be plugged, but only the shared recognition that in attending to the relations between humans and things we can attain a novel and uniquely archaeological understanding of the persistent process of macropolitical association that we have come to gloss as "empire." Likewise, a comparative project pitched on these terms provides the tools for wading through the dense forests of historical particularities across time and space, and giving voice to illuminating points of convergence and divergence in ways that archaeology alone can. Matter furnishes a distinctly archaeological inflection to the cross-disciplinary study of empire.

Yet if a strong case for an archaeological prerogative in the study of empire requires a more confident decoupling from texts, then it also requires a new relationship to time. Once relieved of the duty to fill the gaps in fragmentary historical records, archaeology confronts a new challenge: to critique the underestimated exertions of matter in shaping and subverting today's imperial projects. We thus end where we began, with satrapal conditions in our own time.

IMPERIAL MATTER IN THE PRESENT

This book was completed at a time of unusually heightened concern surrounding the complex relations between imperial agents and things. Let us consider three examples that attest to the importance of a materially aware critique of expansionary political projects. I draw my examples from current affairs of geopolitics and science with no illusion that these will be matters of pressing concern in years or even months hence, but only the confidence, based on humanity's track record over three thousand years, that imperial ambition in some form, familiar or novel, will remain a part of our political repertoire into the future.

Notes from Russia: Little Green Men and the Annexation of Crimea

Russia's 2014 annexation of Crimea witnessed the appearance of a new kind of military being. Dressed in helmets, black masks that covered all but their eyes, and unusual camouflage combat uniforms that bore no trace of political or military insignia, these new beings appeared to be special forces of an anonymous army that belonged to no sovereign state whatsoever. The peculiar military men were anomalous in other respects as well. While always carrying machine guns, the force was unusually polite, frequently seen posing for photo-ops with small children and young women. In Russian they came to be called *vezhlevye zelenye chelovechki,* or the "polite little green men." Alexei Yurchak (2014) has noted that the Russian subtleties of the slang hint at a being that is almost less than human—"small creatures that are like humans, but are not humans." Most observers quickly assumed that the "polite little green men" were surely Russian army troops. But on more than one occasion, Vladimir Putin denied the claim, offering the absurd suggestion that the men "'are probably forces of Crimean self-defense who purchased their uniforms in a local store'" (Yurchak 2014). After the annexation of the peninsula was complete, the Russian president admitted that his troops had indeed been in Crimea to help prepare for the staged referendum that supposedly legitimated Russia's takeover of the region. Yurchak has persuasively described the "little green men" as indicative of a new Russian technology of sovereignty that ironically involves military occupation through nonoccupation. With their nondescript uniforms, the "little green men" were intended to be anonymous yet recognizable, polite yet threatening, identifiably Russian yet not quite so: "They were designed to be a *pure, naked military force*—a force without a state, without a face, without identity, without a clearly articulated goal." They were the advance guard in a resurgent Russian empire's new approach to warfare that uses "the spectacle of dominance" to create "docile populations within the new geographic boundaries of empire in Europe" (Dunn and Bobick 2014: 406).

In the media coverage of the Crimea invasion, the unmarked uniforms and associated paraphernalia of the "little green men" received much attention. And indeed, they merit our scrutiny, for they provide us with a modern instance of a forceful human–thing delegate assemblage deployed in the theater of imperial conquest, in both the dramaturgical and military senses. The "little green men" are but select participants in a broader Russian "theater state" in which, unlike Geertz's Negara, warfare is terrifyingly real (Dunn and Bobick 2014: 409). What is perhaps most intriguing about the unmarked combat uniforms, tactical vests, and composite helmets of the "little green men" is how they assiduously resist interpretation as either material proof or material sign of Russian expansion. Lacking identifying marks, the delegates stand at best as negative evidence and anti-symbols that refuse to speak loudly of imperial ambition. Instead, they work only as quiet but active players in the course of events, helping the men with smiling eyes sway popular opinion and realize military gains that resulted in a questionable referendum strongly in favor of Russian annexation. An understanding of the Russian invasion of Crimea requires careful consideration of these (and no doubt other) material delegates, whose power to create their own effects, apart from the agency of the human commandoes who wore them, was clearly at the forefront of Russian neo-imperial strategy.

Notes from Syria and Iraq: ISIS and the Destruction of Heritage

In the months following Russia's mindfully material takeover of Crimea, the world's gaze turned to another theater of conquest in which *things* are making a difference with terrifying efficacy. In 2014, a radical Sunni militant group known (in one of its appellations) as the Islamic State of Iraq and al-Sham (ISIS) declared itself a worldwide caliphate. The group demanded the allegiance of Muslim communities around the globe, and began to expand territorially from its "heartland" in Syria into northern Iraq, while also establishing an operational presence in many other countries. ISIS's rise to power has entailed unfathomably brutal war crimes and human rights abuses, especially against minorities, justified in the name of jihadist Salafism. Accompanying the human carnage has been a deftly publicized campaign of iconoclasm marked by the shattering of museum artifacts in the Mosul Museum, the destruction of well-known archaeological sites, the detonation of hundreds of Muslim cultural sites, and the burning of archives. All the while, there have been recurrent reports that ISIS relies, even if in only small measure, on the revenues from the illicit looting and trade of antiquities to finance its operations. As of this writing, events continue to unfold rapidly. States and international organizations are scrambling to address the unprecedented humanitarian crisis, the global security threats, and the cultural heritage emergency. On the latter score, heritage practitioners are working to document the wreckage, to assist in stemming the traffic in illicit antiquities, and to decide on the appropriate rhetorical and affective responses. In such a moment of urgency, pausing to contemplate the role of *things* in ISIS's project to recreate a caliphate is not to retreat into the tranquil shelter of scholarly analysis but to ascertain whether our human agencies can check the efforts of both the human and the material participants in this calamity.

It is widely accepted the ISIS's acts of heritage destruction are but one part of a carefully crafted media campaign designed to gain publicity, shock the sensibilities of a world community that assigns value to cultural heritage, and attract and further radicalize sympathizers to its putative utopia. Ömür Harmanşah (2015: 170) has recently critiqued the careful staging of destruction as media performance. He notes how ISIS has coordinated and choreographed the violence into "mediatic spectacles," broadcast to the outside world "through ISIS's own image-making and dissemination apparatus that increasingly utilizes the most advanced technologies of visualization and communication." Once the images of smashed stone sculptures and detonated monuments fall into the juggernaut of mass media, they "go viral" in an information cascade. In a fast-paced virtual age, the images are themselves things with tactile materiality, embedded in the screens of our devices and the folds of our "print" media (Bruno 2014). Apart from their creators, both these *image-things* and the *imaged things* work in concert as a powerful force, capable of creating visceral, embodied effects that incite viewers to action. While the consequential difference made by each specific element of ISIS's expansive media strategy cannot be discriminated, the "mediatic spectacles" of heritage destruction are a major part of that whole, and thus important contributors to the organization's continued success in recruiting militant volunteers transnationally. To the extent that the new "caliphate" aspires to territorial expansion, it is fair to ask whether the monuments and antiquities themselves, along with a vast apparatus of visual technology—from handheld recording devices, to the unseen servers of social media outlets, to the smartphones in our pockets—have become weapons of conquest. If so, repressing such powerful things requires more-than-human strength, the marshaling of human agencies and technological capabilities in confederation to deflect the spectacle and deny its viral spread.

Notes from the Atmosphere: Colonialism and the Anthropocene

In the spring of 2015, a provocative study appeared in the journal *Nature* that brought attention to the shocking planetary reverberations of the complex weaves that stitch together imperial processes and the material world. The study was designed to identify the most likely start date for the human-dominated geological epoch that has come to be known as the Anthropocene. Using the formal criteria for defining a shift in geological time—most importantly a global marker of an event in stratigraphic materials like rock, sediment, or glacial ice—climate scientists Simon Lewis and Mark Masin concluded that the year 1610, roughly a century after Europe's colonization of the Americas, provides a more satisfactory start date for anthropogenic change in the Earth's system than, for example, the advent of agriculture or the spread of industrial technologies. European imperial colonialism in the Americas had geological effects that were without precedent, marked most conspicuously by a dramatic decline in atmospheric carbon dioxide between 1570 and 1620 that is discernable in high-resolution Antarctic ice core records. What accounts for the decline is the regeneration of 50 million hectares of forest, woody savanna, and grassland, which caused a significant carbon uptake. The diseases, war, enslavement, and famine brought on by European imperialism led to a rapid fall in human numbers—a drop from 54–61 million people in 1492 to a minimum of 6 million in 1650—in turn leading to a decline in farming and the use of fire that combined to transform the planetary system (Lewis and Maslin 2015: 175).

Whether or not the "Orbis hypothesis," as Lewis and Masin term it, will hold up to future scientific scrutiny of the Anthropocene is of less immediate relevance here than the opening the authors provide for thinking through the possibilities and limits of a critical "post-humanist" archaeology of imperial formations. On the one hand, the study alerts us to the formidable power of the nonhuman material world—in this case biota—to create consequences of planetary proportions that reverberate far beyond the designs of colonialism's human agents. European imperialism set in motion devastating human harms that had a profound influence on the "natural" world, but, as material ecocritics would note (Iovino and Oppermann 2014), that agentive nonhuman world acted back with an unexpected animacy whose effects are still felt today. The study also alerts us to the fact that the lasting and all-too-vibrant material legacies of imperialism, what Stoler (2013) and others have examined under the frame "imperial debris," lodge themselves not only in minds, bodies, and built landscapes, but in the material fabric of the Earth itself. On the other hand, against such lessons that press forward the high stakes of a materially aware approach to problems of empire and colonialism is a countervailing caution that alerts us to the risks and limits of a "materialist" archaeology of empire. It is with this cautionary note that I conclude these investigations.

ON VIOLENCE AND ACCOUNTABILITY

What Russia's "little green men," ISIS's "mediatic spectacle" of heritage destruction, and the Orbis hypothesis all have in common is a figuration of the material world in relation to acts of political violence, albeit with different agentive implications and under different temporalities. In the case of Russia and ISIS, the unmarked uniforms, demolished monuments, and staged visuals exert themselves in the politics of expansionist polities-in-the-making, in action at the "moment" of violent territorial takeover or jihadist recruitment. In these cases, the work of things not as mere tools in human-orchestrated violence but as participants in dangerous, interlocking human–thing unions is available to recognition when placed under an archaeological gaze. In contrast, the Orbis hypothesis perceives material agency as a *response* to European colonial violence, at work over a considerably protracted timescale. When we read of disease, war, enslavement, and famine in a colonial context, our instinct is to imagine a deplorable human tragedy, with human protagonists and victims. To be sure, disease entails the bustling activity of microscopic infectious agents, war requires unyieldingly solid lethal weapons, enslavement requires a host of physical restraints, and famine entails material refusals. But to invoke the indisputable work of nonhuman players in a human ordeal as devastating as Europe's colonization of the Americas would seem at best to miss the point of humanistic inquiry, at worst to betray the entire enterprise itself. For where then would accountability reside? The question can now be extended to the "little green men" and ISIS's media of heritage carnage: What are the ethical implications of an approach to empire that redistributes efficacies among humans and nonhumans alike? Who or what is then expected to answer for imperialism's manifold harms? Without actionable culpability, is there the risk that imperialism could become natural, inevitable, resistant to critique? While the new ontologies opened up by the material turn may be cogent, even correct, they may at the same time be deeply *wrong*.

The human and nonhuman agencies of violence in Achaemenid Armenia are not at present open to investigation given the scarcity of relevant evidence as might be gleaned, for example, from mortuary assemblages, osteological or artifactual. While the delegates and proxies that figured prominently in this account of the satrapal condition played a part in the transformation of lifeways, they are not themselves brutal things of ruination. But neither this fact, nor the temporal remove of antiquity that invariability divests such an archaeology of imperial matter of an urgent ethical reckoning, renders the question of how to apportion responsibility for imperial production and reproduction any less acute. A critique of satrapal conditions does not absolve humans of moral responsibility, even if causative responsibility may be diffuse. While the redistribution of agency that lies at the heart of the material turn does demote human motivation as agency's defining quality, it does not deny the force of human will. For now at least, it is we humans who get to choose whether intention remains the grounds for deliberation on the dispensation of justice. Allowing ourselves to look closely at imperial matter need not exempt us of culpability; instead, it holds out the promise that if we understand the workings of human–thing assemblages we may stop to ask ourselves, "Do I attempt to extricate myself from assemblages whose trajectory is likely to do harm?" (Bennett 2010: 37). We may also be better positioned to control the vitalities of our nonhuman partners when their efficacies are directed toward the sundry harms associated with the most enduring approach to political life of the last three millennia. One thing is all but certain: there will be future opportunities to try.

NOTES

INTRODUCTION

1. Occurrences are numerous, and include "The Bridge Builder," *The Times,* May 12, 1997; "Raymond Edde . . . ," *The Guardian,* May 24, 2000; "Danger from Damascus," *Jerusalem Post,* July 25, 2002; "The USA Has Made Fools of Us," *Evening Standard,* October 10, 2003; "A Ballot in Beirut," *The Times,* June 9, 2009; and Fisk (2013).

2. "Leading Article: A Strategic Absurdity: Sunnis against Shias," *The Guardian,* January 6, 2014.

3. For example, turning from states to other forms of political association, some have described the European Union as a collection of so many satrapies (Booker 2007; Johnson 2012).

4. To recognize that impossibility is not to encourage facile analogies or the casual application of potentially anachronistic interpretive concepts, as Nicola Terrenato (2005) has cautioned with respect to postcolonialism and Roman studies. See also Dietler (2010), Rowlands (1998), and van Dommelen (2002).

5. We shall return in chapter 1 to the controversial link between the Achaemenids and Zoroastrianism.

6. "Leading Article: Why the Civil Service . . . ," June 2, 1997. The journalist was facetiously critiquing the notion that the British prime minister's private secretary should be an independent civil servant rather than a party appointee, a "wholly politicised satrap."

7. "We shall make the boundary of the land of Persia border on the lofty realm of Zeus," Herodotus ventriloquized the Persian king, Xerxes, as saying to an assembly of Persians in advance of his march on Greece. "The sun will not look down on any territory bordering our own, because after I, together with you, have passed through all of Europe, we shall have made them all one single territory. . . . Thus those we regard as guilty as well as those who are innocent will bear the yoke of slavery" (Herodotus 2007, Hist. 7.8).

8. Margaret Cool Root (2002: 201–202) has spoken of this scene as no simple lion kill but rather "one of symbolic collusion." The image brings together two powerful and noble animals in a pose that "is more reminiscent of leonine mating foreplay than the hunting kill." It thus "projects their union within a symbolic landscape of abundance signifying the combined powers of nature brought together by and for the Achaemenid empire."

9. On ancient Iraq, see Bahrani (2003). On ancient Iran, I have in mind the efforts of a small circle of scholars who came to constitute the field of Achaemenid studies out of a series of important conferences and proceedings dating to the 1980s and 1990s known as the Achaemenid History Workshop (Sancisi-Weerdenburg and Kuhrt 1987, 1988, 1990; Sancisi-Weerdenburg 1987).

10. Much as colonial studies long ago cleaved colonialism from its Latin derivation and Roman origins.

11. As Wiesehöfer (1996) notes, "there was nothing in the Persian empire that might compare with the Roman colonies and municipia, in which . . . there occurred economic and familiar interchange between conquerors and subjects." There is, however, some evidence for the deportation of conquered groups from one area of the empire to another (Briant 2002: 505).

12. For recent histories of the Achaemenid Empire, see Briant (2002), Kuhrt (2001, 2007a, 2007b), and Waters (2014). For historical treatments of the empire's satraps and satrapies, see e.g. Schmitt (1976), Tuplin (1987), and Klinkott (2005).

1. THE SATRAPAL CONDITION

1. Translated by Sadri (2013).

2. On the etymology of *xšaça,* as the cuneiform script is transliterated in the Roman alphabet, see Cheung (2007: 451–452). On a recent suggestion that Old Persian existed well before the Bisitun inscription, see Vallat (2013).

3. Translated by Kent (1953). Following convention, the abbreviations for Achaemenid royal inscriptions used throughout this book are from Kent (1953).

4. For a recent analysis of the many rich complexities of this monument, see Root (2013).

5. "It is both power and the domain where this power is exercised, kingship and kingdom."

6. Gnoli (2007: 113–115) suggests that *xšaça* can be taken to mean "province," much like the word *dahyu,* meaning both "lands" and "peoples," which the Achaemenids used to describe the component parts of their dominion. But the concurrence of *xšaça* and *dahyu* in the Old Persian inscriptions occurs only with respect to Persia, which, as the imperial heartland, was hardly a "province" in the English sense, even if it may have been a *dahyu* in the Old Persian sense. It is also worth noting that the absence of geographic fixity to the role of the *xšaçapāvan* echoes the apparent fluidity with which the Achaemenids may have perceived the imperial center itself. Lincoln's (2012: 54) analysis of the king's royal circuit suggests that "determination of [the empire's] center did not depend on considerations of geometry alone. Rather, the center was relational, being defined by the king himself, and not some administrative structure of fixed geographic locus."

7. Herodotus rarely uses "satrapy" in the *Histories,* or the Greek *ἀρχή* with which he explicitly defines it. The word *νομός* appears more commonly to describe the organizational

elements of the Achaemenid Empire. νομός also carries administrative connotations, perhaps even more strongly than ἀρχή. Prior to the *Histories,* ἀρχή denoted "beginning, origin, first principle," while slightly before or contemporary with Herodotus it was used in an abstract sense to mean "power, sovereignty." Yet Herodotus is credited as the first to use ἀρχή in a governmental sense to mean an office or sphere of jurisdiction, as is clear from the passages cited above and elsewhere (*Hist.* 1.207.3, 3.97.1, 7.19.2).

8. The Achaemenids used a different word to describe the component parts of their dominion, and that was *dahyu,* a term that denotes at one and the same time the incorporated "lands" or "countries" and the "peoples" of the empire (see note 6). It is also worth noting that the stripping away of the metaphysics behind Persian concepts may have been a Greek habit. We find this at work in the case of the paradise (*pairi.daida*), a complex institution linked to Achaemenid cosmogony and eschatology about which more will be said in chapter 4. The Persian paradise was an earthly preserve of original, cosmic perfection that had been broadly lost with the arrival of the Lie, but whose continued cultivation held out the promise of eventual restoration of happiness for mankind at the end of days. This philosophical inflection fell away in the hands of virtually all Greek authors, who reduced the Persian paradise to "a technical term" to describe an exquisite garden for royal repose (Lincoln 2012: 128).

9. This is of course not to suggest that the mundane trappings of government and administration were not of the greatest importance to the Achaemenids, for which we have no better evidence than the Persepolis archives. However, the language of administration and that of political metaphysics were largely, though perhaps not absolutely, distinct. Indeed, of some 8,500 known inscribed tablets from Persepolis, only one is written in Old Persian, the most common languages of administration being Elamite and Aramaic (Stolper and Tavernier 2007).

10. Toward the end of Darius's reign it was replaced by *būmi,* originally a cosmologically inflected word for "earth" or "world" which the Achaemenids later redeployed to refer to an earthly (and distinctly spatial) notion of "empire" (Lincoln 2007: 45). On the language of Persian imperialism, see e.g. Benveniste (1969), Herrenschmidt (1976), and Lincoln (2007). Suffice it to say that *xšaça* is but one term in the Achaemenid political lexicon, and one that occurs relatively rarely in the extant sources.

11. Throughout this book, I follow the Western convention of using the Greek name, Persepolis, to describe a place that the Persians themselves called Parsa.

12. In the tomb reliefs, the figures are labeled with the repeated phrase "this is the Persian," "this is the Egyptian," "this is the Armenian," etc.

13. Translated by Kent (1953).

14. It should be obvious that I use the word "demos" here not strictly in the classical Greek sense but in the sociological sense of a political collective, like those depicted in registers on the throne-bearing scenes.

15. Translated by Kuhrt (2007).

16. Translated by Lincoln (2012).

17. In the final analysis, however, the question largely depends on the relative weight to be placed on the worship of Ahuramazda, the chief deity at the center of both Zoroastrian scripture and Achaemenid inscriptions, versus the prophet Zarathustra, who is nowhere mentioned in the latter corpus (e.g. Lincoln 2012; Skjærvø 2005).

18. A variant of the term Bounteous Immortals (with the word order inverted) makes its first appearance in a set of hymns known as the Yasna Haptanghaiti that are thought to be roughly as old as the Gathas, the earliest corpus of Avestan scripture attributed to the prophet Zarathustra. But in the Yasna Haptanghaiti (39.3) the constituent elements of the group are not there enumerated. Equally interestingly, the entities that would eventually congeal into the Bounteous Immortals are invoked in the Gathas as abstract nouns, but here they are not clearly divine personifications, and they are not distinguished as a collective group of particular significance apart from the numerous other such abstractions in the Gathas.

19. The names of the other Bounteous Immortals are, in approximate English translation, Good Purpose, Best Truth, Holy Devotion, Wholeness, and Immortality. I thank Bruce Lincoln (personal communication) for furnishing the translation Choice Sovereignty; the entity sometimes appears in the relevant literature as Desirable Dominion.

20. In Lommel's (1970 [1959]: 256–257) words: " . . . abstrakt ist in dieser archaischen Geisteswelt nichts. . . . Wir erfassen das Geistige, z. B. Wahrhaftigkeit oder treffliche Gesinnung eines Menschen als etwas ihm Innerliches, das nach außen wirkt. Dort, so glaube ich es zu verstehen, wurde es erfaßt als etwas, das ihn lenkt, eine Kraft, die auf ihn einwirkt. Für uns ist dies etwas Subjektives, dort aber erschien es als ein Objektives, Gegenüberstehendes, und—als geistig—über dem Menschen Stehendes. Und da es als wirkend erfahren wurde, war es ein Lebendiges, somit eine Persönlichkeit."

21. The tribute-procession motif has antecedents in the artistic production of earlier Near Eastern empires, but the Apadana differs from these in many important ways (Root 1979: 240–263). On gifting in the Achaemenid Empire, see Briant and Herrenschmidt (1989) and Sancisi-Weerdenburg (1998).

22. See Root (2007) for a detailed discussion of the tension between absorption and difference through the specific case of the Greek delegation on the Apadana relief.

23. If the two bows that the Elamite delegation brings are of metal, as Walser (1966: 73) thinks possible, as well as the various vessels that the Arian, Arachosians, and Egyptian delegations bring, then all but three of the twenty-three delegations bear metal gifts.

24. In this regard it is also worth noting the strips of gold buried under the paved terrace of the Sacred Precinct of Pasargadae (Stronach 1978: 145, pl. 109a), which Root (2010: 167) has brought into the conversation on Achaemenid foundation deposits.

2. WHERE THINGS STAND

1. Perhaps the earliest such reckoning for which we have evidence was the Elamite king Shutruk-Nahhunte's appropriation of Akkadian things in the twelfth century B.C. (Bahrani 2003: 149–184; Feldman 2009). Later rulers of the Near East would go on to investigate and use the material ruins of imperial pasts in new ways, from the excavation campaigns of the Babylonian king Nabonidus (Winter 2000) to the fortress revitalizations of the Hellenistic kings of Armenia (Khatchadourian 2007).

2. At the time, the very suggestion that empires should be taken seriously in the comparative study of complexity required an apologia. Consider Craig Morris's appeal in *Archaic States* (1998: 294) that the Inca case could reveal the "relatively uncontaminated birth of a

state, though obviously not a pristine state." On the long-standing marginality of empires within anthropological archaeology in the 1970s and 1980s, see Sinopoli (2001: 439).

3. The classic Marxist accounts of Luxemburg, Lenin, and others, in their particular focus on outward material flows from metropoles to colonies—the dumping of Europe's surplus commodities and the export of capital to precapitalist dependencies—had no clear antecedents in humankind's earliest experiments with expansive economic formations (Mommsen 1980).

4. In its more recent deployments (Stark and Chance 2012), talk of strategies has shifted from the strategies of states to the strategies of provincials, though the latter are still very much set within a state-centered framework.

5. But see Wernke (2013) for a particularly effective use of landscape archaeology to expose the limitations of models premised on the distinction between "direct" and "indirect" rule.

6. Although it should be noted that, even with the presence of such roundhouses, other scholars have stressed that the Romano-British landscape remained fundamentally an imperial one, "constructed by and for a colonial society" (Mattingly 2006: 355).

3. IMPERIAL MATTER

1. In one later study, Thomas (2002) more expressly considers the ways in which enlisted objects (particularly missionary-imported cloth) powerfully assisted human projects of colonial transformation, for instance in the conversion to Christianity in nineteenth-century Oceania.

2. Interestingly, when efficacy is afforded directly to the things themselves, it is only by the subjects of the Comaroffs' study, the Tswana and the evangelists, who believed that clothes could change human conduct (Comaroff and Comaroff 1997: 223, 230).

3. Augustus himself may have viewed it rather more metaphorically. After quoting the emperor on his makeover of Rome, Dio (1987: 245) goes on to explain, "In saying this he was not referring literally to the state of the buildings, but rather to the strength of the empire."

4. FROM CAPTIVES TO DELEGATES

1. DSf.20–22, as translated by Vallat (2013b: 284).

2. As listed in inscriptions DSz, DSf, DSaa. For the complexities surrounding the various texts that make up the Susa Foundation corpus, see Root (2010).

3. DsSaa.5, from Kuhrt (2007a: 497). Translations vary. Vallat (2013b: 290) prefers, "By the grace of Ahuramazda, the materials and decoration of this palace were brought from afar and I designed the layout."

4. The Persians might have called this an *apadana*. On the complexities surrounding this and related words, see e.g. Schmitt (1987), Stronach (1985), Lecoq (1997: 115–116), and Razmjou (2010: 231–233).

5. Old Persian *fraša*, e.g. DSj.3.

6. Armenia and Media are mentioned in only one text of the Susa Charters as places that contributed to the centripetal flow of materials. The Babylonian tablet DSaa (4.18–31)

reads: "Here are the countries which brought the materials and decorations of this palace: Persia, Elam, Media, Babylon, Assyria, Arabia, Egypt, the Countries of the Sea, Sardis, Ionian, Urartu," etc. (Vallat 2013b: 290). Urartu is the Babylonian equivalent of the Old Persian, Armina.

7. It may have been at the hands of the Median contingent that a stone relief depicting the Assyrian defeat of the Elamites, a group centered in southwestern Iran with which the Medes may have felt some affinity (but see Henkelman 2003b: 199), was deliberately damaged, the faces of the Assyrian aggressors purposely defaced (Nylander 1980, 1999; Reade 1976). At the Neo-Assyrian capital of Kalhu, Medes have been linked to the destruction of documents recording the oaths of loyalty that Median mercenary bodyguards were forced to swear to the Assyrian overlord, King Esarhaddon (Liverani 1995).

8. Smith (2003: 252–254) has discerned the signs of internal political fragmentation in the architectonics of Urartu's later fortress of Teishebai URU, where, in a departure from earlier spatial practice, complexes are less integrated, suggestive of greater institutional differentiation. At the same time, redundancy of storage practices across complexes suggests a decline in the coordination of fortress administration. Older accounts of Urartu's demise that are based on a section of Herodotus's *Histories* known as the *Medikos logos*, which effectively (although not explicitly) places Urartu's fall at the hands of the Medes at some point between 605 and 585 B.C., today have few proponents (Diakonoff and Medvedskaya 1987; Diakonov 1956; Lehmann-Haupt 1910; Piotrovskii 1969).

9. Some hosted small-scale "squatter" occupations, as at Bastam (Kroll 2013) and Horom (Badaljan et al. 1997; Kohl and Kroll 1999), while others were transformed into mortuary landscapes, as at Tushpa (Tarhan 2007) and Teishebai URU (Martirosyan 1961: 137–148). There are the faintest traces of post-Urartian occupation in the outer town at Ayanis, in the Pınarbaşı area, but not on the citadel itself (Erdem and Batmaz 2008). At Oshakan, on the northern Ararat plain, the Urartian citadel at the summit of a hill was left vacant after Urartu's collapse, despite the presence of a reusable complex of fine ashlar masonry. That said, an unfortified residential structure below the citadel does provide some evidence for continued activity in the area of the site (Esayan and Kalantarian 1988; Ter-Martirosov 2001). At Argishtihinili, settlement activity continued on one of the two hills that makes up the site, the eastern hill of Armavir, but the dating of the post-Urartian occupation is extremely convoluted. The long-time director of the Armavir excavations, Gevork Tiratsyan (1988: 11), noted that there was no clear evidence for an Achaemenid-era stratum at Armavir, despite Felix Ter-Martirosov's (1974) attempt to delineate one as part of his dissertation research. Ter-Martirosov (2001: 156) later argued that a highly irregular columned hall at the east side of the eastern hill dates to the period of Achaemenid rule, but his post-Urartian dating of the structure in question is not widely accepted (see note 18). In any event, there are few signs of activity at Armavir in the seventh century B.C. (but see Kanetsyan 2001).

10. I do not include in this assessment minor fortresses of the Urartian period (and often earlier) that were not significant centers of the polity, and continued to host occupation in subsequent centuries. Examples include Aramus and some of the fortresses that rim the southern shore of Lake Sevan (Biscione et al. 2002; Khatchadourian 2008: 376–377; Kuntner and Heinsch 2010; Kuntner et al. 2012). Even in the case of Aramus, it is interesting to note that archaeologists identified a "transitional unfortified settlement phase" dated to the sixth century B.C. (Kuntner and Heinsch 2010: 342), which supports the argument

that the fortress institution was called into question in the immediate aftermath of Urartu's demise.

11. In the case of Assyria, the beginnings of political association premised on radical social asymmetries, extraction, and violence trace to the earliest emergence of complex polities in Mesopotamia, in the fourth millennium B.C. In the case of Urartu, that tradition reached back to the mid-second millennium B.C., when the region's first complex polities appeared (Biscione 2003: 183; Burney 2002; Smith 2012; Smith and Thompson 2004). Evidence points to discernable linkages between the Late Bronze Age and Urartian political systems on the Armenian highland. The clustering of religious, political, economic, and military institutions within the walls of Late Bronze Age fortresses provided what Smith has called the "the basic blueprint" for the later, more regularized and expansive Urartian political landscape, which likewise combined such institutions within the confines of the regime's hilltop fortresses (Smith 2012: 44, 49).

12. See e.g. Rawlinson (1871–73: 371–431) and Diakonoff (1985).

13. Instead, these sources speak only of "city lords" (Akkadian *bēl āli*—Lanfranchi 2003; Radner 2003).

14. By violence Clastres means the coercive apparatus critical to the reproduction of political authority within the State, and not warfare organized against those outside the political community.

15. The omission of Hasanlu from the main body of this discussion will seem conspicuous to specialists since the site, located in the Solduz Valley just south of Lake Urmia, contains several columned spaces. The most prominent, Burned Building II from Hasanlu IV, may indeed mark an earlier incarnation of the columned-hall tradition discussed at length below. But as others have noted, certain features set it apart from the later halls discussed here, especially the articulation of a wide central aisle, the presence of only two rows of columns, and the axial orientation toward a rather prominent "throne seat" (Gopnik 2010: 197, 2011: 341; Stronach and Roaf 2007: 156; Young 1994). The fact that the Hasanlu IV hall was not revitalized in Period III, after its destruction at the very end of the ninth century B.C. or sometime thereafter (Magee 2008), suggests that it afforded a different, even if somehow antecedent, kind of political interaction from that which I will argue below obtained with the later halls.

16. Gopnik (2011: 345) has suggested on the basis of radiocarbon dates that the site fell into disuse sometime around the middle of the seventh century B.C., after which later settlers built a number of small houses in the ruins of one of the smaller columned spaces. But the radiocarbon dates do not clearly inform the beginning and end of the hiatus between the main occupation and this later resettlement, nor are ceramics particularly helpful. There are three radiocarbon dates from poplar charcoal collected in the North Magazine garbage deposit (345), and all fall on the calibration curve's intractable Hallstatt plateau. Without sound Bayesian modeling, they simply do not permit higher precision. The problem with relative dating based on ceramics is that the pottery from Godin is dated on the basis of comparison with other sites in Iran whose chronology is equally unresolved when it comes to the late seventh through mid-sixth century B.C., leading to "a knot of circular reasoning that is very hard to untangle" (343).

17. John Curtis (2005: 122–123, 2013: xxiv) has suggested that the filling in of the temple at Nush-i Jan may relate to the religious transformations linked to the rise of Darius, namely

the prominence of Ahuramazda, perhaps at the expense of the Mithra and the Median *magi*. Whatever the validity of this interpretation, his point goes to show how fluid and unresolved is the dating of the highland sites of the seventh and sixth centuries.

18. I reserve from this discussion the columned hall at the site of Altıntepe, on Turkey's Erzincan plain; on present evidence, the arguments for a post-seventh-century date for the construction of this hall remain the more compelling, despite recent arguments in favor of a higher chronology (see chapter 5). Also set to one side is the columned hall at Armavir (Argishtihinili), for the simple but unfortunate reason that the few publications are woefully cursory. They are inadequate even for developing a basic understanding of the appearance of the excavated remains, let alone the dating of the hall, on which scholars disagree (compare Kanetsyan 2001: fig. 6; Ter-Martirosov 2001: fig. 2). Scholars have directed more attention to the three fragmentary Elamite inscriptions found at the site, which belong to a private letter. The texts were once thought to be associated with the Epic of Gilgamesh (Diakonov and Jankowska 1990). Koch (1993) subsequently dated them to the period of Achaemenid rule and suggested they may have originated in Persepolis, on comparison with a subset of Elamite administrative tablets in the Persepolis Fortification Archive that are written in a letter format. Vallat (1997) later dated the texts to the second half or third quarter of the sixth century B.C. and argued against a Persepolitan origin. This lower dating seems more likely given details of the syllabary and vocabulary (Henkelman 2003b: 199–200).

19. A passage in the southeast leading to the earlier Urartian temple of Haldi was shuttered and blocked by a bench (Stronach et al. 2010).

20. Elsewhere I have discussed the evidence for this redating, and expressed reservations, in this particular context, with chronological arguments based on architectural style alone, without independent absolute or relative dates (Khatchadourian 2013: 124–126). Since then, the findings of ceramic analysis, coupled with two radiocarbon determinations, appear to corroborate a late-seventh- or early-sixth-century (i.e. "post-Urartian") date for the initial construction of the columned hall (de Clairfontaine and Deschamps 2012: 122). Despite the publication dates, de Clairfontaine and Deschamps's 2012 study appeared in press after Khatchadourian 2013.

21. On the difficulties of identifying a "Median" phase at Hamadan/Ecbatana, see Sarraf (2003) and Boucharlat (2005: 253–254).

22. It is perhaps for these reasons that few have gone as far as Michael Roaf (2008/2010: 10) to read into the multiplication of the columned halls possible evidence for the coercive State—an expansionary Median polity, extending out from its heartland in the Zagros to occupy the Armenian highland (for a historical critique see Rollinger 2003).

23. The use of columns itself was not new by the seventh century B.C. (Gopnik 2010: 200, 2011: 340; Stronach and Roaf 2007: 188–190). Pillared spaces were a more regular feature of Urartian than of Assyrian architecture, but they differed considerably from the columned halls. Urartian columned spaces were rectangular structures, with only two rows of pillars, as for instance at Bastam, Armavir, and Erebuni. In general, Urartian fortresses, like Assyrian cities, were premised on the segmentation of activities. The plan of Erebuni provides but one example of this phenomenon, which is also on view at labyrinthine sites like Teishebai URU, Argishtihinili, and Bastam, where we often find densely compacted rooms separated by long, narrow courtyards (Kleiss 1988; Martirosian 1974; Martirosyan 1961). Promoting

interaction among sizeable numbers of people who enjoyed access to the restricted inner quarters of the fortress was not an element of Urartian or Assyrian political practice.

24. The ceramic evidence from Godin in particular supports an interpretation of these sites as venues for collective feasting among privileged social actors (Gopnik 2010: 199).

25. At Godin Tepe there is evidence for rebuilding of some of the towers, recurrent repair of the northern exterior wall, and renovation of the columned hall (Gopnik 2011: 306–307). On the challenges of maintaining mud brick in this period, see Liverani (2001: 377–378).

26. Quoted in Gopnik (2011: 319).

27. It is uncertain whether a similar range of variability in brick dimensions exists at Tepe Nush-I Jan, for which Stronach and Roaf (2007: 181) provide only average brick size.

28. Chemical composition analysis could test this hypothesis. It is worth mentioning that there is also considerable variability in the walls of the hall at Erebuni, where the socles of the east wall and part of the north wall are made up of finely dressed, gray andesite blocks, while the rest of the north wall had undressed, unshaped stones, which Stronach et al. (2010: 123) maintain "was not a repair, but part of the original construction." These authors explain such variability in utilitarian terms; when builders depleted the fine ashlar blocks that they brought from the nearby abandoned Urartian fortress of Teishebai URU, they had little choice but to resort to coarser materials. We might alternatively speculate that the building was the result of the same kind of cooperative effort that I am suggesting for the hall at Godin Tepe.

29. This interpretation can exist comfortably alongside the presence of the modest and off-centered "seat of honour" at Godin Tepe for a "central figure" (Gopnik 2010: 203), perhaps a single individual of prominence in each region, or perhaps a variety of individuals entitled, in turn, to hold the floor. Nor is there any conflict with the existence of annexes at Godin and Erebuni, in which smaller councils could convene. And of course, there would be little ground for suggesting that the religious structures at Nush-i Jan preclude the possibility that the columned hall at that site served as a venue for political assembly, for where in ancient southwest Asia were power and religion anything but two sides of the same coin?

30. Mario Liverani (2001: 391) has hinted at a similar view, seeing the fall of Assyria at the hands of the Medes as the start of a "real break in political tradition" that led to "an interlude of anti-imperialistic flavor, dominated not by the aggressive and exploitative attitude of the lowland states, but by the highlanders' rules of hospitality and gift exchange, inter-marriage and alliance, chivalry and bravery."

31. Included in this count are only known structures with more than two rows of columns. Excluded from the foregoing discussion is the small hall at Babylon, containing two rows of four columns (Gasche 2013), as well as the possible hall at Hamadan where excavations revealed fragments of Achaemenid-style column bases, some of which were inscribed in the reign of Artaxerxes II and make reference to a structure containing stone columns (Knapton et al. 2001). Also excluded are the halls in the Borazjan area, in the Dashtestan region of southwestern Iran (Boucharlat 2005: 236; Sarfaraz 1971, 1973; Yaghmaee 2010).

32. The redating of Erebuni requires an extension of this sphere of origin to the north, and consequently, as I have attempted here, a broader gaze on post-Urartian/pre-Achaemenid political practice (and hence architecture) in the Near Eastern highlands that transcends

the distinction between a purportedly unified Median and residually Urartian sphere. As Stronach (2012b: 319) has noted, there are lines of evidence, independent of the halls, that suggest linkages between these two arenas, including narrow halls with two long rows of columns, as appear at both at Bastam and Godin Tepe, and possibly the tower-like temples that are so typical of the Urartian tradition and conceivably echoed in the Central Temple at Tepe Nush-i Jan (see also Tourovets 2005). For these reasons, coupled with Stronach's own redating of Erebuni to the second half of the seventh century B.C., and his inclination to similarly date the halls at Altıntepe and Armavir, it is difficult to understand why he would maintain that "there is no need to attempt to revise the present broad understanding that various features in the sixth century and later columned halls at Pasargadae and Persepolis descend from long-established traditions that flourished, at least in the main, within the present-day borders of western Iran" (Stronach 2012b: 317). It should also be noted that the discovery of two, more modest ninth-to-seventh-century columned halls in eastern Arabia, at the sites of Rumeilah and Muweilah (Boucharlat and Lombard 2001; Magee 2001), has not changed this interpretation appreciably, as most suspect that the idea of the hall would have likely reached Arabia through Iran rather than the other way around (Boucharlat 2013b: 417; Curtis and Razmjou 2005: 50; Gopnik 2011: 339; Stronach 2001: 97). Specifically, Stronach (2001: 97) anticipates the eventual discovery of pre-Achaemenid columned halls in southwestern Iran, which would shift the source of the concept in Cyrus's day away from the northern highlands, but, as he acknowledges, there is at present absolutely no evidence for any such architectural tradition in Fars.

33. Regarding the date of conquest, Babylonian records indicate that Cyrus conquered Media in 550 B.C., marking the conventional start date of the Achaemenid Empire. His conquest of Armenia in 547 B.C. is documented on the Nabonidus Chronicle, a cuneiform tablet that details the events during the reign of the Babylonian king Nabonidus, the last to rule before the Persian seizure of Babylon. Recounted in the Chronicle are the successful campaigns of Cyrus in that year against an entity whose name on the tablet is damaged. The defeated entity was long thought to be Lydia, a region of western Asia Minor, but despite its wide acceptance, this reading has long been recognized as a "very doubtful reconstruction" (Cargill 1977: 97). In 1997, Oelsner (1999/2000) reexamined the text and concluded that the damaged word can only be "Urartu" (see also Rollinger 2008). This is the now widely accepted reading of the tablet (Waters 2014: 40), and it places the conquest of Armenia at the very beginning of Cyrus's reign.

34. Sometimes described as a capital, Pasargadae is better understood more neutrally as a royal settlement, given the limited evidence for administration. That said, recent geophysical survey conducted between 1999 and 2008 makes it quite clear that there are substantial subsurface stone constructions that await investigation (Benech et al. 2012), and the Persepolis Fortification tablets hint at the presence of a depot and craft center at Pasargadae (Henkelman 2013: 940).

35. The tall tower finds its closest architectural parallels in the tower temples of Urartu (Stronach 2012b: 315–316), and may represent another captive from the northern highlands, along with the similar square tower that Darius built near Naqsh-i Rustam, known as the Ka'bah-i-Zardusht (Schmidt 1970).

36. Stronach (2008: 161) and Boucharlat (2013b: 417) have maintained that the idea of the portico traced to Ionia, since porticoes do not appear at the Zagros sites after Hasanlu.

This is a reasonable supposition, but it is worth noting that there is a small, outward-facing portico at the entrance to Erebuni, which Ter-Martirosov (2005b: 50) dates to the Achaemenid-era occupation of the site. It remains to be seen whether the recent excavations that have led to a redating of the columned hall will also extend to a reconsideration of the portico, which would open the possibility that Cyrus had both highland and Greek examples in mind when designing the porticoed spaces at Pasargadae. Another portico, which the excavators tentatively date to the early sixth century B.C., has recently come to light on the extramural southeast hill at Erebuni (Stronach 2012b: 318; Stronach et al. 2009).

37. See Boucharlat (2013b: 411–412) for a compelling perspective that emphasizes the simultaneity of the Susa and Persepolis building programs in the last two decades of the sixth century, conventionally thought to be sequential projects within Darius's reign.

38. This hall is called an Apadana on parallel with Susa, although it is nowhere described as such in the inscriptions from Persepolis.

39. Likely a misleading designation, given its small size (Boucharlat 2013b: 419; Razmjou 2010).

40. A trilingual inscription of Artaxerxes II (A2Sa), carved on a column base, reads in part, "Darius my ancestor built this Apadana; afterwards, in the time of my grandfather Artaxerxes, it then burnt down, then by the grace of Ahuramazda, Anahita and Mithra, I had the Apadana rebuilt" (Vallat 2013b: 294).

41. On the translation, see Lincoln (2012: 9), Panaino (2012), and Boucharlat (2008: 558; 2013a: 394).

42. On the organization of labor, including forced labor, see e.g. Briant (2002: 429–439; 2013: 18) and Kuhrt (2007: 766–767).

43. In saying that Cyrus may have developed his political sensibilities in an Elamite sphere I am making no comment on the debated question of his ethnic identity in contrast to Darius's, on which question see e.g. Henkelman (2008a) and the review of the relevant literature therein. There has been much recent discussion on the Elamite "pre-history" of the Achaemenid Empire, on which see also e.g. Henkelman (2008b) and Potts (2005).

44. See Boucharlat et al. (2012) for the recent results of geophysical and other remote-sensing survey techniques around Persepolis that attest to some occupation zones in the areas beyond the terrace.

45. Since the excavations of the citadel at Pasargadae were not completed, it is difficult to account for the fortified component of the settlement.

46. A detailed account of the continuities between Assyrian and Persian models of kingship is beyond the scope of this project, but it suffices to state plainly that, in recognizing Cyrus's captivation with the political landscapes of the highlands, I am by no means envisioning an absolute rupture with Mesopotamian political traditions.

47. Although the audience usually remains unspecified, Perrot (2013a: 452) has emphasized that such spaces were not intended for satrapal delegations from incorporate territories, as the reliefs on the Apadana at Persepolis would suggest, but for Persians alone. As for the Hall of 100 Columns, Schmidt (1953: 129) conjectured that since it would be "senseless" to have two halls on the terrace serving the same function, this hall was intended not for large assembly, but to display royal preciosities. Friedrich Krefter (1971: 59–61) instead proposed that the Hall of 100 Columns hosted military gatherings. Most efforts to reconstruct the function of the halls are based on interpretations of the stone reliefs found in association

with them, which is not necessarily sound given that the buildings may been put to different uses over the centuries (Curtis and Razmjou 2005: 54).

48. Relatedly, Root (2015: 3) has discussed the ways in which, at Persepolis, Darius reformulated an imperial ideology that "offered an implicit alternative to the realities of the Perso-Elamite line of Cyrus, while managing to engage rather than reject Elamite cultural legacies as instruments of historical memory and administrative know-how."

49. Scholars have long speculated on a possible religious break between Cyrus and Darius, which would go part of the way to explaining the shifts in the political entailments of the halls. But the arguments for such a religious rupture are built on scant evidence, as the most recent studies have shown (Frye 2010: 578; Henkelman 2008a; Jacobs 2010).

50. The impression is drawn from a passage of Xenophon's *Oeconomicus* (4.21), which contains the following description of a paradise: "Lysander admired the beauty of the trees in it, the accuracy of the spacing, the straightness of the rows, the regularity of the angles and the multitude of sweet scents that clung round them as they walked" (Xenophon 1979).

51. The Medes, Armenians, and Sagartians are clustered in the same section of the Bisitun inscription (DB24–34), and the absence of a named leader of the Armenian rebellion opens the possibility of alliance with the Medes (Lecoq 1997: 197; Waters 2010: 67–68). On the administrative relationships between the *dahyāva* of Media and Armenia in the Achaemenid Empire, see Khatchadourian (2008: 78–85).

5. DELEGATES AND PROXIES IN THE *DAHYU* OF ARMENIA

1. Quoted in King (2010: 20).

2. Labeling this period Iron 3 is unconventional in the context of highland archaeology. Scholars working in Turkey customarily describe the sixth through fourth centuries as the Late Iron Age, while in Armenia it is variously discussed as the post-Urartian period, the Early Armenian period, or, in local dynastic terms, the Yervandid period. In recognition of the different temporalities that govern the pace of political history, as opposed to that of social and material culture change, my colleagues and I prefer to extend archaeological periodization into the era of Achaemenid rule, rather than adopt the conventions of historical time-telling when dealing with archaeological materials (Smith, Badalyan, and Avetisyan 2009: 41). To a certain extent, currently the distinction between an archaeological versus a historical chronology is semantic, since the basis for the archaeological chronology is derived, in part, from historical ruptures. However, a change in nomenclature is a first step toward pushing archaeological analysis away from the narrow rhythms of royal genealogies. The problem with "Late Iron Age" is that it forecloses the possibility of extending archaeological periodization into later historical phases during which iron remained a defining technology (Khatchadourian 2011: 464–466). We thus follow a sequential system of periodization, which is comparable with that used in the archaeology of Iron Age Iran.

3. Two syntheses of these dispersed discoveries suggest that the material record for the period in question is sufficiently well preserved to support targeted research, while also revealing the obstacles posed by modern political borders. Karapetyan (2003) brings together all known archaeological findings of the period from the territory of the modern Republic of Armenia, while Yiğitpaşa (2016) provides a complete register of sites and materials from museum collections in eastern Anatolia.

4. On the north façade, the Armenian delegation includes five people instead of three, who bring not a horse and amphora but riding garments and a pair of straight-sided vessels. Root (forthcoming) has noted that the Armenians on the north are unique in being the only group to carry the riding costume as the first gift of the delegation, rather than the last. Associations with horse-riding may have been particularly strong. It should be noted that the terms used to describe Achaemenid vessels, including *amphora, rhyton,* and *phiale* (discussed below), are Greek in derivation. Greek craftspeople and consumers enthusiastically replicated and used Achaemenid-style drinking vessels (Hoffmann 1961; Miller 1993). By convention, scholars use the Greek terms also when speaking of such vessels as they occur within the imperial sphere. The Persian terms are not known.

5. Herodotus records Armenia's tribute obligation as 400 talents of silver (Hist. 3.93; see discussion in Briant 2002: 391), while Xenophon (*An.* 4.5.3.34) and Strabo (11.14.9) further attest to payment in the form of horses. Xenophon states that the horse tax was differentially distributed according to a quota system across the villages of the *dahyu.* The village Xenophon visited had to supply 17 colts each year to local leaders, who transferred them to the satrap. The satrap would in turn pass them over to the court. Strabo notes that the *dahyu* supplied the king with 20,000 foals each year, which would be sacrificed in a festival to honor the god Mithra.

6. Between December 522 and June 521 B.C. Darius's army fought five battles in Armenia on two fronts. Rebel forces, sometimes fighting from mountain perches, persistently reassembled after each defeat (DB.I.26–30). In Daniel Potts's (2006–7: 134) words, "the Armenians would not be quelled." The Old Babylonian version of the inscription records 5,097 dead and 2,203 captured, but the accuracy of such statistics is difficult to ascertain, as are the locations of the battles where such casualties were incurred (see Potts 2006–7: 135 and passim). In any event, several elements of the passages dealing with Armenia are unusual in the context of the monument as a whole. For instance, although each battle is punctuated with the formulaic refrain of the text ("by the grace of Ahuramazda did my army utterly overthrow the rebel host"), the subduing of Armenia appears to fall short as an expression of royal triumph. First, we read of no action or boast that definitively concludes the episode, as in the passages about Babylon, Media, and Persia. Nor does an Armenian insurgent appear in the sculptural representation of the bound captives who stand in judgment before Darius (figure 4, p. 3). And finally, Armenia is not included in the summary of successes. When the text is read at face value it is not immediately clear what was the end result or consequence of Armenia's involvement in these events. Leqoc (1997: 197) and Jacobs (1994: 176–177) have attempted to resolve the ambiguities by suggesting that Armenia was administratively nested within the larger entity of Media, and thus the ultimate suppression of the Median revolt and the punishment of its leader would effectively imply the definitive defeat of the Armenian rebels. This is possible, but it still leaves Armenia in an anomalous position in the inscription.

7. On the historical geography of the Armenian *dahyu,* see Khatchadourian (2008: 87–91).

8. Scholars have debated the status of Colchis within the empire. It was never listed as its own *dahyu.* Bruno Jacobs (1994, 2000) and Maria Brosius (2010: 32) have suggested it may have been a part of the *dahyu* of Armenia, though possibly holding a different status with respect to obligations to the crown, and possibly for only a short duration.

9. Such analysis must contend with the ubiquitous challenges of combining survey datasets into a synthetic analysis (Alcock 1993; Alcock and Cherry 2004), plus the specific challenges that attend such efforts on the Armenian highland, where systematic and diachronic surveys are exceedingly few and ceramic chronologies for the centuries after Urartu are nascent (Khatchadourian 2008: 351–356). Surveys (and excavations as well) have struggled to differentiate, on the basis of ceramics alone, the short interval between the collapse of Urartu and the period of Achaemenid rule. For a history of regional-scale investigations on the Armenian highland, see Khatchadourian (2008: 347–356). As with all efforts at "side-by-side" survey (Alcock and Cherry 2004), one must contend with differing collection methods, data recording systems, and degrees of systematicity and intensity. By and large, all too many survey efforts of the last three decades still entail travel by vehicle to known or promising site locations, without intensive prospecting (see Khatchadourian 2008: table 7.1). Soviet land amelioration policies, a program intended to increase the productivity of previously uncultivated areas, often through the use of bulldozers, which cleared fields to make way for industrialized agriculture on collective farms (Smith and Greene 2009), further frustrates systematic survey in regions of the highland that fall within the former USSR.

10. See Khatchadourian (2008: 357–360) for a detailed discussion of the methodology used in this analysis.

11. See Khatchadourian (2008: 360–383) for detailed discussion of each project's methodology and findings.

12. The numbers are striking: in Doğubeyazıt there is a drop in site numbers from 20 to 4; in Erciş, from 26 to 4; and in Lake Urmia, from 142 to 18.

13. Muş, which is also near Lake Van and the center of Urartu, does not fit this pattern, since site numbers there remained constant. Regrettably, however, it is not possible to account for the different situation in Muş, since in the absence of detailed site descriptions it is not even clear whether the Iron 2 sites of this region were fortresses.

14. In the Bayburt region, although two fortresses continued to be occupied during the Iron 3 period, the average elevation of the new, unfortified mound sites is lower than mounds occupied in the Iron 2 (or Urartian) period. In the Lake Sevan area, all of the newly founded Achaemenid-era sites are on low ground or in unfortified locations (while the sites that were continuously occupied from the Iron 2, or Urartian, period are fortress settlements). In the Muş region, we can only go on the statement of the investigator: "The defensive positions the Urartian rulers favored in the hills appear from our current evidence to be less important during the time of the world empires" (Rothman 2004: 149).

15. From the Greek *rhysis,* "flowing." A rhyton is "a vessel with a small aperture (or a short spout) near its lower extremity through which a jet of wine could issue" (Stronach 2012a: 170).

16. See Arakelyan (1971) for photographs of the vessels prior to restoration.

17. The vessel finds numerous parallels, recovered through both illicit and controlled excavations from Asia Minor, to the Caucasus, to the southern Urals (Treister 2007; 2013: 386–387).

18. In his close analysis of this frieze, Treister (2015) details the various features that help situate it within a cultural field that conjoins Persian and Greek formal styles. For instance, the dress of the female figures is variously both Greek and Persian in design. Perhaps most

notable is the upright fingers of the seated man and the woman who approaches him, a manner of holding drinking bowls that scholars generally agree is associated with Persia (Dusinberre 2013: 133; Treister 2012: 120). And yet the probable association of the scene with Greek myth, coupled with the numerous points of comparison with the arts of Greece and Asia Minor, situate this object in that complicated heuristic category that art historians have come to call, not without reservation, Greco-Persian style (for discussion, see Gates 2002).

19. See note 5.

20. The leading candidate in the scholarship seems to be the historically attested satrap, Orontes, on whom see Khatchadourian (2008: 93–101).

21. On which see p. 143 above.

22. In terms of dating, in the long history of scholarship on these vessels, there appears to be consensus that the horse rhyton (without rider) and the fluted goblet fall squarely within the period of Achaemenid rule, sometime after the second half of the fifth century (e.g. Stronach 2011; Treister 2015). There is some disagreement on the other two vessels. Recent arguments for the dating of the horse-protome rhyton with rider range from the second half of the fifth century (Treister 2015) to the end of the fourth century (Stronach 2011), but the weight of the scholarship favors a date within the period of Achaemenid ascendancy. In recent years, the calf-head rhyton has been variously assigned to a date no later than the middle or third quarter of the fourth century (Ter-Martirosov and Deschamps 2007; Treister 2012, 2013, 2015), or to the late fourth to early third century (Hažatrian and Markarian 2003; Stronach 2011), yet Treister's most recent analyses do lend weight to the former dating.

23. Many scholars have accepted a provenience in Armenia—see Muscarella (1980: 30) for citations, as well as Amiet (1983)—but Muscarella is rightly doubtful of information provided by dealers.

24. Other items in the collection include a cylindrical silver box, a shallow silver dish, and two silver scoops, possibly incense ladles (for comparanda from Persepolis, see Simpson 2005: 128).

25. By the same token, the appearance of a rhyton along with the Achaemenid bowls and *phiale* could, at one and the same time, speak to the authenticity of the collection (since such vessels are known to have been associated with one another in use), and to the wile of forgers all too knowledgeable of this association.

26. Once again, for both of these two amphorae many scholars have accepted or advanced a provenience in Armenia—see Muscarella (1980: 29–30) for citations—but Muscarella is understandably doubtful.

27. It is generally thought that the form belongs to a distinctly imperial aesthetic, and is not linked to any particular region of the empire (Dusinberre 2013: 130; Moorey 1985: 33; Sancisi-Weerdenburg 1989: 136). Indeed, apart from the Apadana depictions that link the form with Lydia and Armenia (figure 10, p. 20), metal examples with secure provenience have been found as far afield as the Filippovka burials in the southern Urals, the Kukuva Mogila burial at Duvanli, Bulgaria (Gergova 2010; Treister 2010; Treister and Yablonsky 2012), and (in representational form) on a wall painting in Karaburun Tomb II in Lycia, where a servant carries before a reclining (Persian?) dignitary a double-handled vessel with outward-facing griffin heads (Mellink 1972: 265).

28. Identifying the place of manufacture of these vessels would allow greater understanding of their life cycles. But, as Gunter and Root (1998: 21) note, the available evidence does not currently permit the identification of regionally distinct silver workshops on the basis of vessel styles, variable though Achaemenid silver plate appears to have been. Many have argued for the abundance of argentiferous lead ores in Anatolia and in Armenia, suggesting that these regions may have been major sources for Achaemenid silver production (Gunter and Root 1998: 20; Moorey 1980: 30; 1994: 235). Most scholars conjecture that the Erebuni vessels were produced in these regions, usually offering more localized points of manufacture within that expanse, but strong evidence is in most cases not available. See Treister (2015) for discussion. Given its iconography, it seems reasonable to assign the calf-head rhyton to a workshop in Asia Minor, "in the contact zone between Greece and the Achaemenid state" (Treister 2015: 89). But there is no reason to doubt that silver vessels circulating through the Achaemenid exchange economy could have traveled quite far. It is in this regard worth noting the reliefs of the Tomb of Petosiris in Egypt, which depict the manufacture of metal rhyta and bowls, suggesting if not the actual existence of such Egyptian workshops, then an awareness of such production at the shift from Achaemenid to Ptolemaic control (Muscarella 1980: 28; Root, personal communication).

29. The practice was by no means new in the Achaemenid era, with the earliest evidence in the Near East dating to the second millennium B.C., although the most abundant evidence is from the latter-seventh through fourth centuries B.C. (Kroll 2013; Moorey 1994; Tal 2011).

30. The Apadana relief at Persepolis, discussed in chapter 1, vividly represents this seemingly consensual inflow of silver vessels as no mere obligatory payment of debts but a spectacle glorifying sovereignty itself.

31. The hoards are, however, quite different. The Pasargadae jug contained mainly gold jewelry and various kinds of beads, but very little silver (only two spoons). Moreover, there is no evidence of deliberate damage to the objects (Stronach 1978: 167–177).

32. Using Michael Vickers's (2002) proposed *sigloi* weight ranges, the weight of the horse rhyton (821.5 g) corresponds to 150 *sigloi*. The weight of the goblet (544 g) corresponds to 100 *sigloi*. The weight of the calf-head rhyon (452.1 g) perhaps best corresponds to 100 *drachmai*. The *sigloi* correspondence of the horse-with-rider rhyton cannot be calculated with any precision due to lost fragments.

33. Chemical analysis has yet to be performed on these vessels, yet a characterization study could determine whether the percentage of copper alloy, in particular, falls in the 1.5–2.5% range that Zournatzi (2000) has identified as a possible Achaemenid standard.

34. BM123258 weighs 634.8 g, corresponding to 150 *drachmai*, BM123256 weighs 423.7 g, corresponding to 100 *drachmai*, and BM123255 weighs 214.1 g, corresponding to 50 *drachmai* (Michael Vickers, personal communication). These correspondences are somewhat surprising, given the scarcity of extant plate that is made in terms of *drachmai* rather than *sigloi*.

35. In contrast, rhyta and *phialai* are not to be found on the Apadana relief, suggesting to Gunter and Root (1998: 27) that such silver vessel types principally flowed outward, as royal gifts. The same may also have been true of alabastra with royal name inscriptions (Root, personal communication) and royal name seals (Garrison 2014).

36. M. J. Hughes (1984) conducted energy-dispersive X-ray fluorescence (XRF) and atomic absorption spectrometry (AAS) on several objects in the "Erzincan" collection. The one "Achaemenid bowl" analyzed (by XRF) contained 97.5% silver and 1.8% copper, consistent with Zournatzi's hypothesis of imperially regulated copper alloying in the range of 1.5–2.5%. Of the other six objects analyzed from the same collection, three had higher copper values, including the *phiale* (94.5% silver, 4.7% copper, analyzed by AAS), a scoop (96.6% silver, 3.0% copper, analyzed by AAS), and a lid (96.6% silver, 3.0% copper, analyzed by XRF). Reanalysis using the same instrument on all the objects would be worthwhile.

37. The seal was found by a farmer in the village of Horom, where excavations of a large fortress uncovered evidence for settlement activity during the Iron 3 period (Kohl and Kroll 1999). The provenience of the seal is thus less than secure, though its authenticity has never been called into question. On iconographic grounds, Garrison and Root (2001: 56) have described the Horom seal as an unquestionable product of Achaemenid-era manufacture, not least for its striking similarity to a seal from Pasargadae (Root 1999).

38. Some uncertainty surrounds the terminus for the use of the hall, despite the recent redating of its initial construction. Stronach et al. (2010: 128) have reasoned that the hall was "probably allowed to collapse within the course of the 6th and 5th centuries." But given that the hall's interior was fully excavated to floor level in the 1950s and subsequently renovated into a tourist destination, it is hardly surprising that recent work at the site has found "no visible sign of any post-Urartian [i.e. post-seventh-century] occupation within the limits of the structure" (Stronach et al. 2010: 128). Ceramics recovered from the recent excavations at Erebuni that postdate the seventh century B.C. thus far appear to be few (de Clairfontaine and Deschamps 2012), yet this too is less than meaningful, given the history of excavation. Also, assuming a gradual turn to ruins during the sixth and fifth century leads to a rather implausible picture. For there is securely dated evidence that during this period Erebuni remained a locus of activity for privileged individuals versed in the most rarified practices of the imperial elite, not least of all the silver vessels discussed above. To these can be added wall paintings (Ter-Martirosov 2005a) and a ceramic duck-handled bowl, found in a building to the north of the columned hall (Loseva 1958: 193, fig. 110), which recalls the duck- and swan-headed stone vessels from Persepolis (Karapetyan 2003: 44–45; Pl. 31.43; Schmidt 1957: 88, Pl. 53–84; Tiratsyan 1960: 103). Also notable are the two silver coins from Miletus, which date no later than 478 B.C. (Sargsyan 1998). Found near the long-lived Susi temple, the coins likely played a part in the same far-reaching exchange networks that brought similar Milesian coins to Persepolis (Avetisyan et al. 1998; Schmidt 1957: 110, Pl. 184; Tiratsyan 1960: 103). It is difficult to accept that a structure occupying so much of the built area on the citadel was left to fall into disrepair while Achaemenid modes of commensal politics and economic transactions in the wider currency of the empire were taking place in the close vicinity.

39. It is possible that future findings will one day recommend placing Altıntepe alongside Godin Tepe, Nush-i Jan, and Erebuni as host to one of the seventh-century or post-Urartian halls that marked the initial phase in the emergence of the form. At present, the arguments are quite tenuous on both sides. Until quite recently, scholars maintained that the columned hall at Altıntepe was constructed during the period of Achaemenid hegemony on the highland (e.g. Khatchadourian 2013; Summers 1993), and might have been but one part of a larger settlement complex that included the neighboring hill of Saztepe, where

reconnaissance survey conducted by Charles Burney in 1955 and then again by Mehmet Işıklı in 2006–2007 primarily revealed evidence for Late Iron Age (i.e. Achaemenid-era) rather than Middle Iron Age (i.e. Urartian) occupation in the form of painted pottery belonging to the Triangle Ware tradition (see note 19; Işıklı 2010; Summers 1993: 95). But with recently resumed investigations at the site, this dating has been the subject of some reevaluation. Karaosmanoğlu and Korucu (2012) have made the case for an earlier construction date for the Altıntepe hall, in the "late" Urartian period. Unfortunately, precisely what Karaosmanoğlu and Korucu mean by "late" Urartian is not at all clear, for they provide no absolute dates. Indeed, the absolute dating of the Iron Age occupations at Altıntepe is uncertain in general, but the predominance of evidence does seem to suggest that the first Urartian occupation did not predate the reign of Argishti II (ca. 714–685 B.C.; see a review of the relevant literature in Summers 1993: 94). Insofar as there is consensus that the Urartian occupation entailed two phases, to argue for a third, as do Karaosmanoğlu and Korucu, would require that the site underwent three major reconstructions in the seventy-year period between the reign of Argishti II and the end of the Urartian Kingdom in approximately 640 B.C. Yet, given that not everyone subscribes to the latest proposed dates for the collapse of Urartu (see p. 89), it is possible that Karaosmanoğlu and Korucu are working on the basis of the (now largely discredited) Herodotean date of 585 B.C., in which case the "late" Urartian period of which they speak would more properly belong to the poorly understood interval, extensively discussed in the previous chapter, between the collapse of Urartu and the emergence of the Achaemenid Empire. With that by way of the general problems of absolute chronology, one of the main points of disagreement between a "late Urartian" and an Achaemenid dating pertains to the stratigraphic relationship between the large hall and the temenos to the north. The floor of the hall is approximately 2 m higher than the level of the temple complex. In addition, the northeast corner of the hall sits atop the southeast wall of the earlier temenos. Summers (1993: 93–94) argued that these facts, coupled with the extensive use of Urartian masonry in the foundations of the large hall (much as Urartian building blocks were reused in the reconstruction of the fortification wall) suggest a break of "at least a hundred years before it was reestablished by the Persians." For their part, Karaosmanoğlu and Korucu (2012: 134–135) have deemphasized the significance of the stratigraphic layering of the corner of the hall atop the temenos wall, focusing instead on the fact that a short wall was built during this third phase to attach the temenos to the northeastern wall of the large hall, for which reason they maintain that this "annexation" provides "clear evidence that the temple from this point on functioned together with the . . . 18-columned Apadana [*sic*]." Yet the problem here is that there is no evidence for a passage between the two structures, and thus the argument for the mutual functioning of these buildings is not clear at all. Two forms of evidence complicate matters still further. In the earlier investigations, archaeologists uncovered, both at the site and in the area of the hall, ceramics belonging to a painted tradition known as Triangle Ware. While itself the subject of considerable discussion, there is today little disagreement that Triangle Ware postdated the Iron 2 period, with most scholars placing its emergence in the sixth through fourth centuries B.C. (Summers 1993; Summers and Burney 2012). Ceramics thus provides the one solid basis for an Iron 3 date for the hall. It is of little significance that Karaosmanoğlu and Korucu (2012: 136) found no such pottery in their recent excavations, since the structure had already been excavated to floor level (it is for this same reason that one of the discoveries brought to light by their work is the earlier, Urartian building, beneath the columned hall). Finally, like Özgüç (1966) before them, Karaosmanoğlu and Korucu have taken the existence of wall-painting fragments found within the hall that are stylistically characteristic of Urartian frescos as support for an Urartian date. And yet, as none of the fragments were found *in situ,* and as the building of the last phase was constructed directly atop the earlier Urartian building, it is very difficult to assign these fresco fragments narrowly to the latest phase of occupation. Moreover, even if the Urartian-style paintings *did* belong to the last phase, they do not speak conclusively to an Urartian date; there is every reason to believe that the elite individuals who used the highland halls were not officials sent forth from Persia but leaders of the highland, who could quite plausibly reproduce painting styles of earlier decades, just as we see continuity in certain ceramic forms. In sum, apart from the evidence of the Triangle Ware, all that remains are speculations, and it is thus on the basis of the one piece of artifactual evidence that is reasonably secure that I favor the Achaemenid dating.

40. In the late sixth and fifth centuries B.C., other communities of the *dahyu* appear likewise to have inserted columned spaces into newly reconfigured complexes. Relevant here is Phase X at Tille Höyük, a site located at the approximate westernmost limits of the *dahyu,* on the west bank of the Euphrates River, where excavations uncovered a columned room with two rows of six columns that Stuart Blaylock (2009) assigns squarely to the Achaemenid era.

41. And possibly Hamadan. See note 31 in chapter 4.

42. In his 1993 publication Geoff Summers described the bases as limestone, but as limestone occurs nowhere else at the site, this seemed to me unlikely. Recent casual inspection by Elif Denel (for which I am grateful) suggests that indeed the locally quarried andesite is the only building material at the site.

43. As Jacobs (1994) has noted, the eastern frontier of what he calls the "Central Minor Satrapy Armina/(East) Armenia" is difficult to reconstruct. He includes in the *dahyu* "the region around Lake Sevan." Karačamirli is not far from the northeastern shore of Lake Sevan. According to Jacobs's reconstruction of satrapal boundaries, the other possibility is that Karačamirli and other nearby sites (Sari Tepe and Gumbati) fell within what he calls the "Minor Satrapy Media Minor." In his overall reconstruction, Media and Armenia are closely related, with Armenia in fact a subsidiary unit of the "Great Satrapy Māda/Media." For the present purposes, such historical geography is not particularly important. It suffices to recognize that a site such as Karačamirli could only have fallen within imperial bounds.

44. The suggestion that the partially investigated building at Rizvan Tepe, 550 m south of the *propyleion,* may have stored agricultural surplus extracted from a surrounding subject population is particularly intriguing (Knauss et al. 2013: 20).

45. It is probable that the delegate at Karačamirli did not work alone in these efforts but in assemblage with other nearby frontier complexes at the sites of Gumbati and Sari Tepe in Georgia's Alasani Valley and the Akstafa tributary of the Kura, respectively (Furtwängler 1996; Furtwängler and Knauss 1997; Furtwängler et al. 1995; Gagoshidze 1996; Knauss 1999, 2000, 2001, 2006; Narimanov 1959, 1960; Narimanov and Khalilov 1962). However, the excavated remains at both sites are fragmentary. The exposures of built remains are partial,

and the absence of a published register of artifacts recovered from the limited excavated areas at both sites further hampers any attempt at interpretation. Thus, Gumbati and Sari Tepe do not yet permit analysis in the terms of this discussion, despite the oft-cited discovery of Achaemenid-style bell-shaped column bases at both sites which, at least in some cases, have been shown by petrological analysis to derive from the same workshop as the bases at Karačamirli (Knauss et al. 2013: 26).

46. In Lecoq's (1997: 263–264) translation, the Babylonian version reads "the mountain" instead of "this niche."

47. On his visit to Van in 1849, Austin Henry Layard (1859: 345) remarked that he was unable to copy the trilingual inscription because it simply could not be read without the kind of "strong telescope" that was available to Schultz (1828, 1840), the first scholar who transcribed it, in 1827.

6. GOING UNDERGROUND: AFFILIATES, PROXIES, AND DELEGATES AT TSAGHKAHOVIT

1. "The houses here were underground," Xenophon (*An.* 4.5.25) wrote, "with a mouth like that of a well, but spacious below. And while entrances were tunneled down for the beasts of burden, the human inhabitants descended by a ladder."

2. Very few contemporaneous settlements have received targeted and sustained investigation. Most notable is the site of Beniamin, on the neighboring Shirak Plain (Ter-Martirosov and Deschamps 2007; Ter-Martirosov et al. 2012). In 1999–2007, a French-Armenian team uncovered a large Iron 3 "palace" and two rooms of a nearby, semi-subterranean structure. In its first phase, activities in this area centered on iron metallurgy, later developing into a multifunctional production and dwelling space possibly akin to Tsaghkahovit. In modern Armenia, other contemporary settlements where excavations were either short-lived or not targeted to the Iron 3 period include Karchakhbyur (Karapetyan 1979), Horom (Badaljan et al. 1997; Kohl and Kroll 1999), and several fortress sites in northeastern Armenia (Esayan 1976). Work is still underway in the Vorotan River valley (Mkrditch Zardaryan, personal communication; see also Zardaryan et al. 2007).

3. The investigations of the Iron 3 settlement at Tsaghkahovit are part of a broader effort, underway since 1998, to detail long-term transformations in regional occupation of the Tsaghkahovit Plain through a program of systematic survey and excavation organized under the auspices of the Project for the Archaeology and Geography of Ancient Transcaucasian Societies (ArAGATS). For a complete list of project publications, see http://aragats.arts.cornell.edu.

4. There is some evidence for activity on the plain during the intervening Iron 1 period, represented most visibly by recently discovered burials. But significant settlement activity did not resume until the Iron 3.

5. On the Late Bronze Age occupation of the plain, see Badalyan et al. (forthcoming); Badalyan et al. (2008); Greene (2013); Lindsay (2006, 2011); Lindsay and Greene (2013); Lindsay et al. (2008); Marshall (2014); A. T. Smith (2012, 2015).

6. The absolute chronology of Tsaghkahovit's resettlement is based on Bayesian analysis of radiocarbon dates, which provides a model for the settlement's dating that accords

with historical reconstruction derived from other archaeological analyses (i.e. produces no outliers). For more detailed discussion of Tsaghkahovit's chronology and a list of all radiocarbon dates from the settlement, see Khatchadourian (2014) and Manning et al. (n.d.).

7. In one area, the main wall of the large LB building (WC301) was entirely buried and built over by a new, more modest freestanding stone masonry room. In other areas, Iron 3 walls were dug into and built against the LBA wall, thus partitioning the once monumental structure into smaller informal spaces.

8. Corroborating this picture are the material assemblages from within the Iron 3 citadel, which suggest a nondomestic area, given the paucity of consumption vessels relative to other areas of the site. See Khatchadourian (2008: 293–302) for statistical analyses that support this conclusion. The cumulative weight of the evidence suggests that the fortress served some quite specific needs of the community, perhaps centered on production and storage, and perhaps as a place of shelter in times of threat.

9. For detailed reports on these excavations, see Badalyan et al. (2008) and Khatchadourian (2014).

10. Some radiocarbon samples that were collected from final floor surfaces yielded calibrated dates with the highest probability range (at 1 σ) for a felling date extending into the fifth century B.C. (e.g. WSG.12, WSH.30). On stylistic grounds, artifactual evidence falls more broadly into the "Achaemenid period," resisting further refinement. On the basis of ^{14}C alone, abandonment after the early-to-mid fourth century B.C. is improbable.

11. The same can be said of Precinct B, about which little is known. A single sounding in this area suggests shallow deposits and poor preservation. Avetisyan et al. (2000: 51) have posited that several of the larger rooms may have served as corrals.

12. Preliminary ground penetrating radar survey in the area between Precincts A and C has revealed subsurface rooms. The boundaries of the precincts are thus approximate and open to revision.

13. The clay-packed Iron 3 preparatory surfaces beneath floors are encountered on average 1.35 m below topsoil. The thick deposit of silt overburden above the floors is customarily very rocky, indicative of one or more freestanding courses above the retaining walls. There are no discernable subsequent subsurface cultural deposits.

14. One is reminded of the *kômarch,* or local leader, with whom Xenophon (*An.* 4.5.34) claims to have feasted in a village in Armenia.

15. Another point of entry may have been from Room D, possibly for livestock, judging by the width of the doorway and the room's internal features.

16. Excavations exposed door blockages between Rooms D and G, I and K, M and N, AC and AD, and DA and DB. In Room S of Precinct A, no doorway was identified at all, suggesting either an extremely thorough closure, or a restriction of access through a roof hole.

17. Not pictured in the case of C.

18. For an ethnoarchaeological account of village architecture in the Near East and its relation to kinship ties, see Horne (1994).

19. The exposure of additional doorways since 2006 and their comparison with previously exposed doors makes an early interpretation of these closures as the result of an abandonment practice now seem a less likely interpretation (*contra* Khatchadourian 2008: 232).

20. The former pair may adjoin to one additional room to the south. The latter pair may adjoin to one additional room to the west.

21. The foregoing discussion of the faunal record is based on the work of Belinda Monahan. I draw selectively here on the main findings from her published (Monahan 2014) and unpublished reports.

22. Sheep and goat comprise the largest percentage of the number of identified specimens identified to genus (51.6%), followed by cattle (35.8%). Cattle may be underrepresented in the assemblage because of postdepositional modification, particularly gnawing, which is more pronounced on cattle bones than other animals.

23. There is limited evidence for burning or butchery associated with consumption. Fileting is also not in evidence, suggesting that perhaps meats were stewed in pots on the bone and then removed after cooking. Butchery associated with dismemberment suggests that primary processing of animals was done on site. Utility indices and kill-off patterns suggest that cattle production might have focused less on meat and more on secondary products like milk, as well as traction. Sheep and goat meat appears to have been more important than cattle meat, although maximization of sheep and goat meat and meat-related products, including marrow and bone grease, may not have been a high priority. In Precincts A and C, the cumulative survivorship curve based on tooth eruption and wear suggests that only 30% of sheep/goat herd lived past age three, while epiphyseal fusion points to slightly longer-living herds. Survivorship among cattle is higher, with over three-quarters of the sample surviving to maturity. In neither case is there clear evidence of specialized production or production for exchange.

24. Among equids, which make up 3.9% of the assemblage, horses are more frequent than donkeys, and domesticates are more frequent than wild onagers. There is no evidence of burning or butchery on horse bones, though this does not in itself preclude consumption. Due to the difficulty of distinguishing among equids, the only elements that were identified definitively as horses were teeth and two associated mandibles, so it is not possible to analyze body-part distribution. While the sample is too small to discuss survivorship in a concrete way, many of the teeth were heavily worn, suggesting that most of the animals were killed well into adulthood. This is indicative of a population that was being reared not for food but for riding and/or traction.

25. There is a notable number of cervids, including *Cervus* and *Dama,* in the Tsaghkahovit faunal assemblage. Over 50% of the cervid remains at the site are antlers, and over half of these antlers show evidence of being worked. Moreover, half of all worked bone artifacts are cervid antlers. It would appear that the community was involved in some sort of tool industry focused on cervid (particularly red deer) antlers. Virtually none of the worked antlers has a very clear form. However, they do carry evidence of cutting and smoothing. In a few cases it seems that a rough circular hole was carved through the antler shaft, akin to the complete holes on the one *psalia.* The working or use of antler implements was spread throughout the settlement, although there is a particularly high concentration in Room S. In light of this, it is possible to hypothesize that the worked-antler industry may have been linked to horse riding.

26. The carpological remains of 66 kinds of plants were identified, belonging to at least 32 taxa of higher plants (Hovsepyan 2014). The main cultigens present include bread wheat (*Triticum* cf. *aestivum*) with its common subspecies (*T.* cf. *aestivum* ssp. *vulgare*), macaroni

wheat (*Triticum* cf. *durum*), emmer (*Triticum dicoccum*), and cultivated barley (*Hordeum vulgare*), part of which belongs to a hulled six-rowed variety (*H. vulgare* ssp. *vulgare* convar. *vulgare*). Judging by the samples examined to date, barley was the most intensively cultivated plant at Tsaghkahovit, with a wheat/barley ratio of 36% to 64%. In addition, there are comparably rare occurrences in the sample of rye (*Secale* sp.), possibly lentil (cf. *Lens* sp.), and broomcorn millet (*Panicum miliaceum*), as well as cultivated grape (*Vitis vinifera*). Insofar as climatic conditions at the altitude of the Tsaghkahovit Plain are not amenable to the growth of millet or grape, the presence of these cultigens attests to connections with lowland communities, perhaps in the Ararat Plain.

27. See note 2.

28. Tripartite arrowheads are widely distributed at sites across Eurasia and the Near East in the first millennium B.C. See e.g. Cleuziou (1977), Moorey (1980: 65–66), and Schmidt (1957: 9, table IX, pl. 76). Morphologically, the bracelet fits neatly within the Iron Age tradition of zoomorphic terminal bracelets predominant in the Caucasus, Luristan, and western Iran. Indeed, the earliest appearance of serpent terminals has been assigned to the Early Iron Age Caucasus (Moorey 1971: 220). Animal terminal bracelets of precious metal are a distinctive feature of Achaemenid art. The iron fibula with flat, disc-shaped face is similar to disc-shaped hinged fibulae from Iran (Delougaz, et al. 1996: Pl. 76B; Muscarella 1965), as well as two examples from Karchakhbyur and Makarashen in Armenia, dated to the sixth-to-fourth century B.C. (Karapetyan 2003: 79, figs. 51.78, 79).

29. Leah Minc at the Oregon State University Radiation Center conducted the analysis.

30. The thickness and smoothness of individual sherds tend to be highly uniform and in some cases very thin, suggesting the use of a fast wheel; traces of coil-forming are absent from all but the largest vessels; and firing conditions were clearly highly controlled given the consistency of color across individual sherds within several types, especially bowls.

31. Complete information on each sherd, including Munsell colors, fabric, dimensions, and more, can be found in the Project ArAGATS data portal (https://aragats.gorgesapps.us).

32. The petals appear to have been created through a combination of grooving and the application of pressure on the vessel's interior, or what Miller (1993: 118) calls "petal-grooving."

33. Although minimalism is also encountered on some unprovenanced metal examples (Amandry 1959: fig. 23.21; Historisches Museum der Pfalz Speyer 2006, no. 2242).

34. Some elements of these vessels have antecedents in the ceramics of Assyria, the Armenian highland, Egypt, and prehistoric Iran (Amandry 1959: 39; Paspalas 2000). The overall vessel morphology (minus spout and explicit zoomorphic adornment) does occur in the ceramic repertoires of Urartu and Iron Age sites of northwestern Iran during the eighth through early sixth centuries. There is good reason to look to Urartu for an early production of the form (Paspalas 2000: 160). Abramova (1969) and Medvedskaya (1989) have taken the upright nubs on the handles of Urartian vessels to be highly stylized horns. Such nubbed handles are numerous at Tsaghkahovit, suggesting that the style endured even after the indisputably zoomorphic handles were in circulation. But by the mid-first millennium B.C., the overall form-concept (including animal symmetrical handles, with or without spout) conjoined old and new stylistic elements and appropriated them to an Achaemenid political aesthetic (anchored by the Apadana relief), and thus instances dating to this era are most reasonably situated in relation to a Persepolitan cultural and political arena.

35. One *possibly* belongs to one of the three reference groups for the Tsaghkahovit Plain, the others belonging either definitely or probably. *Possible* group affiliation means that the multivariate probability of membership in one of the three defined reference groups for the Tsaghkahovit was less than 5%, plus the specimen fell outside the 95% confidence interval ellipse for group membership as defined on the primary discriminating elements and on the discriminant function axes; but the specimen is assigned to a group anyway by discriminate function analysis (personal communication, Leah Minc).

36. The two amphorae on which the animals are rendered through relief carving, which is precisely the technical detail that suggests direct descent from the metal forms, are without any parallels. The animal protomes recall the twin-spouted animal-handled amphorae-rhyta from Mingechaur and Glinjanye, which carry either stylized representations of a fully modeled beast or beasts' heads. These have been variously assigned to the fifth–fourth centuries B.C. (Haerinck 1980; Tiratsyan 1964) and the fourth–first centuries B.C. (Abramova 1969). I am not aware of provenience information on a ceramic vessel with modeled ibex handles in the Persepolis Museum (Root, personal communication).

37. These "fronds" are not shown. The fragments that bear them do not join to the restored part of the vessel.

38. The slipped exterior red surface is burnished, while the interior of this restricted vessel was unslipped. The presence of "spalling" of the top portion of the tail may point to a structurally vulnerable appliqued element, but a displacement technique cannot be dismissed. Whatever the technique, it produced an effect that appears very similar to the relief elements on the animal-handled amphorae. There are pronounced striations on the interior of the vessel that could indicate wheel manufacture, although surface features can be polysemic (Roux and Courty 1995: 18).

39. None of the five fragments of serpentine vessels from Susa is inscribed.

40. Scholars have debated the question of their origin. Some have postulated a source in Afghanistan, in part because the inscriptions repeatedly mention a "Treasurer in Arachosia" (see Cahill 1985: 382). Following Schmidt (1957: 88), Cahill somewhat vaguely suggests a possible Egyptian origin for "certain vessels" at Persepolis. This interpretation supports one of Cahill's larger contentions, that the objects in the Treasury are foreign to the imperial heartland, and that this structure served as a storehouse for gift-tribute. The fact that the stone of the Tsaghkahovit plate matches serpentine deposits in the Zagros should occasion a reconsideration that the serpentine examples in the Treasury are gifts from far-flung provinces. As recently as 2005, Simpson (2005: 109) wrote that the sources of the stones from the Treasury remain uncertain.

41. Considering first the inscribed chert vessels, the earliest example is dated to Xerxes's year 7 (479/8 B.C.) and the latest to Artaxerxes I's year 29 (436/5 B.C.—Bowman 1970: 56–62; Cahill 1985: 382). Next, of the non-chert plates that are inscribed, there are two groups: those inscribed with the names of pre-Achaemenid foreign kings (e.g., Ashurbanipal, Amasis, Psamtik); and those inscribed with Xerxes. Of the stone vessels inscribed with the names of foreign kings, none are made of serpentine and only one remotely resembles the plates among which the Tsaghkahovit example belongs (although even in this one case, the vessel is footed, handled, and made of alabaster). The rest are stone objects of other shapes, like lids, pedestals, deep bowls, and bottle-shaped vessels. Of the remaining non-chert inscribed

vessels in the Treasury, all are labeled "Xerxes, the Great King." Kings later than Xerxes do not appear on any of the inscribed non-chert vessels (Cahill 1985: 383), nor are there any earlier Achaemenid kings. Moreover, almost all of these inscriptions appear on footless or footed plates (Schmidt 1957: 87). Thus the single inscribed serpentine plate is also dated to Xerxes. Finally, outside of Persepolis, inscribed stone vessels dating to the reign of Darius I and later Achaemenid kings are mostly cosmetic jars and bottles; none resembles the plates in question here. As of 1957, no inscribed stone vessel dated to Cyrus or Cambyses was known to exist and, as far as I know, this has not changed.

42. In this regard it is also notable that, of the radiocarbon determinations from Precinct A, the single sample with the highest probability range that reaches as far as the end of the fifth century B.C. is from the floor in room G (AA72366).

43. As of 1985, Cahill (1985: 382) wrote that with the exception of a few chance finds, objects such as these chert plates (and associated artifacts) have not been found outside of Persepolis. Stronach (1978: fig. 99.91) documented a footed bowl of "dark green stone" from the surface of the hilltop at Pasargadae, but it is not clear whether the vessel is of chert or serpentine. Five fragments of serpentine vessels are known from Susa, three of which are footless plates (Amiet 1990: 217–219, figs. 215, 216, 219, 222, 223). In 2007, researchers at the site of Qaleh Kali, a possible way station on the road between Susa and Persepolis, discovered fragments of four stone vessels from a dump area associated with a large colonnaded building (Potts 2007: 295 and pers. comm. 2008). Two of the fragments are footed bases of bowls that appear to be made of serpentine.

44. I am aware of only two other stone plates that are comparable to those from the Treasury and were found in a province of the empire. A plate made of jasper was among the finds in a tomb at Ikiztepe in western Turkey (Özgen and Öztürk 1996: no. 85). The jasper plate from the Ikiztepe tomb appears to be one of the objects that Burhan Tezcan discovered in 1966 during the course of his salvage excavations following the partial plundering of the tomb. There is also one green plate with uncertain provenience, said to be from Qasr-i Abu Nasr, near Shiraz (Curtis and Tallis 2005: 130, no. 147).

45. On fire altars in Achaemenid art and religion, see Garrison (1999) and Moorey (1979).

46. Scholars have offered several candidates for the precise plant used (Bowman 1970: 12–14; Falk 1989; Windfuhr 1985).

47. Root has marshaled this evidence to interpret the significance of the use of the color green in various areas of the Apadana, including the benches off the south storerooms, proposing that a ritual involving the *haoma* substance may have taken place here.

48. On three of the Achaemenid country lists (DSe, DNa, XPh), one of the subject territories is called Saka Haumavarga. While the second element of this word—*varga*—has been the subject of debate, scholars nevertheless seem to agree on assigning it a religious significance (see Tavernier 2006: 1.4.15.14). Although commonly translated as "the *hauma*-drinking Saka" (or Scythians), Tavernier has retranslated *haumavarga* as a religious expression meaning "laying *hauma*-plants (instead of the usual grass) around (the fire)." *Hauma* also appears in personal names, such as Haumadāna, meaning "gift of Hauma," Haumadāta, meaning "given by Hauma," and Haumayāsa, meaning "desiring for Hauma" (4.2.730–733; 4.2.735–736). Tavernier translates one name, Haumataxma, as "brave through

Hauma," which recalls some of the cited effects of consuming the *hauma* drink, as known from later practice. Unfortunately, further clarity on a ceremony involving the *hauma* plant or its significance in Achaemenid religion is not to be found in the Aramaic inscriptions on the chert objects. While Bowman (1970: 33–37) suggested that these inscriptions refer to a ceremony, most scholars now agree that they pertain instead to administrative matters (Bernard 1972; Cahill 1985: 382 n350; Hinz 1975; Vogelsang 1992: 169).

49. It is worth adding here that while the precise taxonomy of the *haoma* plant remains uncertain, there is some evidence that it was known to exist in Armenia at least in the fourth century B.C. This suggestion links the plant *omōmi* (hauma) mentioned by Plutarch (*Moralia,* V.26.46) to a plant (*amōmon*) which the fourth-century B.C. writer Theophrastus, as well as the first-century A.D. writer Dioscurides, described in their botanical works as an Armenian and Medo-Persian shrub (Bowman 1970: 13). If Plutarch's *omōmi* is indeed the *amōmon* studied by Theophrastus and Dioscurides, then it is possible that the *haoma* plant was native to Armenia.

50. In the first publication of the stone vessels from the Treasury, Schmidt (1957: 55) proposed a functional affinity between the morphologically identical chert and serpentine plates, even though there were no serpentine mortars and pestles. The assemblage from Tsaghkahovit Room G confirms his supposition.

REFERENCES CITED

Abka'i-Khavari, Manijeh
1988 Die Achämenidischen Metalischalen. *Archaeologische Mitteilungen aus Iran* 21: 91–139.

Abramova, M. P.
1969 O kermike s zoomorfnymi ruchkami. *Sovetskaia Arkheologiia* 2: 69–84.

Aching, Gerard
2002 *Masking and Power: Carnival and Popular Culture in the Caribbean.* University of Minnesota Press, Minneapolis.

Agamben, Giorgio
1998 *Homo Sacer: Sovereign Power and Bare Life.* Stanford University Press, Stanford.

Agnew, John, and Stuart Corbridge
1995 *Mastering Space: Hegemony, Territory and International Political Economy.* Routledge, London.

Ajami, Fouad
2011 US Should Call the Bluff of Brutal Assad Regime and Back Syria's Rebels. *The Australian,* August 16, p. 9.

Akın, Günkut
1996 Two Historical House Types from the Traditional Architecture of Eastern and Southeastern Anatolia: Houses with Corbeled Domes and Lantern Roofs. In *Housing and Settlement in Anatolia: A Historical Perspective,* pp. 248–256. Ekonomik ve Toplumsal Tarih Vakfi, Turkey.

Alberti, Benjamin, Severin Fowles, Martin Hobraad, Yvonne Marshall, and Christopher L. Witmore
2011 "Worlds Otherwise": Archaeology, Anthropology and Ontological Difference. *Current Anthropology* 52(6): 896–912.

Alcock, Susan E.
1993 *Graecia Capta: The Landscapes of Roman Greece.* Cambridge University Press, Cambridge.
2001 The Reconfiguration of Memory in the Eastern Roman Empire. In *Empires: Perspectives from Archaeology and History,* edited by S. E. Alcock, T. D'Altroy, K. D. Morrison, and C. M. Sinopoli, pp. 323–350. Cambridge University Press, Cambridge.
2002 *Archaeologies of the Greek Past: Landscape, Monuments, and Memories.* Cambridge University Press, Cambridge.
Alcock, Susan E., and John F. Cherry
2004 *Side-by-Side Survey: Comparative Regional Studies in the Mediterranean World.* Oxbow, Oxford.
Algaze, Guillermo
1993 *The Uruk World System.* University of Chicago Press, Chicago.
Allen, Lindsay
2005 *The Persian Empire.* University of Chicago Press, Chicago.
Allen, Mitchell Jack
1997 *Contested Peripheries: Philistia in the Neo-Assyrian World-System.* PhD dissertation, Archaeology, University of California, Los Angeles.
Althusser, Louis
2007 [1972] *Politics and History: Montesquieu, Rousseau, Marx.* Verso, London.
Amandry, Pierre
1959 Toreutique Achéménide. *Antike Kunst* 2: 38–56.
Amiet, Pierre
1973 Quelques observations sur le palais de Darius à Suse. *Syria: Revue d'art oriental et d'archéologie* 51: 65–73.
1983 Rhytons iraniens du musée du Louvre. *La revue du Louvre et des Musées de France* 2: 85–88.
1990 Quelques épaves de la vaisselle royale perse de Suse. In *Contribution à l'histoire de l'Iran: Mélanges Jean Perrot,* edited by F. Vallat, pp. 213–224. Editions Recherche sur les civilisations, Paris.
2010 Le palais de Darius à Suse: problèmes et hypothèses. *ARTA* 2010.001. http://www.achemenet.com/document/2010.001-Amiet.pdf.
Ando, Clifford
2000 *Imperial Ideology and Provincial Loyalty in the Roman Empire.* University of California Press, Berkeley.
Appadurai, Arjun
1986 *The Social Life of Things: Commodities in Cultural Perspective.* Cambridge University Press, Cambridge.
Applebaum, Anne
2008 Go Around the Generals. *Washington Post,* May 13: A15.
Arakelyan, Babken N.
1971 Klad serebrianykh izdelii iz Erebuni. *Sovetskaia arkheologiia* 1: 143–158.
Arendt, Hannah
1951 *The Origins of Totalitarianism.* Harcourt, Brace, New York.

Avetisyan, Pavel, Ruben Badalyan, and Adam T. Smith
2000 Preliminary Report on the 1998 Archaeological Investigations of Project ArAGATS in the Tsakahovit Plain, Armenia. *Studi micenei ed egeo-anatolici* 42(1): 19–59.

Avetisyan, Pavel, N. Yengibaryan, and G. Sargsyan
1998 Hayastani norahayt hnagitakan hushardzanner (Artashavani dambaranadasht). *Handes Amsorya* 1(12): 193–247.

Azadpour, M.
2003 Hegel, Georg Wilhelm Friedrich. In *Encyclopaedia Iranica,* Vol. 12, edited by Ehsan Yarshater, pp. 139–141. Encyclopaedia Iranica Foundation, New York.

Babaev, Ilyas A., Iulon Gagoshidze, and Florian Knauss
2007 An Achaemenid "Palace" at Qarajamirli (Azerbaijan): Preliminary Report on the Excavations in 2006. In *Achaemenid Culture and Local Traditions in Anatolia, Southern Caucasus and Iran,* edited by A. I. Ivantchik and V. Licheli, pp. 31–45. Brill, Leiden.

Babaev, Ilyas A., and Florian Knauss
2010 Die achaimenidische Residenz bei Karačamirli: Ausgrabungen auf dem Gurban Tepe und auf dem Rizvan Tepe. *Archäologische Mitteilungen aus Iran und Turan* 42: 237–266.

Babaev, Ilyas A., Gundula Mehnert, and Florian Knauss
2009 Die achaimenidische Residenz auf dem Gurban Tepe. Ausgrabungen bei Karačamirli.3. Vorbericht. *Archäologische Mitteilungen aus Iran und Turan* 41: 283–321.

Badaljan, Ruben S., Philip L. Kohl, and Stephan Kroll
1997 Bericht über die amerikanisch-armenisch-deutche archäologische Expedition in Armenien. *Archäologische Mitteilungen aus Iran und Turan* 29: 191–228.

Badalyan, Ruben, Adam T. Smith, Ian Lindsay, A. Harutyunyan, Alan Greene, M. Marshall, Belinda Monahan, and Roman Hovsepyan
in press A Preliminary Report on the 2008, 2010, and 2011 Investigations of Project ArAGATS on the Tsaghkahovit Plain, Republic of Armeina. *Archäologische Mitteilungen aus Iran.*

Badalyan, Ruben, Adam T. Smith, Ian Lindsay, Lori Khatchadourian, and Pavel Avetisyan
2008 Village, Fortress, and Town in Bronze Age and Iron Age Southern Caucasia: A Preliminary Report on the 2003–2006 Investigations of Project ArAGATS on the Tsaghkahovit Plain, Republic of Armenia. *Archäologische Mitteilungen aus Iran und Turan,* 40: 45–105.

Bahrani, Zainab
2003 *The Graven Image: Representation in Babylonia and Assyria.* University of Pennsylvania Press, Philadelphia.

Barfield, Thomas J.
2001 The Shadow Empires: Imperial State Formation along the Chinese-Nomad Frontier. In *Empires: Perspectives from Archaeology and History,* edited by S. E. Alcock, T. N. D'Altroy, K. D. Morrison, and C. M. Sinopoli, pp. 10–41. Cambridge University Press, Cambridge.

Barry, Andrew
2010 Materialist Politics: Metallurgy. In *Political Matters: Technoscience, Democracy, and Public Life,* edited by B. Braun and S. J. Whatmore, pp. 89–117. Minnesota University Press, Minneapolis.

Bartelson, Jens
1995 *A Genealogy of Sovereignty.* Cambridge University Press, Cambridge.
Bartholomae, Christian
1904 *Altiranisches Wörterbuch.* K. J. Trübner, Strassburg.
Beard, Mary
2007 *The Roman Triumph.* Harvard University Press, Cambridge.
Belgiorno, Maria Rosaria
1984 I dati archeologici. In *Tra lo Zagros e l'Urmia: Ricerche storiche ed archeologiche nell'Azerbaigian iraniano,* edited by P. E. Pecorella and M. Salvini, pp. 137–299. Edizioni dell'Ateneo, Rome.
Benech, Christophe, Remy Boucharlat, and Sebastien Gondet
2012 Organisation et aménagement de l'espace à Pasargades. *ARTA* 2012.003. http://www.achemenet.com/document/2012.003-Benech_Boucharlat_Gondet.pdf.
Benjamin, Walter
1996 *Selected Writings, Volume 1: 1913–1926.* Belknap Press, Cambridge, MA.
Bennett, Jane
2010 *Vibrant Matter: A Political Ecology of Things.* Duke University Press, Durham, NC.
Bennett, Tony, and Patrick Joyce (editors)
2010 *Material Powers: Cultural Studies, History and the Material Turn.* Routledge, London.
Benton, Lauren
2010 *A Search for Sovereignty: Law and Geography in European Empires, 1400–1900.* Cambridge University Press, Cambridge.
Benveniste, Émil
1938 Traditions indo-iraniennes sur les classes sociales. *Journal Asiatique* 38: 529–549.
1969 *Le vocabulaire des institutions indo-européennes, 2. Pouvoir, droit, religion.* Éditions de Minuit, Paris.
Bernard, Paul
1972 Les mortiers et pilons inscrits de Persépolis. *Studia Iranica* 1(2): 165–176.
Bhabha, Homi
1997 Of Mimicry and Man: The Ambivalence of Colonial Discourse. In *Tensions of Empire: Colonial Cultures in a Bourgeois World,* edited by F. Cooper and A. L. Stoler, pp. 152–160. University of California Press, Berkeley.
Biscione, Raffaele
2003 Pre-Urartian and Urartian Settlement Patterns in the Caucasus, Two Case Studies: The Urmia Plain, Iran, and the Sevan Basin, Armenia. In *Archaeology in the Borderlands: Investigations in Caucasia and Beyond,* edited by A. T. Smith and K. S. Rubinson, pp. 167–184. Cotsen Institute of Archaeology, University of California, Los Angeles.
Biscione, Raffaele, Simon Hmayakyan, and Neda Parmegiani
2002 *The North-Eastern Frontier: Urartians and Non-Urartians in the Sevan Lake Basin.* Istituto di studi sulle civiltà dell-egeo e del vicino oriente, Rome.
Black, Conrad
2011 At Year End, a World Stumbling Onward. *National Post* [Toronto], December 31:A16.

Blanton, Richard E., and Gary M. Feinman
1984 The Mesoamerican World System. *American Anthropologist* 8(3): 195–216.
Blaylock, Stuart
2009 *Tille Höyük 3: The Iron Age.* British Institute at Ankara, London.
Boardman, John
2000 *Persia and the West: An Archaeological Investigation of the Genesis of Achaemenid Persian Art.* Thames & Hudson, London.
Booker, Christopher
2007 Sign up to Fight the EU Empire. *Sunday Telegraph* [London], July 15, p. 14.
Boucharlat, Remy
2005 Iran. In *L'archéologie de l'empire achéménide: nouvelles recherches. Actes du colloque organisé au Collège de France par le "Réseau international d'études et de recherches achéménides" (GDR 2538 CNRS), 21–22 novembre 2003,* edited by P. Briant and R. Boucharlat, pp. 221–292. De Boccard, Paris.
2008 Gardens and Parks at Pasargadae: Two "Paradises"? In *Herodot und das Persische Weltreich,* edited by R. Rollinger and R. Bichler, pp. 557–574. Harrassowitz, Wiesbaden.
2013a Mercury in the Walls of the Shaur Palace. In *The Palace of Darius at Susa: The Great Royal Residence of Achaemenid Persia,* edited by J. Perrot, pp. 404–405. I.B. Tauris, London.
2013b Other Works of Darius and His Successors. In *The Palace of Darius at Susa: The Great Royal Residence of Achaemenid Persia,* edited by J. Perrot, pp. 359–407. I.B. Tauris, London.
2013c Susa in Iranian and Oriental Architecture. In *The Palace of Darius at Susa: The Great Royal Residence of Achaemenid Persia,* edited by J. Perrot, pp. 409–433. I.B. Tauris, London.
2014 Achaemenid Estate(s) near Pasargadae? In *Extraction and Control: Studies in Honor of Matthew W. Stolper,* edited by M. Kozuh, W. F. M. Henkelman, C. E. Jones, and C. Woods, pp. 27–35. Oriental Institute Press, Chicago.
Boucharlat, Remy, and Pierre Lombard
2001 Le bâtiment G de Rumeilah (oasis d'Al Ain). Remarques sur les salles à poteaux de l'âge du Fer en Péninsule d'Oman. *Iranica Antiqua* 36: 213–238.
Boucharlat, Remy, T. D. Schacht, and Sebastien Gondet
2012 Surface Reconnaissance in the Persepolis Plain (2005–2008): New Data on the City Organization and Landscape Management. In *Dariush Studies II: Persepolis and Its Settlements: Territorial System and Ideology in the Achaemenid State,* edited by G. P. Basello and A. V. Rossi, pp. 249–290. Università degli studi di Napoli L'Orientale, Napoli.
Bowman, Raymond A.
1970 *Aramaic Ritual Texts from Persepolis.* University of Chicago Press, Chicago.
Boyce, Mary
1982 *A History of Zoroastrianism* 2. E. J. Brill, Leiden.
1983 Aməša Spənta. In *Encyclopaedia Iranica,* pp. 933–936. Routledge & Kegan Paul, New York.

Boyer, Lester L., and Walter T. Grondzik

1987 *Earth Shelter Technology.* Texas A&M University Press, College Station.

Braun, Bruce, and Sarah J. Whatmore (editors)

2010a *Political Matter: Technoscience, Democracy, and Public Life.* University of Minnesota Press, Minneapolis.

2010b The Stuff of Politics: An Introduction. In *Political Matter: Technoscience, Democracy, and Public Life,* edited by B. Braun and S. J. Whatmore, pp. ix–xl. University of Minnesota Press, Minneapolis.

Bray, Tamara L.

2003 To Dine Splendidly: Imperial Pottery, Commensal Politics, and the Inca State. In *The Archaeology and Politics of Food and Feasting in Early States and Empires,* edited by T. Bray, pp. 93–142. Kluwer Academic/Plenum, New York.

Briant, Pierre

1989 Table du roi: Tribut et redistribution chez les Achéménides. In *Le tribut dans l'empire perse,* edited by P. Briant and C. Herrenschmidt, pp. 35–44. Peeters, Paris.

2002 *From Cyrus to Alexander: A History of the Persian Empire.* Eisenbrauns, Winona Lake, IN.

2005 Milestones in the Development of Achaemenid Historiography in the Era of Ernst Herzfeld. In *Ernst Herzfeld and the Development of Near Eastern Studies, 1900–1950,* edited by A. C. Gunter and S. R. Hauser, pp. 263–280. Brill, Leiden.

2010 The Theme of 'Persian Decadence' in Eighteenth-Century European Historiography: Remarks on the Genesis of a Myth. In *The World of Achaemenid Persia: History, Art and Society in Iran and the Ancient Near East,* edited by J. Curtis and S. J. Simpson, pp. 1–16. I.B. Tauris, London.

2013 Susa and Elam in the Achaemenid Period. In *The Palace of Darius at Susa: The Great Royal Residence of Achaemenid Persia,* edited by J. Perrot, pp. 3–25. I.B. Tauris, London.

Briant, Pierre, and Remy Boucharlat

2005 Introduction. In *L'archéologie de l'empire achéménide: nouvelles recherches. Actes du colloque organisé au Collège de France par le "Réseau international d'études et de recherches achéménides" (GDR 2538 CNRS), 21–22 novembre 2003,* edited by P. Briant and R. Boucharlat, pp. 17–25. De Boccard, Paris.

Briant, Pierre, and C. Herrenschmidt (editors)

1989 *Le tribut dans l'Empire perse: actes de la table ronde de Paris, 12–13 décembre 1986.* Peeters, Paris.

Brosius, Maria

2010 *Pax Persica* and the Peoples of the Black Sea Region: Extent and Limits of Achaemenid Imperial Ideology. In *Achaemenid Impact in the Black Sea: Communication of Power,* edited by J. Nieling and E. Rehm, pp. 29–40. Aarhus University Press, Aarhus.

Brown, Bill

2001 Thing Theory. *Critical Inquiry* 28(1): 1–22.

Brown, Stuart C.

1986 Media and Secondary State Formation in the Neo-Assyrian Zagros: An Anthropological Approach to an Assyriological Problem. *Journal of Cuneiform Studies* 38: 107–119.

Brumfiel, Elizabeth M.

1987 Elite and Utilitarian Crafts in the Aztec state. In *Specialization, Exchange, and Complex Societies,* edited by E. M. Brumfiel and T. K. Earle, pp. 102–118. Cambridge University Press, Cambridge.

1991 Weaving and Cooking: Women's Production in Aztec Mexico. In *Engendering Archaeology: Women and Prehistory,* edited by J. M. Gero and M. W. Conkey, pp. 224–251. Blackwell, Oxford.

1996 Figurines and the Aztec State: Testing the Effectiveness of Ideological Domination. In *Gender and Archaeology,* edited by R. P. Wright, pp. 143–166. University of Pennsylvania Press, Philadelphia.

1997 Tribute Cloth Production and Compliance in Aztec and Colonial Mexico. *Museum Anthropology* 21(2): 55–71.

1998 The Multiple Identities of Aztec Craft Specialists. In *Craft and Social Identity,* edited by C. L. Costin and R. P. Wright, pp. 145–152. American Anthropological Association, Arlington, VA.

Bruno, Giuliana

2014 *Surface: Matters of Aesthetics, Materiality, and Media.* University of Chicago Press, Chicago.

Burbank, Jane, and Fredrick Cooper

2010 Imperial Trajectories. In *Empires in World History: Power and the Politics of Difference,* edited by J. Burbank and F. Cooper, pp. 1–22. Princeton University Press, Princeton.

Burney, Charles Allen

2002 Urartu and Its Forerunners: Eastern Anatolia and Trans-Caucasia in the Second and Early First Millennia BC. *Ancient West & East* 1(1): 51–54.

Burney, Charles Allen, and David Marshall Lang

1971 *The Peoples of the Hills: Ancient Ararat and Caucasus.* Weidenfeld and Nicolson, London.

Bynum, Caroline Walker

2011 *Christian Materiality: An Essay on Religion in Late Medieval Europe.* Zone Books, New York.

Cahill, Nicholas

1985 The Treasury at Persepolis: Gift-Giving at the City of the Persians. *American Journal of Archaeology* 89: 373–389.

Calhoun, Craig, Fredrick Cooper, and Kevin W. Moore

2006 Introduction. In *Lessons of Empire: Imperial Histories and American Power,* edited by C. Calhoun, F. Cooper, and K. W. Moore, pp. 1–15. New Press, New York.

Callon, Michel, and Bruno Latour

1981 Unscrewing the Big Leviathan: How Actors Macrostructure Reality, and How Sociologists Help Them to Do So. In *Advances in Social Theory and Methodology,* edited by K. Knorr and A. Cicourel, pp. 277–303. Routledge, London.

Calmeyer, Peter

1993 Die Gefäße aus den Gabenbringer-Reliefs in Perspolis. *Archäologische Mitteilungen aus Iran* 26: 147–160.

Cargill, Jack

1977 The Nabonidus Chronicle and the Fall of Lydia: Consensus with Feet of Clay. *American Journal of Ancient History* 2: 97–116.

Carradice, Ian
1987 *Coinage and Administration in the Athenian and Persian Empires: The Ninth Oxford Symposium on Coinage and Monetary History.* British Archaeological Reports 167. British Archaeological Reports, Oxford.

Carter, Elizabeth
1994 Bridging the Gap between the Elamites and the Persians in Southeastern Khuzistan. In *Achaemenid History VIII: Continuity and Change,* edited by H. Sancisi-Weerdenburg and M. C. Root, pp. 65–95. Nederlands Instituut voor het Nabije Oosten, Leiden.

Champion, Marc
1994 Reeling in the Ex-Republics. *Moscow Times,* February 4.

Charlton, Thomas H.
1994 Economic Heterogeneity and State Expansion. In *Economies and Polities in the Aztec Realm,* edited by M. G. Hodge and M. Smith, pp. 221–256. University of Texas Press, Austin.

Cheung, Johnny
2007 *Etymological Dictionary of the Iranian Verb.* Brill, Leiden.

Çilingiroğlu, Altan
2002 The Reign of Rusa II: Towards the End of the Urartian Kingdom. In *Mauerschau: Festschrift für Mafred Korfmann,* edited by R. Aslan, pp. 483–489. Bernhard Albert Greiner, Remshalden-Grunbach.

Clastres, Pierre
1987 *Society against the State: Essays in Political Anthropology.* Zone Books, New York.

Cleuziou, Serge
1977 Les pointes de flèches "Scythiques" au proche et myen Orient. In *Le Plateau iranien et l'Asie centrale des origines à la conquête islamique,* pp. 187–199. Éditions du Centre national de la recherche scientifique, Paris.

Cobo, Bernabe
1990 *Inca Religion and Customs.* Translated and edited by Roland Hamilton. University of Texas Press, Austin.

Cohen, Jeffery Jerome
2000 Midcolonial. In *The Postcolonial Middle Ages,* edited by J. J. Cohen, pp. 1–17. St. Martin's Press, New York.

Cohn, Bernard
1996 *Colonialism and Its Forms of Knowledge: The British in India.* Princeton University Press, Princeton.

Colás, Alejandro
2007 *Empire.* Polity, Cambridge.

Collon, Dominique
1996 A Hoard of Sealings from Ur. In *Archives et sceaux du monde Hellénistique,* edited by M. Boussac and A. Invernizzi, pp. 65–84. Ecole Française d'Athènes, Athens.

Comaroff, Jean, and John L. Comaroff
1991 *Of Revelation and Revolution, Volume 1: Christianity, Colonialism, and Consciousness in South Africa.* University of Chicago Press, Chicago.

1997 *Of Revelation and Revolution, Volume 2: The Dialectics of Modernity on a South African Frontier.* Chicago University Press, Chicago.

Cook, Anita G.

2001 Huari D-Shaped Structures, Sacrificial Offerings, and Divine Rulership. In *Ritual Sacrifice in Ancient Peru,* edited by E. P. Benson and A. G. Cook, pp. 137–163. University of Texas Press, Austin.

Coole, Diana, and Samantha Frost

2010 Introducing the New Materialisms. In *New Materialisms: Ontology, Agency, and Politics,* edited by D. Coole and S. Frost, pp. 1–43. Duke University Press, Durham, NC.

Cooper, Fredrick

2005 Postcolonial Studies and the Study of History. In *Postcolonial Studies and Beyond,* edited by A. Loomba, S. Kaul, M. Bunzl, A. Burton, and J. Etsy, pp. 401–422. Duke University Press, Durham, NC.

Cooper, Fredrick, and Ann Laura Stoler

1997a Preface. In *Tensions of Empire: Colonial Cultures in a Bourgeois World,* edited by F. Cooper and A. L. Stoler, pp. vii–x. University of California Press, Berkeley.

1997b *Tensions of Empire: Colonial Cultures in a Bourgeois World.* University of California Press, Berkeley.

Coronil, Fernando

2007 After Empire: Reflections on Imperialism from the Americas. In *Imperial Formations,* edited by A. L. Stoler, C. McGranahan and P. C. Perdue, pp. 241–271. School for Advanced Research Press, Santa Fe.

Costin, Cathy L.

1993 Textiles, Women, and Political Economy in Late Prehispanic Peru. In *Research in Economic Anthropology,* vol. 14, edited by B. L. Isaac, pp. 3–28. JAI Press, Greenwich, CT.

1996 Craft Production and Mobilization Strategies in the Inka Empire. In *Craft Specialization and Social Evolution: In Memory of V. Gordon Childe,* edited by B. Wailes, pp. 211–225. University Museum of Archaeology and Anthropology, University of Pennsylvania, Philadelphia.

1998 Housewives, Chosen Women, Skilled Men: Cloth Production and Social Identity in the Late Prehispanic Andes. In *Craft and Social Identity,* edited by C. L. Costin and R. P. Wright, pp. 123–141. American Anthropological Association, Arlington, VA.

2001 Production and Exchange of Ceramics. In *Empire and Domestic Economy,* edited by T. D'Altroy and C. A. Hastorf, pp. 203–242. Kluwer Academic, New York.

Costin, Cathy L., and Timothy Earle

1989 Status Distinction and Legitimation of Power as Reflected in Changing Patterns of Consumption in Late Prehispanic Peru. *American Antiquity* 54(4): 691–714.

Costin, Cathy L., Timothy Earle, Bruce Owen, and Glenn Russell

1989 The Impact of Inca Conquest on Local Technology in the Upper Mantaro Valley, Peru. In *What's New? A Closer Look at the Process of Innovation,* edited by S. E. Van der Leeuw and R. Torrence, pp. 107–139. Unwin Hyman, London.

Covey, R. Alan

2000 Inka Administration of the Far South Coast of Peru. *Latin American Antiquity* 11(2): 119–138.

2008 The Inca Empire. In *Handbook of South American Archaeology,* edited by H. Silverman and W. H. Isbell, pp. 809–830. Springer, New York.

Curtis, John

2005 Iron Age Iran and the Transition to the Achaemenid Period. In *Birth of the Persian Empire,* vol. 1, edited by V. S. Curtis, pp. 112–129. I.B. Tauris, London.

2013 Introduction. In *The Palace of Darius at Susa: The Great Royal Residence of Achaemenid Persia,* edited by J. Perrot, pp. xv–xxix. I.B. Tauris, London.

Curtis, John, and Shahrokh Razmjou

2005 The Palace. In *Forgotten Empire: The World of Ancient Persia,* edited by J. Curtis and N. Tallis, pp. 50–55. British Museum Press, London.

Curtis, John, and Nigel Tallis (editors)

2005 *Forgotten Empire: The World of Ancient Persia.* British Museum Press, London.

D'Altroy, Terence N.

1992 *Provincial Power in the Inka Empire.* Smithsonian Institution Press, Washington, DC.

1994 Public and Private Economy in the Inka Empire. In *The Economic Anthropology of the State,* edited by E. M. Brumfiel, pp. 169–221. University Press of America, Lanham.

2001 Empires in a Wider World. In *Empires: Perspectives from Archaeology and History,* edited by S. E. Alcock, T. D'Altroy, K. D. Morrison, and C. M. Sinopoli, pp. 125–127. Cambridge University Press, Cambridge.

D'Altroy, Terence N., and Ronald L. Bishop

1990 The Provincial Organization of Inka Ceramic Production. *American Antiquity* 55(1): 120–138.

D'Altroy, Terence N., and Timothy K. Earle

1985 Staple Finance, Wealth Finance, and Storage in the Inka Political Economy. *Current Anthropology* 26(2): 187–206.

D'Altroy, Terence N., Ana M. Lorandi, Veronica I. Williams, Milena Calderari, C.A. Hastorf, Elizabeth DeMarrais, and Melissa B. Hagstrum

2000 Inka Rule in the Northern Calchaquí Valley, Argentina. *Journal of Field Archaeology* 27(1): 1–26.

D'Altroy, Terence N., Veronica I. Williams, and Ana M. Lorandi

2007 The Inkas in the Southlands. In *Variations in the Expression of Inka Power: A Symposium at Dumbarton Oaks, 18 and 19 October 1997,* edited by R. L. Burger, C. Morris, and R. Matos Mendieta, pp. 85–133. Dumbarton Oaks Research Library and Collection, Washington, DC.

Dalton, Ormonde M.

1964 *Treasure of the Oxus: With Other Examples of Early Oriental Metal-Work.* 2nd ed. British Museum, London.

Daston, Lorraine

2008 Speechless. In *Things That Talk: Object Lessons from Art and Science,* edited by L. Daston, pp. 9–24. Zone Books, New York.

Dawdy, Shannon Lee
2000 Preface. *Historical Archaeology* 34(3): 1–4.
de Certeau, Michel
1984 *The Practice of Everyday Life*. University of California Press, Berkeley.
de Clairfontaine, François F., and Stéphane Deschamps
2012 La céramique ourartéenne et post-ourartéenne du secteur du temple de Haldi (milieu VIIe—débit VIe siècle avant J.-C.). *Aramazd: Armenian Journal of Near Eastern Studies* VII(1): 105–143.
Deagan, Kathleen
1983 *Spanish St. Augustine: The Archaeology of a Colonial Creole Community*. Academic Press, New York.
1995 *Puerto Real: The Archaeology of a Sixteenth-Century Spanish Town in Hispaniola*. University Press of Florida, Gainesville.
2001 Dynamics of Imperial Adjustment in Spanish America: Ideology and Social Integration. In *Empires: Perspectives from Archaeology and History*, edited by S. E. Alcock, T. N. D'Altroy, K. D. Morrison, and C. M. Sinopoli, pp. 179–194. Cambridge University Press, Cambridge.
Deleuze, Gilles, and Felix Guattari
1987 *Thousand Plateaus: Capitalism and Schizophrenia*. Minnesota University Press, Minneapolis.
Delougaz, Pinaz, Helene J. Kantor, and Abbas Alizadeh
1996 *Chogha Mish Volume I: The First Five Seasons of Excavations 1961–1971*. Oriental Institute of the University of Chicago, Chicago.
DeMarrais, Elizabeth
2005 A View from the Americas: "Internal Colonization", Material Culture and Power in the Inka Empire. In *Ancient Colonizations: Analogy, Similarity and Difference*, edited by H. Hurst and S. Owen, pp. 73–96. Duckworth, London.
DeMarrais, Elizabeth, Luis Jaime Castillo, and Timothy K. Earle
1996 Ideology, Materialization, and Power Strategies. *Current Anthropology* 37(1): 15–31.
Deschamps, Stéphane, François F. de Clairfontaine, and David Stronach
2011 Erebuni: The Environs of the Temple of Haldi during the 7th and 6th Centuries BC. *Aramazd: Armenian Journal of Near Eastern Studies* VI(2): 121–140.
Diakonoff, Igor
1985 Media. In *The Median and the Achaemenian Periods: The Cambridge History of Iran*, vol. 2, edited by G. Gershevitch, pp. 36–148. Cambridge University Press, London.
Diakonoff, Igor, and I. N. Medvedskaya
1987 The History of the Urartian Kingdom. *Bibliotheca orientalis* 44(3–4): 385–394.
Diakonov, Igor
1956 *Istoriia Midii (History of Media)*. Izdatel'stvo Akademii Nauk SSSR, Moscow.
Diakonov, Igor, and N. B. Jankowska
1990 An Elamite Gilgameš Text from Argištihenale, Urartu (Armavir-blur). *Zeitschrift für Assyriologie und Vorderasiatische Archäologie* 80(1): 102–123.
Diehl, Jackson
2011 Retreat Roulette. *Washington Post*, July 18, p. A15.

Dietler, Michael

2001 Theorizing the Feast: Rituals of Consumption, Commensal Politics, and Power in African Contexts. In *Feasts: Archaeological and Ethnographic Perspectives on Food, Politics, and Power,* edited by M. Dietler and B. Hayden, pp. 65–114. Smithsonian Institution Press, Washington, DC.

2010 *Archaeologies of Colonialism: Consumption, Entanglement, and Violence in Ancient Mediterranean France.* University of California Press, Berkeley.

Dio, Cassius

1987 *The Roman History: The Reign of Augustus.* Penguin Books, London.

Dirks, Nicholas B. (editor)

1992 *Colonialism and Culture.* University of Michigan Press, Ann Arbor.

Doyle, Michael W.

1986 *Empires.* Cornell University Press, Ithaca, NY.

Dunn, Elizabeth Cullen, and Michael S. Bobick

2014 The Empire Strikes Back: War without War and Occupation without Occupation in the Russian Sphere of Influence. *American Ethnologist* 41(3): 405–413.

Dusinberre, Elspeth R. M.

1999 Satrapal Sardis: Achaemenid Bowls in an Achaemenid Capital. *American Journal of Archaeology* 103(1): 73–102.

2003 *Aspects of Empire in Achaemenid Sardis.* Cambridge University Press, Cambridge.

2005 *Gordion Seals and Sealings: Individuals and Society.* University of Pennsylvania Museum of Archaeology and Anthropology, Philadelphia.

2013 *Empire, Authority, and Autonomy in Achaemenid Anatolia.* Cambridge University Press, Cambridge.

Dyson, Stephen L.

2006 *In Pursuit of Ancient Pasts: A History of Classical Archaeology in the Nineteenth and Twentieth Centuries.* Yale University Press, New Haven.

Earle, Timothy K.

1994 Wealth Finance in the Inka Empire: Evidence from the Calchaqui Valley, Argentina. *American Antiquity* 59(3): 443–460.

Ebbinghaus, Susanne

1999 Between Greece and Persia: Rhyta in Thrace from the Late 5th to the Early 3rd Centuries B.C. In *Ancient Greeks West and East,* edited by G. Tsetskhladze, pp. 385–425. Brill, Leiden.

2000 A Banquet Scene at Xanthos: Seven Rhyta on the Northern Cella Frieze of the "Nereid" Monument. In *Periplous: Papers on Classical Art and Archaeology Presented to Sir John Boardman,* edited by G. Tsetskhladze, A. J. N. W. Prag, and A.M. Snodgrass, pp. 98–109. Thames & Hudson, London.

Edens, Christopher

1992 Dynamics of Trade in the Ancient Mesopotamian "World System." *American Anthropologist* 94: 118–139.

Eisenstadt, Shmuel N.

1963 *The Political Systems of Empires.* Free Press of Glencoe, London.

Ekholm, Kajsa, and Jonathan Friedman

1979 "Capital" Imperialism and Exploitation in Ancient World Systems. In *Power and Propaganda: A Symposium on Ancient Empires,* edited by M. T. Larsen, pp. 41–58. Akademisk Forlag, Copenhagen.

Ellis, Richard

1968 *Foundation Deposits in Ancient Mesopotamia.* Yale University Press, New Haven.

Erdem, Aylin Ü., and Atilla Batmaz

2008 Contributions of the Ayanis Fortress to Iron Age Chronology. *Ancient Near Eastern Studies* 45: 65–84.

Esayan, Stepan A.

1976 *Drevnaia kul'tura plemen severo-vostochnoi Armenii (III-I tyc. do n.e.).* Izdatel'stvo Akademii Nauk Armianskoi SSR, Yerevan.

Esayan, Stepan A., and Aram Kalantarian

1988 *Oshakan.* Izdatel'svto Akademii Nauk Armianskoi SSR, Yerevan.

Euben, Roxanne L.

1999 *Enemy in the Mirror: Islamic Fundamentalism and the Limits of Modern Rationalism.* Princeton University Press, Princeton.

Ewen, Charles R.

1991 *From Spaniard to Creole: The Archaeology of Cultural Formation at Puerto Real, Haiti.* University of Alabama Press, Tuscaloosa.

Fahlander, Fredrik

2007 Third Space Encounters: Hybridity, Mimicry and Interstitial Practice. In *Encounters, Materialities, Confrontations: Archaeologies of Social Space and Interaction,* edited by F. Fahlander and P. Cornell, pp. 15–41. Cambridge Scholar Press, Newcastle.

Falk, Harry

1989 Soma I and II. *Bulletin of the School of Oriental and African Studies, University of London* 52(1): 77–90.

Fedoseev, N. F..

1997 Zum achämenidischen Einfluß auf die historische Entwicklung der nordpontischen griechischen Staaten. *Archäologische Mitteilungen aus Iran und Turan* 29: 309–319.

Feldman, Marian H.

2009 Knowledge as Cultural Biography: Lives of Mesopotamian Monuments. In *Dialogues in Art History, from Mesopotamian to Modern: Readings for a New Century,* edited by E. Cropper, pp. 40–55. National Gallery of Art, Washington, DC.

Ferguson, Leland

1992 *Uncommon Ground: Archaeology and Early African America, 1650–1800.* Smithsonian Institution Press, Washington, DC.

Ferguson, T. J.

2002 Dowa Yalanne: The Architecture of Zuni Resistance and Social Change during the Pueblo Revolt. In *Archaeologies of the Pueblo Revolt,* edited by R. W. Preucel, pp. 33–44. University of New Mexico Press, Albuquerque.

Fisk, Robert

2011 The Brutal Truth about Tunisia. *The Independent* [London], January 17: 1.

2013 The Last Time I Spoke to Abbas's Family He Was Alive. What Went Wrong? *The Independent* [London], December 18, p. 4.

Frow, John

2010 Matter and Materialism: A Brief Pre-History of the Present. In *Material Powers: Cultural Studies, History, and the Material Turn,* edited by T. Bennett and P. Joyce, pp. 25–37. Routledge, London.

Frye, Richard Nelson

2010 Cyrus the Mede and Darius the Achaemenid? In *The World of Achaemenid Persia: History, Art and Society in Iran and the Ancient Near East,* edited by J. Curtis and S. J. Simpson, pp. 17–19. I.B. Tauris, London.

Furtwängler, Adolf

1909 *Griechische Vasenmalerei: auswahl hervorragender Vasenbilder.* F. Bruckmann, Munich.

Furtwängler, Andreas

1996 Gumbati: Archäologische Expedition in Kachetien 1994. *Eurasia Antiqua* 2. Vorbericht: 363–381.

Furtwängler, Andreas, and Florian Knauss

1997 Gumbati: Archäologische Expedition in Kachetien 1995: Ausgrabungen in den Siedlungen Gumbati und Ciskaraant-Gora. *Eurasia Antiqua* 3. Vorbericht: 353–387.

Furtwängler, Andreas, Florian Knauss, and A. Egold

1995 Gumbati: Archäologische Expedition in Kachetien 1994. *Eurasia Antiqua* 1. Vorbericht: 177–212.

Gafni, Isaiah

2002 Babylonian Rabbinic Culture. In *Cultures of the Jews: A New History,* edited by D. Biale, pp. 223–266. Schocken Books, New York.

Gagoshidze, Julon

1996 The Achaemenid Influence in Iberia. *Boreas* 19: 125–136.

Gardner, Andrew

2002 Social Identity and the Duality of Structure in Late Roman-Period Britain. *Journal of Social Archaeology* 2(3): 323–351.

Garraty, Christopher P., and Michael A. Ohnersorgen

2009 Negotiating the Imperial Landscape: The Geopolitics of Aztec Control in the Outer Provinces of the Empire. In *The Archaeology of Meaningful Places,* edited by B. J. Bowser and M. N. Zedeño, pp. 107–131. University of Utah Press, Salt Lake City.

Garrison, Mark B.

1999 Fire Altars. In *Encyclopaedia Iranica,* edited by E. Yarshater, pp. 613–619. Columbia University, New York.

2014 The Royal-Name Seals of Darius I. In *Extraction & Control: Studies in Honor of Matthew W. Stolper,* edited by M. Kozuh, W. F. M. Henkelman, C. E. Jones, and C. Woods, pp. 67–104. Oriental Institute of the University of Chicago, Cicago.

Garrison, Mark B., and Margaret Cool Root

2001 *Seals on the Persepolis Fortification Tablets: Images of Heroic Encounter.* 2 vols. Oriental Institute, Chicago.

Gasche, Herman
2013 The Achaemenid Persian Palaces of Babylon. In *The Palace of Darius at Susa: The Great Royal Residence of Achaemenid Persia,* edited by J. Perrot, pp. 436–450. I.B. Tauris, London.

Gates, Jennifer E.
2002 The Ethnicity Name Game: What Lies behind "Graeco-Persian"? In *Medes and Persians: Reflections on Elusive Empires. Ars Orientalis,* vol. 32, edited by M. C. Root, pp. 105–132.

Geertz, Clifford
1980 *Negara: The Theatre State in Nineteenth-Century Bali.* Princeton University Press, Princeton.

Geiger, Bernhard
1916 *Die Ameša Spentas: ihr Wesen und ihre ursprüngliche Bedeutung.* A. Hölder, Vienna.

Gell, Alfred
1998 *Art and Agency: An Anthropological Theory.* Clarendon Press, Oxford University Press, Oxford.

Gergova, Diana
2010 Orphic Thrace and Achaemenid Persia. In *Achaemenid Impact in the Black Sea: Communication of Powers,* edited by J. Nieling and E. Rehm, pp. 67–86. Aarhus University Press, Aarhus.

Giddens, Anthony
1995 *Politics, Sociology and Social Theory: Encounters with Classical and Contemporary Social Thought.* Stanford University Press, Stanford.

Given, Michael
2004 *The Archaeology of the Colonized.* Routledge, London.

Glatz, Claudia
2012 Bearing the Marks of Control? Reassessing Pot Marks in Late Bronze Age Anatolia. *American Journal of Archaeology* 116(1): 5–38.
2013 Negotiating Empire: A Comparative Investigation into the Responses to Hittite Imperialism by the Vassal State of Ugarit and the Kaska of Pontic Anatolia. In *Empire and Diversity: On the Crossroads of Archaeology, Anthropology, and History,* edited by G. Areshian, pp. 21–56. Cotsen Institute of Archaeology Press, Los Angeles.

Glatz, Claudia, and A.M. Plourde
2011 Landscape Monuments and Political Competition in Late Bronze Age Anatolia: An Investigation of Costly Signaling Theory. *Bulletin of the American School of Oriental Research* 361: 33–66.

Gluckman, Max
1983 Essays on Lozi Land and Royal Property. In *Research in Economic Anthropology,* vol. 5, edited by G. Dalton, pp. 1–94. JAI Press, Greenwich, CT.

Gnoli, Gherardo
1972 Note su *xšāyaθiya-* e *xšaça-*. *Studies in the History of Religions* 22: 88–97.
2005 Ancora su antico-Persiano xšaça. In *Scritti in onore di Giovanni M. D'Erme,* vol. 1, edited by M. Bernardini and N. L. Tornesello, pp. 557–582. Università degli studi di Napoli "L'Orientale," Naples.

2007 Old Persian *xšaça-*, Middle Persian *šahr*, Greek *εθνος*. In *Iranian Languages and Texts from Iran and Turan,* edited by M. Macuch, M. Maggi, and W. Sundermann, pp. 109–118. Harrassowitz, Wiesbaden.

Goethe, Johann Wolfgang von, Martin Bidney, and Peter Anton von Amim

2010 *West-East Divan: The Poems, with "Notes and Essays": Goethe's Intellectual Dialogues.* State University of New York Press, Albany, NY.

Gopnik, Hilary

2003 The Ceramics from Godin II in the Late 7th to Early 5th Centuries BC. In *Continuity of Empire (?): Assyria, Media, Persia,* edited by G. B. Lanfranchi, M. Roaf and R. Rollinger, pp. 249–267. S.a.r.g.o.n. Editrice e Libreria, Padova.

2010 Why Columned Halls? In *The World of Achaemenid Persia: History, Art and Society in Iran and the Ancient Near East,* edited by J. Curtis and S. J. Simpson, pp. 195–206. I.B. Tauris, London.

2011 The Median Citadel of Godin Period II. In *On the High Road: The History of Godin Tepe, Iran,* edited by H. Gopnik and M. Rothman, pp. 285–364. Royal Ontario Museum, Toronto.

Gosden, Chris

2004 *Archaeology and Colonialism: Cultural Contact from 5000 BC to the Present.* Cambridge University Press, Cambridge.

Gramsci, Antonio

1971 *Selections from the Prison Notebooks.* Lawrence & Wisehart, London.

Grant, Bruce

2009 *The Captive and the Gift: Cultural Histories of Sovereignty in Russia and the Caucasus.* Cornell University Press, Ithaca, NY.

Greene, Alan

2013 *The Social Lives of Pottery on the Plain of Flowers.* PhD dissertation, Anthropology, University of Chicago, Chicago.

Grillot-Susini, Françoise

1990 Les textes de fondation du palais de Suse. *Journal Asiatique* 278: 213–222.

Gunter, Ann

1988 The Art of Eating and Drinking in Ancient Iran. *Asian Art* 1(2): 7–52.

Gunter, Ann C., and Margaret Cool Root

1998 Replicating, Inscribing, Giving: Ernst Herzfeld and Artaxerxes' Silver *Phiale* in the Freer Gallery of Art. *Ars Orientalis* 28: 2–38.

Haerinck, Ernie

1980 Twinspouted Vessels and Their Distribution in the Near East from the Achaemenian to the Sasanian Periods. *Iran* 18: 43–54.

Haig, Ian

1991 Peace Must Mean a New Kuwait. *Australian Financial Review,* February 4: 10.

Hall, Thomas D., and Christopher Chase-Dunn

1993 The World-Systems Perspective and Archaeology: Forward into the Past. *Journal of Archaeological Research* 1(2): 121–143.

Hall, Thomas D., P. N. Kardulias, and Christopher Chase-Dunn

2011 World-Systems Analysis and Archaeology: Continuing the Dialogue. *Journal of Archaeological Research* 19: 233–279.

Hansen, Thomas Blom, and Finn Stepputat

2006 Sovereignty Revisited. *Annual Review of Anthropology* 35: 295–315.

Harman, Graham

2002 *Tool-Being: Heidegger and the Metaphysics of Objects.* Open Court, Chicago.

2010 *Toward Speculative Realism: Essays and Lectures.* Zero Books, Winchester, UK.

Harmanşah, Ömür

2015 ISIS, Heritage, and the Spectacles of Destruction in the Global Media. *Near Eastern Archaeology* 78(3): 170–177.

Harris, William

2013 Laying the Blame at the Right Doorstep in Syria. *Washington Post,* July 29:A15.

Harrison, Thomas

2010 *Writing Ancient Persia.* Duckworth, London.

Harrison, Timothy P.

2005 The Neo-Assyrian Governor's Residence at Tell Ta'yinat. *Bulletin of the Canadian Society for Mesopotamian Studies* 40: 23–32.

Haselgrove, Colin

1987 Culture Process on the Periphery. In *Centre and Periphery in the Ancient World,* edited by M. J. Rowlands, M. T. Larsen, and K. Kristiansen, pp. 104–124. Cambridge University Press, Cambridge.

Hassig, Ross

1985 *Trade, Tribute, and Transportation: The Sixteenth-century Political Economy of the Valley of Mexico.* 1st ed. University of Oklahoma Press, Norman.

Hastorf, Christine A.

1990 The Effect of the Inka State on Sausa Agricultural Production and Crop Consumption. *American Antiquity* 55(2): 262–290.

2001 Agricultural Production and Consumption. In *Empire and Domestic Economy,* edited by T. D'Altroy and C. A. Hastorf, pp. 155–178. Kluwer Academic/Plenum, New York.

Hayashida, Frances M.

1999 Style, Technology, and State Production: Inka Pottery Manufacture in the Leche Valley, Peru. *Latin American Antiquity* 10(4): 337–352.

Hažatrian, Ž., and A. Z. Markarian

2003 I rhyta di Erebuni nel contesto dell'arte achemenide e greco-persiana. *Parthica* 5: 9–20.

Hegel, Georg W. F.

1956 *The Philosophy of History.* Translated by J. Sibree. Dover, New York.

Hellwag, Ursula

2012 Der Niedergang Urartus. In *Biainili-Urartu: The Proceedings of the Symposium Held in Minch 12–14 October 2007,* edited by S. Kroll, C. Gruber, U. Hellwag, M. Roaf, and P. Zimansky, pp. 227–241. Peeters, Leuven.

Henkelman, Wouter F. M.

2003a "Dit paleis dat ik in Susa bouwde." Bouwinscriptie(s) van koning Dareios I (DSf, DSz, DSaa). In *Zij schreven Geschiedenis: Historische documenten uit het Oude Nabije Oosten (2500–100 v.Chr.),* edited by R. J. Demarée and K. R. Veenhof, pp. 373–386. Peeters, Leuven.

2003b Persians, Medes and Elamites: Acculturation in the Neo-Elamite period. In *Continuity of Empire (?): Assyria, Media, Persia,* edited by G. B. Lanfranchi, M. Roaf, and R. Rollinger, pp. 181–231. S.a.r.g.o.n. Editrice e Libreria, Padova.

2008a Cyrus the Persian and Darius the Elamite: A Case of Mistaken Identity. In *Herodot und das Persische Weltreich,* edited by R. Rollinger and R. Bichler, pp. 577–634. Harrassowitz, Wiesbaden.

2008b *The Other Gods Who Are: Studies in Elamite-Iranian Acculturation Based on the Persepolis Fortification Texts.* Achaemenid History XIV. Nederlands Instituut voor het Nabije Oosten, Leiden.

2010 "Consumed before the King": The Table of Darius, That of Irdabama and Irtaštuna, and That of His Satrap, Karkiš. In *Der Achämenidenhof / The Achaemenid Court,* edited by B. Jacobs and R. Rollinger, pp. 667–775. Harrassowitz, Wiesbaden.

2013 The Achaemenid Heartland: An Archaeological-Historical Perspective. In *A Companion to the Archaeology of the Ancient Near East,* edited by D. T. Potts, pp. 931–962. Wiley-Blackwell, Malden, MA.

Herodotus

2007 *The Landmark Herodotus.* Translated by A. L. Purvis. Pantheon Books, New York.

Herrenschmidt, Clarisse

1976 Désignation de l'empire et concepts politiques de Darious Ier d'après ses inscrptions en Vieux Perse. *Studia Iranica* 5: 33–65.

Hingley, Richard

1982 Roman Britain: The Structure of Roman Imperialism and the Consequences of Imperialism on the Development of a Peripheral Province. In *The Romano-British Countryside: Studies in Rural Settlement and Economy,* edited by D. Miles, pp. 17–52. BAR British Series, Oxford.

1997 Resistance and Domination: Social Change in Roman Britain. In *Dialogues in Roman Imperialism: Power, Discourse, and Discrepant Experience in the Roman Empire,* edited by D. J. Mattingly, pp. 81–100. Cushing-Malloy, Portsmouth, RI.

2005 *Globalizing Roman Culture: Unity, Diversity and Empire.* Routledge, London.

Hinz, Walther

1975 Zu Mörsern und Stösseln aus Persepolis. *Acta Iranica* 2(2): 371–385.

Historisches Museum der Pfalz Speyer

2006 *Das persische Weltreich: Pracht und Prunk der Grosskönige.* Catalog of an exhibition at the Historical Museum of the Palatinate (Speyer, Germany), July 9—October 29, 2006. Theiss, Stuttgart.

Hodder, Ian

2012 *Entangled: An Archaeology of the Relationships between Humans and Things.* Wiley-Blackwell, Malden, MA.

Hodge, Mary G., and Michael Ernest Smith

1994 *Economies and Polities in the Aztec Realm.* Studies on Culture and Society, vol. 6. Institute for Mesoamerican Studies, University at Albany, State University of New York; distributed by University of Texas Press, Albany.

Hoffmann, Herbert

1961 The Persian Origin of the Attic Rhyta. *Antike Kunst* 1: 21–26.

1989 Rhyta and Kantharoi in Greek Ritual. In *Greek Vases in the J. Paul Getty Musuem*, pp. 131–166. Occasional Papers on Antiquities, vol. 4. Getty Museum, Malibu.

Holland, Tom

2005 *Persian Fire: The First World Empire and the Battle for the West.* Doubleday, New York.

Horne, Lee

1994 *Village Spaces: Settlement and Society in Northeastern Iran.* Smithsonian Institution Press, Washington, DC.

Hovhannisyan [Oganesyan], Konstandin

1961 *Arin-Berd I: Architektura Erebuni.* Izdatel'stvo Akademii Nauk Armianskoi SSR, Yerevan.

1973 *Rospisi Erebuni.* Akademii Nauk Armianskoe SSSR, Yerevan.

Hovsepyan, Roman

2014 Appendix 1: Archaeobotanical Investigations at Iron III Tsaghkahovit, in the Everyday: A Preliminary Report on the 2008–2011 Excavations at Tsaghkahovit, Armenia. *American Journal of Ancient History* 118(1): 163.

Hughes, John

2011 Freedom May Be Messy, but It Beats Despotism. *Christian Science Monitor,* November 2.

Hughes, M. J.

1984 Appendix I: Analysis of Silver Objects in the British Museum. In *Nush-i Jan III: The Small Finds,* edited by J. Curtis, pp. 58–60. British Institute of Persian Studies, London.

Humphrey, Caroline

2004 Sovereignty. In *A Companion to the Anthropology of Politics,* edited by D. Nugent and J. Vincent, pp. 418–436. Blackwell, Malden, MA.

Ingold, Tim

2000 Making Culture and Weaving the World. In *Matter, Materiality and Modern Culture,* edited by P.M. Graves-Brown, pp. 50–71. Routledge, London.

2007 Materials against Materiality. *Archaeological Dialogues* 14(1): 1–16.

Iovino, Serenella, and Serpil Oppermann (editors)

2014 *Material Ecocriticms.* Indiana University Press, Bloomington.

Isaac, Benjamin H.

1992 *The Limits of Empire: The Roman Army in the East.* Clarendon Press, Oxford.

Işıklı, Mehmet

2010 The Results of Surveys in the Environs of the Urartian Fortress of Altıntepe in Erzincan, Eastern Anatolia. In *Proceedings of the 6th International Congress of the Archaeology of the Ancient Near East,* edited by P. Matthiae, F. Pinnock, L. Nigro, and N. Marchetti, pp. 265–273. Harrassowitz, Wiesbaden.

Jacobs, Bruno

1994 *Die Satrapienverwaltung im Perserreich zur Zeit Darius' III.* L. Reichert, Beihefte zum Tübinger Atlas des Vorderen Orients. Reihe B, Geisteswissenschaften Nr. 87. Wiesbaden.

2000 Achaimenidenherrschaft in der Kaukasus-Region und in Cis-Kaukasien. *Archäologische Mitteilungen aus Iran und Turan* 32: 93–102.

2010 From Gabled Hut to Rock-Cut Tomb: A Religious and Cultural Break between Cyrus and Darius? In *The World of Achaemenid Persia: History, Art and Society in Iran and the Ancient Near East,* edited by J. Curtis and S. J. Simpson, pp. 91–101. I.B. Tauris, London.

Jennings, Justin

2003 Inca Imperialism, Ritual Change, and Cosmological Continuity in the Cotahuasi Valley of Peru. *Journal of Anthropological Archaeology* 59(4): 433–462.

Johnson, Boris

2011 The Lessons for Europe from the Beach to Arromanches. *Daily Telegraph* [London], October 24, p. 26.

2012 Europe Is Driving Full-Tilt, Foot on the Pedal, into a Brick Wall. *Daily Telegraph* [London], May 21, p. 18.

Kanetsyan, Amina G.

2001 Urartian and Early Achaemenid palaces in Armenia. In *The Royal Palace Institution in the First Millennium BC: Regional Development and Cultural Interchange between East and West,* edited by I. Nielsen, pp. 145–152. Aarhus University Press, Aarhus.

Karaosmanoğlu, Mehmet, and Halim Korucu

2012 The Apadana of Altıntepe in the Light of the Second Season of Excavations. In *Anatolian Iron Ages 7: The Proceedings of the Seventh Anatolian Iron Ages Colloquium Held at Erdine, 19–24 April 2010,* edited by A. Çilingiroğlu and A. G. Sagona, pp. 131–147. Peeters, Leuven.

Karapetyan, Inesa A.

1979 Karchaghbyuri peghumncrc (1975–1978 ll.). *Putma-banasirakan handes* 3(86): 268–277.

2003 *Hayastani nyutakan mshakuyte m.t.a. VI-IV dd.* H.H. G.A.A. Gitutyun Hratarakchutyun, Yerevan.

Keane, Web

2005 Signs are Not the Garb of Meaning: On the Social Analysis of Material Things. In *Materiality,* edited by D. Miller, pp. 182–205. Duke University Press, Durham, NC.

Kellens, Jean

1992 *La religion iranienne à l'époque achéménide: actes du colloque de Liège, 11 décembre 1987.* Irana antiqua, Gent.

2002 L'idéologie religieuse des inscriptions achéménides. *Journal Asiatique* 290(2): 417–464.

2014 Sur l'origine des Aməša Spəntas. *Studia Iranica* 43: 163–175.

Kent, Roland G.

1953 *Old Persian: Grammar, Texts, Lexicon.* 2nd ed. American Oriental Society, New Haven, CT.

Kepecs, Susan, and P. Kohl

2003 Conceptualizing Macroregional Interaction: World-Systems Theory and the Archaeological Record. In *The Postclassic Mesoamerican World,* edited by M. E. Smith and F. F. Berdan, pp. 14–20. University of Utah Press, Salt Lake City.

Khatchadourian, Lori

2007 Unforgettable Landscapes: Attachments to the Past in Hellenistic Armenia. In *Negotiating the Past in the Past: Identity, Memory, and Landscape in Archaeological Research,* edited by N. Yoffee, pp. 43–75. University of Arizona Press, Tuscon.

2008 *Social Logics under Empire: The Armenian "Highland Satrapy" and Achaemenid Rule, ca. 600–300 BC.* PhD dissertation, Classical Art & Archaeology, University of Michigan, Ann Arbor.

2011 The Iron Age in Eastern Anatolia. In *The Oxford Handbook of Ancient Anatolia,* edited by S. Steadman and G. McMahon, pp. 464–499. Oxford University Press, Oxford.

2012 The Achaemenid Provinces in Archaeological Perspective. In *A Companion to the Archaeology of the Ancient Near East,* edited by D. T. Potts, pp. 963–983. Blackwell, Malden, MA.

2013 An Archaeology of Hegemony: The Achaemenid Empire and the Remaking of the Fortress in the Armenian Highlands. In *Empires and Diversity: On the Crossroads of Archaeology, Anthropology, and History,* edited by G. Areshian, pp. 108–145. Cotsen Institute of Archaeology, Los Angeles.

2014 Empire in the Everyday: A Preliminary Report on the 2008–2011 Excavations at Tsaghkahovit, Armenia. *American Journal of Archaeology* 118(1): 137–169.

forthcoming From Copy to Proxy: The Politics of Matter and Mimesis in Achaemenid Armenia. In *The Art of Empire in Achaemenid Persia: Festschrift in Honor of Margaret Cool Root,* edited by M. B. Garrison and E. R. M. Dusinberre. Nederlands Instituut voor het Nabije Oosten, Leiden.

King, Charles

2010 *The Ghost of Freedom: A History of the Caucasus.* Oxford University Press, Oxford.

Kleiss, Wolfram

1973 Planaufnahmen Urartäischer Burgen in Iranisch-Azerbaidjan im Jahre 1972. *Archaeologische Mitteilungen aus Iran* 6: 81–89.

1974 Planaufnahmen Urartäischer Burgen. *Archaeologische Mitteilungen aus Iran* 7: 79–106.

1975 Planaufnahmen Urartäisher Burgen und Urartäische Neufunde in Iranisch-Azerbaidjan im Jahre 1974. *Archaeologische Mitteilungen aus Iran* 8: 51–70.

1979 Früharmenische Burgen in nordwest-Azerbaidjan. *Archaeologische Mitteilungen aus Iran* 12: 289–302.

1980 Zur Entwicklung der achaemenidischen Palastarchitektur. *Iranica Antiqua* 15: 199–211.

1988 *Bastam II: Ausgrabungen in den Urartäischen Anlagen 1976–1978.* Mann, Berlin.

1992 Beobachtungen auf dem Burgberg von Persepolis. *Archäologische Mitteilungen aus Iran* 25: 155–167.

Kleiss, Wolfram, and Stephan Kroll

1976 Zwei Plätze des 6. Jahrhunderts v. Chr. in iranisch Azerbaidjan. *Archaeologische Mitteilungen aus Iran* 9: 107–124.

1979 Vermessene Urartäische Plätze in Iran (West Azerbaidjan) und Neufunde (Stand der Forschung 1978). *Archaeologische Mitteilungen aus Iran* 12: 183–243.

Klinkott, Hilmar

2005 *Der Satrap: ein achaimenidischer Amtsträger und seine Handlungsspielräume.* Verlag Antike, Frankfurt am Main.

Knäpper, Katharina

2011 *Die Religion de frühen Achaimeniden in ihrem Verhältnis zum Avesta.* Herbert Utz, Munich.

Knappett, Carl

2008 The Neglected Networks of Material Agency: Artifacts, Pictures and Texts. In *Material Agency: Towards a Non-anthropocentric Approach,* edited by C. Knappett and L. Malafouris, pp. 139–156. Springer, Berlin.

Knapton, P., Mohammad Rahim Sarraf, and John Curtis

2001 Inscribed Column Bases from Hamadan. *Iran* (31): 99–117.

Knauss, Florian

1999 Die Achämeniden im Transkaukasus. In *Fenster zur Forschung: Museumsvorträge der Museen der Westfälischen Wilhelms-Universität Münster,* edited by S. Lausberg and K. Oekentorp, pp. 81–114. Universität Münster, Münster.

2000 Der "Palast" von Gumbati und die Rolle der Achaimeniden im transkaukasischen Iberien. *Archäologische Mitteilungen aus Iran und Turan* 32(2000): 119–130.

2001 Persian Rule in the North: Achaemenid Palaces at the Periphery of the Empire. In *The Royal Palace Institution in the First Millennium BC: Regional Development and Cultural Interchange between East and West,* edited by I. Nielsen, pp. 125–143. 4th ed. Monograph of the Danish Institute at Athens. Aarhus University Press, Aarhus.

2005 Caucasus. In *L'archéologie de l'empire achéménide: nouvelles recherches. Actes du colloque organisé au Collège de France par le "Réseau international d'études et de recherches achéménides" (GDR 2538 CNRS), 21–22 novembre 2003,* edited by P. Briant and R. Boucharlat, pp. 197–220. De Boccard, Paris.

2006 Ancient Persia and the Caucasus. *Iranica Antiqua* 41: 80–118.

Knauss, Florian, Iulon Gagošidze, and Ilyas A. Babaev

2013 Karačamirli: Ein persisches Paradies. *ARTA* 004. http://www.achemenet.com/document/ARTA_2013.004-Knauss-Gagosidse-Babaev.pdf.

Knauss, Florian, Julon Gagošidze, and Ilyas A. Babaev

2010 A Persian Propyleion in Azerbaijan: Excavations at Karacamirli. In *Achaemenid Impact in the Black Sea Communication of Powers,* edited by J. Nieling and E. Rehm, pp. 111–122. Aarhus University Press, Aarhus.

Koch, H.

1993 Feuertempel oder Verwaltungszentrale? *Archaeologische Mitteilungen aus Iran* 26: 175–186.

Kohl, Philip L.

1979 The "World Economy" of West Asia in the Third Millennium BC. In *South Asian Archaeology, 1977,* edited by M. Taddei, pp. 55–85. Istituto universitario orientale, Naples.

1987 The Ancient Economy, Transferable Technologies, and the Bronze Age World-System: A View from the Northeastern Frontier of the Ancient Near East. In *Centre and Periphery in the Ancient World,* edited by M. J. Rowlands, M. T. Larsen, and K. Kristiansen, pp. 13–24. Cambridge University Press, Cambridge.

1989 The Use and Abuse of World Systems Theory: The Case of the "Pristine" West Asian State. In *Archaeological Thought in America,* edited by C. C. Lamberg-Karlovsky, pp. 218–241. Cambridge University Press, Cambridge.

Kohl, Philip L., and Stephan Kroll

1999 Notes on the Fall of Horom. *Iranica Antiqua* 34: 243–259.

Kotwal, Firoze M. P.

1969 *The Supplementary Texts to the šayrdy nē-šāyest.* Munksgaard, Copenhagen.

Krefter, Friedrich

1971 *Persepolis Rekonstruktionen; der Wiederaufbau des Frauenpalastes, Rekonstruktionen der Paläste, Modell von Persepolis.* Teheraner Forschungen, Gebr. Mann, Berlin.

Kroll, John H.

2013 Hacksilber. In *The Encyclopedia of Ancient History,* edited by R. S. Bagnall, K. Brodersen, C. B. Champion, A. Erksine, and S. R. Heubner, pp. 3016–3017. Blackwell, Malden, MA.

Kroll, Stephan

1976 *Keramik Urartäischer Festungen in Iran.* Archaeologische Mitteilungen aus Iran Ergänzungsband 2. Reimer, Berlin.

1984 Urartus Untergang in anderer Sicht (La chute de l'Urartu: Une autre vue). *Istanbuler Mitteilungen* 34: 151–170.

2003 Medes and Persians in Transcaucasia? Archaeological Horizons in North-Western Iran and Transcaucasia. In *Continuity of Empire (?): Assyria, Media, Persia,* edited by G. B. Lanfranchi, M. Roaf and R. Rollinger, pp. 281–287. S.a.r.g.o.n. Editrice e Libreria, Padova.

2013 Notes on the Post-Urartian Horizon at Bastam. In *Tarhan Armağani: Essays in Honour of M. Taner Tarhan,* edited by O. Tekin, M. H. Sayar, and E. Konyar, pp. 247–255. Ege Yayinlari, Istanbul.

Kuhrt, Amélie

2001 The Achaemenid Persian Empire (c. 550–330 BCE): Continuities, Adaptations, Transformations. In *Empires: Perspectives from Archaeology and History,* edited by S. E. Alcock, T. N. D'Altroy, K. D. Morrison, and C. M. Sinopoli, pp. 93–123. Cambridge University Press, Cambridge.

2007 *The Persian Empire: A Corpus of Sources from the Achaemenid Empire.* 2 vols. Routledge, New York.

Kuntner, Walter, and Sandra Heinsch

2010 The Ostburg or Aramus, an Urartian and Achaemenid Fortress: The Stratigraphical Evidence. In *Proceedings of the 6th International Congress of the Archaeology of the Ancient Near East: 5 May—10 May 2009, "Sapienza", Università di Roma,* edited by P. Matthiae, F. Pinnock, L. Nigro, and N. Marchetti, pp. 339–345. Harrassowitz, Wiesbaden.

Kuntner, Walter, Sandra Heinsch, and H. G. Avetisyan

2012 The Fortress of Aramus in Achaemenid Times. In *Dariush Studies II: Persepolis and Its Settlements: Territorial System and Ideology in the Achaemenid State,* edited by G. P. Basello and A. V. Rossi, pp. 403–416. Università degli studi di Napoli L'Orientale, Napoli.

Kuznar, Lawrence A.

1999 The Inca Empire: Detailing the Complexities of Core/Periphery Interaction. In *World-Systems Theory in Practice: Leadership, Production, and Exchange,* edited by P. N. Kardulias, pp. 223–240. Rowman & Littlefield, Lanham.

La Lone, Darrell E.

1994 An Andean World-System: Production Transformations under the Inka Empire. In *The Economic Anthropology of the State,* edited by E. M. Brumfiel, pp. 17–41. University Press of America, Lanham.

Ladiray, Daniel

2013 The Archaeological Results. In *The Palace of Darius at Susa: The Great Royal Residence of Achaemenid Persia,* edited by J. Perrot, pp. 139–204. I.B. Tauris, London.

Lanfranchi, Giovanni B.

2003 The Assyrian Expanion in the Zagros and the Local Ruling Elites. In *Continuity of Empire (?): Assyria, Media, Persia,* edited by G. B. Lanfranchi, M. Roaf, and R. Rollinger, pp. 79–118. S.a.r.g.o.n. Editrice e Libreria, Padova.

Latour, Bruno

1992 Where Are the Missing Masses? The Sociology of a Few Mundane Artifacts. In *Shaping Technology/Building Society: Studies in Sociotechnical Change,* edited by W. E. Bijker and J. Law, pp. 225–258. MIT Press, Cambridge, MA.

1993 *We Have Never Been Modern.* Harvard University Press, Cambridge.

2000 The Berlin Key or How to Do Words with Things. In *Matter, Matteriality and Modern Culture,* edited by P.M. Graves-Brown, pp. 10–21. Routledge, London.

2004 *Politics of Nature: How to Bring the Sciences into Democracy.* Harvard University Press, Cambridge.

2005a From Realpolitik to Dingpolitik. In *Making Things Public: Atmospheres of Democracy,* edited by B. Latour and P. Weibel, pp. 14–41. MIT Press, Cambridge, MA.

2005b *Reassembling the Social: An Introduction to Actor-Network-Theory.* Oxford University Press, Oxford.

Latour, Bruno, and Peter Weibel (editors)

2005 *Making Things Public: Atmospheres of Democracy.* MIT Press, Cambridge, MA.

Layard, Austen Henry

1859 *Discoveries among the Ruins of Nineveh and Babylon: With Travels in Armenia, Kurdistan, and the Desert.* Harper & Brothers, New York.

Lechtman, Heather

1993 Technologies of Power: The Andean Case. In *Configurations of Power: Holistic Anthropology in Theory and Practice,* edited by J. Henderson and P. J. Netherly, pp. 244–280. Cornell University Press, Ithaca, NY.

Lecoq, Pierre

1997 *Les Inscriptions de la Perse achéménide.* L'Aube des peuples. Gallimard, Paris.

Lehmann-Haupt, Ferdinand Friedrich Carl

1910 *Armenien: Einst und Jetzt.* B. Behr, Berlin.

Leone, Mark

2007 Beginning for a Postmodern Archaeology. *Cambridge Archaeological Journal* 17(2): 203–207.

Lewis, Simon L., and Mark. A. Maslin

2015 Defining the Anthropocene. *Nature* 519: 171–180.

Liddle, Rod

2011 Here's My Plan B, McSmug: Pay for Your Own Country. *Sunday Times* [London], September 18: 19.

Liebmann, Matthew

2012 *Revolt: An Archaeological History of Pueblo Resistance and Revitalization in 17th Century New Mexico.* University of Arizona Press, Tucson.

2013 Parsing Hybridity: Archaeologies of Amalgamation in Seventeenth-Century New Mexico. In *The Archaeology of Hybrid Material Culture*, edited by J. J. Card, pp. 25–49. Occasional Paper No. 39, Center for Archaeological Investigations, Southern Illinois University.

Lincoln, Bruce

2007 *Religion, Empire and Torture: The Case of Achaemenian Persia, with a Postscript on Abu Ghraib*. University of Chicago Press, Chicago.

2012 *"Happiness for Mankind": Achaemenid Religion and the Imperial Project*. Peeters, Leuven.

Lindsay, Ian

2006 *Late Bronze Age Power Dynamics in Southern Caucasia: A Community Perspective on Political Landscapes*. PhD dissertation, Department of Anthropology, University of California, Santa Barbara.

2011 Holding Down the Fort: Landscape Production and the Sociopolitical Dynamics of Late Bronze Age Fortress Regimes in the Southern Caucasus. In *The Archaeology of Politics: The Materiality of Political Practice and Action in the Past*, edited by P. G. Johansen and A.M. Bauer, pp. 151–185. Cambridge Scholars Press, Newcastle-upon-Tyne.

Lindsay, Ian, and Alan Greene

2013 Sovereignty, Mobility, and Political Cartographies in Late Bronze Age Southern Caucasia. *Journal of Anthropological Archaeology* 32: 691–712.

Lindsay, Ian, Leah Minc, Christophe Descantes, Robert J. Speakman, and Michael D. Glascock

2008 Exchange Patterns, Boundary Formation, and Sociopolitical Change in Late Bronze Age Southern Caucasia: Preliminary Results from a Pottery Provenance Study in Northwestern Armenia. *Journal of Archaeological Science* 35: 1673–1682.

Lisitsyan, Stepan Danilovich

1955 Ocherki etnografii dorevoliutsionnoi armenii. *Kavkazskii etnographicheskii sbornik* 1: 182–264.

Liverani, Mario

1995 The Medes at Esarhaddon's court. *Journal of Cuni* 47: 57–62.

2001 The Fall of the Assyrian Empire. In *Empires: Perspectives from Archaeology and History*, edited by S. E. Alcock, T. D'Altroy, K. D. Morrison, and C. M. Sinopoli, pp. 374–391. Cambridge University Press, Cambridge.

2003 The Rise and Fall of Media. In *Continuity of Empire (?): Assyria, Media, Persia*, edited by G. B. Lanfranchi, M. Roaf, and R. Rollinger, pp. 1–12. S.a.r.g.o.n. Editrice e Libreria, Padova.

Lommel, Herman

1970 [1959] Symbolik der Elemente in der zoroastrische Religion. In *Zarathustra*, edited by B. Schlerath, pp. 253–269. Wissenschaftliche Buchgesellschaft, Darmstadt.

1970 [1964] Die Elemente im Verhältnis zu den Aməša Spəntas. In *Zarathustra*, edited by B. Schlerath, pp. 377–396. Wissenschaftliche Buchgesellschaft, Darmstadt.

Long, Leah

2012 *Urbanism, Art, and Economy: The Marble Quarrying Industries of Aphrodisias and Roman Asia Minor*. PhD dissertation, Classical Art and Archaeology, University of Michigan, Ann Arbor.

Loomba, Ania, Suvir Kaul, Matti Bunzl, Antoinette Burton, and Jed Esty
2005 Beyond What? An Introduction. In *Postcolonial Studies and Beyond,* edited by A. Loomba, S. Kaul, M. Bunzl, A. Burton, and J. Esty, pp. 1–38. Duke University Press, Durham, NC.

Loseva, Irena M.
1958 Novye arkheologicheskie issledovaniia otriada GMII im. A.S. Pushkina na kholme Arin-berd (New Excavations of a Detachment of the State Pushkin Museum on the Hill of Arin-Berd). *Sovetskaia Arkheologiia* 2: 179–195.

Luttwak, Edward
1976 *The Grand Strategy of the Roman Empire from the First Century A.D. to the Third.* Johns Hopkins University Press, Baltimore.

Lynch, Harry F. B.
1901 *Armenia: Travels and Studies,* vol. 2. Longmans, Green, London.

Lyons, Claire L., and John K. Papadopoulos
2002 *The Archaeology of Colonialism.* Getty Research Institute, Los Angeles.

MacKenzie, John
1995 *Orientalism: History, Theory, and the Arts.* Manchester University Press, Manchester.

Magee, Peter
2001 Excavations at Muweilah, 1997–2000. *Proceedings of the Seminar for Arabian Studies* 31: 115–130.
2008 Deconstructing the Destruction of Hasanlu: Archaeology, Imperialism and the Chronology of the Iranian Iron Age. *Iranica Antiqua* 43: 89–106.

Malafouris, Lambros
2008 At the Potter's Wheel: An Argument *for* Material Agency. In *Material Agency: Towards a Non-Anthropocentric Approach,* edited by C. Knappett and L. Malafouris, pp. 19–36. Springer, Berlin.

Malandra, William W.
1983 *An Introduction to Ancient Iranian Religion: Readings from the Avesta and Achaemenid Inscriptions.* University of Minnesota Press, Minneapolis.

Malpass, Michael Andrew
1993 *Provincial Inca: Archaeological and Ethnohistorical Assessment of the Impact of the Inca State.* University of Iowa Press, Iowa City.

Mamdani, Mahmood
1996 *Citizen and Subject: Contemporary Africa and the Legacy of Late Colonialism.* University of Princeton Press, Princeton.

Manassero, Niccolò
2010 La Purezza nella Libazione: Proposte di Interpretazione des Rhyta a Protome Animale. In *Mazzo di fiori: Festschrift for Herbert Hoffmann,* edited by D. Metzler, pp. 240–261. Verlag Franz Philipp Rutzen, Ruhpolding.

Mann, Michael
1986 *The Sources of Social Power.* Cambridge University Press, Cambridge.

Manning, Sturt W., Adam Smith, Lori Khatchadourian, Ian Lindsay, Ruben Badalyan, Alan Greene, and Kate Seufer
n.d. A New Chronological Model for the Bronze and Iron Age Caucasus.

Mantha, Alexis

2013 Shifting Territorialities under the Inka Empire: The Case of the Rapayáan Valley in the Central Andean Highlands. *Archaeology Papers of the American Anthropological Association* 22: 164–188.

Marro, Catherine, and Aynur Özfirat

2003 Pre-Classical Survey in Eastern Turkey, First Preliminary Report: The Agri Dag (Mount Ararat) Region. *Anatolia Antiqua* 11: 385–422.

2004 Pre-Classical Survey in Eastern Turkey, Second Preliminary Report: The Ercis Region. *Anatolia Antiqua* 12: 227–266.

2005 Pre-Classical Survey in Eastern Turkey, Third Preliminary Report: Doğubeyazit and the Eastern Shore of Lake Van. *Anatolia Antiqua* 13: 319–356.

Marshall, Maureen

2014 *Subject(ed) Bodies: A Bioarchaeological Investigation of Late Bronze—Iron 1 (1500–800 BC) Armenia.* PhD dissertation, Anthropology, University of Chicago, Chicago.

Martirosyan, Arutiun A.

1961 *Gorod Teishebaini: po raskopkam 1947–1958gg.* Akademiya Nauk Armyanskoi S.S.R., Yerevan.

1974 *Argishtihinili.* Izdatel'stvo Akademii Nauk Armianskoi SSR, Yerevan.

Marutyan, Harutyun

2001 Settlements, Dwellings, and Inhabitants. In *Armenian Folk Arts, Culture, and Identity,* edited by L. Abrahamian and N. Sweezy, pp. 73–97. Indiana University Press, Bloomington.

Matthews, Roger

2003 *The Archaeology of Mesopotamia: Theories and Approaches.* Routledge, London.

Mattingly, David J. (editor)

1997a Dialogues in Roman Imperialism: Power, Discourse, and Discrepant Experience in the Roman Empire. *Journal of Roman Archaeology,* Supplement 23.

1997b Imperialism and Territory: Africa, a Landscape of Opportunity. In "Dialogues in Roman Imperialism: Power, Discourse and Discrepant Experience in the Roman Empire," edited by D. J. Mattingly. *Journal of Roman Archaeology,* Supplement 23, pp. 115–138.

2006 *An Imperial Possession: Britain in the Roman Empire, 54 BC-AD 409.* Allen Lane, London.

2011 *Imperialism, Power, and Identity: Experiencing the Roman Empire.* Princeton University Press, Princeton.

Mattingly, David J., and John Salmon (editors)

2001 *Economies beyond Agriculture in the Classical World.* Routledge, London.

Mauss, Marcel

1990 *The Gift: The Form and Reason for Exchange in Archaic Societies.* Translated by W. D. Halls. Routledge, London.

McClintock, Anne

1995 *Imperial Leather: Race, Gender and Sexuality in the Colonial Contest.* Routledge, New York.

Medvedskaya, I. N.

1989 The End of Urartian Presence in the Region of Lake Urmia. In *Archaeologia iranica et orientalis,* edited by L. De Meyer and E. Haerinck, pp. 439–454. Peeters Press, Gent.

Mehta, Uday Singh

1999 *Liberalism and Empire: A Study in Nineteenth-Century British Liberal Thought.* University of Chicago Press, Chicago.

Mellink, Machteld

1972 Excavations at Karataş-Semayük and Elmali, Lycia. *American Journal of Archaeology* 76(3): 257–269.

Miller, Daniel

1987 *Material Culture and Mass Consumption.* Basil Blackwell, Oxford.

2010 *Stuff.* Polity, Cambridge.

Miller, Margaret Christina

1993 Adoption and Adaption of Achaemenid Metalware Forms in Attic Black-Gloss Ware of the Fifth Century. *Archaeologische Mitteilungen aus Iran* 26: 109–146.

Mills, Barbara

2002 Acts of Resistance: Zuni Ceramics, Social Identity, and the Pueblo Revolt. In *Archaeologies of the Pueblo Revolt,* edited by R. W. Preucel, pp. 85–98. University of New Mexico Press, Albuquerque.

Minc, Leah

2009 A Compositional Perspective on Ceramic Exchange among Late Bronze Age Communities of the Tsaghkahovit Plain, Armenia. In *The Archaeology and Geography of Ancient Transcaucasian Societies,* edited by A. Smith, R. S. Badalyan, and P. Avetisyan, pp. 381–391. Oriental Institute Press, Chicago.

Mintz, Sidney Wilfred

1985 *Sweetness and Power: the Place of Sugar in Modern History.* Viking, New York.

Mitchell, Timothy

1988 *Colonizing Egypt.* Cambridge University Press, Cambridge.

Mommsen, Wolfgang J.

1980 *Theories of Imperialism.* Random House, New York.

Monahan, B.

2014 Appendix 2: Zooarchaeological Investigations at Iron III Tsaghkahovit. In Empire in the Everyday: A Preliminary Report on the 2008–2011 Excavations at Tsaghkahovit, Armenia. *American Journal of Archaeology* 118(1): 163–166.

Moorey, P. R. S.

1971 *Catalogue of the Ancient Persian Bronzes in the Ashmolean Museum.* Clarendon Press, Oxford.

1979 Aspects of Worship and Ritual on Achaemenid Seals. In *Akten des VII. Internationalen Kongresses für Kunst und Archäologie, München 1976,* pp. 218–226. Archäologische Mitteilungen aus Iran Ergänzungsband 6. Dietrich Reimer, Berlin.

1980 *Cemeteries of the First Millennium B.C. at Deve Hüyük, Near Carchemish, Salvaged by T.E. Lawrence and C.L. Woolley in 1913.* B.A.R., Oxford.

1985 The Iranian Contribution to Achaemenid Material Culture. *Iran* 23: 21–37.

1994 *Ancient Mesopotamian Materials and Industries: The Archaeological Evidence.* Clarendon Press, Oxford University Press, Oxford.

Moreland, John

2001 *Archaeology and Text.* Duckworth, London.

Morris, Craig

1998 Inka Strategies of Incoporation and Governance. In *Archaic States,* edited by G. M. Feinman and J. Marcus, pp. 293–309. School of American Research Press, Santa Fe.

2004 Enclosures of Power: The Multiple Spaces of Inca Administrative Palaces. In *Palaces of the Ancient New World,* edited by S. T. Evans and J. Pillsbury, pp. 299–323. Dumbarton Oaks Research Library and Collections, Washington, DC.

Morris, Craig, and Julian Idilio Santillana

2007 The Inka Transformation of the Chincha Capital. In *Variations in the Expression of Inka Power: A Symposium at Dumbarton Oaks, 18 and 19 October 1997,* edited by R. L. Burger, C. Morris, and R. Matos Mendieta, pp. 135–163. Dumbarton Oaks Research Library and Collection, Washington, DC.

Morrison, Kathleen D.

2001a Coercion, Resistance, and Hierarchy: Local Processes and Imperial Strategies in the Vijanagara Empire. In *Empires: Perspectives from Archaeology and History,* edited by S. E. Alcock, T. N. D'Altroy, K. D. Morrison, and C. M. Sinopoli, pp. 252–278. Cambridge University Press, Cambridge.

2001b Sources, Approaches, Definitions. In *Empires: Perspectives from Archaeology and History,* edited by S. E. Alcock, T. N. D'Altroy, K. D. Morrison, and C. M. Sinopoli, pp. 1–9. Cambridge University Press, Cambridge.

Muscarella, Oscar White

1965 A Fibula from Hasanlu. *American Journal of Archaeology* 69(3): 233–240.

1977 Unexcavated Objects and Ancient Near Eastern Art. In *Mountains and Lowlands: Essays in the Archaeology of Greater Mesopotamia,* edited by L. D. Levine and T. C. Young, pp. 153–207. Undena, Malibu, CA.

1980 Excavated and Unexcavated Achaemenian Art. In *Ancient Persia: The Art of an Empire,* edited by D. Schmandt-Besserat, pp. 23–42. Undena, Malibu, CA.

2000 *The Lie Became Great: The Forgery of Ancient Near Eastern Cultures.* STYX, Groningen.

Myers, Steven Lee

2009 America's Scorecard in Iraq. *New York Times,* February 8, p. 1.

Narimanov, I. G.

1959 Arkheologicheskie raskopki na poselenii kholma Sarytepe (1956–1957). *Izvestiia Akademii nauk Azerbaidzhanskoi SSR* Seriia obshchestvennykh nauk(3).

1960 Nakhodki baz kolonn V—IV vv. do n.e. v Azerbaidzhane. *Sovetskaia Arkheologiia* 4: 162–164.

Narimanov, I. G., and D. A. Khalilov

1962 Arkheologichiskie raskopki na kholme Sarytepe (1956 g.). *Material'naia kul'tura Azerbaidzhana* 4: 6–69.

Narten, Johanna

1982 *Die Ameṣ̌a Spəṇtas im Avesta.* Harrassowitz, Wiesbaden.

Nash, Donna J., and Patrick Ryan Williams

2009 Wari Political Organization: The Southern Periphery. In *Andean Civilization: A Tribute to Michael E. Moseley,* edited by J. Marcus and P. R. Williams, pp. 257–276. Cotsen Institute of Archaeology, Los Angeles.

Nichols, Deborah L.

1994 The Organization of Provincial Craft Production and the Aztec City-State of Otumba. In *Economies and Polities in the Aztec Realm,* edited by M. G. Hodge and M. Smith, pp. 175–193. University of Texas Press, Austin.

Nylander, Carl

1970 *Ionians in Pasargadae: Studies in Old Persian Architecture.* Almqvist & Wiksell, Uppsala.

1974 Masons' Marks in Persepolis: A Progress Report. *Proceedings of the IInd Symposium on Archaeological Research in Iran: Tehran, 29th October-1st November 1973,* pp. 216–222. Iranian Centre for Archaeological Research, Tehran.

1975 Anatolians in Susa—and Persepolis? *Acta Iranica* 3: 317–323.

1980 Earless in Nineveh: Who Mutilated "Sargon's" Head? *American Journal of Archaeology* 84: 329–333.

1999 Breaking the Cup of Kingship: An Elamite coup at Nineveh? *Iranica Antiqua* 34: 71–83.

2006 Stones for Kings: Stone-Working in Ancient Iran. In *Architetti, Capomastri, Artigiani: l'organizzazione dei cantieri e della produzione artistica nell'Asia ellenistica: studi offerti a Domenico Faccenna nel suo ottantesimo compleanno,* edited by P. Callieri, pp. 121–136. Istituto italiano per l'Africa e l'Oriente, Rome.

Oelsner, Joachim

1999/2000 Review. *Archiv für Orientforschung* (46/47): 373–380.

Ohnersorgen, Michael A.

2006 Aztec Provincial Administration in Cuetlaxtan, Veracruz. *Journal of Anthropological Archaeology* 25: 1–32.

Olsen, Bjønar

2010 *In Defense of Things.* Altamira Press, Walnut Creek, CA.

Olsen, Bjønar, Michael Shanks, Timothy Webmoor, and Christopher L. Witmore

2012 *Archaeology: The Discipline of Things.* University of California Press, Berkeley.

Overholtzer, Lisa

2013 Archaeological Interpretation and the Rewriting of History: Deimperializing and Decolonizing the Past at Xaltocan, Mexico. *American Anthropologist* 115(3): 481–495.

Özgen, Ilknur, and Jean Öztürk

1996 *The Lydian Treasure: Heritage Recovered.* Published by Uğur Okman for Republic of Turkey, Ministry of Culture, General Directorate of Monuments and Museums.

Özgüç, Tahsin

1966 *Altıntepe.* Türk Tarih Kurumu Basımevi, Ankara.

1969 *Altıntepe II.* Türk Tarih Kurumu Basımevi, Ankara.

Panaino, Antonio

2012 No Room for the "Paradise"? About Old Persian <pa-ra-da-ya-da-aa-ma>. In *Dariush Studies II: Persepolis and Its Settlements: Territorial System and Ideology in the Achaemenid State,* edited by G. P. Basello and A. V. Rossi, pp. 139–153. Università degli studi di Napoli L'Orientale, Napoli.

Parker, Bradley J.

2003 Archaeological Manifestations of Empire: Assyria's Imprint on Southeastern Anatolia. *American Journal of Archaeology* 107(4): 525–557.

Paspalas, Stavros A.
2000 A Persianizing Cup from Lydia. *Oxford Journal of Archaeology* 19(2): 135–174.
Pauketat, Timothy R.
2007 *Chiefdoms and Other Archaeological Delusions.* AltaMira Press, Lanham, MA.
Payne, Richard
2013 Cosmology and the Expansion of the Iranian Empire, 502–628 CE. *Past & Present: A Journal of Historical Studies* 220: 3–33.
Perrot, Jean
2013a Darius in His Time. In *The Palace of Darius at Susa: A Great Royal Residence of Achaemenid Persia,* edited by J. Perrot, pp. 453–474. I.B. Tauris, London.
2013b Restoration, Reconstruction. In *The Palace of Darius at Susa: The Great Residence of Achaemenid Persia,* edited by J. Perrot, pp. 210–239. I.B. Tauris, London.
2013c Stoneworking. In *The Palace of Darius at Susa: The Great Royal Residence of Achaemenid Persia,* edited by J. Perrot, pp. 189–191. I.B. Tauris, London.
Petrie, Cameron, Peter Magee, and M. Nasim Khan
2008 Emulation at the Edge of Empire: The Adoption of Non-local Vessel Forms in the NWFP, Pakistan during the Mid-Late 1st Millennium BC. *Gandaharan Studies* 2: 1–16.
Piotrovskii, Boris
1969 *The Ancient Civilization of Urartu.* Cowles, New York.
Pitts, Jennifer
2005 *A Turn to Empire: The Rise of Imperial Liberalism in Britain and France.* Princeton University Press, Princeton.
2010 Political Theory of Empire and Imperialism. *Annual Review of Political Science* 13: 211–235.
Pollock, Sheldon
2006 Empire and Imitation. In *Lessons of Empire: Imperial Histories and American Power,* edited by C. Calhoun, F. Cooper, and K. W. Moore, pp. 175–188. New Press, New York.
Pollock, Susan
2011 Imperial Ideologies and Hidden Transcripts: A Case from Akkadian-Period Mesopotamia. In *Ideologies in Archaeology,* edited by R. Bernbeck and R. H. McGuire, pp. 130–150. University of Arizona Press, Tucson.
Potts, Daniel T.
2005 Cyrus the Great and the Kingdom of Anshan. In *Birth of the Persian Empire,* vol. 1, edited by V. S. Curtis and S. Stewart, pp. 7–28. I.B. Tauris, London.
2006–7 Darius and the Armenians. *Iranistik: Deutschsprachige Zeitschrift für iranistische Studien* 10(1&2): 133–146.
2007 The Mamasani Archaeological Project, Stage Two: Excavations at Qaleh Kali (Tappeh Servan/Jinjun [MS 46]). *Iran* 45: 287–300.
Preucel, Robert W. (editor)
2002 *Archaeologies of the Pueblo Revolt.* University of New Mexico Press, Albuquerque.
Radner, Karen
2003 An Assyrian View on the Medes. In *Continuity of Empire (?): Assyria, Media, Persia,* edited by G. B. Lanfranchi, M. Roaf and R. Rollinger, pp. 37–64. S.a.r.g.o.n. Editrice e Loibreria, Padova.

Rawlinson, George

1871–73 *The Five Great Monarchies of the Ancient Eastern World.* 2nd ed. Murray, London.

Razmjou, Shahrokh

2001 Des traces de la déesse Spenta Ārmaiti à Persépolis: Et proposition pour une nouvelle lecture d'un logogramme élamite. *Studia Iranica* 30: 7–15.

2005 Religion and Burial Customs. In *Forgotten Empire: The World of Ancient Persia,* edited by J. Curtis and N. Tallis, pp. 150–156. British Museum Press, London.

2010 Persepolis: A Reinterpretation of Palaces and Their Function. In *The World of Achaemenid Persia: History, Art and Society in Iran and the Ancient Near East,* edited by J. Curtis and S. J. Simpson, pp. 231–245. I.B. Tauris, London.

Reade, Julian E.

1976 Elam and the Elamites in Assyrian sculpture. *Archäologische Mitteilungen aus Iran* 9: 97–106.

1986 A Hoard of Silver Currency from Achaemenid Babylon. *Iran* 24: 79–89.

Reeves, Phil

1995 Moscow's Man Escapes Chechen Bomb Attack Try to Blow Up Satrap. *The Independent* [London], November 21: 14.

Rempel, Alexandra R., and Alan W. Rempel

2013 Rocks, Clays, Water, and Salts: Highly Durable, Infinitely Rechargeable, Eminently Controlable Thermal Batteries for Buildings. *Geosciences* 3: 63–101.

Revell, Louise

2009 *Roman Imperialism and Local Identities.* Cambridge University Press, Cambridge.

Rice, Prudence M.

2005 *Pottery Analysis: A Sourcebook.* University of Chicago Press, Chicago.

Roaf, Michael

1973 The Diffusion of the *Salles à Quatre Saillants. Iraq* 35: 83–91.

2003 The Median Dark Age. In *Continuity of Empire (?): Assyria, Media, Persia,* edited by G. B. Lanfranchi, M. Roaf and R. Rollinger, pp. 13–22. S.a.r.g.o.n. Editrice e Libreria, Padova.

2008 Medes beyond the Borders of Modern Iran. *Bāstānpazhuhi: Persian Journal of Iranian Studies (Archaeology)* 3(6): 9–11.

2010 The Role of the Medes in the Architecture of the Achaemenids. In *The World of Achaemenid Persia: History, Art and Society in Iran and the Ancient Near East,* edited by J. Curtis and S. J. Simpson, pp. 247–253. I.B. Tauris, London.

Robinson, E. S. G.

1950 A "Silversmith's Hoard" from Mesopotamia. *Iraq* 12: 44–51.

Rollinger, Robert

2003 The Western Expansion of the Median Empire: A Reexamination. In *Continuity of Empire (?): Assyria, Media, Persia,* edited by G. B. Lanfranchi, M. Roaf and R. Rollinger, pp. 289–320. S.a.r.g.o.n. Editrice e Libreria, Padova.

2008 The Median "Empire", the End of Urartu and Cyrus the Great's Campaign in 547 B.C. (*Nabonidus Chronicle* II 16). *Ancient West & East* 7: 51–65.

Root, Margaret Cool

1979 *The King and Kingship in Achaemenid Art: Essays on the Creation of an Iconography of Empire.* Brill, Leiden.

1999 The Cylinder Seal from Pasargadae: Of Wings and Heels, Date and Fate. *Iranica Antiqua* 34: 157–190.

2000 Imperial Ideology in Achaemenid Persian Art: Transforming the Mesopotamian Legacy. *Bulletin of the Canadian Society for Mesopotamian Studies* 35: 19–28.

2002 Animals in the Art of Ancient Iran. In *A History of the Animal World in the Ancient Near East,* edited by B. J. Collins, pp. 169–209. Brill, Leiden.

2007 Reading Persepolis in Greek: Gifts of the Yauna. In *Persian Responses: Political and Cultural Interaction with(in) the Achaemenid Empire,* edited by C. Tuplin, pp. 177–224. Classical Press of Wales, Swansea.

2010 Palace to Temple—King to Cosmos. In *From the Foundations to the Crenellations: Essays on Temple Building in the Ancient Near East and Hebrew Bible,* edited by M. J. Boda and J. Novotny, pp. 165–210. Ugarit, Munster.

2013 Defining the Divine in Achaemenid Persian Kingship: The View from Bisitun. In *Every Inch a King: Comparative Studies on Kings and Kingship in the Ancient and Medieval Worlds,* edited by L. Mitchell and C. Melville, pp. 23–65. Brill, Leiden.

2015 Achaemenid Imperial Architecture: Performative Porticoes of Persepolis. In *Persian Kingship and Architecture,* edited by S. Babaie and T. Grigor, pp. 1–63. I.B. Tauris, London.

forthcoming Medes in the Imperial Imagination. In *Festschrift for Alireza Shapour Shahbazi,* edited by K. Abdi, Tehran.

Rossi, Adriano V.

2006 Colours and Lexical Taxonomies: Linguistic and Cultural Categories in Iranian. In *Proceedings of the 5th Conference of the Societas Iranologica Europaea, Ravenna, 6–11 ottobre,* edited by A. Panaino and A. Piras, pp. 459–480. Mimesis, Milan.

Rothman, Mitchell

1992 Preliminary Report on the Archaeological Survey in the Alpaslan Dam Reservoir Area and Muş Plain 1991. *Araştırma Sonuçları Toplantısı* 10: 269–295.

2004 Beyond the Frontiers: Muş in the Late Bronze to Roman Periods. In *A View from the Highlands: Archaeological Studies in Honour of Charles Burney,* edited by A. Sagona, pp. 121–178. Peeters, Dudley, MA.

Rothman, Mitchell, and Kozbe Gülriz

1997 Muş in the Early Bronze Age. *Anatolian Studies* 47: 105–126.

Roux, Valentine, and M. Courty

1995 Identification of Wheel Throwing on the Basis of Ceramic Surface Features and Micro-fabrics. *Journal of Archaeological Science* 22(1): 1–29.

Rowlands, Michael J.

1998 The Archaeology of Colonialism. In *Social Transformations in Archaeology: Global and Local Perspectives,* edited by K. Kristiansen and M. J. Rowlands, pp. 327–333. Routledge, London.

Rowlands, M. J., Mogens Trolle Larsen, and Kristian Kristiansen

1987 *Centre and Periphery in the Ancient World.* Cambridge University Press, Cambridge.

Russell, David S.

1964 *The Method and Message of Jewish Apocalyptic (200 BC—AD 100).* Westminster Press, Philadelphia.

Sadri, Ahmed
2013 *Shahnameh: The Epic of the Persian Kings.* Quantuck Lane Press, New York.
Sagona, Antonio, and Claudia Sagona
2004 An Archaeological Survey of the Bayburt Province. In *Archaeology at the North-East Anatolian Frontier, I: An Historical Geography and a Field Survey of the Bayburt Province,* edited by A. Sagona and C. Sagona, pp. 111–233. Peeters, Dudley.
Sagona, Claudia
2004 Did Xenophon Take the Aras High Road? Observations on the Historical Geography of North-East Anatolia. In *A View from the Highlands: Studies in Honour of Charles Burney,* edited by A. G. Sagona, pp. 299–333. Peeters, Dudley.
Said, Edward
1978 *Orientalism.* Pantheon Books, New York.
Sancisi-Weerdenburg, Heleen
1987a The Fifth Oriental Monarchy and Hellenocentrism. In *Achaemenid History II: The Greek Sources,* edited by H. Sancisi-Weerdenburg and A. Kuhrt, pp. 117–131. Nederlands Instituut voor het Nabije Oosten, Leiden.
1987b Introduction. In *Achaemenid History I: Sources, Structures and Synthesis. Proceedings of the Groningen 1983 Achaemenid History Workshop,* edited by H. Sancisi-Weerdenburg, pp. xi–xiv. Neederlands Instituut voor het Nabije oosten, Leiden.
1988 Was There Ever a Median Empire? In *Achaemenid History III: Method and Theory,* edited by A. Kuhrt and H. Sancisi-Weerdenburg, pp. 197–212. 3rd ed. Achaemenid History. Nederlands Instituut voor het Nabije Oosten, Leiden.
1989 Gifts in the Persian Empire. In *Le tribut dans l'Empire perse: actes de la table ronde de Paris, 12–13 décembre 1986,* edited by P. Briant and C. Herrenschmidt, pp. 129–145. Peeters, Paris.
1998 Bāji. In *Achaemenid History XI: Studies in Persian History: Essays in Memory of David M. Lewis,* edited by M. Brosius and A. Kuhrt, pp. 23–24. Nederlands Instituut voor het Nabije Oosten, Leiden.
Sancisi-Weerdenburg, Heleen, and Amelie Kuhrt (editors)
1987 *The Greek Sources: Proceedings of the Gronigen 1984 Achaemenid History Workshop.* Nederlands Instituut voor het Nabije Oosten, Leiden.
1988 *Achaemenid History III: Method and Theory.* Nederlands Instituut voor het Nabije Oosten, Leiden.
1990 *Achaemenid History IV: Centre and Periphery.* Nederlands Instituut voor het Nabije Oosten, Leiden.
Sarfaraz, A. A.
1971 Un pavillion de l'époque de Cyrus le Grand à Borasdjan. *Bāstān-Šenāsī va Honar-e Īrān* 7–8: 22–25.
1973 Borazjān. *Iran* 11: 188–189.
Sargsyan, H. V.
1998 Hayastani dramashrch'anarut'yan vaghaguyn vkayut'iinneri masin. *Hay dramagitakan handes* 24: 11–24.
Sarraf, Mohammad Rahim
2003 Archaeological Excavations in Tepe Ekbatana (Hamadan) by the Iranian Archaeological Mission between 1983 and 1999. In *Continuity of Empire (?): Assyria,*

Media, Persia, edited by G. B. Lanfranchi, M. Roaf and R. Rollinger, pp. 269–279. S.a.r.g.o.n. Editrice e Libreria, Padova.

Schaffer, Simon

2008 A Science Whose Business is Bursting: Soap Bubbles as Commodities in Classical Physics. In *Things That Talk: Object Lessons from Art and Science,* edited by L. Daston, pp. 147–192. Zone Books, New York.

Schmidt, Erich Friedrich

1953 *Persepolis I.* University of Chicago Press, Chicago.

1957 *Persepolis II: Contents of the Treasury and Other Discoveries.* University of Chicago Press, Chicago.

1970 *Persepolis III: The Royal Tombs and Other Monuments.* Oriental Institute, Chicago.

Schmitt, Carl

2003 *The Nomos of the Earth.* Telos Press, New York.

Schmitt, Rüdiger

1976 Der Titel 'Satrap'. In *Studies in Greek, Italic, and Indo-European Linguistics: Offered to Leonard R. Palmer on the Occasion of his Seventieth Birthday, June 5, 1976,* edited by A.M. Davies and W. Meid, pp. 373–390. Inst. f. Sprachwissenschaft d. Univ. Innsbruck, Innsbruck.

1987 Apadana, i. Term. In *Encyclopaedia Iranica,* vol. 2, edited by E. Yarshater, pp. 145–146. Routledge & K. Paul, London.

1998 Tradition und Innovation: Zu indoiranischen Formeln und Fügungen im Altpersischen. In *Mír Curad: Studies in Honor of Calvert Watkins,* edited by J. Jasanoff, H. C. Melchert, and L. Oliver, pp. 635–644. Innsbrucker Beiträge zur Sprachwissenschaft, Innsbruck.

Schnapp, Alain

1997 *The Discovery of the Past.* Harry N. Abrams, New York.

Schneider, Jane

1977 Was There a Pre-capitalist World System? *Peasant Studies* 7(1): 20–29.

Schreiber, Katharina

1992 *Wari Imperialism in Middle Horizon Peru.* Museum of Anthropology, University of Michigan, Ann Arbor.

2001 The Wari Empire of Middle Horizon Peru: The Epsitemological Challenge of Documenting an Empire without Documentary Evidence. In *Empires,* edited by S. E. Alcock, T. N. D'Altroy, K. D. Morrison, and C. M. Sinopoli, pp. 70–92. Cambridge University Press, Cambridge.

2005a Imperial Agendas and Local Agency: Wari Colonial Strategies. In *The Archaeology of Colonial Encounters: Comparative Perspectives,* edited by G. Stein, pp. 237–262. School of American Research Press, Santa Fe.

2005b Sacred Landscapes and Imperial Ideologies: The Wari Empire in Sondondo, Peru. In *Foundations of Power in the Prehispanic Andes,* edited by K. J. Vaughn, D. Orgburn, and C. A. Conlee, pp. 131–150. American Anthropological Association, Arlington, VA.

Schultz, F. E.

1828 Notice sur le voyage litteraire de M. Schultz en Orient et sur les decouvertes qu'il a faites récomment dans les ruines de la ville de Semiramis en Armenie; par M. Saint-Martin. *Journal Asiatique* 2: 161–188.

1840 Sur le lac Van et ses environs, par M. Fr. Ed. Schultz. *Journal Asiatique* 3: 257–299.

Scott, James C.

1985 *Weapons of the Weak: Everyday Forms of Peasant Resistance.* Yale University Press, New Haven.

1990 *Domination and the Arts of Resistance: Hidden Transcripts.* Yale University Press, New Haven.

1998 *Seeing Like a State: How Certain Schemes to Improve the Human Condition Have Failed.* Yale University Press, New Haven, CT.

2009 *The Art of Not Being Governed: An Anarchist History of Upland Southeast Asia.* Yale University Press, New Haven, CT.

Service, Elman Rogers

1975 *Origins of the State and Civilization: The Process of Cultural Evolution.* 1st ed. Norton, New York.

Sewell, William Hamilton, Jr.

2005 *Logics of History: Social Theory and Social Transformation.* University of Chicago Press, Chicago.

Simpson, St John

2005 The Royal Table. In *Forgotten Empire: The World of Ancient Persia,* edited by J. Curtis and N. Tallis, pp. 104–111. British Museum Press, London.

Simpson, St John, M. R. Cowell, and S. La Niece

2010 Achaemenid Silver, T.L. Jacks, and the Mazanderan Connection. In *The World of Achaemenid Persia: History, Art and Socetiy in Iran and the Ancient Near East,* edited by J. Curtis and S. J. Simpson, pp. 429–442. I.B. Tauris, London.

Sinopoli, Carla M.

1994a The Archaeology of Empires. *Annual Review of Anthropology* 23: 159–180.

1994b Political Choices and Economic Strategies in the Vijayanagara Empire. In *The Economic Anthropology of the State,* edited by E. M. Brumfiel, pp. 223–242. University Press of America, Lanham.

1998 Identity and Social Action among South Indian Craft Producers of the Vijayanagara Period. In *Craft and Social Identity,* edited by C. L. Costin and R. P. Wright, pp. 161–172. American Anthropological Association, Arlington, VA.

2001 Empires. In *Archaeology at the Millennium: A Sourcebook,* edited by G. M. Feinman and T. D. Price, pp. 439–471. Kluwer Academic, New York.

2003 *The Political Economy of Craft Production.* Cambridge University Press, Cambridge.

Skjærvø, Prods Oktor

2005 The Achaemenids and the *Avesta.* In *Birth of the Persian Empire,* vol. 1, edited by V. S. Curtis and S. Stewart, pp. 52–84. I.B. Tauris, London.

Smith, Adam T.

2003 *The Political Landscape: Constellations of Authority in Early Complex Polities.* University of California Press, Berkeley.

2012 The Prehistory of the Urartian Landscape. In *Biainili-Urartu: The Proceedings of the Symposium Held in Munich 12–14 October 2007,* edited by S. Kroll, C. Gruber, U. Hellwag, M. Roaf, and P. Zimansky, pp. 39–52. Peeters, Leuven.

2015 *The Political Machine: Assembling Sovereignty in the Bronze Age Caucasus.* Princeton University Press, Princeton.

Smith, Adam T., Ruben Badalyan, and Pavel Avetisyan

2009 *The Archaeology and Geography of Ancient Transcaucasian Societies: Vol. I, Regional Survey in the Tsaghkahovit Plain, Armenia.* Oriental Institute, Chicago.

Smith, Adam T., and Alan Greene

2009 Remote Sensing Data and Analysis. In *The Archaeology and Geography of Ancient Transcaucasian Societies: Vol. 1 Regional Survey in the Tsaghkahovit Plain, Armenia,* edited by A. T. Smith, R. S. Badalyan, and P. Aventisyan, pp. 373–380. Oriental Institute, Chicago.

Smith, Adam T., and Tiffany T. Thompson

2004 Urartu and the Southern Caucasian Political Tradition. In *A View From the Highlands: Trans-Caucasus, Eastern Anatolia and Northwestern Iran, Studies in Honor of C.A. Burney,* edited by A. G. Sagona, pp. 557–580. Peeters, Dudley.

Smith, Mark

2001 *The Origins of Biblical Monotheism: Israel's Polytheistic Background and the Ugaritic Texts.* Oxford University Press, New York.

Smith, Michael E.

2001 The Aztec Empire and the Mesoamerican World System. In *Empires: Perspectives from Archaeology and History,* edited by S. E. Alcock, T. D'Altroy, K. D. Morrison, and C. M. Sinopoli, pp. 128–154. Cambridge University Press, Cambridge.

Smith, Michael, and Francis Berdan

1996 Introduction. In *Aztec Imperial Strategies,* edited by F. F. Berdan, R. E. Blanton, E. Boone, M. G. Hodge, M. E. Smith, and E. Umberger, pp. 1–9. Dumbarton Oaks Research Library and Collection, Washington, DC.

Smith, Michael, and Cynthia Heath-Smith

1994 Rural Economy in Late Postclassic Morelos. In *Economies and Polities in the Aztec Realm,* edited by M. G. Hodge and M. Smith, pp. 349–376. University of Texas Press, Austin.

Smith, Michael E., and Lisa Montiel

2001 The Archaeological Study of Empires and Imperialism in Pre-Hispanic Central Mexico. *Journal of Anthropological Archaeology* 20: 245–284.

Smith, Michael E., Jennifer B. Wharton, and Jan Marie Olson

2003 Aztec Feasts, Rituals, and Markets: Political Uses of Ceramic Vessels in a Commercial Economy. In *The Archaeology and Politics of Food and Feasting in Early States and Empires,* edited by T. Bray, pp. 235–268. Kluwer Academic/Plenum, New York.

Smith, Stuart Tyson

2003a Pharaohs, Feasts, and Foreigners: Cooking, Foodways, and Agency on Ancient Egypt's Southern Frontier. In *The Archaeology and Politics of Food and Feasting in Early States and Empires,* edited by T. Bray, pp. 39–64. Kluwer Academic/Plenum, New York.

2003b *Wretched Kush.* Routledge, London.

South, Stanley

1988 Santa Elena: Threshold of Conquest. In *The Recovery of Meaning: Historical Archaeology in the Eastern United States,* edited by M. Leone and P. B. Potter, pp. 27–72. Smithsonian Institution Press, Washington, DC.

Stanish, Charles

1997 Nonmarket Imperialism in the Prehispanic Americas: The Inka Occupation of the Titicaca Basin. *Latin American Antiquity* 8(3): 195–216.

Stanish, Charles, and Brian S. Bauer

2007 Pilgrimage and the Geography of Power in the Inka Empire. In *Variations in the Expression of Inka Power: A Symposium at Dumbarton Oaks, 18 and 19 October 1997*, edited by R. L. Burger, C. Morris, and R. Matos Mendieta, pp. 45–83. Dumbarton Oaks Research Library and Collection, Washington, DC.

Stark, Barbara L.

1990 The Gulf Coast and the Central Highlands of Mexico: Alternative Models for Interaction. In *Research in Economic Anthropology*, edited by B. L. Isaac, pp. 243–285. JAI Press, Greenwich.

Stark, Barbara L., and John K. Chance

2012 The Strategies of Provincials in Empires. In *The Comparative Archaeology of Complex Societies*, edited by M. E. Smith, pp. 192–237. Cambridge University Press, Cambridge.

Stein, Gil

1999 *Rethinking World-Systems: Diasporas, Colonies, and Interaction in Uruk Mesopotamia*. University of Arizona Press, Tucson.

Stengers, Isabelle

2010 Including Nonhumans in Political Theory: Opening Pandora's Box? In *Political Matter: Technoscience, Democracy, and Public Life*, edited by B. Braun and S. J. Whatmore, pp. 3–33. University of Minnesota, Minneapolis.

Steward, Julian

1955 *Theory of Culture Change: The Methodology of Multilinear Evolution*. University of Illinois Press, Urbana.

Steward, Julian, and Louis C. Faron

1959 *Native Peoples of South America*. McGraw-Hill, New York.

Stoler, Ann Laura

1997 Sexual Affronts and Racial Frontiers: European Identities and the Cultural Politics of Exclusion in Colonial Southeast Asia. In *Tensions of Empire: Colonial Cultures in a Bourgeois World*, edited by F. Cooper and A. L. Stoler. University of California Press, Berkeley.

2006a Imperial Formations and the Opacities of Rule. In *Lessons of Empire: Imperial Histories and American Power*, edited by C. Calhoun, F. Cooper, and K. W. Moore, pp. 48–60. New Press, New York.

2006b On Degrees of Imperial Sovereignty. *Public Culture* 18(1): 125–146.

2008 Imperial Debris: Reflections on Ruins and Ruination. *Cultural Anthropology* 23(2): 191–219.

2013 *Imperial Debris: On Ruins and Ruination*. Duke University Press, Durham, NC.

Stoler, Ann Laura, and Fredrick Cooper

1997 Between Metropole and Colony: Rethinking a Research Agenda. In *Tensions of Empire: Colonial Cultures in a Bourgeois World*, edited by F. Cooper and A. L. Stoler, pp. 1–56. University of California Press, Berkeley.

Stoler, Ann Laura, and Carole McGranahan

2007 Introduction: Refiguring Imperial Terrains. In *Imperial Formations,* edited by A. L. Stoler, C. McGranahan, and P. C. Perdue, pp. 3–42. School for Advanced Research Press, Santa Fe.

Stolper, Matthew, and Jan Tavernier

2007 From the Persepolis Fortification Archive Project, 1: An Old Persian Administrative Tablet from the Persepolis Fortification. *ARTA* 001. http://www.achemenet.com/document/2007.001-Stolper-Tavernier.pdf.

Strabo

1932 *Geography, Books 10–12.* Translated by Horace Leonard Jones. Harvard University Press, Cambridge.

Stronach, David

1978 *Pasargadae: A Report on the Excavations Conducted by the British Institute of Persian Studies from 1961 to 1963.* Clarendon Press, Oxford.

1985 The Apadana: A Signature of the Line of Darius I. In *De l'indus aux balkans,* edited by J. Huot, M. Yon, and Y. Calvet, pp. 433–445. Éditions Recherche sur les Civilizations, Paris.

2001 From Cyrus to Darius: Notes on Art and Architecture in Early Achaemenid Palaces. In *The Royal Palace Institution in the First Millennium BC: Regional Development and Cultural Interchange between East and West,* vol. 4, edited by I. Nielsen, pp. 95–112. Monographs of the Danish Institute at Athens.

2008 The Building Program of Cyrus the Great at Pasargadae and the Date of the Fall of Sardis. In *Ancient Greece and Ancient Iran: Cross-Cultural Encounters,* edited by S. M. R. Darbandi and A. Zournatzi, pp. 149–173. National Hellenic Research Foundation, Athens.

2011 A Pipes Player and a Lyre Player: Notes on Three Achaemenid or Near-Achaemenid Silver Rhyta found in the Vicinity of Erebuni, Armenia. In *Strings and Threads: A Celebration of the Work of Anne Draffkorn Kilmer,* edited by W. Heimpel and G. Frantz-Szabó, pp. 251–274. Eisenbrauns, Winona Lake, IN.

2012a The Silver Rhyta from Erebuni Revisited. In *Archaeology of Armenia in Regional Context: Proceedings of the International Conference Dedicated to the 50th Anniversary of the Institute of Archaeology and Ethnography Held on September 15–17, 2009 in Yerevan,* edited by P. Avetisyan and A. Bobokhyan, pp. 170–184. Gitutyun, Yerevan.

2012b Urartu's Impact on Achaemenid and Pre-Achaemenid Architecture in Iran. In *Biainili-Urartu: The Proceedings of the Symposium Held in Munich 12–14 October 2007,* edited by J. H. Kroll, C. Gruber, U. Hellwag, M. Roaf, and P. Zimansky, pp. 309–320. Peeters, Leuven.

Stronach, David, and Michael Roaf

2007 *Nush-i Jan I: The Major Buildings of the Median Settlement.* British Institute of Persian Studies, Peeters, London.

Stronach, David, Felix Ter-Martirosov, A. Ayvazian, W. Collins, C. Demos, and S. Ghanimati

2009 Erebuni 2007. *Iranica Antiqua* 44: 181–206.

Stronach, David, Henrik Thrane, Clare Goff, and Alan Farahani
2010 Erebuni 2008–2010. *Aramazd: Armenian Journal of Near Eastern Studies* 5(2): 98–133.
Summers, G. David
1993 Archaeological Evidence for the Achaemenid Period in Eastern Turkey. *Anatolian Studies* 43: 85–108.
Summers, G. David, and Charles Allen Burney
2012 Late Iron Age Pottery from Northwestern Iran: The Evidence from Yanik Tepe. In *Anatolian Iron Ages 7: The Proceedings of the Seventh Anatolian Iron Ages Colloquium Held at Edirne, 19–24 April 2010,* edited by A. Çilingiroğlu and A. G. Sagona, pp. 269–315. Peeters, Leuven.
Tal, Oren
2011 Negotiating Indentity in an International Context under Achaemenid Rule: The Indigenous Coinage of Persian-Period Palestine as an Allegory. In *Judah and the Judeans in the Achaemenid Period: Negotiating Identity in an International Context,* edited by O. Lipschits, G. N. Knoppers, and M. Oeming, pp. 445–459. Eisenbrauns, Winona Lake, IN.
Tarhan, Taner
2007 Median and Achaemenid Periods at Tušpa. In *The Achaemenid Impact on Local Populations and Cultures in Anatolia,* edited by I. Deleman, pp. 117–130. Turkish Institute of Archaeology, Istanbul.
Taussig, Michael
1993 *Mimesis and Alterity: A Particular History of the Senses.* Routledge, New York.
Tavernier, Jan
2006 *Iranica in the Achaemenid Period (ca. 550–330 B.C.): Linguistic Study of Old Iranian Proper Names and Loanwords in Non-Iranian Texts.* Peeters, Dudley, MA.
Ter-Martirosov, Felix I.
1974 K stratigrafii Armavirskogo kholma. *Vestnik obshchestvennykh nauk Akademii nauk Armianskoi SSR* 1: 57–67.
2001 The Typology of the Columnar Structures of Armenia in the Achaemenid Period: Regional Development and Cultural Interchange between East and West. In *The Royal Palace Institution in the First Millennium BC,* edited by I. Nielsen, pp. 155–163. Monographs of the Danish Institute at Athens, vol. 4. Aarhus University Press, Aarhus.
2005a Freski erebuni urartskogo i akhemenidskogo vremeni. *Vestnik obshchestvennykh nauk Akademii nauk Armianskoi SSR* 1: 40–65.
2005b Raskopki na severnom sklone kreposti Erebuni. *Kul'tura drevnei Armenii* 13: 147–153.
Ter-Martirosov, Felix, and Stéphane Deschamps
2007 Données récentes sur l'Arménie et l'empire perse achéménide. *Les dossiers d'archéologie* 321: 68–72.
Ter-Martirosov, Felix, Stéphane Deschamps, F. F. de Clairfontaine, and V. Mutarelli
2012 Beniamin (5–4th Centuries BC): A Palace and Its Dependencies during the Achaemenid Period. In *Archaeology of Armenia in Regional Context: Proceedings of the International Conference Dedicated to the 50th Anniversary of the Institute of*

Archaeology and Ethnographic Held on September 15–17, 2009 Yerevan, edited by P. Avetisyan and A. Bobokhyan, pp. 197–207. Gitutyun, Yerevan.

Terrenato, Nicola

2005 The Deceptive Archetype: Roman Colonialism in Italy and Postcolonial Thought. In *Ancient Colonizations: Analogy, Similarity and Difference*, edited by H. Hurst and S. Owen, pp. 59–72. Duckworth, London.

Thomas, Nicholas

1991 *Entangled Objects: Exchange, Material Culture, and Colonialism in the Pacific*. Harvard University Press, Cambridge.

2002 Colonizing Cloth: Interpreting the Material Culture of Nineteenth-Century Oceania. In *The Archaeology of Colonialism*, edited by C. L. Lyons and J. K. Papadopoulos, pp. 182–198. Getty Research Institute, Los Angeles.

Thompson, Damian

2011 A Scramble for Africa Ignored by the Left. *Daily Telegraph* [London], November 26: 26.

Tilia, Ann B.

1978 *Studies and Restorations at Persepolis and Other Sites in Fars, 2*. IsMEO, Rome.

Tiratsyan, Gevork A.

1960 Arin-berdi syunazard dahliche ev satrapayin kentronneri harts'e haykakan lernashkharhum. *Teghekagir hasarakakan kitut'yunneri* 7–8: 99–114.

1964 Nekotorye cherty material'noi kul'tury armenii i zakavkaz'ia V-IV vv. do n.e. *Sovetskaia Arkheologiia* 3: 64–78.

1988 *Kul'tura drevnei Armenii: VI v. do n.e.-III v. n.e.: po arkheologicheskim dannym*. Izdadtel'stvo Akademii Nauk Armianskoi SSR, Erevan.

Tourovets, Alexandre

2001 Nouvelles propositions et problèmes relatifs à l'identification des délégations de l'escalier est de l'Apadana (Persépolis). *Archäologische Mitteilungen aus Iran und Turan* 33: 219–256.

2005 Some Reflections about the Relation between the Architecture of Northwestern Iran and Urartu: The Layout of the Central Temple of Nush-i Djan. *Iranica Antiqua* 40: 359–369.

Tozer, H. F.

1881 *Turkish Armenia and Eastern Asia Minor*. Longmans, Green & Co., London.

Traynor, Ian

2008 War in the Caucasus. *The Guardian* [London], August 12, p. 6.

Treister, Mikhail Yu

2007 The Toreutics of Colchis in the 5th-4th Centuries BC: Local Traditions, Outside Influences, Innovations. In *Achaemenid Culture and Local Traditions in Anatolia, Southern Caucasus and Iran*, edited by A. I. Ivantchik and V. Licheli, pp. 67–107. Brill, Leiden.

2010 "Achaemenid" and "Achaemenid-Inspired" Goldware and Silverware, Jewellery and Arms and Their Imitations to the North of the Achaemenid Empire. In *Achaemenid Impact in the Black Sea: Communication of Power*, edited by J. Nieling and E. Rehm, pp. 223–279. Aarhus University Press, Aarhus.

2012 The Treasure of Silver Rhyta from Erebuni: The Calf-Head Rhyton. In *Изкуство и идеология*, edited by K. Rabadzhiev, pp. 117–145. Унив. изд. Св. Климент Охридски, Sofia.

2013 Klad cerebrianykh ritonovakhemenidskogo kruga iz Erebuni. *Scripta Antiqua: Ancient History, Philology, Arts and Material Culture* 3: 341–422.

2014 Akhemenidskie "importy" u kochevnikov evrazii. In *Sarmaty i vneshnii mir: materialy VIII Vcerossiiskoi (c mezhdunarodnym uchastiem) nauchnoi konferentsii "Problemy sarmatskoi arkheologii i istorii" IIIAL UNTS RAN, 12–15 maia 2014 g,* edited by L. T. Yablonsky and N. C. Savel'ev, pp. 235–244. Institut istorii, iazyka i literatury ufimskogo nauchogo tsentra, Ufa.

2015 A Hoard of Silver Rhyta of the Achaemenid Circle from Erebuni. *Ancient Civilizations from Scythia to Siberia* 21: 23–119.

Treister, Mikhail Yu, and L. T. Yablonsky

2012 *Vliianiia akhemenidskoi kul'tury v iuzhnom priural'e (V-III vv. do n.e.),* tom 1. TAUS, Moscow.

Trenin, Dmitri, and Boris Dolgin

2010 *Russia's Foreign Policy: Modernize or Marginalize.* Carnegie Moscow Center. http://carnegie.ru/2010/01/21/russia-s-foreign-policy-modernize-or-marginalize.

Trigger, Bruce G.

1989 *A History of Archaeological Thought.* Cambridge University Press, Cambridge.

Tully, James

2008 *Public Philosophy in a New Key: Volume II, Imperialism and Civic Freedom.* Cambridge University Press, Cambridge.

Tuplin, Christopher

1987 The Administration of the Achaemenid Empire. In *Coinage and Administration in the Athenian and Persian Empires: The Ninth Oxford Symposium on Coinage and Monetary History,* edited by I. Carradice, pp. 109–158. BAR International Series 343. B.A.R., Oxford, England.

Umberger, Emily

1996 Aztec Presence and Material Remains in the Outer Provinces. In *Aztec Imperial Strategies,* edited by F. F. Berdan, R. E. Blanton, E. Boone, M. G. Hodge, M. E. Smith, and E. Umberger, pp. 151–179. Dumbarton Oaks Research Library and Collection, Washington, DC.

Vallat, François

1997 La lettre élamite d'Arménie. *Zeitschrift für Assyriologie und Vorderasiatische Archäologie* 87: 258–270.

2013a Darius the Great King. In *The Palace of Darius at Susa: The Great Royal Residence of Achaemenid Persia,* edited by J. Perrot, pp. 29–48. I.B. Tauris, London.

2013b The Main Achaemenid Inscriptions at Susa. In *The Palace of Darius at Susa: The Great Royal Residence of Achaemenid Persia,* edited by J. Perrot, pp. 281–295. I.B. Tauris, London.

Van De Mieroop, Marc

2011 *A History of the Ancient Near East ca. 3000–323 BC.* 2nd ed. Blackwell, Malden, MA.

van Dommelen, Peter

2002 Ambiguous Matters: Colonialism and Local Identities in Punic Sardinia. In *The Archaeology of Colonialism,* edited by C. L. Lyons and J. K. Papadopoulos, pp. 121–147. Getty, Los Angeles.

Vickers, Michael
2002 "Shed No Tears?" Three Studies in Ancient Metrology. In *Essays in Honor of Dietrich von Bothmer,* edited by A. J. Clark and J. Gaunt, pp. 333–339. Allard Pierson Series 14, Allard Pierson Museum, Amsterdam.
Villa, Susie Hoogasian, and Mary Allerton Kilbourne Matossian
1982 *Armenian Village Life before 1914.* Wayne State University Press, Detroit.
Vogelsang, Willem J.
1992 *The Rise and Organisation of the Achaemenid Empire: The Eastern Iranian Evidence.* Brill, Leiden.
Voss, Barbara
2008a *The Archaeology of Ethnogenesis: Race and Sexuality in Colonial San Francisco.* University of California Press, Berkeley.
2008b Domesticating Imperialism: Sexual Politics and the Archaeology of Empire. *American Anthropologist* 110(2): 191–203.
Voss, Barbara, and E. C. Vasella (editors)
2010 *The Archaeology of Colonialism: Intimate Encounters and Sexual Effects.* Cambridge University Press, Cambridge.
Wallerstein, Immanuel Maurice
1974 *The Modern World-System: Capitalist Agriculture and the Origins of the European World-Economy in the Sixteenth Century.* Academic Press, New York.
Walser, Gerold
1966 *Die Völkerschaften auf den Reliefs von Persepolis: Historische Studien über den sogenannten Tributzug an der Apadanatreppe.* Tehraner Forschungen 2. Mann, Berlin.
Waters, Matthew
2010 Cyrus and the Medes. In *The World of Achaemenid Persia: History, Art and Society in Iran and the Ancient Near East,* edited by J. Curtis and S. J. Simpson, pp. 63–71. I.B. Tauris, London.
2014 *Ancient Persia: A Concise History of the Achaemenid Empire, 550–330 BCE.* Cambridge University Press, Cambridge.
Webmoor, Timothy
2007 What about "One More Turn after the Social" in Archaeological Reasoning? Taking Things Seriously. *World Archaeology* 39(4): 563–578.
Webster, Jane
2001 Creolizing the Roman Provinces. *American Journal of Archaeology* 105(2): 209–225.
2003 Art as Resistance and Negotiation. In *Roman Imperialism and Provincial Art,* edited by S. Scott and J. Webster, pp. 24–51. Cambridge University Press, Cambridge.
Wells, Peter
1999a *The Barbarians Speak.* Princeton University Press, Princeton.
1999b Production within and beyond Imperial Boundaries: Goods, Exchange, and Power in Roman Europe. In *World-Systems Theory in Practice: Leadership, Production, and Exchange,* edited by P. N. Kardulias, pp. 85–101. Rowman & Littlefield, Lanham.
Wernke, Steven A.
2007 Analogy of Erasure? Dialectics of Religious Transformation in the Early *Doctrinas* of the Colca Valley, Peru. *International Journal of Historical Archaeology* 11(2): 152–182.

2013 *Negotiated Settlements: Andean Communities and Landscapes under Inka and Spanish Colonialism.* University of Florida Press, Gainesville.

Wiesehöfer, Josef

1996 *Ancient Persia: From 550 BC to 650 AD.* I.B. Tauris, London.

Wilkinson, Tony J., Jason Ur, Eleanor Barbanes Wilkinson, and Mark Altaweel

2005 Landscape and Settlement in the Neo-Assyrian Empire. *Bulletin of the American School of Oriental Research* 340: 23–56.

Windfuhr, Gernot L.

1985 Haoma/Soma: The Plant. *Acta Iranica* XI: 699–726.

Winichakul, Thongchai

1994 *Siam Mapped: A History of the Geo-body of a Nation.* University of Hawaii Press, Honolulu.

Winter, Irene

2000 Babylonian Archaeologists of The(ir) Mesopotamian Past. In *Proceedings of the First International Congress of the Archaeology of the Ancient Near East,* edited by P. Matthiae, A. Enea, L. Peyronel, and F. Pinnock, pp. 1785–1798. Università degli studi di Roma "La Sapienza," Rome.

Witmore, Christopher L.

2007 Symmetrical Archaeology: Excerpts of a Manifesto. *World Archaeology* 39(4): 546–562.

Wolf, Eric R.

1982 *Europe and the People without History.* University of California Press, Berkeley.

Woolf, Greg

1990 World-Systems Analysis and the Roman Empire. *Journal of Roman Archaeology* 3: 44–58.

Woollacott, Martin

1991 The Gulf War: America's True War Aim is Laid Bare—The Remaking of the Middle East. *The Guardian* [London], February 16.

Wright, Gwendolyn

1991 *The Politics of Design in French Colonial Urbanism.* University of Chicago Press, Chicago.

Wright, Henry Tutwiler, and G. A. Johnson

1975 Population, Exchange, and Early State Formation in Southwestern Iran. *American Anthropologist* 77: 267–289.

Xenophon

1979 Xenophon in Seven Volumes, 4. Harvard University Press Cambridge, Mass.

Yaghmaee, Ehsan

2010 Excavations in Dashtestan (Borazjan, Iran). In *The World of Achaemenid Persia: History, Art and Society in Iran and the Ancient Near East,* edited by J. Curtis and S. J. Simpson, pp. 317. I.B. Tauris, London.

Yiğitpaşa, Davut

2016 *Doğu Anadolu Geç Demir Çağı Kültürü.* Gece Kitaplığı, Ankara.

Yoffee, Norman

2005 *Myths of the Archaic State: Evolution of the Earliest Cities, States and Civilizations.* Cambridge University Press, Cambridge.

Young, Hugo
1997 Quite Simply Independent. *The Guardian,* April 7: 19.

Young, T. C.
1994 Architectural Developments in Iron Age Western Iran. *Bulletin of the Canadian Society for Mesopotamian Studies* 27: 25–32.

Yurchak, Alexei
2006 *Everything Was Forever, Until It Was No More: The Last Soviet Generation.* Princeton University Press, Princeton.
2014 Little Green Men: Russia, Ukraine, and Post-Soviet Sovereignty. *Anthropoliteia,* March 31. http://anthropoliteia.net/2014/03/31/little-green-men-russia-ukraine-and-post-soviet-sovereignty/.

Zardaryan, Mkrdich H., Armen V. Tonikyan, Susan E. Alcock, and John F. Cherry
2007 Les investigations du projet "Vorotan" dans la région de Suynik. *Les dossiers d'archéologie* 321: 60–63.

Zimansky, Paul E.
1995 Xenophon and the Urartian Legacy. In *Dans les pas des Dix-Mille: peuples et pays du Proche-Orient vus par un Grec,* edited by P. Briant, pp. 255–268. Presses universitaires du Mirail, Toulouse.

Zournatzi, Antigoni
2000 The Processing of Gold and Silver Tax in the Achaemenid Empire: Herodotus 3.96.2 and the Archaeological Realities. *Studia Iranica* 29: 241–271.

INDEX